SANDINISTA

SANDINISTA

Carlos Fonseca *and the* Nicaraguan Revolution

MATILDE ZIMMERMANN

DUKE UNIVERSITY PRESS Durham and London 2000

© 2000 DUKE UNIVERSITY PRESS
Third printing, 2004
All rights reserved
Printed in the United States of America
on acid-free paper ∞
Typeset in Minion by Keystone Typesetting, Inc.
Library of Congress Cataloging-in-Publication
Data appear on the last printed page of this book.

To Arnold

CONTENTS

Acknowledgments / ix

Introduction / 1

1. Matagalpa: The Early Years, 1936–1950 / 12

2. A Rebellious Student, 1950–1958 / 28

3. The Cuban Revolution, 1958–1961 / 50

4. Founding the FSLN, 1960–1964 / 69

5. The Evolution of a Strategy, 1964–1968 / 88

6. Underground and Prison Life, 1968–1970 / 111

7. The Sandino Writings, 1970–1974 / 143

8. A Fractured Movement, 1972–1975 / 162

9. The Montaña and the Death of Fonseca, 1975–1976 / 185

10. The Revolution of 1979 / 205

Epilogue / 222

Notes / 229

Glossary of Organizations / 257

Bibliography / 259

Index / 271

Acknowledgments

I can name only a few of the many Nicaraguans who led me to documents by and about Fonseca and shared with me their memories of him. Lt. Col. Ricardo Wheelock Roman, Juana Quintana, and Soraya Sánchez unlocked the doors to the large archive of Fonseca's unpublished writings at the Nicaraguan army's Centro de Historia Militar. Margarita Vannini and her staff at the Instituto de Historia de Nicaragua made available the rich collection of manuscripts, newspapers, and published works at the IHN and the Instituto de Historia Centroamericana and provided a comfortable and collegial workplace during my three trips to Nicaragua. Miguel Ángel Herrera of the IHN, who has studied the writings of Carlos Fonseca with love and respect for almost two decades, shared his insights and his considerable knowledge. Of the many friends and *compañeros* of Fonseca who granted me interviews, I want to single out his high school friend Ramón Gutiérrez Castro and his widow María Haydeé Terán. I went back again and again to their homes in Rivas and León and each time came away with a better understanding of Fonseca and his times. Sylvia Torres provided crucial assistance, both in Nicaragua and in Pittsburgh.

Grants and fellowships from the Andrew Mellon Foundation, Center for Latin American Studies at the University of Pittsburgh, and the Cole and Marty Blazier Award financed the field research for the Ph.D. dissertation on which this book is based.

A number of scholars and friends read part or all of the dissertation or book manuscript (and in the case of a few heroic souls, both): Reid Andrews, John Beverley, Barry Carr, Deborah Higdon, Donald Hodges, Michael Jiménez, Jim Miller, Aaron Ruby, James Sanders, Larry Seigle, Bob Schwarz, Volker Wuenderich, and the anonymous readers of Duke University Press.

Their knowledge of the subject and attention to detail stimulated my thinking and saved me from a variety of errors. The thoughtful comments and criticisms of my students at Vassar College helped make the book more accessible to nonspecialists. Kikombo Ilunga Ngoy of the Vassar College Geography Department created the map for this volume. Readers will appreciate the intelligence and meticulous care with which Bob Schwarz produced the index. My editor at Duke University Press, Valerie Millholland, patiently steered a novice author through the mysteries of publishing a book.

My love and gratitude go to my parents, Mildred and Virgil Zimmermann, and my son Darryl Miles.

Without the encouragement and sharp criticism of colleagues, friends, and family, this book would have been infinitely weaker. Without Arnold, it could never have been written at all.

Introduction

On 7 November 1979, more than one hundred thousand people packed the Plaza de la Revolución in Managua, Nicaragua, to honor Carlos Fonseca Amador, the founder of the Sandinista National Liberation Front (Frente Sandinista de Liberación Nacional, FSLN). The demonstrators were overwhelmingly young men and women from poor barrios and rural villages, participants in the insurrection that, only a few months before, had toppled the four-decade-long Somoza dictatorship and swept the FSLN into power. Many thousands came to the rally armed, and they waved their rifles in the air when the crowd chanted, "Comandante Carlos, Ordene!" [At your command!].

It was the third anniversary of the date Fonseca died fighting Somoza's army, and his remains had been exhumed and brought to the capital for reburial. The FSLN had planned a more low-key event, one that would commemorate not just Fonseca but several of the movement's most important martyrs. But the announcement of plans to rebury Fonseca, like the call for a "final offensive" against Somoza six months earlier, generated a response that went beyond anything FSLN leaders anticipated. A simple ceremony planned for the remote town of Waslala, near the forested hillside where Fonseca died, was overwhelmed by the hundreds of peasants who arrived on mule, on horseback, and on foot, some walking for more than a day. A helicopter flew Fonseca's remains to the town of Matagalpa, his birthplace. Nearly fifty thousand turned out, virtually the entire population of the town plus many who trekked in from the surrounding countryside. People gathered beside the highway and in small villages along the way as a car caravan carried the bones from Matagalpa to Managua.

Carlos Fonseca, though no longer alive, was the popular hero of the

HONDURAS

EL SALVADOR

Rio Coco

Rio Bocay

Puerto Cabezas ★

★ Siuna

★ Ocotal

★ Somoto

★ Waslala

Estelí ★   ★ Jinotega

Matagalpa ★   ★ Rio Blanco

Chinandega
★
★ Corinto

León
★

★ Boaco

ATLANTIC OCEAN

★ Managua

Masaya ★   ★ Juigalpa

★ Granada

Jinotepe
★

Rivas
★

Rama ★

Bluefields ★

PACIFIC OCEAN

★ San Carlos

0   25   50   Kilometers

0   25   50 Miles

COSTA RICA

Nicaragua. Map by Kikombo Ilunga Ngoy.

Nicaraguan revolution of 1979. He was much better known to the ordinary citizen than any of the people who made up the new revolutionary government. The young men and women who fought the National Guard in the insurrections of 1978 and 1979 considered themselves Sandinistas, but many knew only a few basic facts about the FSLN: its colors were the black and red of Sandino, its leader was Carlos Fonseca, it was serious about taking power, and it fought on the side of workers and peasants. That was enough.

Carlos Fonseca was also the FSLN leader who most epitomized the radical and popular character of the revolution, its anticapitalist and antilandlord dynamic. Two sayings of Fonseca's were especially prominent at the 7 November rally and preceding events. The first he appropriated from nationalist hero and guerrilla general Augusto César Sandino: "Only the workers and peasants will go all the way." The second, featured on the front page of the FSLN newspaper on 8 November, declared: "It is not simply a question of changing the individuals in power, but rather of changing the system, of overthrowing the exploiting classes and bringing the exploited classes to victory."[1]

For nearly twenty years, Fonseca had been the central ideological and strategic leader of the revolutionary movement in Nicaragua. The writings that defined the political ideology of the Frente Sandinista—programmatic documents, historical and social analyses, key speeches, and manifestos—were almost without exception his work. Until his death, Carlos Fonseca also played a crucial role, even from prison or exile, in organizing the day-to-day work of the FSLN, recruiting to its ranks, expanding its political influence, and planning its military operations.

Before 1979, most people in North America and Europe, and many in Latin America, had never heard of Nicaragua, but the revolution captured the imagination of people around the world. The scruffy young FSLN guerrillas, affectionately referred to as *muchachos,* "kids," had won an armed revolution against an entrenched dictatorship. Television viewers far from Central America were shocked by the brutal violence of the Somoza government and National Guard and were impressed by the sight of ordinary people—students, housewives, workers—standing up to government tanks with homemade bombs and cobblestone barricades. Most participants in the urban and rural uprisings of early 1979 came from the lower classes, but at the end there was also widespread support for the revolution from the middle class, the Catholic Church, and even sections of the Nicaraguan bourgeoisie. A genuine popular uprising finally forced President Anastasio Somoza to flee the country and destroyed the hated institution of the National Guard. Of all the socialist and nationalist guerrilla movements that sprang up around Latin America in the decades following the Cuban revolution of 1959, only the FSLN of Nicaragua ever came to power.

It is impossible to understand this revolution or Carlos Fonseca's role in it without knowing something of Nicaragua and its history. Nicaragua in 1979 was an impoverished, underdeveloped, sparsely populated country in the middle of Central America, a region of poor and economically backward countries. The size of Illinois, Nicaragua had a population of less than 2.5 million.

When the Spanish conquered Nicaragua in the early sixteenth century, they found a land of lakes and volcanoes, of pine-covered mountains, tropical jungle, and hot, fertile plains, of vast forests of precious hardwoods. They did not, however, find what they wanted: gold and silver available for easy plunder. The most important economic activity carried out by the new rulers of Nicaragua in the early years was slave raiding, the capture and transportation of Indians to work in the silver and mercury mines of Peru. The violence of slaving, combined with the devastation of new diseases introduced by the Europeans, reduced the population of western Nicaragua from an estimated six hundred thousand to a few tens of thousands by about 1600. It took more than two centuries for the population to recover to preconquest levels.

Independence from Spain was won in the early 1820s, but the economic patterns of the colonial era persisted well into the twentieth century. Cattle raising on large haciendas was the most important commercial activity until the coffee boom of the 1880s. The production of agricultural goods for European and North American consumers dominated the market economy, making Nicaragua dependent on the vagaries of world prices, demand, and competition, and ensuring that, even in boom years, profits went mostly to wealthy landowners and merchants. The majority of the population continued to grow beans and corn much as their ancestors had before the conquest, although the decreasing size of peasant landholdings forced many into seasonal labor as well. The indigenous communities enjoyed a significant amount of autonomy, but the Indian population was also subject to coerced labor on public works and coffee plantations. Precapitalist labor relations and primitive technology were common in Nicaragua much longer than in other parts of Latin America. It was not until the cotton boom of the 1950s that fully capitalist agricultural production came to the country.

The political life of Nicaragua from independence to 1979 was characterized by the exclusion of workers and peasants from political power, the use of violence to resolve conflicts between different factions of the dominant class, and intervention by the United States. Frequent wars between Liberals and Conservatives had little to do with ideology but rather were fueled by a jockeying for power among wealthy families and geographic rivalries between the two great colonial cities of Granada and León. In the 1850s, William Walker, an American adventurer backed initially by the U.S. government, took advantage of a war between Liberals and Conservatives to make himself president of Nicaragua, legalize slavery, and declare English the official language, before being defeated by popular resistance and a joint Central American army. In the decades before the construction of the Panama Canal, U.S. industrialist Cornelius Vanderbilt made a fortune exploiting the geographic advantages of Nicaragua to transport passengers and freight across a short land-and-water route between the Atlantic and Pacific Oceans. At the beginning of the twentieth century, the United States intervened militarily to overthrow Liberal president José Santos Zelaya, impose Conservative Adolfo Díaz in his place, and begin a military occupation of the country that lasted, with only a few years interruption, until 1933. Nicaragua's banks, customs office, and railroads were signed over to American bankers, and the Bryan-Chamorro Treaty of 1914 gave the United States exclusive rights in perpetuity to build a canal across Nicaraguan territory.

In 1927 Augusto César Sandino, one of the Liberal generals fighting an imposed Conservative president, refused to sign a U.S.-brokered truce and went on to lead a six-year war against the U.S. Marines. The efforts of Sandino's peasant army, combined with growing opposition to the intervention inside the United States, led to the withdrawal of the American troops in 1933. Sandino was assassinated in 1934 at the orders of Anastasio Somoza García, the commander of a new U.S.-trained military force called the Guardia Nacional (National Guard). In the 1960s and 1970s, Carlos Fonseca resurrected the example of Sandino to inspire a new generation to fight against a government and National Guard led by Anastasio Somoza's sons.

Who was Carlos Fonseca? What aspects of his life and surroundings drove him to rebellion? How and why did his ideas change over time? What impact did Nicaraguan history and culture have on his political views, and to what extent was he influenced by events in the world outside Central America? Was he a Marxist? Nationalist? Internationalist? Castroist? Sandinista? How did he understand the class structure of Nicaragua, and what role did he envision for different social classes in the revolution? What was his view of the role of women in the guerrilla struggle and in postrevolution society? How did his ideas differ from those of others in the FSLN and in the broader

Left and opposition movements in Nicaragua? What difference did Carlos Fonseca make in the eventual victory of the Nicaraguan revolution, which came several years after his death?

This work, drawing on a sizable collection of hitherto unknown Fonseca writings, tells Carlos Fonseca's story by placing the development of his ideas in the context of the world in which he lived and the Nicaraguan reality he studied and fought to change. It stresses two dominant influences on Fonseca's life and political philosophy: the Cuban socialist revolution, and particularly the writings and actions of Ernesto "Che" Guevara; and the long tradition of resistance and courage on the part of Nicaraguan workers and peasants, exemplified especially by the anti-imperialist general Sandino. Carlos Fonseca followed in the footsteps of two individuals above all others, Che Guevara and Augusto César Sandino. They were Fonseca's personal heroes, and he also saw them as representing broader historical processes. Following in Che's footsteps also meant following Fidel Castro, the July 26 Movement, and the rebels who attacked the Moncada Barracks in 1953. Studying and emulating Sandino also meant learning from Indians who fought Spanish conquistadores, youths who hurled rocks at invader William Walker, and patriots who led the resistance to U.S. intervention in the decades before Sandino.

Carlos Fonseca's contribution lay in the interweaving of two themes: on the one hand, the fight for national liberation and against U.S. imperialism, and on the other the struggle for socialist revolution. His vision of a "Sandinista popular revolution" included both military victory over the U.S.-backed Somoza dictatorship and a social transformation to end the exploitation of Nicaraguan workers and peasants. Fonseca's goal was to build a movement that was deeply rooted in the material reality of Nicaragua and its rebel traditions symbolized by Sandino while looking to Cuba—and behind Cuba, the Russian Revolution—for inspiration and a sense of what was possible.

"It is not our job," Fonseca wrote in 1975, "to discover the universal laws that lead to the transformation of a capitalist society into a society of free men and women; our modest role is to *apply* these laws, which have already been discovered, to the conditions of our own country."[2] The task he set himself was not "modest"; it was difficult and dangerous, and success was far from guaranteed. Indeed, of all the guerrilla groups formed around Latin America in the years immediately following the Cuban revolution of 1959, the one that seemed at first to have the *worst* prospects for success was probably the FSLN. The transformation of a handful of radical students into a movement leading a popular insurrection took almost two decades and was marked by more defeats than victories, prolonged periods of isolation, and the accumulation of a long list of martyrs. Even among students, the Sandinistas did not win hegemony until the decade of the sixties was well over. In the broad movement of opposition to Somoza and in the labor movement, more moderate voices than the FSLN's prevailed until the late 1970s.

Throughout this period, the FSLN was slowly winning to its ranks young students and workers, one or two at a time. Creating the kind of collective leadership that could take power at the head of a popular uprising was a long process involving sharp debate, discussion, conflicting proposals, experimentation, detours, and shared responsibilities. When the revolution occurred in 1979, everyone—friends and enemies—agreed that it was led by the FSLN. One of the themes of my work is that this experienced and committed leadership, this "vanguard" in the vocabulary of the time, was a necessary ingredient to the success of the Nicaraguan revolution. Like Che Guevara, I am convinced that one of the most important preconditions for revolution is the human one. The focus of this book is the men and women who struggled to build the FSLN through the 1960s and 1970s, and in particular the central role played by Carlos Fonseca.

Most books about the Nicaraguan revolution are by social scientists who are primarily interested in analyzing the FSLN's behavior after it came to power. They describe the ideology and program of the FSLN as it existed in the early 1980s, based on interviews and speeches of various party and government leaders, combined with some historical material from Carlos Fonseca and others. This approach enables them to show the complexity of Sandinista ideology in the early 1980s, but it does not reveal the organic development of this political ideology, the learning process, zigzags, debates, and rejection of failed strategies. It has led to several common errors, including a mystification of the process by which Sandino was chosen as a symbol, an overestimation of the importance of liberation theology in the formative period of the FSLN, and an insufficient appreciation of the role played by Carlos Fonseca at key junctures. The literature's focus on the FSLN in power creates the impression that the victory of the Nicaraguan revolution was somehow inevitable, whereas a more historical approach recovers the contingency and the drama of the process. Readers of this book may be surprised by the strength and stability of the Somoza regime during the 1960s and early 1970s, the numerical and military weakness of the FSLN and its marginalization within the broader opposition movement, and the number of instances when the guerrilla movement could have been annihilated or just given up on the prospect of revolution.

The Nicaraguan revolution—like all revolutions—was the product of a particular national experience, history, body of traditions, and political culture. The key to developing a revolutionary nationalist ideology and program for Nicaragua was the resurrection and reinterpretation of Augusto César Sandino. In retooling the lessons of the 1920s for the needs of the 1970s, Fonseca stressed two main themes: the FSLN had to be anchored in the working class and peasantry, and it had to be prepared to take on U.S. imperialism, which he considered the main obstacle both to Nicaraguan national independence and to the struggle of the country's lower classes for social justice.

A necessary part of this process was the FSLN's rejection of the political perspectives and methods of the Communist Party. Fonseca, originally a member of the pro-Moscow party in Nicaragua, led this split at the beginning of the 1960s with his criticisms of the Communists' electoralism, their unwillingness to commit to armed struggle, and their lack of confidence in the ability of Nicaraguan workers and peasants to carry out a socialist revolution. This orientation to reform rather than revolution and to alliances with parties that represented the interests of capitalist and middle-class forces developed under Soviet leader Joseph Stalin in the 1930s and was common to all the Latin American parties that looked to Moscow for direction. Scholars of Nicaragua refer to this political philosophy as "Stalinism" or "popular frontism," or "the Third International tradition"; Carlos Fonseca called it "Browderism."[3] Fonseca led a break from the Communist Party to the Left, rejecting the conservatism and bureaucratic methods of the Nicaraguan CP in favor of the revolutionary Marxism of Che Guevara and Fidel Castro. Fonseca saw this turning point as a move toward, not away from, Marxism.

Some scholars argue that it was Fonseca's rejection of Marxism in favor of a more pragmatic nationalism that made the revolution of 1979 possible.[4] Fonseca's political writings over a two-decade period show him, to the contrary, becoming more committed over time both to scientific socialism and to revolutionary Nicaraguan nationalism. Marxism and nationalism were two intertwined aspects of Fonseca's political philosophy, held together by the glue of anti-imperialism and symbolized by his constant pairing of Che Guevara and Augusto César Sandino.

I argue that the Cuban revolution of 1959 was the crucial turning point in Fonseca's political evolution, opening up the possibility of a deep-going social revolution in his own country, turning him to a study of Sandino's history, and leading directly to the formation of the FSLN. "We are the *fidelista* generation," Fonseca said, with the goal of establishing in Nicaragua "the second free territory of the Americas."[5]

It should be noted that in the eyes of those who speak for what remains of the FSLN in the late 1990s, this is the most controversial argument of the book. Fonseca's writings, including his historical writings on Sandino and his last strategic document, written less than a month before his death, continually stress the importance of the Cuban revolution and its relevance for Nicaragua. At the time of the Nicaraguan revolution, the material aid and political inspiration of Cuba were both widely acknowledged. The FSLN—to the delight and astonishment of the Cubans—sent *twenty-six* of its thirty-six highest-ranking military officers to Havana for a celebration on 26 July 1979, only seven days after the Nicaraguan victory.[6] At the November 1979 Managua rally commemorating Carlos Fonseca, and at other political demonstrations in the first months of the revolution, the crowd burst into chants of "Cuba! Cuba! Cuba!" and "Viva Fidel!" In the course of the 1980s, however, leaders of the FSLN mentioned Cuba less and less often, finally rewriting their own history by substituting a Swedish or Mexican model for Cuba.

Perhaps following the lead of these FSLN leaders, scholars of the revolution tend to downplay the importance of Cuba. They argue that after an early infatuation with Cuba, lasting perhaps until the defeat of Che Guevara in Bolivia in 1967, the Sandinistas abandoned the Cuban model and set out to make a different type of revolution, one that was multiclass, Christian, and nonsocialist.[7] My study of Carlos Fonseca shows that the FSLN under his leadership, as it became more deeply rooted in Nicaraguan reality, continued at the same time to look to the Cuban revolution as an example of what was possible.

The reader should know that I have brought more than academic curiosity to this research project. I was already an active supporter of the Nicaraguan revolution when I first heard of Carlos Fonseca. In February 1980, only a few months after the rally welcoming Fonseca's remains to the capital, I made the first of many trips to Nicaragua. I lived in Managua during the early 1980s and wrote a series of pro-revolution articles chronicling the first few years of the FSLN government. During the U.S.-backed contra war, I spent one harvest picking cotton on a state farm near the war zone, and I gave talks in the United States in solidarity with the Sandinista revolution. At the end of the decade, I moved back to Nicaragua to help on an FSLN project in the autonomous region of the northern Atlantic Coast. I was disappointed, although not surprised, when the FSLN was voted out of office in February 1990.

In the Nicaragua of the 1980s, Carlos Fonseca's image was everywhere on murals and posters. He looked a little ethereal, even snooty—half aristocrat and half Jesus Christ. As the FSLN began to publish some of Fonseca's writings, I was struck by the contrast between the way he was portrayed in these ubiquitous murals and the plain-talking radicalism of his own speech, his embrace of revolutionary violence, and his identification with the daily hardships and concerns of Nicaraguan workers and peasants. Unlike most Latin American Marxists, Carlos Fonseca wrote and spoke a language ordinary people could understand. I was impressed with his clarity and singleness of purpose, and sorry when the FSLN rather abruptly stopped publishing Fonseca's work after 1985 and let his *Obras* go out of print.

When I returned to Nicaragua in the 1990s, the revolutionary murals had been sandblasted or painted over, and speeches by FSLN politicians never mentioned Carlos Fonseca. But I met many Nicaraguans from what they themselves call the "humble classes" whose memory of him was vivid. Men and women of various ages, encountered in the market, on buses, in small towns, in a clinic waiting room, responded in virtually identical terms to the news that I was writing a biography of Carlos Fonseca. "Carlos—he was one of us. He spoke our language." And often, "He would never have let this happen to our revolution."

By the time this book was written, the FSLN had become a center-left electoral party whose platform and actions were similar to those of other reform-minded parties in and out of office around Latin America. Some of the idealistic young guerrillas who had fought alongside Fonseca had become millionaire businessmen, large landowners, or corrupt politicians. The Nicaraguan revolution was over. Most books about Latin American revolutions published in the 1990s start from this framework. These post–Cold War postmortems are primarily concerned with explaining the *defeats* of all revolutionary efforts after Cuba, including Nicaragua. Insofar as they deal with Nicaragua, their starting point is the electoral defeat of 1990, not the victorious revolution of 1979. My purpose is to try, through the central figure of Carlos Fonseca, to reconstruct the events and ideas that produced the FSLN and the revolution of 1979. What drove Fonseca and his followers? What did they say and write at the time, and how did they end up the undisputed leaders of a popular insurrection? I think it is more interesting, important, and unusual that many thousands of Nicaraguans were ready to die for the FSLN in 1979 than that they were unwilling to vote for it a decade later.

The fictional Irish bartender Mr. Dooley once criticized the kind of history that only "tells ye what a countrhy died iv." Like Mr. Dooley, "I'd like to know what it lived iv."[8]

Matagalpa: The Early Years, 1936–1950

In early July 1936, a Matagalpa seamstress stopped by City Hall to register the birth of a baby boy to her neighbor Augustina Fonseca, an unmarried twenty-six-year-old washerwoman from the countryside. The clerk took down the information that the infant, born 23 June, was named Carlos Alberto Fonseca and was illegitimate.[1]

As the child grew up, he came to see his world as dominated by sharp and sometimes violent contrasts: between his country of Nicaragua and United States imperialism, between the white coffee growers and merchants of the Matagalpa region and the overwhelmingly Indian coffee pickers and *campesinos*, between the tiny revolutionary group he founded and the powerful and well-armed Somoza government.

But the first contrast Carlos Fonseca Amador became aware of must have been within his own family. He lived with his mother, older brother Raúl, and eventually three younger siblings in a single windowless room about twelve feet on a side, off the kitchen patio of an aunt's house. Half a mile away was the mansion where his father, Fausto Amador Alemán, lived with his wife and children. One of the few two-story buildings in Matagalpa, the Amador residence, along with the cathedral facade half a block away, dominated the north end of town. Inside were shining mahogany floors and cabinets, mosaic tiles, a garden of flowers and trees, and elegant imported furnishings, all kept immaculate by live-in servants.

Carlos's mother, Augustina Fonseca Ubeda, had arrived in Matagalpa in about 1930 from the rainy mountain village of San Rafael del Norte. According to a local resident and distant relative of Carlos, San Rafael del Norte was "an area of simple folk, the majority of them fair-skinned, where those who had land used it to keep cattle and grow sugar cane," and the Ubeda family were "cattle keepers, who grew some cane and some garden crops, hard-working people who lived austerely; they were extremely religious and sometimes only appeared in town for Holy Week celebration."[2]

Like many country people from the North, Augustina Fonseca, who was twenty years old in 1930, came to the city looking for work and fleeing the disruption of war. San Rafael del Norte was the home of Blanca Aráuz, the wife of guerrilla leader Augusto César Sandino,[3] and the Segovian Mountains around the town became a war zone in the late 1920s.

Augustina, or Tina as she was known, arrived in Matagalpa with her two aunts, only slightly older than herself, Isaura and Victoria Ubeda. Tina found work as a maid at the Hotel Bermúdez, where in 1933 she gave birth to twin boys, Raúl and Carlos. (This first Carlos died as an infant.) The twins' father was reportedly U.S. Marine Lieutenant Pennington, an officer of the anti-Sandino forces stationed in northern Nicaragua.[4] When Isaura Ubeda acquired a comfortable corner house near Plaza Laborio at the south end of town, she allowed Tina and baby Raúl to move into a back room. This is the house in which Carlos Fonseca Amador was born.[5]

Tina's neighbor Benita Alvarado has described her friend's life as being "constant hard work, nothing but washing and ironing." But Alvarado also described herself and Tina as *fiesteras*, "party girls," in their youth. "We all liked to dress up fancy to go out to the dance halls on the road to Jinotega," said Alvarado, "but with Tina, the more simply she dressed, the more beautiful she was and the more she attracted men." Augustina's daughter-in-law said she had the "double misfortune of being both poor and beautiful." Among Tina's suitors in 1935 was Carlos's father, Fausto Amador, a wealthy twenty-two year old who had just returned from school in the United States and had a reputation as a playboy and daredevil.[6]

Still unmarried, Augustina Fonseca had three more children over the next fifteen years. Each time she became pregnant—when Carlos was four and then again when he was about ten and again when he was in his midteens—Tina and her children were thrown out of Isaura's house. Penniless and with no help from the children's fathers, the family each time searched for a shack to stay in until the new baby was born. Carlos later described one of these temporary dwellings to a friend: around the corner from Isaura's house, the hovel rented for forty córdobas (about five dollars) a month, and "the door wasn't even attached—at night we had to push the beds up against it to keep it from opening."[7] Isaura always relented afterward, when Tina promised to change her ways, and each time she allowed the growing family to return.

In Nicaragua at the time, working-class and peasant couples commonly lived together for many years and had children without going through the formality of marriage. Isaura Ubeda herself had this type of relationship with the saddle maker Agustín Castillo. Augustina Fonseca's pregnancies, however, all seem to have resulted from short-lived sexual encounters rather than the more stable relationships in which society recognized a family tie. Her five children all had different fathers. Friends and family members I have interviewed do not believe that any of Augustina Fonseca's pregnancies resulted from rape. At the same time, they describe her as having few options in life after she bore her first illegitimate child—especially one whose father was reputed to be a Yankee. Regarded as "damaged goods," she had little chance of marrying or entering into a stable common-law relationship.[8]

Fonseca's strict attitude toward matrimony and monogamy may be traced in part to these early childhood experiences. At age eighteen Carlos told his close friend Ramón Gutiérrez that he had never had sexual intercourse. When Ramón asked in some astonishment why, Carlos said that he would never do to any woman what had been done to his mother. A poem Fonseca wrote for the magazine *Segovia* in 1954 contains the lines "It's good that . . . Tomasa is going to have a child. / But it's bad that . . . Tomasa's child is not going to have a father." On trial in 1964, Fonseca was questioned about a National Guard report that he had needed treatment for venereal disease after his arrest. "Look, compañeros," he insisted, "I am an ascetic, almost a mystic. Every minute of my time is dedicated to the revolution and to the fatherland. What you were told is false. It is pure invention."[9]

When Carlos Fonseca registered at the national university in 1956, he wrote "servant" in the space for parent's occupation. The clerk looked up and said, "Don't you mean housewife?"

"No, I don't mean housewife," replied Fonseca testily. "I am the son of a servant."[10]

Writing to his father in 1960, Fonseca described his mother's life as "nothing but sadness, a constant tragedy." Carlos asked for help, not for himself but for his mother:

> The poor woman, at this stage of her life, has never known what it means to live in a room of her own. She has always been a slave in the kitchens of those she has worked for, and the kitchen has been the only home I have known. . . . For my mother it is a bitter experience to live with my aunt. Besides, in Matagalpa she could live in a little rented place with running water and electricity for the sum of only 100 córdobas a month. She would have my younger maternal brother and sister with her of

course. I assured her that you would help us, not really because you had any obligation to do it but because you would recognize that it would give me immeasurable satisfaction to have this dream of mine realized. When she comes to your office, I hope that you will remember that she has known nothing but sadness in this life, and that therefore she suffers deeply every time someone looks at her in a disparaging way.[11]

Amador did not respond favorably to this plea. Augustina Fonseca lived in Isaura Ubeda's kitchen until she died from a stroke in 1967. She died penniless, and her sons had to borrow money for a simple box in which to bury her.

Carlos's father, Fausto Amador, belonged to one of the wealthiest and politically most powerful families of the region. Although no father was listed on Carlos Alberto's birth certificate or baptismal record, his Amador grandparents did appear on his baptismal certificate in 1937,[12] and sometime during Carlos's elementary school years his father began to acknowledge his parentage.

The Amador family of Matagalpa had been prominent coffee growers, merchants, and politicians since the nineteenth century. Fausto Amador's father and Carlos's grandfather was Horacio Amador, an important coffee trader who also owned coffee plantations and several houses in Matagalpa. One of Fausto's uncles, Sebastián Amador, had been the *jefe político* (political boss) of the Matagalpa region from 1915 to 1917 during the administration of Conservative president Adolfo Diaz. The Amadors, like most of the aristocratic families of Matagalpa, traditionally supported the Conservative Party, but Fausto switched his allegiance to the Nationalist Liberal Party (Partido Liberal Nacionalista, PLN) of President Anastasio Somoza García. In 1950 Fausto Amador moved with his family to Managua to administer several large Somoza enterprises. By the 1970s he owned a large amount of agricultural land in the Matagalpa and Managua regions and four luxurious homes in Managua, in addition to the Matagalpa family mansion.[13]

Shortly after the birth of Carlos Fonseca, Fausto Amador married Lola Arrieta, the daughter and granddaughter of prominent Matagalpa professionals and *cafetaleros* (coffee planters). Between 1939 and 1950, Fausto Amador and Lolita Arrieta had one daughter and three sons: Gloria, Iván, Fausto Jr., or Faustito, and Cairo. Coincidentally, Carlos Fonseca also had three brothers and a sister on his mother's side: Raúl, René, Juan Alberto, and Estela. He developed the closest relationship with Faustito Amador and Juan Alberto Fonseca, both about a decade his junior.

Carlos had a voracious appetite and would later recall the poverty, humiliation, and constant hunger of his early years, when he sold the weekly newspaper *Rumores* in the street and peddled candies to bring home a few centavos or some bread for his little brothers. One of his mother's employers, Salvador Pineda, caught her slipping leftover food to her son, and according to Carlos, "He kicked me out like a dog." A line in a 1955 poem by Fonseca reads: "The rich feed you with leftovers." In 1956, when Carlos was working as a school librarian, he was sometimes able to sneak a hungry day student into the school cafeteria as his "guest."[14]

Carlos had fonder memories of another of his mother's employers, Nacho Lay, the owner of the Shanghai Restaurant. The Chinese restaurant owner noticed that Carlos had to go right up to a huge wall clock to tell the time and sent him to get his first eyeglasses at the age of about ten or twelve. Fonseca wore heavy glasses for the rest of his life, and some of his letters express concern about his deteriorating vision. A high school friend remembered once asking Carlos why he looked so sad. "Well, Poet," answered Carlos, "I just got back from Managua, where I saw the eye doctor. He told me I have to stop studying or I'll be blind."

"So, Poet, what are you going to do?" asked the friend.

"Nothing, I guess I'll just go blind, because studying is my life." A gloating—and false—National Guard surveillance report assured Somoza in 1968 that "the communist Fonseca Amador is now almost completely blind."[15]

By the late 1940s, Carlos's poverty was relieved by some financial help from his father. Fausto Amador's wife Lolita convinced him to take responsibility for Carlos, who bore a striking physical resemblance to his father and paternal brothers and was acquiring a reputation as a brilliant student.[16] Carlos visited the Amador mansion and got to know his paternal siblings and his father's wife. During this period, Fausto Amador managed the U.S.-owned La Reyna gold mine in the town of San Ramón, about thirty kilometers away (where he had a mistress and another young son), spending only weekends at the family house in Matagalpa. When Carlos began high school in 1950, according to Lolita's sister Nellie Arrieta, Fausto paid for his tuition of about ten córdobas a month, his meals at a food stall near the school, and the clothes he bought from a local shopkeeper. In 1960 Fonseca wrote to Lolita Arrieta expressing gratitude for her affection and assuring her that "the goodness you have shown both to me and to all those who have had the opportunity to be close to you, is being rewarded by the fine children you have been given." He went on to praise Iván's good-heartedness and Fausto Orlando's brilliance and to express concern that Gloria's values would be corrupted by attending school in the United States.[17]

Writers associated with the FSLN often deny that Carlos Fonseca had any relationship with his Somocista father.[18] But Fonseca's own letters and other documents reveal a different and more complicated reality. His personal letters indicate that at least until the late 1960s, Fonseca craved his father's understanding and felt intense, if tortured, affection for him. "I want to speak frankly to you," Fonseca said in a 1960 letter, "because I cannot speak to the people I love in any other way." He went on: "This isn't the first time I have told you that it is more important to me that my father understand me spiritually than that he help me financially. . . . I would be extremely happy if you could make a little trip to this country [Costa Rica], even if it were for just one day, so that I could see you and talk to you at length. Or do I have to get shot to see you?"[19]

In the same letter, Carlos attempted to find justification for his father's links to the Somoza dictatorship:

> It sometimes makes me unhappy to think about the position you have, but I also feel justly proud of the fact that no one has ever proved to me that my father has committed a wrongful act. I say justly proud, because it is rare for anyone to get to my father's position without being buried in horrible misdeeds. And for this reason I believe that if my father had lived in a better time and place he would have put his talent at the service of society, of humanity, of progress. The voice of reason tells me that it wasn't intrigue and ambition that got my father to the high position he has today but rather simply his own abilities.

As late as 1967, by which time he had long since committed himself to revolutionary politics, Fonseca wrote a passionately personal letter to his father. He explained why he had not written for seven long years: "I found out that you had said you expected a letter from me any day because I would surely write as soon as I needed money. And a proof of how I am sometimes too sensitive is the fact that this comment of yours hurt me and prevented me from either writing you or asking for your help, even though I have needed this help more than once." Carlos did in fact ask his father in this letter for a C$ 10,000 loan, which he promised to repay in six months with interest at the rate of "a million thank-yous percent." Fonseca told his father he appreciated "the respect you have shown for the path I have chosen in life," which appears to be filial wishful thinking, and ended his letter with a hope that the period of estrangement was over:

I want to talk to you about all the things swirling around in my head. I have wanted to see you, to talk to you at length, wanted to hear you and have you hear me. Again I want to tell you that I know you understand me, but if you could hear me talk you would understand me even better. I am not suggesting a face-to-face meeting, which I know is impossible right now for a variety of reasons. . . . For many years you were the person I dreamed about most often when I was sleeping. And these dreams were always unpleasant. But for some time this hasn't been the case. Now the dreams I have about you are pleasant. I have finally managed to understand you and to acknowledge and appreciate your fraternal [sic] affection.[20]

Carlos Fonseca identified with his mother's social class. His feelings for Augustina Fonseca seem to have been a mixture of love, loyalty, and pity—and not a little guilt. He jeopardized his own safety to visit her during his years underground, and he asked his young comrades in the FSLN, at considerable risk, to bring his mother to Costa Rica and Honduras for visits. But he saw his father as a more kindred intellectual spirit. Fonseca's letters to his father are full of historical and literary analysis, as he tried to convey his evolving political ideas and motivations. Educated in the United States, Fausto Amador was bilingual in English and Spanish, and he had a reputation as a brilliant administrator. Augustina Fonseca, on the other hand, was known as much for her silence as for her beauty. Even when she was young, according to her neighbor, "she was known as someone who almost didn't talk." Some of Carlos's contemporaries who had met his mother assumed that she was illiterate, although in fact she could read and write.[21]

Less than a year after Augustina Fonseca's death, in a Mother's Day message dedicated to women whose sons and daughters had been killed by the National Guard, Fonseca claimed that she eventually came to terms with his revolutionary activity: "On this day, allow me to mention the mother of the writer of this message, my proletarian mother, whose days on earth have ended. That humble woman came to understand and say with pride that this son of hers was a true patriot."[22] Other Matagalpa residents of the era remember her as pained and confused by Carlos's radicalism, and there is unfortunately no testimony from Augustina herself on the subject.

The personal anguish and social pressure the teenage Carlos suffered because of his family background were exacerbated by the small-town atmosphere of his birthplace. Matagalpa in the 1940s was a ribbon-shaped municipality of some 12,000 to 15,000 people. Almost 2,500 feet above sea level, it resembled the highland settlements of South America or Guatemala more than it did hot, swampy Managua or León, which baked in 100-degree heat for much of the year. Located in a narrow valley along the Río Grande de Matagalpa, the town was dominated by two parallel paved streets connecting the cathedral toward the north end of town with the Plaza Laborio at the south. Green hillsides rose a block or two east of the Avenida Central; just to the west were the marketplace and the river. From June to December it rained almost every day, mud flowed down the hillsides into town, and the Río Grande filled with cold, fast-moving water from the mountains.

In the late nineteenth century, the Nicaraguan government had offered 500 *manzanas* of good coffee land in the highlands around Matagalpa free to any investor who would plant 25,000 coffee trees and maintain them at his own expense until they began to produce. This attracted nearly 200 well-to-do immigrants from Germany, the United States, England, Italy, and France.[23] Coffee plantations with names such as La Bavaria and Washington appeared in the hills around Matagalpa. Carlos Fonseca had friends called Bütsching and LeCler in high school.

Matagalpa boasted a more cosmopolitan atmosphere than other Nicaraguan towns its size. The Deutscher Club, founded at the turn of the century, formed the basis for the Club de Extranjeros (Foreigners' Club), where wealthy immigrants and their children socialized. The Germans also had their own hunting lodge and club in the mountains, named after the Black Forest of their homeland. Aristocratic families like the Amadors would have been welcome at the Club de Extranjeros, but the Nicaraguan elite also had their own Club Social on a hill near the cathedral. A small Chinese community, led by several merchant families, had its own club and cemetery. Some of the most important businesses in town were Hüper's tools and textiles, Lau's housewares, the Leyton nursery, Mixter industrial supply store, the Siles transport company, and María Uebersezig's "Tante Mari" restaurant. Mr. Potter expected his guests to wear formal dress for dinner at his hacienda, and Mr. Wiley organized the first truck transport from Matagalpa down to the lowlands. Dr. Josephson treated the medical problems of Matagalpan high society. Among the families with the largest coffee plantations were the Italian Vitas, the North American Hawkinses and Sullivans, and the German Boesches. A half century ago Matagalpa had its own movie theater, bullfight ring, and train station, none of which exist today.[24]

A Matagalpa high school newspaper described the town in 1954, with "its irregular barrios, rocky and wet."

Sunk in a hole, Matagalpa is buffeted by the winds that blow cold through its streets. Most of the houses seem to be built of cement; they belong to rich coffee growers. The daughters of these gentlemen go to the best schools in Managua, Granada, León and the United States; they don't want anyone to think they are dummies from Matagalpa. There is nothing provincial about Matagalpa. Here the Chinese, the Turks, the Yankees, the Germans and even a Russian all consider themselves natives. The only ones not native are the Indians.

Matagalpa has two long streets lined with houses, and in almost every house there is a shop. The town seems like a shopping center—everybody is selling something. Commercially, Matagalpa is second only to Managua. The Old Market, which is actually a new market and very pleasant and varied, has barber shops, shoemakers, places to eat, food stores, and a crush of people that constantly makes it necessary to expand in new directions.[25]

Matagalpa and the entire north-central region was affected more than most areas of Nicaragua by political, economic, and cultural developments in Honduras, El Salvador, and Guatemala. The long border with Honduras was exceedingly porous, and many families in the frontier regions had members on both sides. For more than a century, smugglers, immigrant workers, and dissident intellectuals had carried goods and ideas back and forth across the borders. Carlos Fonseca and Augusto César Sandino were only two of the thousands who took refuge across a border because they were in trouble with the police in their own country. The Matagalpa region was also the gateway to the northern Atlantic Coast, with its gold mines and settlements of Miskito and Sumo Indians.

In spite of its international character, Matagalpa had aspects of a frontier town as Carlos Fonseca was growing up in the 1940s. Horses were more common than automobiles in its streets, and goods were transported in ox carts. Every hotel, even the fanciest, had a hitching post for horses and a pile of hay. The roads leading out of town into the coffee-growing areas were passable for trucks and cars only during the dry season, from January to May. Most businesses were connected to agriculture—coffee merchants, tool and feed stores, veterinary suppliers. Matagalpinos of all social classes were closely connected to the countryside and familiar with rural life. Wealthy families such as the Vogls and Vitas had their primary residences on their coffee plantations, although they also kept houses in town. Many of Fonseca's classmates in high school, who came from lower-middle-class families, spent their weekends and school vacations on the family *finca* (farm). Carlos himself spent time with his great-aunt in the remote town of Matiguás.

The commercial life of Matagalpa revolved around the coffee cycle. The three-to-four-month harvest season usually started in December, and by February the *beneficios* (processing plants) bulged with coffee beans, and both workers and plantation owners had money to spend in town. Most labor was seasonal; the coffee planters employed very few year-round workers and contracted with temporary workers, often whole families, for the harvest months. During the off-season, called in Matagalpa the "silent season," most coffee pickers returned to their own small landholdings to grow beans and corn.

As coffee production increased in the Matagalpa highlands during the late nineteenth and early twentieth centuries, formerly self-sufficient peasants were forced into tenancy arrangements or further inland onto the agricultural frontier. Between the two world wars, coffee production in the department of Matagalpa tripled while the number of people identified in the census as *agricultores* (farmers) was cut in half. But this expropriation was neither abrupt nor complete. Although commercial coffee growing favored the large producers, a significant number of midsize farms remained into the post–World War II period, growing small amounts of coffee as well as food crops for local consumption and sale.

The coffee pickers and campesinos of the mountains around Matagalpa were largely Indian, although their indigenous languages had been supplanted by Spanish. There has been some scholarly debate over the extent to which the rural population of the highlands retained its Indian identification into the twentieth century. The traditional view has been that an Indian revolt in 1881 in Matagalpa represented the last instance of resistance with a strong ethnic dynamic, and that by the first decade of the twentieth century the entire population of the Pacific region could be considered mestizo. In *Viva Sandino*, written in 1974, Carlos Fonseca said the so-called Indian War of 1881 "was not really about Indians at all, but rather mestizo campesinos who spoke Spanish, who had lost their mother tongue, even though their appearance showed them to be primarily of indigenous origin."[26]

Recent historical studies by Jeffrey Gould portray a considerably more complex reality. Drawing to a significant extent on evidence from the Matagalpa region, Gould has shown that in spite of the pressures of loss of communal land, racial discrimination, and military defeats, the indigenous population retained some aspects of their culture and forms of social organization well into the twentieth century. Not until World War II did Matagalpa

Indians abandon their distinctive dress, when a wartime agreement with the United States on cotton production led to the uprooting of the cotton plants that grew wild in the highlands. At least until the 1940s, the indigenous population of Matagalpa, although considerably smaller than at the turn of the century, still identified itself as Indian and spoke a distinctive dialect— "almost like singing" is the way the city's folk historian Doña Pinita described it. Writing in the early 1960s, Doña Pinita gave a detailed description of Indian dress, customs, language, and tools, observing that Indians who once lived closer to town had been retreating further and further into the mountains.[27] Members of the indigenous *comunidades* were identified as Indians by their neighbors and employers and were discriminated against socially and economically. In the postwar period, elements of ethnic consciousness persisted, interwoven with class consciousness, among the coffee pickers and campesinos of the Matagalpa region.[28]

During Carlos Fonseca's youth in the 1930s and 1940s, Indians from the countryside gathered in the Plaza Laborio a block from his house to look for work. Several of the rural Indian settlements, or *cañadas,* maintained houses in town for their members. The Cementerio de los Indios stood not far from where the ladinos, or Spanish speakers, were buried. Every New Year's Day, Indians marched into Matagalpa, some in traditional dress. At the end of each parade, the next year's designated leader of the Indian population received the symbol of authority, a tasseled wand. By the 1940s, these Indian leaders had been to a large extent co-opted and turned into state agents. One of the responsibilities of the man chosen to receive the wand each year, for example, was to turn out the vote for the Somocista candidate in elections. Indian involvement in Liberal and Conservative politics had a tangled history going back at least to the turn of the century. The coffee growers of Matagalpa aggressively fought their Indian workers for two types of legal powers. The cafetaleros wanted the prohibition of communal land ownership, traditionally a Liberal cause, but they also wanted laws sanctioning coerced labor, usually a Conservative demand. Gould has shown how both Liberal and Conservative politicians tried to implement the land and labor policies demanded by the coffee growers, while at the same time seeking to avoid Indian resistance and when possible appeal for indigenous electoral support.

Labor relations in the coffee highlands had more in common with the colonial past than with fully capitalist production. Precapitalist forms, including coerced Indian labor and debt peonage, persisted in Matagalpa and the neighboring department of Jinotega through the first half of the twentieth century. With much lower yields and higher transportation costs than other Central American coffee producers, Nicaraguan growers could compete only by paying extremely low wages, requiring pickers to work long days of back-breaking physical labor without the machinery available elsewhere, and forcing workers to accept wages in food from the grower's own high-priced store. Anti-Indian racism was used to justify paying labor in Matagalpa even less than elsewhere in Nicaragua, only half the piecework wages of pickers in the coffee-growing regions near Managua. Usurious credit policies helped the cafetaleros acquire the land of smallholders, and a cooperative National Guard rounded up and jailed Indians who accepted *adelantos* (cash advances) and tried to leave before the harvest was over.[29]

One month before Carlos Fonseca's birth, the head of the Nicaraguan National Guard, *Jefe Director* Anastasio Somoza García, overthrew elected Liberal president Juan Sacasa in a coup backed by sections of the labor movement. Two years earlier, Somoza had ordered the assassination of guerrilla general Augusto César Sandino and supervised the hunting down of most of the leaders of Sandino's army. As soon as he became president in 1936, Somoza embarked on policies designed to consolidate his rule through strengthening the state apparatus and its police force, the National Guard. He enjoyed considerable success incorporating popular sectors, in particular urban workers, into the electoral machinery of his Nationalist Liberal Party. Somoza's enforcement of credit and labor policies benefiting export capital as a whole laid the basis for a series of political agreements with the Conservative Party.

Post-1979 scholarship on Nicaragua has emphasized the political and economic conflict between the Somoza family and other sections of the Nicaraguan bourgeoisie, but historian Knut Walter argues persuasively that Somoza García's twenty-year rule (1936–1956) was "an uninterrupted effort at social and political alliance formation" that met with considerable success. Carefully constructed power sharing between Liberals and Conservatives, according to Walter, laid the foundations for a stable state "within which coffee and cotton growers, ranchers and dairymen, industrialists and merchants all could prosper in a secure environment." Jaime Biderman's study of the state and agricultural development in twentieth-century Nicaragua similarly concludes that the Nicaraguan government, in addition to serving the interests of the Somoza family, "was also responsive to the general requirements of capital accumulation and to the needs of various fractions of the capitalist class." Amalia Chamorro has applied the Gramscian concept of hegemony to Nicaragua, arguing the Somozas ruled not only through a highly developed repressive apparatus but also through a "partial hege-mony," based on broad support from the bourgeoisie of both political parties, the backing of the United States, regularly scheduled elections that were formally democratic, the image of a modernizing state, and populist appeals to the lower classes, particularly labor. Jeffrey Gould has examined in some detail the populist rhetoric and pro-labor image cultivated by Somoza in the 1940s.[30] This revisionist scholarship concerning the administrations of Somoza García and his sons Luis and Anastasio Somoza Debayle represents a convincing challenge to the stereotype of Somocista Nicaragua as the fiefdom of one all-powerful family, a nation ruled by a "dynasty," a "Mafia-cracy," or in the words of one scholar, a "patrimonial praetorian regime" based on "the political exclusion of the upper class."[31]

The consolidation of Somocista rule in Matagalpa in the 1930s and early 1940s mirrored the process underway in the rest of the country. Matagalpa, traditionally a Conservative Party stronghold, prospered under the Liberal Somoza government. Coffee prices rose, agricultural labor costs were kept low, and the state put money into building the kind of infrastructure that exporters needed.

Somoza's methods did produce resentment and opposition. His friends and relatives and members of his Nationalist Liberal Party got preferential treatment for high-ranking new jobs and received more than their share of the land and businesses confiscated from Germans during World War II. Some young members of the Conservative Party objected to their leadership's power-sharing deals with Somoza. Anti-Somoza demonstrations broke out in Managua and León in 1944, led by young Conservatives and dissident Liberals who defected from Somoza's party to form the Independent Liberal Party (Partido Liberal Independiente, PLI).[32] These mobilizations found an echo among the Conservative youth in Matagalpa. Students at Matagalpa's National Institute of the North (Instituto Nacional del Norte, INN) published several issues of a newspaper called *Vanguardia Juvenil* in the late 1940s. These student protesters may have influenced Fonseca, although he did not enter the INN until 1950. In 1947, when Carlos was just eleven, he and a young friend, Manuel Baldizón, walked out of grade school because their anti-Somoza teacher Lucidia Mantilla was fired. The boys finished the school year attending classes at Mantilla's house.[33]

Doris Tijerino, born in Matagalpa in 1943 and later a leader of the FSLN, has described her Conservative mother's involvement in radical opposition activities.[34] Tijerino's mother was, however, something of an exception among Matagalpa landowning Conservatives. In Matagalpa, as elsewhere in the country, wealthy Conservative families had made their peace with the Somoza government by the late 1930s. The propertied immigrant families, for their part, had always avoided lining up with either Liberals or Conservatives. And some Matagalpa aristocrats, like Fonseca's father, Fausto Amador, simply switched their allegiance from the Conservative to Liberal camps. They were in good company: Nicaragua's most powerful Liberal of all, Anastasio Somoza García, was the son of a Conservative coffee grower. The programmatic differences between the two parties were minimal in any case.

Riding the wave of post–World War II capitalist expansion, the Nicaraguan economy boomed during the 1950s and well into the following decade. Cotton production exploded, to become the nation's main export; coffee prices and production rose; and there was a rapid increase in middle-class jobs in the state bureaucracy and professions. In the mid-1950s, Carlos Fonseca and a group of teenage friends would begin to voice their moral outrage about the miserable living conditions, illiteracy, and poor health of workers, campesinos, and coffee pickers in the Matagalpa region. In the context of unprecedented wealth for the dominant classes, especially export capitalists, and complacent comfort for the middle class, the poverty and exploitation suffered by the majority of Nicaragua's population seemed intolerable to these high school students.

The young Fonseca's political and social ideas emerged in a setting where a variety of opposition traditions resonated. By the early 1950s, at least five different types of anti-Somoza or antigovernment sentiment had a hearing in Matagalpa and the surrounding region.

The first was the traditional or bourgeois opposition, represented especially by the Conservative Party but also by the anti-Somoza wing of the Liberal Party, the PLI. The willingness of wealthy Nicaraguans, Liberal or Conservative, to oppose the regime was limited by the fact that they profited from a system administered quite effectively by Somoza. In 1950 the U.S.-brokered "Pact of the Generals" formalized the power-sharing arrangement between Somoza's Liberals and the mainstream Conservatives. Nonetheless a generational divide existed within the traditional opposition, with a younger, more action-oriented, less subservient group coming on the scene in the 1940s. In Matagalpa this was represented by youths such as Tomás Borge, Guillermo McEwan, the Vargas brothers, and Ramón Gutiérrez— mostly students at the INN in the late 1940s and mostly from Conservative families.

The region also had a long history of Indian resistance to Spanish and ladino domination, represented especially by the 1881 Indian rebellion in

Matagalpa. In the early decades of the twentieth century, the indigenous population of the northern highlands looked to different wings of the Liberal and Conservative parties for protection against encroachments on their land and political rights. In the 1920s, Fonseca's own great-uncle Sebastián Amador had carried out a wave of terror against the indigenous communities around Matagalpa. Carlos and his teenage friends understood that much of the rural population of their region still considered itself Indian, but the students tended to see Indian resistance as something of historic interest rather than a living tradition. They were repelled by the racism and brutality with which the cafetaleros and the National Guard treated the indigenous population, but the students' own attitudes tended to be paternalistic. Even after the formation of the FSLN, Fonseca and his followers never really understood the depth of ethnic identity in Nicaragua or advanced much beyond this paternalistic approach.

A bipartisan resentment of United States military and economic intervention lay at the heart of the third tradition. Matagalpa and its surrounding province had been a center of the U.S. Marine occupation from mid-1927 to late 1932, and even two decades later, the occupiers' mistreatment of Nicaraguans, and especially their abuse of Nicaraguan women, still aroused anger. Although the Somoza regime had done much to wipe out the history of Sandino's struggle against the marines, at least in the urban areas, this more general anti-interventionist mood persisted. Ideologues of both traditional parties appealed to anti-Yankee sentiment, although at the same time both had close business and political relationships with the United States. The Conservatives accurately portrayed the Liberal Somoza and his National Guard as creatures of the United States, and the Liberals, with equal justification, pointed out that Conservative presidents had signed over Nicaragua's canal rights in the unpopular Bryan-Chamorro Treaty and had been the ones to call in the marines. There was no cultural counterpart to these expressions of political nationalism by Conservative and Liberal leaders. The Nicaraguan bourgeoisie and middle class, perhaps because of their small size, never developed a national culture and remained very much oriented to the United States. Wealthy Nicaraguans often went to school in the United States, bought their clothes there, preferred to speak English on social occasions, read the original versions of North American romance and mystery novels, and furnished their houses as if they lived in Miami or New Orleans. Nicaraguan theaters showed Hollywood movies, often in English without subtitles. The cultural norms of the wealthy were passed on to the poor—the only decoration in rough peasant shacks far from the capital was often tacked-up pages from *Life* magazine. Before the FSLN, the only challenge to U.S. domination over intellectual life came from the Right, through the attraction of some leading Nicaraguan intellectuals of the 1930s and 1940s to Catholic Falangism.

The fourth opposition tradition, and the only one with significant working-class support, was the Communist Party of Nicaragua (Partido Socialista de Nicaragua, PSN).[35] When first established as a legal organization during World War II, the party had given qualified support to Somoza. It was then able to use its legality and the space opened up by Somoza's labor code to stake out a significant role in the labor movement to the Left of the Somocista unions.[36]

The final tradition, the one most important to Fonseca in the 1960s and 1970s, was epitomized by Augusto César Sandino. In the early 1950s, in spite of a violent campaign to wipe out Sandino's combatants and an ideological crusade to paint him as a bandit, there remained country folk who had fought in Sandino's army or supported him. Nearly a decade later, Carlos Fonseca would set himself the task of searching out these old Sandinistas throughout northern Nicaragua and learning everything he could from them. But that was still ahead. As Fonseca went into his last years of high school, the Sandinista tradition was less real to him than any of the others. And there would be no references to Sandino in the cultural magazine in which Fonseca first expressed his political and social ideas in 1954 and 1955.

A Rebellious Student, 1950–1958

In 1950, at the age of fourteen, Carlos Fonseca entered the only public secondary school in Matagalpa, the National Institute of the North (INN). None of his maternal brothers went to high school: Raúl had only a year or two of schooling, and René and Juan Alberto at most finished fourth grade. Carlos had graduated at the top of his class from the only free elementary school in town, the Escuela Superior de Varones, a few blocks from his home. The student body of the INN was mostly male, although the school started to admit a few girls as day students in the early 1950s. Some scholarships were available to cover the small tuition, and boarding students from poor families received a modest government stipend. A student in the mid-1950s said the INN was "more like a reformatory than an institute, and the boarding student, if he wanted to survive, learned fast how to steal food." A 1955 article in the INN student magazine *Segovia* emphasized the working-class character of the student body:

> This little factory of ours that we call an institute will always be ready to produce more qualified youth for us—poor youth, the sons and daughters of humble people. The students who have graduated from the I.N.N. are all harvested from among the masses, the children of mechanics, masons, shoemakers, seamstresses, shopkeepers, etc. The children of the rich and the nearly-rich have plenty of money to go to the U.S. and to the major educational centers.[1]

As a public institution, the INN had links to the Somocista state, with preference given to the children of state bureaucrats, National Guard officers, and electoral supporters of Somoza's Nationalist Liberal Party. Carlos's connection to the Amador family weighed as heavily as his academic accomplishments in the school's decision to award him a full scholarship. Although later in life he preferred to use only the surname Fonseca, he was always Carlos Fonseca Amador at the INN.

In spite of its semiofficial status, the INN had a tradition of student oppositional activity. The short-lived *Vanguardia Juvenil* of 1946 was published by INN students, as was the equally ephemeral *Espártaco* of 1947 to 1948. Tomás Borge, an INN student who later helped found the FSLN, wrote stridently anti-Somocista articles for *Vanguardia Juvenil*. He described the bloc that backed Somoza's candidate in the 1947 elections as "a Front . . . composed of reactionaries, flunkies and cowards, whose goal is to perpetuate the power of the Nicaraguan Fuehrer and the Nicaraguan Gestapo, so that it can continue spilling the blood of our young rebels, continue with its persecutions, jails and beatings."[2] During the same pre-election period, Borge, Ramón Gutiérrez, and other dissident youths draped in black a bridge that Somoza was about to cross.

The radical INN students suffered a few nights in jail for their activity. Gutiérrez described one time when "they made us sweep the streets around the Parque Central with our hands, gather up shit with our bare hands. Some of the youth were sent under guard to throw feces in the Río Grande on the edge of town. There were no latrines in the town jail, and feces and urine were collected in four-gallon cans and thrown in the river." In 1952 the INN was the only secondary school in the country to join a university students' strike demanding that a plaque honoring Somoza be removed from the national university.[3]

During the early 1950s, Fonseca attended several meetings of a Conservative youth group and for a while worked with the National Union of Popular Action (Unión Nacional de Acción Popular, UNAP), a movement led by intellectuals who had participated in the anti-Somoza demonstrations of the mid-1940s. But around the same time, he came into contact with an organization that would have a much more important political influence on him, Nicaragua's Communist Party, the PSN. As Fonseca explained to a judge in 1957, "I came to see that the UNAP and its national leaders were too well off economically, they were too perfumed, too bourgeoisified, and that turned me off." He went on to link his disillusionment with the UNAP with a growing interest in Marxism:

> As my democratic concerns continued and weren't being satisfied by the
> UNAP, I looked for answers in Marxism, and I started looking in every
> bookstore I went to for Marxist books, whether they were philosophy,

politics, novels, or poetry. And my curiosity was aroused and led me to look in the newspapers every day for news about the communist countries and about the communist movement around the world, even though my budding sympathy for Marxism already made me suspect that the news about communism put out by the news agencies was fabricated.[4]

In 1953 or possibly early 1954 he told a leader of the UNAP that he could no longer support the organization because he had become a Marxist.[5]

Although he could not have found many Marxist books in the bookstores and libraries of Matagalpa, Fonseca did have a teacher at the INN, Rafael Antonio Díaz, who secretly lent interested students radical books from his own library. When Carlos traveled to Managua to visit his father's family, he found a bookstore linked to the Communist Party.

There is some dispute about when Fonseca joined the PSN and how seriously he took his membership. A detailed chronology prepared by the Instituto de Estudio del Sandinismo (IES) says he joined in July 1955, after he left Matagalpa for Managua. Carlos's employer in Managua also says he joined the party there. In 1956 Fonseca helped organize the first student cell of the PSN in León, and this date is sometimes given for his entry into the party. An even later date might be indicated by the fact that Fonseca, returning from Moscow in 1957, told his National Guard interrogators that he was not a member of the Communist Party although he sympathized with its ideas.[6] But the evidence is convincing that Fonseca joined the PSN in Matagalpa around 1954. According to Tomás Pravia ("Colocho"), the principal leader of the Matagalpa cell in the 1950s, Carlos attended weekly meetings as a voting member, paid the party dues of one córdoba a week, and was formally transferred to the jurisdiction of the party national office in Managua and then to León when he left Matagalpa in 1955. Colocho, another Communist worker named Santos Sánchez ("El Camarada"), and Fonseca's friend Ramón Gutiérrez all agree that Carlos's relationship with the cell was different from that of Ramón, who attended as an observer but did not vote or present resolutions.[7]

Jesús Blandón, a student at the INN during the mid-1950s, says two INN students were members of the PSN—Fonseca and Marcos Altamirano.

The main thing they did was sell the party newspaper *Unidad,* of which [the Matagalpa cell] received a bundle of 300. The sale lasted two days, since they would go through the barrios, enter into people's houses, and read the prospective customer an article from the paper. They used to invite the buyer's family to participate in the discussion about the newspaper as well, so that in this way the buyer would develop into a party sympathizer.

According to Colocho, the teenage Carlos sometimes sold as many as a hundred copies of an issue, carrying the paper around in his book bag through working-class neighborhoods and to market vendors and workplaces.[8]

Fonseca's mature political writings were extremely critical of the PSN, which he condemned as class collaborationist and bureaucratic, unable and unwilling to lead a revolution in Nicaragua. He called the PSN "Browderist" after CPUSA general secretary Earl Browder, the Western Hemisphere's leading advocate of communists joining with bourgeois forces in "popular fronts." Once Fonseca decided that the PSN was not genuinely Marxist, he had little patience with workers who were drawn to it. To understand his own attraction to the PSN, it helps to look concretely at where and when he joined. About fifteen young workers constituted the PSN cell in Matagalpa in the early 1950s. Colocho, age twenty-six in 1950, was the oldest. Except for Carlos Fonseca and one or two other high school students, all the members were workers, primarily in construction. Involved in union activities, they also had contacts with coffee workers in the countryside. This contrasts with the middle-class leadership of the party in the capital city: the seven Managua Communists charged with producing an illegal leaflet in the early 1950s included two doctors, one writer, and one businessman.[9]

That the PSN was not a legal organization in the early 1950s would have added to its revolutionary credibility for Carlos. Meetings in Matagalpa were held at a different member's house each week, and the newspaper had to be sold surreptitiously. "We used to arrive in a super-secret way, we would give a knock at the door and wait a long time; we would go with our collars turned up, covered right up to our chins, the way we had read about in a book about conspiracies against the dictator Rosas in Argentina," remembered one of Carlos's friends later. The PSN had been banned and some of its leaders arrested in the late 1940s, as the Cold War began and Somoza moved out of his "pro-labor," populist stage of 1944 to 1946 and into mending fences with the elite opposition.[10]

Fonseca may have had moments of doubt about the revolutionary potential of the PSN even as early as the Matagalpa years. According to Ramón Gutiérrez, in late 1954 or early 1955, Carlos convinced the rest of the PSN cell in Matagalpa to pass a resolution calling for an armed workers' and peasants' revolution in Nicaragua. Because Carlos could not go, Ramón went alone to

Managua to present the resolution to the Political Bureau. PSN chief Manuel Pérez Estrada received Gutiérrez at his house and began to ridicule the resolution, calling it "adventurist," threatening to invoke "party discipline," and complaining about the backwardness of the peasantry. "This lowered the level of our enthusiasm," said Gutiérrez in a 1994 interview. Matagalpa cell leader Colocho has insisted that this incident never took place and that Fonseca never voiced these opinions until after the Cuban revolution. Presenting such radical ideas in a Communist Party cell in the mid-1950s would have been, according to Colocho, "not acceptable, not in the interests of national unity."[11] Gutiérrez's story has the ring of truth, however. Carlos's ideas were in a state of flux—he was, after all, seventeen years old. It is not so hard to imagine his getting a burst of enthusiasm for armed revolution, even within the context of overall loyalty to the PSN's more cautious and moderate approach, and carrying the young workers of the Matagalpa cell with him.

A description of Fonseca at gatherings in the home of Marxist intellectual Manolo Cuadra in the mid-1950s is that of a restless, questioning teenager, totally lacking in social graces. Interviewed in 1986, one of Cuadra's guests remembered a skinny, reserved, serious youth, who spoke only to his host and generally did not even sit down but "took up his position in a corner of the room, leaning against a wall, and from there watched the different participants in the discussion." Occasionally Carlos would take advantage of a lull in the conversation to interject a question like "Manolo, do you think the bourgeoisie will rule this country forever?" or "Manolo, do you think an alliance of the workers, campesinos and intellectuals is possible?" and then retreat to his corner to wait for an answer from his embarrassed host.[12]

During Carlos Fonseca's fifth and final year of high school, he began collaborating with two young friends whose ideas about the world and budding desire to change it were similar to his own. Ramón Gutiérrez, whose father owned a small shoemaking operation, had been involved in oppositional activities half a decade earlier. When he was about sixteen, Ramón was excommunicated by the Catholic Church and forced to leave town after publishing a skit involving a masturbation contest among a group of archangels. Living in Guatemala during the presidency of Jacobo Arbenz, Ramón obtained a copy of *The Communist Manifesto* in French and some writings by Mao Zedong in Spanish, which he brought back to Matagalpa with him in 1954. Ramón, sometimes called "Moncho," took up his studies again at the INN and began to discuss with his new friend Carlos Fonseca the pamphlets he had brought back. Ramón and Carlos look very much alike in a snapshot taken at Christmas in 1955—tall, thin, and fair skinned, they appear studious and serious behind identical dark-framed eyeglasses. Carlos's second new friend looked quite different. Shorter, darker, and younger, Francisco "Chico" Buitrago moved to Matagalpa from the northern village of Terrabona to finish high school. Because he had been a seminary student and always dressed in white, his friends at the INN sometimes called him "Cura" (priest), but Buitrago, like his two older friends, no longer accepted the teachings of the church. In early 1954, Fonseca was seventeen, Buitrago fifteen, and Gutiérrez twenty.[13]

The three friends organized a student group at the INN, the Centro Cultural, with Carlos as president and Ramón keeping a low profile to avoid bringing down the wrath of the church. In August 1954 the Centro began to publish a cultural journal called *Segovia*, with new issues following almost every month until editor Fonseca graduated and left Matagalpa in the spring of 1955. Buitrago put out four more issues of the magazine before following Carlos to Managua in early 1956, at which point *Segovia* ceased publication. The students financed their project through newspaper sales and advertisements by local businesses, sometimes supplemented by a loan from Matilde Morales, a sympathetic teacher in whose house they met to plan each issue.

Segovia did not take on the Somoza government directly; the dictator's name hardly appeared in the journal, and one article even had modest praise for a government-sponsored public housing program. The writers avoided overtly political subjects, conscious of the vulnerability of an official student publication at a public institution. After only a few issues appeared, the influential opposition daily *La Prensa* published a short article entitled "The Red Seeds of Matagalpa," simultaneously patronizing and Red-baiting the *Segovia* youth. In an emergency meeting, the editorial group discussed this unwelcome national attention and worried about how their parents and teachers would react and whether they would lose their scholarships.[14] But *Segovia* weathered this storm. By the end of its run in 1956, its student writers had moved away or lost interest, not succumbed to government repression.

The twelve articles written by Carlos Fonseca include poetry, editorials on student life, and analytical pieces on female suffrage and on the nineteenth-century independence wars. The *Segovia* collection has never been published and has received almost no attention from scholars.[15] Yet these youthful writings offer valuable insight into Carlos Fonseca's political and social ideas. Producing the journal represented his first experience with collective political activity. He was at the center of a core group of four or five teenage boys who directed the endeavor politically and organized twenty or more youths, male and female, to write articles and sell the magazine. Besides Carlos,

Chico, and Ramón, the central organizers included Raúl LeCler, whose father was a professor, and Cipriano Orúe, from a family of Conservative intellectuals. The broader circle included students such as Carlos's neighbor Bertha Prado, the daughter of a National Guard colonel. Besides selling *Segovia*, Bertha also borrowed political books from Carlos and took sewing courses so that she could someday give vocational training to women workers.[16] Fonseca's role in the *Segovia* group presaged in several ways his later involvement in university politics and in the FSLN. Although the project represented a collective effort, Carlos was indisputably its central organizer, and it suffered when he was not present. All the secondary leaders who worked closely with him were male. The other activists were all extremely loyal to Fonseca and impressed with his level of political and academic commitment, even when they did not share it.

"The youth of Matagalpa is fired up," began Fonseca's editorial launching the first issue of *Segovia*. "Isn't a bullet hot when it is fired? We are a bullet fired out of longing to serve our nation." This short paragraph introduced the two interrelated central themes of *Segovia*: the key role of youth, and the close relationship between education and the nation, or *patria*. The theme of violence is also present but was not as prevalent in *Segovia* as it would become in Carlos's later writings.

Carlos contrasted his own generation with earlier ones, saying that "the cold activity of Nicaraguan intellectuals will be heated up by the youth." He returned to this theme in the lead editorial several months later. It was not enough to be young and energetic; students also had to be united, well-read, and conscious about their role in society. "We are sure that Matagalpa has a young population of great talent, but in other eras Matagalpa had equally talented youth who, for lack of cultural orientation, produced bad results."[17]

The most important role students could play, according to Fonseca and the other youths who put out *Segovia*, was to bring literacy and therefore civilization to poor workers and peasants. At the time more than 80 percent of the rural population of Nicaragua was illiterate, and these students considered it their patriotic duty to spread learning in the countryside. Articles by Francisco Buitrago, in particular, developed the close relationship between education, civilization, industrialization, and nationhood. He titled his call for a national literacy campaign "Let's Build a Nation!" [Hagamos Patria]. "Thoughts of a Segovian Student" in the first issue called on students to take up "the position of a soldier, ready for the Patria's call and anxious to take up the weapons of the intellect." Buitrago returned to this theme again and again; in one of the last issues, he wrote: "We must do everything we can to teach campesinos, small landowners, and field hands to read and write; if we accomplish this it won't just mean we have fewer illiterates, it will also mean we have a more advanced Nation." Buitrago had harsh words for apathetic students "who don't care about the Vampire who is sucking drop by drop the blood of their fellow citizens, who because they don't have money are thrown into the workplace, making themselves into fresh meat for exploitation." Students were not the only ones urged to help their country by teaching the illiterate to read and write. Scattered through the eleven issues of the magazine were exhortations to landlords and employers such as "If you own a hacienda, find out which of your workers are illiterate and teach them to read and write," and "Teach your servant to read and you will be doing the best deed of your life." The final issue of *Segovia*, in early 1956, reprinted a letter from Carlos Fonseca to the minister of public education, in which Fonseca proposed establishing popular libraries in barbershops around the country for the use of "the poor people who will come to these barbershops looking for newspapers and magazines, that is, working people."[18]

Over the course of *Segovia*'s existence, ever greater attention was paid to social issues, particularly to working-class living conditions. Colonial patterns still prevailed, especially in the countryside, making Nicaragua, in Fonseca's words, "unfit for living like a human being." Articles highlighted the problems of hunger, dilapidated and overcrowded housing, and the lack of social security coverage and union protection. *Segovia* greeted 1956 with an article saying: "For the poor the New Year is one of tears, of sadnesses, but also one of hopefulness for those who have a redeeming ideology, for those who understand that the popular masses have the strength of the majority."[19]

Fonseca frequently used mother-child metaphors, with Nicaragua or the nation as the mother and the socially minded student as the good child. He was not the first to use the convention, but he put his own youthful spin on this gendered nationalist vision. In an article entitled "The Future," Carlos called Nicaraguan cities "half-naked virgins," then went on confidently to assert that with the advent of industrialization, these cities "will get married. They will no longer be virgins! They will not be ravished! And they will form households. They will bear children! The revolution will be here. And it will be Nicaraguans who will be the main ones to enjoy the fruits of Nicaraguan resources."[20] The contrast could hardly be more stark: on the one hand, virgins who are half-naked, backward, dangerous, liable to be ravished and taken advantage of by unnamed foreigners; on the other, married women with children, living in households, Nicaraguans enjoying their nation's bounty, modern and even revolutionary.

An article entitled "The Women's Vote" appeared in the December 1955 issue, signed by Carlos as "former editor of *Segovia*." This short contribution, which Fonseca mailed from Managua, was clearly a response to Ramón Gutiérrez's essay of the previous June, "The Female Vote and Women's Lack of Productivity." Gutiérrez had taken a sectarian position, couched in Marxist terminology, implying that female suffrage was "premature" until an industrial revolution had transformed women into wageworkers. "The women of northern Nicaragua," wrote Ramón, "cannot know what the nation needs if they do not even know what to do in order to survive. They are nonproductive women because the work they do does not produce anything." The issue was not an academic one—the Somoza government had just extended the vote to women, as part of a constitutional reform package that also allowed for reelection of the president. The PSN was at best lukewarm to the idea of women voting. Fonseca countered: "In the next elections, Nicaraguan women will have the right to vote. Unfortunately there is a large sector that is against this fact and thinks Nicaraguan women should not get involved in politics. We are against this idea. Because we believe that all those who are directly affected by politics must have the right to vote." After pointing to the fact that two-thirds of Nicaraguan children were raised by single mothers, Fonseca called on women to cast their first votes in favor of policies that would guarantee all Nicaraguans "beans, clothes and freedom."[21]

At the heart of the writings of Fonseca and Buitrago was the concept of progress and modernization as nearly inevitable, the automatic result of the spread of education. Although very aware of Nicaragua's poverty and backwardness, and especially the harsh lives of its working classes, these young men believed that their country would follow the path of Western Europe and the United States to modern nationhood through industrialization and economic progress. As long as students and intellectuals fulfilled their educational responsibilities, cultural advancement and improving social conditions would come through capitalist development. The ideas of the Enlightenment, as interpreted by the Liberal tradition of their own country going back to the nineteenth century, made sense to these young men of the mid-1950s. A decade later, under the influence of the Cuban revolution, Fonseca would reject the idea of modernization through capitalist development, but it was quite compatible with the version of Marxism that he had learned from the PSN in his youth. The Communists believed that countries like Nicaragua were destined to pass through a prolonged period of economic development along Western lines, and that socialism, like capitalism, would eventually come to these backward countries from outside.

Segovia did represent something new in its rejection of the framework of traditional Conservative and Liberal party politics. Unlike the PSN or the Conservative opposition youth of the late 1940s the INN youth had little interest in elections. The only articles that mentioned voting were those on female suffrage.

Two other aspects of *Segovia* deserve mention: its fiery, youthful enthusiasm and its regional character. In its writing style, subject matter, and dependence on the editors' exam schedules, the journal constantly reflected its student origins, with poetry, satire, short stories, sports news, historical articles, and reports on school assemblies and celebrations. *Segovia* performed as a cultural magazine in the broadest sense. Fonseca presented his own belligerent definition of culture when he wrote of *Segovia:* "Our culture-bearing function is analogous to that of a combatant who in a dangerous situation goes right up to where the opposing army is just in order to punch an enemy soldier in the nose."[22] There is something almost childish about the sentence, although it is not atypical of Fonseca's lifelong bluntness in writing and speaking. Both Fonseca and Buitrago frequently employed military metaphors in their *Segovia* writings.

The opening editorial of the magazine promised that this "cultural organ born in the Segovias" would show the rest of Nicaragua that the north-central region could produce something besides farm crops and dairy cows.[23] An article in the first issue by Francisco Buitrago referred to "the virgin nature of these cold mountains, not yet completely exploited by the greedy and commercial foreigner. . . . We come out of this land, overflowing with the fertility of these hillsides, filled up with ideals as hugely majestic as these gigantic pines that caress us and with the courageous spirit that belongs to every Segovian."

What is missing from *Segovia* is also significant. Augusto César Sandino's name never appears in the eleven issues. It is true that the Segovias were the center of support for Sandino's uprising, so at first glance the title seems to be an indirect (and therefore safe) way of identifying with Sandino's struggle. But young Conservatives such as Tomás Borge had written articles about Sandino nearly a decade earlier, and Fonseca could have found some way to make reference to Sandino. Even Fonseca's history of the fight for Nicaraguan national liberation from the Spanish conquest to his own day, which stretched over two issues, did not mention the war of 1926 to 1933. The journal's name was probably chosen simply because Segovia was where this group of youth lived. They identified with their own region's lush mountain scenery, its history of Indian resistance, and its democratic tradition compared to the old aristocratic capitals of Granada and León. Fonseca had certainly heard of Sandino by this time. But he was at least a sympathizer and more likely already a member of the PSN, which considered Sandino a petit bourgeois adventurer.[24] Fonseca's own writings never mentioned Sandino until the end of the 1950s, when his name came up in the context of the Cuban revolution.

When Carlos graduated in 1955, he won a gold star for being first in his class every year for five years. He also won first prize in French, a language he had learned to read *The Communist Manifesto.* The *Manifesto* helped him through his final exam, in which he wrote an essay entitled "Capital and Labor." Fonseca wrote that "for communists there's no such thing as a just wage. Karl Marx, in his work *Capital* explained: 'The worker has a right to the entire product of his labor.' The Marxist formula, for all its extremism, seems to us the only solution to the enormous economic crisis that has brought down such misery and . . . [illegible] . . . and ignorance upon the proletariat."

Even on his high school final exam, Carlos Fonseca displayed the insolence and class hatred that would mark his dealings with social superiors for the rest of his life:

> The owners of the instruments of production must be the workers themselves. So, for that to happen, does the property of the capitalists have to be taken away? Yes, it must be stripped away. What difference does it make if a few people suffer who have always lived high by exploiting proletarian labor? . . . Our people have a saying: "The only way to get rich is to be a thief." And they don't say that because some communist demagogue has been talking to them. Our people talk that way because they know the hacienda owner is afraid to walk on his own land for fear the campesinos he stole it from will shoot him down.[25]

After graduation, Carlos moved to Managua, residing briefly in his father's house before persuading the director of the Instituto Ramírez Goyena, Guillermo Rothschuh Tablada, to hire him to organize the school's library. "He suddenly turned up in my office at the Goyena one morning and declared, 'I'm a poet,'" said Rothschuh. "I asked him what he had written and he recited his poem 'The Molendero Bird's Sixteen Verses.'"[26]

"El Goyena," founded in 1893, was one of the leading secular high schools in Nicaragua. Like the INN in Matagalpa, the school had close links to the Somocista Liberal Party, giving preference in admission and financial aid to the sons of Liberal politicians and military officers. Rothschuh Tablada, the young director of the Goyena, had a reputation for encouraging critical thinking in his students. Under his influence, a group of students in the mid-1950s were studying the Mexican revolution and dreaming "that in Nicaragua there would be changes, that the dictatorship would fall and that the people would have knowledge, health, shelter, and bread." Rothschuh had created a storm when he commissioned the painting of a mural at the school entitled "La Raza," and *La Prensa* once referred to him as a "communist element." But as an employee of the Ministry of Education, Rothschuh did not criticize Somoza directly. He had been a member of the Somocista Youth in his hometown, and one of his published poems was a hymn of praise to Somoza's wife. Rothschuh might have found it difficult to explain his decision to hire Fonseca Amador if the radical youth were not also the son of a prominent Somocista.[27]

A boarding student described the arrival of the new librarian, only a couple years older than most of the students:

> He unpacked just a few pieces of clothing, one pair of shoes and plenty of books, along with some copies of *Segovia*. . . . he was tall and skinny, with a wide forehead and a big Adam's apple, with poor but clean clothes. . . . Carlos rapidly became part of the discussions that took place almost every evening on the school's patio. At first he only made a few observations, but later he became a leader of the sizable group that gathered. The group wasn't restricted to Goyena people but often included artists and poets; those who attended most frequently were [the journalist] Manuel Diaz y Sotelo and Manolo Cuadra.[28]

Fonseca encouraged his student charges to study Nicaraguan history. Once he assigned them to find out everything they could about an unknown figure named Cleto Ardóñez. "You have to look him up in the archives," Carlos instructed, "until you come up with a biography that will rescue him from the disdain and neglect the fake historians have condemned him to."[29] Carlos himself would later take on the same project with Augusto César Sandino.

But Fonseca was no mere archivist. He was also doing political contact work with the students. At the end of the day, commented one youth, "Carlos closed the Goyena library, only to open the one he had in his own locker. Fewer books but of higher quality. . . . It was a locker without much clothing and with nothing to eat in it, but it was full of books, magazines and leaflets. He never went anywhere without a book under his arm."[30]

Fonseca's extracurricular political activity did not escape the attention of the director of the institute. "He founded his own Recruitment School at Goyena," said Rothschuh later. "That's where he fished for his first disciples."

> I think of Carlos, with a bunch of books under his arm, coming and going in the poor neighborhoods of Managua, passing Goyena's books to union workers and then from the union to an even more private hiding place. . . . Or selling the magazine *Segovia* that he had founded, or selling *Orientación Popular* [the PSN newspaper] on the Managua buses, coming and going on the buses every night, and then getting off at exactly 10 o'clock at Fray Bartolomé de las Casas Park, opposite the Fishermen's Barrio, where he had a meeting at 10:10 with the shoemakers.[31]

Fonseca impressed many Goyena students with his self-discipline and his abstinence from drinking, smoking, and sexual activity, but few were prepared to follow his example. In this they were similar to their counterparts at the INN in Matagalpa, where some students had begun to drift away from the *Segovia* group in 1955 because of Carlos's strictness and his tendency to criticize them for going to a party instead of a meeting.[32]

Carlos's most important recruit at the Goyena was Jorge Navarro, a gentle and hardworking student from a small town in the North, who, according to a classmate, "was so serious he never went out, he spent his whole time reading and playing basketball." Navarro is the FSLN member most often compared to Fonseca in terms of moral rectitude. Navarro allegedly used to walk from one end of Managua to the other to save the twenty-five-centavo bus fare, even when he had in his possession C\$ 50,000 that the FSLN had "recovered" by robbing a bank.[33] Sometime in the fall of 1955, Francisco Buitrago moved from Matagalpa to Managua to work with Fonseca and Navarro.

Fonseca still hoped to build a national movement of high school students. He pressed the Goyena Institute to admit students who had been expelled from other schools. Under his direction, students at the Goyena put out a short-lived mimeographed newsletter called *Diriangén* after an Indian chief who had fought the Spanish. On 14 September 1955, in celebration of the Nicaraguan national holiday, Fonseca, Buitrago, and Rothschuh organized a march in which students from three public high schools converged on the San Jacinto hacienda, site of a famous mid-nineteenth-century battle against the invader William Walker. Although Fonseca was beginning to try to reach out to students at the private Catholic high schools, his contacts in the mid-1950s were all at public institutions.

In March 1956, at the end of the Nicaraguan school year, Fonseca left the

Instituto Goyena and moved to León, where he enrolled in the National University of Nicaragua as a law student. León, a colonial city sixty miles northwest of the capital on the hot coastal plain, was the traditional stronghold of the Liberal wing of the Nicaraguan oligarchy and, since the eighteenth century, the rival of Conservative Granada. León was famous as much for its cathedrals as for its university, and the Catholic Church played a prominent and public role in the life of the city. In other parts of Latin America, the Conservatives were known as the party of the church and the Liberals generally associated with secularism, but ideological lines were blurry in Nicaragua.

León, the nation's second-largest city, was a bastion of electoral support for Somoza's Nationalist Liberal Party and had its own Liberal newspapers. Two other wings of Liberalism were based in León: Liberal *obrerismo*, representing the concerns of artisans and other urban workers, and the Independent Liberal Party, or PLI, formed in León in 1944 by middle-class and bourgeois opponents of Somoza.

Traditionally an area of cattle, grain, and sugar production, the departments of León and its northern neighbor Chinandega were transformed by an explosion of cotton production in the decade after World War II. By 1955 the fiber had replaced coffee as Nicaragua's leading export. Cotton acreage increased more than five times between 1951 and 1955, and production increased almost ten times. Once the breadbasket of Nicaragua, the area around León was transformed into a dust bowl as plantation owners cut down forests and expelled tenant farmers and Indian communities from their land. During the spring dry season, hot winds blew dust into every corner of the city, and the air in León stank of pesticide.[34]

Wealthy cotton planters lived in León mansions hidden behind modest exteriors. Even today, walking down a León street, one seems to pass by three or four small row houses, each with a door and one or two windows fronting right on a treeless street. But an open door or window will reveal that the three or four houses are actually a single luxurious dwelling, with living and sleeping rooms distributed around a courtyard the size of a small park, filled with trees and flowers and surrounded by four wide corridors set off by arched pillars.

Nicaragua in the 1950s had only about a thousand university students and one institution of higher education, the National University in León (called the Universidad Nacional de Nicaragua until 1958, thereafter the Universidad Nacional Autónoma de Nicaragua, UNAN). Like the secular high schools where Carlos Fonseca had studied and worked, the National University had close ties to the Somocista state apparatus. Students who were the offspring of, or came recommended by, Liberal Party stalwarts were listed in the "Red Book" and received preferential treatment when it came to financial aid and grades. Nevertheless a movement for university autonomy began to gain force in the mid-1950s. At this stage, autonomy activists' goal was a "non-political" university: a manifesto of the early 1950s insisted that a university that tolerated student organizing *against* Somoza would be just as bad as one affiliated with the regime.[35] Autonomy was finally granted in March 1958, at the urging of the school's rector, Mariano Fiallos Gil, with a law modeled on the university autonomy won in Córdoba, Argentina, in 1918—a full four decades earlier.

Nicaraguan university students were a privileged minority, and most were headed for a career in the professions or state bureaucracy. Not all the students at the UNAN came from wealthy families, however. Some scholarships went to the children of relatively low-level supporters of Somoza, and the richest Nicaraguan families tended to send their sons and daughters to college in the United States and Europe—or at least to Mexico.

On his arrival in León in the spring of 1956, Carlos Fonseca moved into a subsidized room near the university and paid by the month to eat at the cheapest food stand in León. The Student Center (CUN, later CUUN) named him editor in chief of its newspaper, *El Universitario*. Octavio Robleto, a friend from the Goyena Institute who lived nearby, remembers that Fonseca again had more books than clothes and had already found a sympathetic professor to lend him the Marxist books that were hard to find in Somoza's Nicaragua. When Carlos visited Octavio, the two would spend half the night discussing politics and literature—Cervantes, Neruda, Rubén Darío, Manolo Cuadra.[36]

In 1957 Fonseca described with pride the intense political activity of his first year in León: "I threw myself into [student activism] with all the energy I had. Because I believed that newspapers, meetings and leaflets constituted the civil, peaceful campaign that was decisive in the struggle against any antipopular dictatorship. This correct thesis was maintained also by a courageous group of independent liberals, as well as by the popular masses."[37] When this passage was written, Fonseca still thought change could be won through a "civil, peaceful campaign," an idea against which he would argue vigorously in subsequent decades.

In León, Fonseca put together the first all-student cell of the PSN in Nicaragua. Its members included Tomás Borge, a fellow Matagalpan and occasional writer for the opposition newspaper *La Prensa*, and Silvio Mayorga, a fourth-year law student from a family of modest landowners in the provincial town of Nagarote. Borge had the most extensive political experience. He had been involved in the Conservative youth in Matagalpa in the late 1940s, and he had attended a Latin American student conference in Bogotá, Colombia, in 1948, where he met Cuban student leader Fidel Castro and had a chance to observe the urban uprising known as the "Bogotazo."

The campus-based PSN group in León organized the study of Marxist classics and sent Silvio Mayorga to the 1956 World Federation of Democratic Youth conference in Ceylon. The initiative for the all-student cell came from Fonseca rather than from the PSN national leadership. Fonseca later complained that his party paid little attention to campus organizing. "This cell tried to establish a relationship with the Communist Party that existed in Nicaragua, with the idea of following its instructions, of being directed by it. But in fact the PSN had nothing to do with the student movement." This was also true of Fonseca's earlier work among students in Matagalpa and Managua; Ramón Gutiérrez called the Matagalpa Communist cell "stupid" because he and Carlos "had twenty students who followed our lead and the socialists never gave us any direction."[38] In any case, the student cell in León lasted only a few months.

Nicaraguan president Anastasio Somoza García was assassinated in León in September 1956. Founder and first chief of the National Guard, diplomatic ally of the United States in World War II and the Cold War, Somoza García had been president of Nicaragua almost without interruption for two decades. When he was killed, his older son, Luis Somoza Debayle, was immediately named president. His second son, West Point–educated Anastasio, was already the head of the National Guard. (Anastasio Somoza Debayle is known in Nicaragua as "Tachito," to distinguish him from his father, Anastasio Somoza García, whose nickname was "Tacho.")

Somoza's killer, Rigoberto López Pérez, was slain on the spot by presidential bodyguards. A twenty-seven-year-old poet, López Pérez had loose ties to the dissident PLI, and he had been trained and armed by anti-Somoza former National Guardsmen who lived in exile in El Salvador. Sixteen years later, in his "Notes on the Testimonial Letter of Rigoberto López Pérez," Fonseca described López Pérez as a "legitimate child of Sandino," characterizing his action as "not just understandable but also justifiable" because "in the whole country there was no organization, no leadership, no revolutionary consciousness."[39] Fonseca had no praise for López Pérez in 1956, however, when he was still committed to nonviolent methods and believed that the PSN provided the leadership Nicaragua needed.

President Luis Somoza declared a state of siege after his father's killing and began a roundup of suspected conspirators that was particularly intense in León. The area surrounding the university was turned into an armed camp, its streets blocked off by barbed wire and patrolled by the National Guard. Hundreds of students and other dissidents were arrested, including Carlos Fonseca, who had never met López Pérez and knew nothing about the assassination plot. Held from 27 September to 14 November, Carlos was eventually released without charges, probably as a result of his father's intervention. Tomás Borge remained in jail more than two years, winning release only after sustained student protests.

When the *Guardia* arrested Fonseca, they confiscated eighty books, leaflets, and newspapers, including writings of Marx and Engels, Pablo Neruda's poetry, novels by Faulkner, Balzac, and Dostoyevsky, and essays on religion and on politics. Following his release, Fonseca—who identified himself as "son of Fausto F. Amador"—wrote to National Guard chief Anastasio Somoza Debayle, demanding the return of the confiscated material, "none of which has any usefulness for the National Guard, while for me it represents the fruit of ten years of disquiet." Fonseca expressed his confidence that Col. Somoza would return his "valued books and beloved pictures," and that thus the colonel "will avoid the growth of useless resentment on my part."[40]

This request prompted a letter from a National Guard security officer to "Chief Director" Somoza. Written on the letterhead of the Office of National Security (OSN), the letter is a fascinating document, written entirely in English. The signature is illegible, but the author's fluent and correct English suggests he was an American. Somoza apparently found it perfectly normal to receive a communication from his secret police in English, scrawling on the bottom of the page in the same language, "Return those things which are not comunistic. ASD." The security officer's conclusion that Fonseca was too radical and too open about his politics to be a member of the Communist Party was astute and even prophetic, although factually incorrect at the time.

> 1. Attached is a copy of the list of personal property which was taken from FONSECA Amador at the time of his arrest. Most of the literature is communistic. The subject is an admitted supporter of Communist doctrine, although he denies being a member of the Communist Party. It is believed that he is *not* a member of the Communist Party, since one who is so outspoken in matters concerning Communism in a country in which Communism is illegal would probably be shunned by the covert members of the Party.

2. The subject's father, Fausto F. AMADOR, has stated that he feels that his natural son has become a much more outspoken exponent of Communism since his recent imprisonment. FONSECA stated during his interrogation that he and Tomas BORGE planned to continue their activities in Matagalpa and León after his release.[41]

Despite his seven weeks in jail, Fonseca finished near the top of his class at the end of his first year at the UNAN. The report card he received after his February 1957 exams contained many perfect scores and nothing lower than eight on a scale of ten. That was his last good report card, however. Fonseca was out of the country for much of the 1957 to 1958 school year, so his second year of law school did not begin until June 1958. After the final exams in February 1959, Fonseca's report card simply noted after every subject, "No se presentó" [failed to show up].[42]

In 1957 the PSN sent Fonseca to the Soviet Union as its delegate to the Sixth World Congress of Students and Youth for Peace and Friendship. Some 35,000 young people attended the Moscow festival, and about 700 the subsequent conference in Kiev. In the book Fonseca wrote about his visit, he made the decision to attend seem almost accidental. He was suffering acute "mental fatigue," he said, the result of intense student activism, followed by fifty days in jail and two months cramming for final exams. Six feet tall, he weighed only 140 pounds in June 1957. A doctor prescribed a long vacation, and Fonseca went to Costa Rica to recuperate. There he looked up Manolo Cuadra, who told him about the youth festival and arranged his airfare to the Soviet Union. It is more likely that Fonseca's trip was organized the same way as the other Latin American delegations, by the local Communist Party. Fonseca was a member of the PSN and its best-known student leader; he was the logical person to be sent by a small party that could only field a delegation of one to a major international event. He was listed at the conference (under the pseudonym Pablo Cáceres) as a representative of the "Jeunesse Parti Socialiste" of Nicaragua.[43] The Salvadoran revolutionary Roque Dalton, who met him in Moscow, said Fonseca was a member of the Communist Party at the time.

In *Un Nicaragüense en Moscú*, written in early 1958, Fonseca presented an uncritical journalistic account of his trip to the Soviet Union and East Germany. He described the Soviet Union as a workers' paradise, its five-year plans accomplished in full, social evils like prostitution abolished completely, unemployment and discrimination eliminated for all time. "The purpose of my booklet," he explained at the beginning, "is to add a Nicaraguan grain to the construction of world peace. . . . I hope to contribute to peaceful coexistence between the great powers that have different social systems." The book's only criticism of the United States was that it refused to recognize the Soviet Union's peaceful intentions. Fonseca praised the "humble" lifestyle of top Soviet officials and claimed that "the newspapers are one of the main means of criticism." He insisted that "contrary to what people might think these days, the Russians don't like to hide any mistakes they make or defects they have." Fonseca brushed aside the Khrushchev revelations and repeatedly praised Stalin as a great leader: "I saw monuments to Stalin everywhere I went in the Soviet Union. But I never saw a single one to Nikita." Fonseca claimed to have learned the truth about the Hungarian uprisings of 1956, quoting a Hungarian youth as "grateful to the Soviets for the help they gave us in preventing fascist criminals from taking over in Hungary."[44]

Fonseca throughout his life was scrupulously honest and often remonstrated with fellow Sandinistas who exaggerated the strengths or hid the defects of their own movement. Why, then, did he paint such a rosy and one-sided picture of the Soviet Union in 1957? His hosts undoubtedly arranged tours and interviews that presented Soviet society in the best possible light, but this only partly explains Fonseca's failure to uncover any negative features. The explanation that fits best with his character is that he was simply swept away by the technological and social achievements of the Soviet Union, by the fact that it had become a major world power in the four decades since the Russian Revolution. He was like thousands of other students and workers, especially from underdeveloped countries, who saw socialism as practiced in the Soviet Union as a way out of the backwardness and inequality of their own societies. Except for its title, *Un Nicaragüense en Moscú* could easily have been created by a young Communist Party member in Indonesia or Bolivia or even the United States. Although written in Fonseca's own direct and folksy style, the book had none of the revolutionary content of his writings after the Cuban revolution. The closest it came was in his enthusiasm for the "youth culture" aspect of the festival. "The Festival brought together in Moscow the world's best—its Youth. I think that the greatest thing about Panama isn't its canal, but rather its youth. And the greatest thing about Cuba isn't its sugar industry, but rather its youth."[45]

The name Augusto César Sandino does not appear in *Un Nicaragüense en Moscú*. At one point Fonseca noted that many of the delegates from other countries gave him pins and buttons with pictures of their national heroes and asked him for similar mementos. "Because my trip was organized in such a hurry," Fonseca wrote, "I didn't have time to collect mementos of my country, such as coins, stamps, empty cigar boxes, etc."[46] There is no indication here that Nicaragua might have a national hero of its own.

Un Nicaragüense en Moscú is most striking for its discontinuity with all Fonseca's later writings.[47] It glorified the USSR, failed to mention Sandino, and accepted without question the PSN's theory that Nicaragua needed not a revolutionary transformation but a long process of reform in which organized labor would play the key role. Fonseca gave several talks about the situation in Nicaragua during his trip to the Soviet Union and East Germany. The only one that has survived is his message to the Fourth Congress of the World Federation of Trade Unions in Leipzig in October 1957, where he gave some statistics about the poverty and lack of education of Nicaraguan workers and praised the strength of the union movement between 1944 and 1947 (when, under the leadership of the PSN, it gave qualified support to Somoza). Fonseca did not even mention that a state of siege had existed in his country for nearly a year, stressing instead the openings for labor organizing and the circulation of the PSN's pro-labor newspaper.[48]

The PSN assigned Rodolfo Romero to edit Fonseca's book "for political errors." Only a few years older than Fonseca, Romero had been a Communist for almost a decade and had worked with both the PVP of Costa Rica and the PGT of Guatemala. He made few suggestions, aside from telling Carlos to drop the passage where an elementary school girl gave a speech that sounded like it came from Lenin. As they worked on the book, the two men became friends. Rodolfo told Carlos about his experiences in 1954 during the military coup against Guatemalan president Jacobo Arbenz. Although not instructed by the PSN to stay, Romero remained in Guatemala for a time to participate in the short-lived and disorganized resistance to the coup. There he met a young Argentine doctor who was also looking for a way to fight the military takeover. The doctor had no combat experience, and Rodolfo taught him how to clean and fire an automatic weapon. Romero knew the Argentine as Ernesto Guevara, but he told Fonseca in 1958 that Guevara had joined up with Cuban rebel Fidel Castro and that the Cubans had begun to call him "Che."[49]

When Carlos Fonseca wrote *Un Nicaragüense en Moscú*, he was a loyal member of the PSN. The book was published by the party in early 1958, with an introduction by Secretary-General Manuel Pérez Estrada. Fonseca aggressively sold the book at meetings, train stations, and public squares, and he gave copies to friends and relatives. He even mailed a copy to Anastasio Somoza, in a letter asking for the return of the books and camera taken from him on his return to Nicaragua.[50]

There is no evidence that Fonseca disagreed with the PSN's politics in 1958. One of the party's most important projects that year was organizing support for Somoza's new labor legislation, which provided for increased social security while raising taxes on workers' wages. Fonseca later condemned PSN chief Pérez Estrada for speaking on the same platform with "the discredited hacks of the Somocista unions" and called the PSN's behavior proof of its "chronic tendency to follow along at the tail of the traditional political groups controlled by the exploiting classes."[51] This criticism came long after 1958, however.

Fonseca started his second year of law school at the UNAN in June 1958. He was elected to the executive committee of the CUUN, where he worked closely with Fernando Gordillo, at age seventeen already known as a poet and orator. The UNAN had finally won its autonomy in March 1958 and was no longer officially linked to the Somocista state and Nationalist Liberal Party. UNAN rector Mariano Fiallos Gil and young academic Carlos Tunnerman chose Carlos Fonseca to give the welcoming speech to new students for the first year of university autonomy.

Carlos used his position as a campus leader to involve students in national and international politics, helping to organize the July 1958 protests that prevented the UNAN from granting the U.S. president's brother Milton Eisenhower an honorary degree. Many of Fonseca's duties had to do with more mundane student affairs. Among the letters signed by him that made their way into the secret police's new Carlos Fonseca Amador file were requests for rooms for student meetings, a reminder to an interurban bus company about student discounts, and a schedule announcement for the August 1958 annual university fair.[52]

In October 1958 the first national student strike in Nicaraguan history demanded that the government release Tomás Borge and other students imprisoned since the assassination of Somoza García more than two years earlier. Together with other campus leaders, Fonseca met with President Luis Somoza in Managua on 15 October to present the strikers' demands. Student activism could well have been the reason Carlos was suddenly arrested at the end of November, "for no known reason," he said later. This time he was quickly released, probably because his father interceded.

High school students' participation in the October strike led to a December conference in León to organize a national association of secondary school students. Fonseca, who would throughout his life stress the importance of reaching out to Nicaraguan high school students, played a central role in organizing this conference. He wrote to student groups encouraging them to elect delegates, and he convinced the rector of the UNAN to reassure high school principals who were hesitant to allow students to attend. According to the delegate from a Catholic high school in nearby Chinandega, some of the university students did not seem to think autonomy extended to high school students. When it came time to draft the traditional final communique on the results of the conference, this delegate recalled, "A couple of college students came up to us with something they had all worked out, which we were supposed to accept." The conference almost broke up when high school students protested this high-handed treatment. Carlos Fonseca intervened, however, "affirming that the new high school leadership had the right to draw up its own final communique absolutely without interference from anybody." The CUUN continued to reach out to secondary school students after Fonseca left León. René Núñez, later a leader of the FSLN, has described how college students came to his public high school in the early 1960s to give talks, organize meetings, and build support for demonstrations and rallies.[53]

Fonseca remained a member of the PSN but received little attention from the party leadership, despite his loyal efforts to involve students in actions in solidarity with labor struggles. Fonseca wrote an editorial for *El Universitario* supporting a dockworkers' strike in the nearby port of Corinto, spoke at a Corinto strike meeting as a representative of the student movement, and continued to sell the PSN newspaper *Unidad*. The PSN was also involved in struggles over land rights in the Indian neighborhood of Subtiava, which involved mobilizations of as many as a thousand people and won support from the broader university community as well.[54] As a prominent student leader and member of the PSN, Fonseca almost certainly participated in this struggle. He was resident in León in 1958, and the central square of Subtiava is less than a mile from the university.

Events during the course of 1958 were, however, pushing Fonseca in the direction of a break with the PSN. Like other radical students in Nicaragua and around Latin America, he was following with growing excitement what was happening on the Caribbean island of Cuba.

The Cuban Revolution, 1958–1961

When Fidel Castro and his July 26 Movement overthrew Cuban dictator Fulgencio Batista on 1 January 1959, celebrations broke out around Nicaragua. A religious procession at a Catholic boys school in Managua turned into a demonstration of support for the Cuban guerrillas. According to the Conservative daily *La Prensa*, the 1 January victory "was met with celebration and widespread joy throughout the Republic, especially in Managua, where fireworks and rockets were set off all day long." The youth groups of the Conservative Party, Independent Liberal Party, and Social Christian Party organized a demonstration that same afternoon, chanting "Viva la Libertad," "Viva Cuba Libre," and "Viva Fidel" until the National Guard broke up their march. The police also stopped a pro-Cuba demonstration a few days later, each time briefly detaining several opposition politicians. Celebrations were not limited to the major cities. According to a newspaper dispatch from the agricultural town of El Viejo, near Chinandega, "Here too, the news of the fall of the Cuban dictator filled people with joy. The news poured out of all the houses, and there were smiling faces and clapping hands and mutual congratulations. Firecrackers were set off in various parts of town. It was clear that the leader Fidel Castro is very much admired by all those who want freedom." A 10 January *La Prensa* article from a heavily Conservative town revealed more about the bourgeois opposition's goals for Nicaragua than about anything happening in Cuba:

> From the early hours of the morning of 1 January, there were enthusiastic exchanges of rejoicing around town, among the numerous Conservatives and opposition Liberals, when they learned of the fall of the despot Batista and definitive victory of the redemptory cause of the hero

Fidel Castro, standard-bearer of justice and democracy. In the various circles of this town everyone is talking about how, when the victorious revolutionaries arrived in the Cuban cities, they did it in a completely orderly way and with the greatest respect for life and property.[1]

The rapid unfolding of the guerrilla war against Batista's army had already spurred an increase in armed anti-Somoza activity inside Nicaragua. Germán Pomares, a peasant who became a guerrilla leader of the FSLN, described this period as one in which "everybody in the world went around cooking up a conspiracy." A disproportionate number of these efforts were led by rebels from the Matagalpa area and concentrated in the northern mountains. Julio Alonso, a schoolteacher from San Ramón near Matagalpa, organized a series of armed actions. Alonso had participated in an abortive military coup against Somoza in 1954, was in contact with Carlos Fonseca during the late 1950s, and received aid from the Cubans in 1959. Chale Haslam, a twenty-six-year-old farmer from Matagalpa province, put together in late 1958 the only majority-campesino guerrilla band since Sandino's time. Enrique Montoya, another young Matagalpa landowner, got involved after he was unjustly arrested and personally saw the National Guard shoot two of his farmworkers. The guerrilla José de Jesús López, nicknamed "The Miskito" because of his dark skin, was a student at the INN just after Carlos Fonseca. A Matagalpa builder named Fanor Rodríguez Oscrío conspired with former members of the National Guard and was wounded alongside Fonseca at El Chaparral.[2]

Although Matagalpa was the hotbed of rebellion, the entire Pacific zone saw armed actions against the Somoza dictatorship during 1958 and 1959. Most of these were similar to coup attempts that had been going on sporadically since 1940 and quite different from the armed movement Fonseca would lead in the 1960s and 1970s. They all resembled military coups in that disillusioned members and former members of the National Guard and Air Force played important roles. Even the uprising Fonseca joined in 1959 was commanded by a former National Guard officer. In addition, they were all very much within the framework of the two traditional parties of the Nicaraguan oligarchy: each tendency of the Conservative Party and anti-Somoza Liberals had its own miniconspiracy, led by its most prominent politicians, with its particular military allies and exile support committees in Mexico, Venezuela, or the United States. Another characteristic of these rebellions, especially those associated with the Conservative Party, was that they usually surrendered without seeing any real combat. Finally, insofar as they had any political program, these armed movements sought only to remove Somoza from office and replace him with their own leaders.

The guerrilla campaign organized by veteran Sandinista general Ramón Raudales was a partial exception. Raudales had fought alongside Sandino in the war of 1927 to 1933 and tried to resurrect Sandino's campaign in 1948.[3] Inspired by events in Cuba, the sixty-eight-year-old Raudales in 1958 recruited a band of twenty-five young fighters who called themselves the Revolutionary Army of Nicaragua and swore to fight to the death in an oath modeled after that taken by Sandino's soldiers. Raudales's program, although calling only for a Liberal-Conservative government of national conciliation, raised fundamental democratic demands for land reform, nationalization of foreign-owned mines, and expropriation of the wealth of Somoza and his friends. Raudales was killed in combat in mid-October 1958 in the mountains north of Matagalpa, and his little army disbanded.

In the midst of this upsurge in anti-Somoza plots and uprisings, dozens of Nicaraguans found their way to Havana in the first months of the Cuban revolution. Among them was Carlos Fonseca, who may well have been there during the February 1959 exams he failed to attend in León. The enthusiasts who flocked to Havana included not only radical students and members of all the opposition tendencies—Conservatives, Independent Liberals, Socialists, and Social Christians—but also con men, opportunists, and the simply curious. A Nicaraguan named Ignacio Pastora, self-declared General of the Rebel Army, arrived with a Spaniard he introduced as commander of the Revolutionary Air Force and a Frenchman he said was head of the Navy; the three lived it up in the Havana Riviera hotel and sold "bonds" to support the coming revolution in Nicaragua until the Cubans arrested them. Chester Lacayo, commander of another phantom army, signed up a thousand Cubans to fight Somoza—collecting five dollars from each of them—and then defected to the United States, where he accused Fidel Castro of trying to export revolution to Central America.[4]

Carlos Fonseca was not yet prominent enough in Nicaraguan opposition politics to be included in any of the groups who met with Cuban revolutionary leaders Fidel Castro and Che Guevara. At least two groups came to ask for help in organizing an armed uprising against the Somoza dictatorship: a delegation of young Conservatives, led by Pedro Joaquín Chamorro and organized into a Revolutionary Directorate, and a more radical Revolutionary Committee. According to one leader of the Directorate, Adán Selva Ramírez, the moderates received a chilly response. Selva paraphrased Che Guevara's response to their requests as follows: "Look, you guys, I agree with

Fidel. I don't think you are capable of making a revolution in Nicaragua, and in fact I tend to think we should throw our support to the more progressive group. But if you are set on organizing a movement, go ahead and do it, and if you do manage to get yourselves onto Nicaraguan territory and liberate a piece of it, then we would be jackasses if we didn't support you."[5] According to Selva, the young Conservatives then met with the U.S. ambassador in Costa Rica, who promised his support as long as the expedition brought down Somoza without bloodshed and without calling a general strike. The Chamorro-Selva group went on to organize the ill-planned and ineffective Olama y Mollejones operation, which entered Nicaragua from Costa Rica at the end of May 1959 and was quickly quashed.

The group that received Cuban support grew out of the Committee for the Liberation of Nicaragua, which in February 1959 published a call to arms known as the "Havana Letter."[6] Made up of Nicaraguans and supportive Cubans, it drew together members of the PSN and PLI, radical students, and delegates from an exile group based in Venezuela. Che Guevara helped organize the military operation and chose its commander Rafael Somarriba, a former member of the Nicaraguan National Guard who had lived in exile in the United States for a dozen years. Guevara also assigned to the expedition several veterans of the recent Cuban revolutionary war. Some survivors of Ramón Raudales's guerrilla band joined the group, including a childhood friend of Carlos Fonseca's from Matagalpa, twenty-two-year-old Manuel Baldizón.

Guevara knew little about the Nicaraguan opposition, but he regarded Augusto César Sandino as a hero, and he hated the Somoza dictatorship for its intimate relationship with U.S. imperialism. In March 1959 he invited Rodolfo Romero, his friend from the short-lived 1954 Guatemala resistance, to come to Havana and advise him about the prospects for revolution in Nicaragua. According to Romero, he told Che that the PSN was politically "prostrate," and that the only road forward for Nicaragua was "the road of Cuba," at which point Guevara directed him to the Somarriba training camp. Romero understood that Guevara planned to join the guerrilla operation himself once he returned from a trip to Indonesia.[7]

Around the time his friend Rodolfo joined Somarriba's expedition, Fonseca left Cuba, only to be arrested in Managua on 8 April and deported by helicopter to Guatemala City. There he got in touch with groups of Guatemalan students and Nicaraguan exiles, including Fanor Rodríguez, a member of the Cuban-supported Committee for the Liberation of Nicaragua. Fonseca told relatives that he planned to enroll in law school in Guatemala and continue his studies, but instead he went to Honduras and began training for the anti-Somoza expedition. By May, Somarriba's group, now baptized the 21st of September Rigoberto López Pérez Brigade, had fifty-five members at a farm in southern Honduras and another twenty-seven men in training. Only the Cubans and those who had fought with Raudales had any combat experience. The expedition was an open secret in the Honduran capital, and the Nicaraguan ambassador there made regular reports to Somoza on its activity. On 29 May, President Luis Somoza said, "in Costa Rica an invasion is being prepared by people it is possible to have a dialogue with. But in Honduras another one—of communist style—is being cooked up, which will have to be exterminated."[8]

Carlos Fonseca had trouble getting accepted into the Rigoberto López Pérez Brigade. The fullest account of his participation is in a long four-part article by Ignacio Briones Torres, based on interviews with survivors in Havana in 1960.[9] According to this account, Somarriba grilled Fonseca about his preparation and motivation. When the youth complained that other volunteers were not being subjected to the same interrogation, Somarriba "explained it was Fonseca's physical appearance that worried him, that the coming days, the battle, the risks, the weather, would all be very difficult and would require great sacrifices. . . . [Fonseca] was invited to go back to Tegucigalpa and take up the revolutionary fight in some other trench, like in training cadre, for example."

"It is true that I am a student," Carlos answered, "but I'm a revolutionary student. I know I can take it. Let me prove it." Somarriba, greatly worried about the new recruit's obvious nearsightedness, urged him several more times to turn back, suggesting he would do better in urban warfare because "the mountain is a cruel enemy."

"I want to fight," Carlos answered him. "Don't forget that no one brought me here, no one sent me, I came on my own account."

Somarriba finally accepted Fonseca and assigned him to the rear column, commanded by the Cuban Onelio Hernández. According to his diary, Hernández thought that "the kid could turn out to be a problem" because of his physical weakness, but the commander was favorably impressed with Fonseca's familiarity with firearms. "The young student seemed to have made up his mind some time earlier to learn how to shoot, which he did with fluency and precision, in spite of his nearsightedness." On the second day, Fonseca had to see the expedition doctor because "his face was all swollen up in an incredible way, so much that his eyes looked like they were crusted over, buried in the inflammation. Mosquitoes had practically destroyed his face."

The column marched all that day and the next (Carlos's twenty-third birthday), only to be ambushed by Honduran army troops and the Nicaraguan National Guard at El Chaparral, Honduras, on 24 June 1959. Six of the rebels died in the firefight, including the Cuban commander Hernández and Fonseca's friend Manuel Baldizón, and three more wounded guerrillas were executed by their captors. Fifteen other wounded combatants, including Carlos Fonseca, were captured and taken by the Honduran army to a prison hospital in Tegucigalpa. Fonseca, who had been shot through the left lung, wrote from his hospital bed three weeks later: "That first day an enormous amount of blood poured out from my mouth, and by the afternoon of that same day, I looked so bad that—they now tell me—my compañeros never thought I would survive. Their only question was who would die first, me or another compañero. He lost because he died." Expedition commander Somarriba, unharmed and protected by his U.S. passport, quickly left the country.

"It wasn't a battle, it was *the most terrible of massacres,*" wrote Fonseca in the same letter. Words scrawled across the top of his handwritten letter gave his explanation for the massacre: "Rafael Somarriba, the traitor responsible for the death and disaster." Fonseca did not think Somarriba was actually an agent of Somoza, only that he was inadequate to the task: "It may be that Rafael is an honorable man, *but that is not enough to be a leader in times like ours.*" Fonseca went on to write that his first guerrilla experience had taught him "lessons that it is impossible to learn even from a thousand books or a hundred teachers."[10]

The main lesson Fonseca drew from El Chaparral concerned the leadership required for a successful revolution. In the context of the recent victory in Cuba, this was the line of analysis that would lead him to study Sandino and would also lead to his break with the PSN. Less than a year after El Chaparral, Fonseca developed this theme clearly in a long letter to his friend and mentor Professor Edelberto Torres, a longtime enemy of Somoza and a member of the Committee for the Liberation of Nicaragua. "Whenever a struggle develops," wrote Fonseca, "there are always people with the serious defects of Rafael Somarriba, but they can't cause much mischief when there are other leaders who are clearly superior to them." The "backwardness" of the movement in Nicaragua, according to Fonseca, meant that "our people has not yet produced its natural leaders, . . . its indisputable leaders."[11]

"It is we, the youth, who have the responsibility for moving the struggle forward," he continued. But, he noted, young people's ignorance about their own history prevented them from fulfilling their revolutionary responsibility. He recounted how he had to go to Costa Rica to learn about his own history, referring to the writings of virtually unknown nineteenth- and twentieth-century Nicaraguan intellectuals but making no mention in this letter of Sandino.

El Chaparral may also have been the final straw in Fonseca's deteriorating relationship with the PSN. Although still a member, he had during 1958 increasingly carried out his own activity in the student movement independent of the PSN. Then came the victory of the Cuban revolution, led by a movement that had been organized outside the framework of the Cuban Communist Party. The Nicaraguan Communists were part of the committee sponsoring the Rigoberto López Pérez Brigade, but they did not encourage Fonseca to join the expedition, and he for his part never asked their permission. Fonseca later said the PSN took El Chaparral as confirmation of their pessimistic outlook on revolution: "After the defeat at El Chaparral, the Socialist Party grouping, the leading elements in the party, totally and absolutely abandoned any idea of carrying out an armed struggle." The party leadership went into the operation under the illusion that a revolutionary victory would be quick and easy, according to Fonseca. Afterward they decided it would be "extremely difficult, extremely unlikely—in fact, impossible."[12] El Chaparral was a decisive juncture for Carlos Fonseca as well, but he was moving in a different direction.

Rodolfo Romero, still a member of the PSN when he participated in the Rigoberto López Pérez Brigade, said that "after the events of El Chaparral, the party expelled both Carlos and me. They had a formal meeting of the Central Committee, and they expelled the two of us because they disagreed with our approach, which they said was 'guerrilla-ist.' "[13]

Whether Carlos Fonseca was formally expelled from the PSN or just drifted away because of political differences, the break represented an important shift in his own political thinking. The PSN had been a major influence in his life for several years. When he wrote *Un Nicaragüense en Moscú*, Fonseca agreed with the political perspectives of the PSN, which it shared with other Communist parties around Latin America. He saw the international task of Nicaraguan Communists as defending the diplomatic interests of the existing socialist states, primarily the Soviet Union, and their domestic task as organizing within the existing capitalist system around economic demands and democratic reforms. Social revolution was not on the agenda in countries like Nicaragua and was not likely to be for some time. The victory of the Cuban revolution convinced Carlos Fonseca that revolution was possible and that a new organization was needed to lead it. The FSLN and the PSN would develop along different philosophical lines and in competition with each other throughout the 1960s and 1970s, with the Communists condemning the Sandinistas as "adventurists" and "suicidal" right up to the eve of the 1979 insurrection.

Rigoberto Palma, the PSN Central Committee member in charge of the party's work in the Rigoberto López Pérez Brigade, was interviewed shortly before his death in the early 1980s. He said that even though Carlos was a member of the PSN, "the youth refused" the party's order to return to Managua, "because he had decided to follow his own road." In Palma's words, "I came to Managua and he returned to Cuba."[14]

Before Fonseca left Honduras, he spent several weeks in the San Felipe hospital in Tegucigalpa, where his mother and father separately visited him. Simon Delgado, a prominent Nicaraguan oppositionist and the uncle of Silvio Mayorga, went to Tegucigalpa to transport the El Chaparral prisoners to Havana. Interviewed in the early 1980s, Delgado said that Fonseca was still in such bad shape that the Pan American Airlines captain at first refused to allow him and another wounded guerrilla to board. Fonseca spent the flight lying on a stretcher "vomiting blood, with his wounds bleeding, in an extremely critical state."[15]

Around the time Fonseca left Honduras, an event occurred in León that was a direct result of El Chaparral and would alter the history of the Nicaraguan student movement. On 23 July 1959, the National Guard attacked unarmed protesters, killing four students and two spectators and wounding nearly a hundred people. From this point on, radical-minded students around Fonseca's age would be called the "Generation of '59," or the "Generation of the 23rd of July," and would be sharply distinguished from the "Generation of '44" that had been made up of Conservative and dissident Liberal students.

The initial reports from Honduras after El Chaparral indicated that Carlos Fonseca was one of several Nicaraguan students killed, leading to a large protest meeting at the UNAN in late June. By mid-July Fonseca was known to be in a Tegucigalpa military hospital, and the CUUN called for a peaceful march on 23 July, to demand respect for his life and to protest the killings at El Chaparral. Both the university administration and the local jurisdiction of the National Guard granted legal permits for the march.

The 23 July march grew from several hundred to some three thousand. "It wasn't just us university students any more," wrote protest leader Fernando

Gordillo. "We had been joined by students from high schools and technical schools." Even when the National Guard tried to block their path, the students felt confident and almost festive, according to Gordillo.

> Besides the speeches, there were "Vivas" and all kinds of shouts, and finally, to demonstrate their determination not to back down, the compañeros sat down in the street. In spite of the difficulty of being in a confrontation with the steel-helmeted Guard, and in spite of their threats (which, to tell the truth, we did not put much stock in), an air of contentment prevailed—something like what an athlete feels when going all out in a difficult competition—both among those sitting in the street and among those of us discussing what to do.[16]

Just as one student leader proposed returning to the University Center, the Guard attacked, first firing tear gas and then shooting rifles into the crowd of fleeing students. Four students between the ages of seventeen and twenty-one were killed, all from families of modest means. Twelve thousand people—virtually the entire city of León—turned out for the funeral march the next day. The university did not reopen until 31 August, at which time students and faculty waged a successful campaign to expel the National Guard from campus. A few months later, the first national conference of university students was held in León. Carlos Fonseca did not attend, although rumors persisted for decades that he had been there in disguise. He would have agreed with the resolutions adopted, which included the repudiation of the pro-U.S. Bryan-Chamorro Treaty, "condemnation of the sell-out behavior of the two traditional parties," and support for students around Latin America concerned about working-class issues.[17]

Although all sections of the opposition protested the 23 July massacre, there were already different views on the university's relationship to social and political change and especially on the role of radicals in the student movement. The two approaches can be seen in the different eyewitness accounts published by Fonseca's friend Fernando Gordillo and the more moderate La Prensa correspondent Rolando Avedaña Sandino. Avedaña condemned the National Guard's murder of unarmed protestors, but he was also extremely critical of student leaders whom he called "demagogues who arrive with an agenda they have been given by old-style politicians, who control them by remote control." He believed the Guard was provoked by these unnamed leaders of student organizations, "some of whom even like to call themselves Communists."[18]

Carlos Fonseca was recuperating in Cuba during the months following the 23 July march in León. He and the other wounded Nicaraguans had been taken to the Calixto García hospital on their arrival in Havana. There he met Cuban Communist Pedro Monett, who, along with his wife Rosa García, was to provide crucial support and friendship in Havana. Monett saw Fonseca and his roommate Fanor Rodríguez in a tiny room with no visitors: "Carlos's room was pitiful—even the clothes they had given him looked totally ridiculous. Too short for someone his height, the pants only reached a little below his knees." When Carlos was well enough to leave the hospital, he was given a place to live in Miramar, a middle-class neighborhood. He asked Pedro and Rosa if he could receive mail and hold meetings at their house, to which they responded, "Don't you realize, kid, that this is your house and you can do whatever you want here." Interviewed shortly before his death in the mid-1980s, Monett said the room in his house was "so small that we hardly fit inside. There was a little table and four beer cartons we used as chairs. . . . And that's where they began to have their meetings." Carlos and Silvio Mayorga arrived first every Sunday, to be joined by Tomás Borge, Noel Guerrero, and others.[19]

It was during this period in Cuba that Carlos Fonseca began a serious study of Sandino. It is likely that the only book he had read about Sandino before late 1959—the only one available in Nicaragua—was Anastasio Somoza García's ghostwritten *The Truth about Sandino, or The Ordeal of the Segovias*.[20] The theme of Somoza's book was, not surprisingly, that "the scourge of the Segovias" was a bandit, terrorist murderer, and communist, but the volume also included the texts of many of Sandino's letters and war communiques. Fonseca may have read this book sometime in 1958, that is, when he was already avidly following the progress of the guerrillas in Cuba's Sierra Maestra mountains. Fonseca went from Cuba to Costa Rica in late 1959 or early 1960, where he doubtless pursued his interest in Sandino. In a 1960 letter to his father, Fonseca said he discovered in Costa Rica information about the history of his own country he had never known before, although he did not mention Sandino by name. Fonseca had the Cuban revolution to thank for the Sandino biography he found most useful. Gregorio Selser's two-volume *Sandino: General of Free Men* was first published in Buenos Aires in 1957 and then reprinted in Havana in 1960, the first project of the new publishing house set up by the Cuban revolutionary government. It is improbable that Fonseca had access to the earlier Argentine edition.

Scholars have devoted considerable attention to analyzing the Sandinista philosophy of the FSLN.[21] Steven Palmer's groundbreaking 1988 essay draws out the implications of Fonseca's idea that Sandino represented a "path," acknowledges the impact of the Cuban revolution, and recognizes the fundamental conflict between Fonseca's revolutionary Marxism and the politics of the PSN. But he shares with other scholars the error of dating Carlos Fonseca's identification with Sandino to 1955 or 1956, for which they cite Tomás Borge's poetic prison journal *Carlos, the Dawn Is No Longer beyond Our Reach*. On this subject and others, students of Nicaragua have followed the lead of the postrevolution FSLN leadership in accepting Tomás Borge as the most authoritative source on Carlos Fonseca and the early history of the FSLN, and they have, perhaps without realizing it, accorded the poet Borge a considerable measure of poetic license. This has led to some jarring misrepresentations of Fonseca's ideas in otherwise conscientious and well-researched studies, such as the idea that he was a disciple of Peruvian Marxist José Carlos Mariátegui and that he thought student members of the FSLN were "driven more by shame than by conscience."[22] In Borge's defense, it should be noted that his description of Carlos Fonseca as already a committed Sandinista in the mid-1950s was written when the author was locked up in solitary confinement, subjected to the torture of being kept hooded for extended periods, with no books, notes, calendars, or opportunity to compare his own memory with that of others.

If Carlos Fonseca in early 1956 were already well-informed about Sandino, already saw him as the "path" to be followed, surely this would have found expression in his writings and political activities. Where did he find the books on Sandino, and where did he hide them? The entire library of eighty books and pamphlets confiscated from Fonseca by the National Guard in September 1956 contained not a word about Sandino. And why would Carlos remain for two or three more years in a party that despised his hero? There is no mention of Sandino in any of Fonseca's writings, letters, or speeches until early 1960, after which there is no example of a political writing by him that does not feature Sandino.

More is involved here than just details of chronology. The question of when, how, and why Fonseca started to study Sandino is central to understanding the development of his political ideology, the relationship between Marxism and national liberation in the Nicaraguan case, and the impact of the Cuban revolution on Nicaraguan revolutionary thought. To project Fonseca's *sandinismo* back to 1955 is to mystify it, to turn it into an article of faith, to separate it from his own experience and behavior.

One of the advantages of analyzing the ideology and strategy of the FSLN through a biography of its central leader is that it demands a historical framework. Carlos Fonseca's ideas changed and developed over time, under the influence of his personal and family experiences, observations of the reality of Matagalpa and then the rest of Nicaragua, the stances of organizations he belonged to, his study of history, discussions and debates with contemporaries, and big national and world events. He went through a process of trial and error, looking to the Communist Party for a time, for example, before rejecting its approach as too conservative. This dynamic process is obscured when the ideology of the mature Fonseca is projected back to his adolescence.

The period from 1958 to 1960 represented a major turning point in Fonseca's political ideas. In early 1958 he was still eulogizing Stalin, and by 1960 he was already pointing to the example of Sandino and reading Che Guevara's book *Guerrilla Warfare*. In less than two years, Fonseca went from being a campus activist who read books about Marxism to being a practitioner of revolutionary war. The impetus for this sea change in Fonseca's approach was the Cuban revolution, starting with the guerrilla war of 1958. The victory of the July 26 Movement, more than anything else, convinced him that something more radical than the PSN's perspective of electoral blocs and labor organizing was possible in his own country. His conviction that a socialist revolution was also possible in Nicaragua drove him to study his nation's history—already a personal interest—and made him take a more careful look at the figure of Sandino.

In Havana in 1959, Fonseca discovered that the leaders of the Cuban revolution already knew about Augusto César Sandino and took him seriously. In the late 1940s, Fidel Castro had joined the ill-fated Sandino Battalion with the goal of overthrowing Dominican dictator Rafael Trujillo. Castro and Che Guevara studied Sandino's guerrilla war experiences with Spanish-born strategist Alberto Bayo in Mexico in 1956. When the El Chaparral expeditionaries left Cuba for Central America in the spring of 1959, Guevara reportedly sent them off with the words "I love the land of Sandino and I want to fight there too."[23] Sandino's only child, Blanca Sandino Aráuz, lived in Havana from 1960 to 1979 as an honored guest of the Cuban government.

The Cuban revolution had a national hero and anti-imperialist symbol in José Martí, who was killed fighting Spanish colonialism in 1895, the year of Sandino's birth. Martí played much the same role in the ideology of the July 26 Movement that Sandino would come to play in that of the FSLN. A manifesto edited by Fonseca and published as a wall poster in July 1960 praised and quoted both Martí and Sandino; this was the first public statement of support for Sandino inside Nicaragua by the group around Fonseca.

In the years after 1953, and especially after 1959, the Cuban leaders resurrected Martí as a revolutionary anti-imperialist fighter, overlaying the image of poet, teacher, and spiritual "apostle" that had prevailed during the first half of the century. Carlos Fonseca followed the propagation of the revolutionary image of Martí and publication of his political writings during subsequent decades as Fonseca was pursuing his own study of Sandino. In a 1974 speech in Havana, Fonseca said the Cuban and Nicaraguan peoples were "bound together by indestructible historical ties. The thought and action of José Martí and Augusto César Sandino point out to us a path of common struggle." A letter from Fonseca to the Cuban magazine *Bohemia* in the mid-1970s praised an article on Sandino for drawing a parallel with José Martí, while pointing to several places where the author had made errors of interpretation and fact concerning the writings of both Sandino and Martí.[24]

During late 1959 and early 1960, eight or ten Nicaraguan students who had first started working together in Matagalpa or León began to meet regularly in Havana to discuss the situation in their country. In effect, the center of operations for the most radical wing of the Nicaraguan student movement had moved temporarily from León to Havana. In June 1960 a Havana newspaper published a statement by Nicaraguan students condemning the expulsion of Cuban diplomats from Nicaragua. The signers for the León student center CUUN were Tomás Borge ("delegate in Cuba") and Carlos Fonseca ("delegate in Costa Rica"). Revolutionary students and former students Silvio Mayorga, Rodolfo Romero, and Noel Guerrero signed on behalf of a Nicaraguan exile group based in Venezuela. No signers were identified as residing in Nicaragua.[25] Considering that the CUUN represented the students at a small university—the poorest in Central America—the student council had substantial international connections. In addition to its delegates in Cuba and Costa Rica, in 1960 the CUUN sent Fernando Gordillo to an international student conference in Baghdad and Jorge Navarro, not even a student, to a conference in North Vietnam.

As had been the case with the core group that had published *Segovia* in Matagalpa five years earlier, all these students and former students were male. Young Nicaraguan women from the university and surrounding community participated in celebrations of the Cuban victory and protests following El Chaparral, but they did not travel to Havana or play a direct role in organizing the groups that led up to the FSLN. The male conspirators, if they gave any thought to the matter at all, apparently saw female participation as providing support and swelling the ranks of demonstrations, and this may well be how young women activists themselves understood their role at the time. Fonseca was interested in the involvement of Cuban women in two organizations that took shape while he was in Havana in 1959, the community-based Committees for Defense of the Revolution and the Federation of Cuban Women (FMC). Immediately after he was released from the hospital, he asked to accompany Rosa García to an FMC meeting, where he gave a fiery speech about conditions in Nicaragua. It was his first political activity in Cuba.

Carlos Fonseca would never again be a student or consider the university his main arena of activity. This momentous decision came as a direct result of the Cuban revolution. His friend Roque Dalton, whom Fonseca visited in El Salvador just before the El Chaparral disaster, said that Fonseca's decision to "abandon his university studies and join an anti-Somoza guerrilla movement" was "a higher type of decision than the simple membership in a political party that we both were involved in already." It was a decision that brought pain to Augustina Fonseca. A friend of Carlos from Matagalpa ran into him on a plane to Havana in 1962 and told him: "I see your mother all the time. She comes to my house to talk. She is miserable because you are involved in this business. She said that by this time you should have been a lawyer."

"Look, brother," Carlos replied, "Nicaragua has plenty of lawyers, what it needs is some genuine revolutionaries."[26]

In the course of 1960, Carlos Fonseca and the other Nicaraguan students who had been meeting in Havana moved back to their own country or to adjacent Costa Rica, leaving Rodolfo Romero to represent them in Cuba. They helped organize demonstrations in Managua and León on the first anniversary of the 23 July student massacre. The protests were attacked by police, and the student movement acquired two more martyrs. The CUUN in León published a manifesto called "23 July 1960," addressed to the people of Nicaragua, to commemorate the anniversary. The wall poster version of this manifesto preserved in the secret police files bears the handwritten notation "Edited by C. F. Amador" across the top. Although Carlos Fonseca was not in Nicaragua on 23 July 1960, the political content of the manifesto indicates that he may well have had a hand in its drafting. Its central themes are the commemoration of the student martyrs, the condemnation of the "democratic farce" of the Somoza government, the need for a radical social revolution, the identification of student interests with those of the worker and peasant majority, a call for revolutionary land reform, the responsibility of U.S. imperialism for imposing dictatorial regimes in Central America, the inspiration of the Cuban revolution, the example of Sandino, and the historic role of youth as the agent of change.[27]

The period between the Cuban revolution of 1959 and the founding of the FSLN more than three years later was a time of intense debate and ideological change on the part of Fonseca and his friends. The manifesto of July 1960 represented a certain stage in this process, with Cuba and Sandino's war against the marines clearly projected as models. In terms of the possibility of revolutionary change in Nicaragua, a definitive break had been made with the ideology and strategy of the PSN.

The issue over which Fonseca and his followers broke from the PSN is sometimes said to be the younger revolutionaries' commitment to armed struggle. But this oversimplifies. The use of violence to resolve political disputes or remove a president was part of the political culture of Nicaragua. Long before either the FSLN or the PSN was formed, groups and parties from across the political spectrum accepted armed struggle in principle and employed it in practice. The PSN itself claimed to be committed to armed struggle and had participated in various coup attempts and violent uprisings. The same was true of opposition forces within the Conservative and Liberal parties. Although the abortive El Chaparral and Olama y Mollejones invasions of the spring of 1959 turned out to be the last significant armed operations ever led by the traditional Communist, Liberal, and Conservative parties in Nicaragua, these groups did continue to give verbal support to armed struggle—and even to carry out a few violent actions—through the first year or two of the new decade. The first months of 1960 saw guerrilla actions in the Las Trojes area near the border with Honduras, as well as an abortive uprising in the mountains north of Matagalpa, led by an individual linked to the Conservative Party. Sporadic armed actions, combined with student protests and strikes, led President Luis Somoza to declare his second state of siege in November 1960 (the first had been imposed after his father's assassination in 1956). Young Conservatives responded to the 1960 declaration with violent attacks in several cities, actions that, Fonseca said, "gave them a certain authority among the urban petit bourgeoisie." In early 1961 Nicaraguan banana workers with ties to the Communist Party of Costa Rica launched guerrilla actions in the extreme south of Nicaragua. Fonseca said later that the fact that a grouping inside the PSN started to advocate armed struggle in 1961 caused confusion and made it more difficult for him to win recruits to an independent course.[28] By far the most influential group talking about armed struggle in 1962 was not the tiny group of rebels around Fonseca but the Conservative Party. The Conservative candidate for president in

1963, Fernando Agüero, threatened to launch an armed revolution if he lost the election.

For a year or two following the Cuban revolution, the young revolutionaries thought their differences with the PSN, including the important issue of armed struggle, could be resolved without a decisive break. Fonseca later described the first stage of the debate over strategy as "an internal struggle that took place inside the Socialist Party," because he still saw himself, at least nominally, as a member of the party in late 1959 and early 1960. In another reference to his own role, he wrote, "following El Chaparral, several months of arguing our case in the PSN finally convinced us that any possibility of organizing inside the party to carry out a revolutionary armed struggle was completely dead—was, we repeat, completely dead." Some of his followers still believed it would be possible to win the PSN over to a revolutionary course. Fonseca said the group with whom he secretly entered Nicaragua from Costa Rica in 1960 had

> certain illusions that there was still something to discuss with the dominant elements in the leadership of the Socialist Party. That is, even though there wasn't much hope of bringing those leaders around to a more radical and forthright position, we still did not go ahead, as we have explained, to project a completely independent existence. That failure contributed, played a role, in slowing down the progress of our nascent, or we could say embryonic, clandestine activity in Nicaragua.

Looking back on this period a few years later, Fonseca wrote:

> From 1959 to 1962 some people among those who made up the FSLN held onto the illusion that it was possible to bring about a change in the pacifist line of the leadership of the Nicaraguan Socialist Party. In practical terms this illusion came to an end in 1962, with the formation of the Frente Sandinista as an independent organization, even though for a while the idea persisted that it was possible to achieve some kind of unity with the leadership of the Socialist Party—something which reality itself has proven to be impossible.[29]

No documents have survived from the crucial period from 1959 to 1962 to give a picture of how either Fonseca's group or the PSN officials saw their growing estrangement. Fonseca's earliest reference to the split came in a mid-1963 interview. Asked by a Mexican journalist to define the ideology of the FSLN, Fonseca explained: "We who are now the leaders of the movement are socialists. But we have invited all Nicaraguans with clean hands, from any party, to fight along with us, from the Conservative Party, which has on occasion taken a pro-insurrection position, to the Communist Party, which here is called the Socialist Party of Nicaragua."

"So does that mean the Communists aren't part of the FSLN?" the journalist pressed him.

"For now, they are not," Fonseca answered.[30]

Fonseca later analyzed the rupture with the PSN as involving not just the issue of revolutionary violence but also different goals, an orientation to different social classes, and even a different concept of internationalism. He wrote that following the 23 July 1959 student massacre,

> a situation developed in the country in which the little groupings of revolutionary-minded youth began to discuss the idea of building an armed revolutionary movement, while, on the other hand, the dominant elements in the socialist party proposed carrying out the same types of activities they always had, in which the party would go out and hook up with the traditional petit bourgeois sectors.

In the same document, he took issue with the view of pro-Moscow parties such as the PSN that internationalism meant subordinating local struggles to the diplomatic needs of the Soviet government: "It is a stupid kind of internationalism that only pays attention to the workers in certain parts of the world, ignoring the interests of workers in other regions, including workers in one's own country. Really that is a caricature of internationalism."[31]

Fonseca never saw his differences with the PSN as a rejection of Marxism, although some of the other early leaders of the FSLN may have perceived it this way. He, in fact, always claimed that leaders of the pro-Moscow party were "false Marxists" and that his own organization represented historic continuity with Marx, Lenin, and the Russian Revolution. In a 1970 interview, he insisted: "For the campesino in the mountains, for the poor of the sprawling slums around our cities, for the student in a rural village—the revolutionaries, the rebels, the communists, are the members of the Frente Sandinista, even though in some international gathering across the seas our right to this legitimate title is, against all reason, denied us." As early as 1961, after the break with the PSN but before the formation of the FSLN, Fonseca said, "I am not a communist because I still have many defects and frankly I don't consider myself an exemplary revolutionary, while the communists with a heart, the genuine communists, are people without equal, are the true revolutionaries." Despite the existence of a party that called itself Marxist in the years before the formation of the FSLN, Fonseca claimed there was a palpable "absence in Nicaragua of any instrument of struggle endowed with a scientific method with which the proletariat could fortify itself for its task of carrying out a social transformation."[32] He in part blamed the absence of immigration by pro-socialist European workers for the backwardness of the socialist movement in his country compared to elsewhere in Latin America.[33]

The FSLN was founded, in Fonseca's view, to provide such an "instrument of struggle," to reknit a continuity with the past, to pick up a historical thread dropped in the 1930s. He believed that even though revolutionary Marxist ideas had arrived late to his country, the fact that "the Nicaraguan people have rich traditions of rebellion that have caused our capitalist class many sleepless nights . . . is a base that will enable us quickly to make up the time the revolutionary movement has lost."[34] His historical writings on Sandino all emphasized this theme.

Fonseca was proud that he and his followers understood before any other group in Latin America that one of the lessons of the Cuban revolution was the need to break with the conservatism of the pro-Moscow Communist parties.

> It is worth stressing the fact that this internal struggle inside the PSN took place when in Latin American countries generally the struggle against these opportunist policies was not yet on the agenda. . . . In 1959 there were no signs yet of this conflict that would break out later. We stress this fact because it is worth thinking about how early we in Nicaragua were able to make the transition to a consistent revolutionary approach for the fight against the reactionary regime. It would be years before a similar understanding would be achieved in other Latin American countries.[35]

For Carlos Fonseca, genuine Marxism reached Nicaragua only in the wake of the Cuban revolution. In a 1970 interview, he said: "In my country it wasn't really until the triumph of the Cuban revolution that people began to talk about socialism, and an ideology that was revolutionary began to reach the minds of our intellectuals." The same year, he told another journalist that 1958 represented the end of "a quarter-century of darkness, of paralysis, of atrophy in the Nicaraguan popular movement. . . . For a quarter century there was neither revolutionary consciousness, nor revolutionary organization. . . . This is because for a variety of reasons it took many many years for Marxism to appear in Nicaragua; it finally appeared and caught on with a broad sector of the Nicaraguan lower classes and youth with the victory of the Cuban revolution."[36]

The Cuban revolution convinced Fonseca that a new type of Marxist organization was needed in Nicaragua. The first few years of the 1960s were devoted to that task.

Founding the FSLN, 1960–1964

Carlos Fonseca and his followers began the 1960s as a heterogeneous group of young rebels inspired by the Cuban victory and fired with the will to do *something* to bring down Somoza. This mood lent itself to desperate and adventuristic actions, Fonseca acknowledged at the time, while insisting, in language reminiscent of Che Guevara, that "the danger of adventurism must not become an excuse for moving at a turtle's pace."[1]

Fonseca and those around him were rapidly losing faith that the Nicaraguan Communist Party would ever lead a revolution. A new type of political movement was needed, one that did more than run in elections and lobby for legal reforms. In a 1960 manifesto, Fonseca argued that in the case of Nicaragua, "legal struggle cannot lead to victory," and that "papelitos y reunioncitas" [scraps of paper and little meetings] could not change the social order.[2] Fonseca spoke the language of the Nicaraguan masses; his dismissive use of the word *reunioncitas* would have struck a chord among common people in his country. But neither he nor any of his companions had a clear idea in 1960 what it would take to apply the example of Cuba to the concrete reality of Nicaragua. It would take years of experimentation, debate, and struggle against the Somoza regime before they reached a collective position on the type of organization needed, and on a program of demands.

Following the Cuban victory of January 1959, Fonseca and his student friends experimented with a variety of different organizational forms to pull together the cadre that could sustain an underground revolutionary movement. In early 1959, students with ties to the PSN, including Fonseca and Silvio Mayorga, founded the Democratic Nicaraguan Youth (Juventud Democrática Nicaragüense, JDN) in an effort to reach out to nonstudent urban youth. The organization was open to all youths who were "honest and against Somoza," and its activities consisted of painting revolutionary slogans on walls and participating in the demonstrations in support of the Cuban revolution organized by the bourgeois opposition in January 1959. The JDN ceased to exist, and later in 1959, some of the same individuals formed an organization called Revolutionary Nicaraguan Youth (Juventud Revolucionaria Nicaragüense, JRN). This group originated either in Havana or San José, Costa Rica, and most of its activities took place in Costa Rica, where it published ten issues of a little paper called *Juventud Revolucionaria*.[3] The young activists of the JRN worked with Nicaraguan banana workers and shoe workers in Costa Rica and had an uneasy relationship with the Costa Rican Communist Party, the PVP.

The JRN attended a conference of Nicaraguan exiles in Maracaibo, Venezuela, on 21 February 1960, the twenty-sixth anniversary of the assassination of Sandino. This meeting was sponsored by the Nicaraguan United Front (Frente Unitario Nicaragüense, FUN), a loose coalition of a dozen exile groups from Mexico, Central America, the United States, and Venezuela, many of them with links to the PLI or the Conservative opposition. Silvio Mayorga attended the convention as the delegate of the JRN, and Carlos Fonseca as a representative of the student government at the National University in León. They both signed the FUN's manifesto "Bloody Intervention: Nicaragua and Its People" and its "Minimum Program." Fonseca and Mayorga were able to present their own more radical analysis of the Nicaraguan situation in a report to students at the Central University of Venezuela, and they also met two young Nicaraguans in Venezuela who would become early members of the FSLN.[4]

The JRN had no real presence inside Nicaragua. In early 1960, however, JRN leaders established contact with a new student group based inside the country, the Patriotic Nicaraguan Youth (Juventud Patriótica Nicaragüense, JPN), made up largely of the children of Conservative Party oppositionists. This movement arose somewhat spontaneously in the context of Nicaraguan student excitement about the Cuban revolution and a temporary waning of the influence of the Conservatives and dissident Liberals following the El Chaparral and Olama y Mollejones debacles. In two rather vague 1960 documents, "Principles of the JPN" and "The Why, For What, and How of the JPN," the organization defined itself as a group of youth committed to democracy and social justice who "follow no party banner."[5] Activists in the JPN included two working-class youths from Managua who were to become leaders of the FSLN, Julio Buitrago, still in his early teens in 1960, and José

Benito Éscobar. The JPN played a major role in the July 1960 actions marking the first anniversary of the student massacre in León, and for several months afterward it sponsored protests against the murder of a student protester, against Nicaraguan government harassment of Cuban diplomats, and for changing the name of Roosevelt Avenue in Managua to Sandino Avenue. The JPN mounted protests not only in the capital but also in Matagalpa and Carazo and even, to some extent, in rural areas around Managua. Fonseca asked Marcos Altamirano, his political ally from their days at the Matagalpa INN, to get involved in the activities of the JPN, and Altamirano soon became the organization's secretary-general. The leadership of the JPN and other radical student groups of the era was all male, although young women participated in demonstrations and protest activities.

Fonseca would later praise the JPN's initiative, the enthusiasm of its followers, and its ability to mobilize youth against the dictatorship, all of which mattered more, he said, than the individuals who found themselves "by accident" at the head of the movement. He blamed the inexperienced leadership of the JPN for the organization's rapid disappearance when President Luis Somoza responded to the upsurge in radical activity by declaring a state of siege in November 1960. But Fonseca had harsher criticisms for the PSN, which used some poorly organized actions by the JPN (possibly involving agents provocateurs) as an excuse to condemn all militant street actions and justify its own do-nothing approach.[6]

Most of the activists in the short-lived student groups of the early 1960s did not go on to become members of the FSLN. But the groups were important precursors of the FSLN in their emphasis on militant street actions, solidarity with the Cuban revolution, and independence from both the traditional bourgeois parties and the Communist Party.

Repression was not the Somoza regime's only response to the upsurge in militant oppositional activity that began in 1959. To counter the growing radicalization at the public university in León, the Somoza administration in 1960 backed the foundation of a new private Jesuit university in Managua. The Central American University (Universidad Centroamericana, UCA) was built on Somoza family land, and the priest who served as its first rector was President Somoza's uncle. The CUUN of León issued a statement attacking the new university at a conference of Central American students in Panama in May 1960. It predicted that only "students who come from the dominant classes" would be able to afford tuition at the private school, and that its religious character would "impede research of a scientific nature, which should be the real basis of a university education." León student leaders charged that Somoza had created the UCA "to use as an arm of the dictatorial government of Nicaragua in order to destroy the National University." President Luis Somoza was using a tactic adopted by his father in the 1940s to counter the influence of Communists in the union movement, although, as Jeffrey Gould has explained, the Somocista unions turned out to be a mixed blessing for Anastasio Somoza García.[7] Luis Somoza's attempt to undercut the radicals by setting up an alternative university was for him an unqualified disaster. Within a few years, some middle-class parents were sending their sons and daughters to León to get them away from the radicals at the UCA.

This period of increased oppositional activity, a direct result of the success of the Cuban revolution, provided Fonseca and his circle with a broader arena in which to carry out political activities and recruit supporters. The window of opportunity started to close in 1962 as almost all opposition forces were drawn into the presidential campaign of Conservative Party candidate Fernando Agüero. The diminished attractiveness of revolutionary politics then continued for a few years as students tested the possibilities of legal activity under the new president René Schick, the first Nicaraguan president in three decades who was not a member of the Somoza family.

Throughout 1959 and 1960, Fonseca worked primarily in the student movement, and the organizations he helped found were made up almost exclusively of students. But he had broader aspirations. In Venezuela in March 1960, Fonseca spoke of the "Internal Resistance Front" (Frente Internal de la Resistencia, FIR) and its "immense possibilities of developing into an organization that could lead the Nicaraguan insurrection." Another 1960 writing referred to the FIR and the "Defending Army of the People" (Ejército Defensor del Pueblo, EDP), the latter apparently named after Sandino's Defending Army of National Sovereignty, or EDSN. There is, however, no evidence that either the FIR or the EDP ever existed outside Fonseca and Mayorga's imaginations.[8]

Sometime in early 1961, a major step toward the formation of the FSLN was taken with the launching of the Movement for a New Nicaragua (Movimiento Nueva Nicaragua, MNN). Its membership list contained familiar names of student and former student leaders such as Fonseca, Mayorga, Borge, Gordillo, Navarro, and Francisco Buitrago, but it also included working-class youths such as José Benito Éscobar, a small businessman named Julio Jérez Suárez, and peasant activist Germán Pomares. Most important, the founders of the MNN included a few survivors of Sandino's war against the U.S. Marines. Santos López, who had fought alongside Sandino as part of his "Angels' Choir" of very young soldiers, was almost fifty in 1961. He brought to the youthful MNN not only valuable military experience and the moral authority of Sandino's struggle but also the incorporation of a different generation.[9] Although primarily based in Honduras, the MNN established three small cells inside Nicaragua—in Managua, Estelí, and León—and made its first public appearance with a protest against Washington's escalating anti-Cuba campaign a month before the April 1961 Bay of Pigs invasion.

The MNN soon disappeared into another organization with largely the same membership that sometime in late 1961 or early 1962 began calling itself the National Liberation Front (Frente de Liberación Nacional, FLN). The FLN took its name from the organization that fought French colonial rule in Algeria, at the time regarded by the young Nicaraguans as second only to the Cuban revolution in importance. Early on, Carlos Fonseca proposed adding the word *Sandinista* and calling the group the FSLN, but it took him more than a year to convince his comrades of this addition. The first communiqués signed by the FSLN were issued in September and October 1963. The earliest appearance of the name FSLN in print is in a November 1963 interview with Fonseca in the Mexican magazine *Siempre*.[10]

Why did the revolutionaries around Fonseca hesitate to call their organization Sandinista in 1962? Sandino's name had already begun to resonate in the broader student movement, as shown by the 1960 demonstrations demanding that Roosevelt Avenue be renamed Sandino Avenue. Starting in early 1960, Fonseca pointed to the model of Sandino in his own writings, calling his own generation "the children of Sandino" and naming his proposed army of liberation after Sandino's Defending Army of National Sovereignty. Fonseca's 1960 essay "Nicaragua, Bitter Land" praised the heroism of Sandino and quoted some of his best-known sayings.[11]

The strongest opposition to Fonseca's proposal to name the new group after Sandino came from Noel Guerrero Santiago, a lawyer from León. Guerrero, although somewhat older than most of the students around Fonseca, was part of the core leadership of the groups that led up to the FSLN. Guerrero spent most of his life in Mexico and was a member of the Communist Party there, joining the PSN when he returned to Nicaragua in the late 1950s. Guerrero left the PSN with Carlos Fonseca in the aftermath of El Chaparral, but he seems to have retained the conservative politics of the PSN. Tomás Borge has described the early stages of the discussion about Sandino:

> The guy from León was erudite, he knew his Marxism. In those days he was very patient and fraternal toward us; he had discussions with us.
>
> "Sandino," Carlos said once, "is a kind of path. I think it would be a

mistake to dismiss him as someone only worth mentioning once a year on his anniversary. I think we ought to be studying his thought."

Noel Guerrero answered: "A path? That's just poetry! Don't forget about the suspicious praise for this guerrilla on the part of various bourgeois ideologues. Sandino fought against foreign occupation, not against imperialism. He was no Zapata—that is, he didn't address the land question.[12]

At the time, Guerrero was considered more "erudite" than Fonseca. He may have convinced the others that it was more radical to identify with the Algerian revolution than with Sandino. The important decision to identify the organization finally as Sandinista was the result of three processes that were just getting under way in 1961 and 1962: the organized study of Sandino's life and ideas, growing commitment to the idea of making a revolution that would be genuinely Nicaraguan in character, and the emergence of Carlos Fonseca as undisputedly the movement's central leader.

When Fonseca later described the formation of the FSLN, he emphasized that what came first was action, not theory:

The FSLN wasn't born at an assembly or a congress, nor did it issue a proclamation announcing its creation. It did not even present a program. For the Frente, what came first was action, and, based on its first experiences it went on formulating and reformulating—because it has always had a sense of the importance of self-criticism—its program, strategy, and tactics. The FSLN was a genuine product of the history of the Nicaraguan masses.

When Fonseca pointed to the importance of action, he was not talking about the uncoordinated action of an individual. "I think we have a duty to act," he wrote in 1964, "but without organization there can be no action."[13]

Fonseca's life in those years exemplified this ideal of action. Constantly on the move, he worked with groups of youths in Havana, Costa Rica, and Honduras, occasionally slipping into Nicaragua to meet with potential recruits. Heriberto Rodríguez Marín, who was a few years older than Fonseca and part of the group that founded the FSLN, gave a firsthand account of this process in a 1996 interview. From a family of Liberal small landowners in the area around Ocotal, close to the Honduran border, Rodríguez described himself as "born Sandinista." Members of his family had fought under Sandino, and Rodríguez grew up knowing the secret network of veterans of Sandino's army in the area around Ocotal.

Starting in 1960, Rodríguez lived in a small house in Tegucigalpa, Honduras, with several other Nicaraguan revolutionaries, including, much of the time, Carlos Fonseca. As Rodríguez described their activities: "Carlos was looking for all the old Sandinistas, for anyone who knew Sandino. I would introduce him and they would introduce us to others. And since I was more experienced than some of the others in military matters and also because I was from the countryside and from the border area, I was given the responsibility of opening up a clandestine route from Tegucigalpa to Estelí, establishing contacts there, distributing study materials." A 1961 letter to Fonseca from another member of the group described the danger of trying to make political contacts and distribute anti-Somoza propaganda in a border area constantly patrolled by the National Guard.[14]

In Tegucigalpa, Fonseca was "always talking about how we had to get things organized," according to Rodríguez. "And he was constantly telling us how important it was to study, to prepare for the time when it would be possible to organize a massive popular insurrection." Rodríguez was impressed with Fonseca's attention to detail, especially when it came to security questions. "I remember how Carlos used to say to me: 'Always have a plan, even for little things. Don't just go out and say you are going for a Coke. Decide ahead of time—if they don't have a Coke, then a Pepsi. If no Pepsi, then a Fanta. Don't ever get caught by surprise, learn to always think ahead, be prepared.'"

According to Rodríguez, Fonseca called him back to Tegucigalpa from Ocotal sometime in 1962, saying that things were finally getting organized. Others came in from Cuba and elsewhere—Rodríguez remembers Borge, Guerrero, Iván Sánchez, Bayardo Altamirano, and Faustino Ruiz. Rodríguez's memory is that the group stopped calling itself the MNN at this point and took the name FLN. This corresponds closely to Fonseca's own declaration to a Managua court in July 1964. Asked by a judge to describe in detail his participation in the FLN and FSLN from the beginning, Fonseca started out, "Around the first half of 1962, Noel Guerrero Santiago, Tomás Borge Martínez, Pedro Pablo Ríos and Faustino Ruiz arrived in Honduras" (from Cuba, joining those already in Tegucigalpa, he said in response to a subsequent question), "and we all began to discuss the political situation in Nicaragua."[15]

The formation of the FSLN took several years and involved many meetings and discussions in at least four countries. In terms of both organizational form and political program, the FSLN went through an initial period of experimentation, false starts, and blocs with different forces. The group constantly sought out new cadres, without yet a very clear idea what recruits were supposed to do. It published several issues of an underground newspaper called *Trinchera* (Trench): an article in the January 1963 issue shows that the organization was still using the name FLN and that its politics were heterogeneous.[16]

The most lasting accomplishment of the FLN/FSLN during this period was a new organization to coordinate work in the student movement, the Federation of Revolutionary Students (Federación de Estudiantes Revolucionarios, FER). The FER, a legal entity although often persecuted by the regime, existed right up to 1979 and was always an important source of recruits and influence for the FSLN. Its first victory came with the 1963 election of FSLN members Casimiro Sotelo, Julio Buitrago, and David Tejada to head the student government at the UCA in Managua. The student council issued a fourteen-point manifesto at its first congress, calling for "an organized revolutionary movement which will support a genuine revolutionary system," and pledging that UCA students would

> Fight to rescue the exploited classes from the clutches of the oligarchy and capitalism; . . . Advocate a just distribution of wealth, the elimination of illiteracy, and the creation of a new education system; . . . Stand up for thoroughgoing land reform, urban reform, the nationalization of foreign businesses; and . . . Struggle to do away with the traditional political parties, which are largely responsible for the tragedy faced by the people of Nicaragua.[17]

The version of the history of the FSLN that has become part of the popular tradition in Nicaragua and appears in virtually all books about the Nicaraguan revolution is that the organization was founded at a meeting in Tegucigalpa in June or July 1961, attended by Silvio Mayorga, Carlos Fonseca, and Tomás Borge.[18] This founding meeting appears to be a post-1979 construction. Participants' accounts of the early days of the FSLN written before 1979, including Fonseca's writings and a long testimonial by Tomás Borge in 1976, do not mention any founding meeting. It was only after the 1979 revolution that speeches and articles by and about Tomás Borge began to present him as the only survivor of a founding meeting of three. Borge has even proposed specific dates for the meeting. In the middle of a speech in late 1979, he suddenly recalled the FSLN's founding on 19 July 1961, the exact date the FSLN overthrew Somoza eighteen years later.[19]

Rodolfo Romero, one of the few survivors of the initial years of the FSLN, said in a 1994 interview that the three-founders meeting was a myth. Romero, who is Borge's age, left the PSN with Fonseca in the aftermath of El Chaparral and was a prominent activist in the JPN, MNN, FLN, and early FSLN. "There was never a formal meeting to found the Frente," Romero said with considerable emphasis. "Everything you read about this is false."

"In spite of the affection I hold for the comandante [Borge]," Romero went on, "I must tell you that the Frente Sandinista never had any official anniversary; there was never any congress, any convention, any founding assembly. There just wasn't. Not ever. The FSLN was created in the heat of battle."[20]

The FSLN, born in action, did not publish a programmatic document until 1969. The discussions and debates of the early years did, however, hammer out a consensus on certain fundamental political tenets: the example of Cuba; independence from the Conservative, Liberal, and Communist parties; the need for a clandestine organization; commitment to armed struggle; and, after some initial disagreement, identification with the struggle of Augusto César Sandino.

For the embryonic FSLN, the Cuban revolution provided not just military but—even more importantly—political lessons. Fonseca later stressed the impact on the young Nicaraguans of the increasing radicalization of Cuba's revolution in the years following the overthrow of Batista. The Cuban leadership's "growing identification with the ideology of the proletariat in the course of 1961 was very important for the Nicaraguan revolutionaries," he explained, "because it gave us the idea that the best way to defend a successful revolution against attacks by reactionary forces and by imperialism was through identification with the exploited classes." Events in Cuba in late 1960 and early 1961, he went on, "made it clearer than ever that the policy of the socialist party [of Nicaragua] was to turn its back on revolutionary armed struggle, to refuse to pay any attention to it."[21]

The FSLN's formative political period coincided not with the military campaigns of the Sierra Maestra or the march of bearded guerrillas into Havana in January 1959 but rather with the massive working-class mobilizations in Cuba during 1960 and 1961, the increasing nationalization of the economy, the sharp polarization of society along class lines, and Castro's 1961 declaration of the socialist character of the revolution. Fonseca himself was in Havana during the Cuban Missile Crisis of October 1962. He participated in the popular mobilizations in support of the Cuban government and understood the Cubans' anger when the Soviets decided to withdraw the missiles without consulting them. He was impressed with the fact that Algerian president Ben Bella, alone among world leaders, literally stood at

Castro's side during the crisis. By the end of the 1960s, the FSLN had concluded that following the Cuban road meant not just overthrowing the U.S.-backed Somoza dictatorship but also beginning the socialist transformation of Nicaragua. As Fonseca told a Cuban journalist in 1970, "Inspired by the victorious Cuban revolution, inspired by sublime Vietnam, inspired by the heroic comandante Ernesto Che Guevara . . . the Frente Sandinista has the profoundly revolutionary goals of wiping out *not only* imperialist domination in Nicaragua but also the domination of all the exploiting classes."[22]

Julio Buitrago, the head of the FSLN urban underground, explained in 1968 that he was fighting to win for Nicaraguan workers and peasants the rights he had seen with his own eyes in socialist Cuba. He wrote to his father, who had offered to help him settle safely out of danger in Costa Rica.

> I left my country, not to make a living but because I had to prepare myself to do battle against this tyranny that every day drowns the exploited masses of our country in hunger and poverty. My experience overseas, where men live like human beings, where the *pueblo* governs, where children do not know hunger or cold, where farmland belongs to those who work it, where there are no gangs of thugs giving tenants two hours to vacate their homes, where the prisons have been converted into schools, and a new world is being opened up through the labor of workers and campesinos—that experience is what has given me the strength to carry on.[23]

The goal of the group that came together around Fonseca in Honduras was to duplicate the Cuban revolution. But they had a variety of explanations for that victory. Most, probably including Fonseca, overestimated its military component and underestimated the contribution of political organizing, strikes, and mass actions. They based this on a misinterpretation of Che Guevara's and Fidel Castro's insistence on the primacy of the *sierra* over the *llano,* of the Sierra-based Rebel Army command over the July 26 Movement apparatus in the lowland cities. The Nicaraguans' model, as they planned their own uprising in 1962, was that of a rural guerrilla war, with peasant support and a mountain base camp, leading rapidly to a nationwide insurrection and military defeat of the dictator's army. This approach came to be known as *foquismo* or *foco* theory, after Régis Debray's analysis of the Cuban experience.[24]

More than a decade later, Fonseca would attribute the military strategy adopted in 1963 to "youthful zeal and lack of experience," and to a misunderstanding of the lessons of the Cuban revolution.

The view we had at that time of the Cuban experience was that all it took was launching the armed struggle to call into being an uprising on a mass scale. That's what we set out to do in Nicaragua, in the period leading up to Ríos Coco y Bocay and during that operation itself. A little more careful attention to the experiences of the Russian and Chinese peoples in their revolutions would have helped us avoid in part our exclusive preoccupation with the armed revolutionary struggle.[25]

But excessive emphasis on military actions without corresponding political work among the lower classes continued to be a problem in the FSLN, dominating the strategy of one section of the FSLN in the 1970s and causing political difficulties after the 1979 revolution.

On the level of military accomplishments, the Cuban revolution proved impossible to duplicate. After only a few months in the Sierra Maestra, the Rebel Army had a permanent base camp and communications network, successfully attacked enemy positions, recruited and trained local peasants, and set up rudimentary production and distribution systems in territory it controlled. The Sandinistas engaged in guerrilla operations off and on for seventeen years without ever having a radio transmitter, sometimes going years without bringing down a single enemy soldier; during most of this time, the guerrilla "army" shrank through death and desertion faster than it could be built up by student recruits from the city; the FSLN never established control over any territory until 1979, when the liberated zones were towns and cities in western Nicaragua, far from the area of guerrilla operations.

In 1963, however, the founders of the FSLN still hoped to reproduce the Cuban experience. They even mechanically drew up a twenty-five-month timetable for their own revolutionary war, based on the length of time that elapsed between the outbreak of guerrilla warfare in the Sierra Maestra mountains and the Rebel Army's triumphant march into Havana. They prepared themselves in the course of 1961 and 1962 by seeking out veterans of Sandino's army to provide military training and adapt the Cuban model to Nicaraguan terrain.

Except for Santos López, named the head of military operations for the new FSLN, and a few like Fonseca who had taken part in El Chaparral or one of the other abortive uprisings of 1959 to 1960, the guerrillas assembled for the 1963 operation had no previous combat experience inside Nicaragua. Many of them had, however, received military training in Cuba, even before the formation of the FSLN. Toward the end of 1960, Rodolfo Romero personally approached his old friend Che Guevara about providing military training for the young Nicaraguans then in Cuba. Twenty or thirty Nicaraguans completed artillery camp in January or February 1961. Then Fidel Castro granted their request for a small group of them (including Fonseca, Mayorga, Borge, and Romero) to spend some weeks with the Cuban forces fighting against counterrevolutionary bands in the Escambray Mountains. This combat experience—probably Borge's and Mayorga's first—took place in the months immediately before the Bay of Pigs invasion. Mayorga was then put in charge of all the Nicaraguans who participated in the organized defense of Havana during the invasion in April 1961.[26]

The guerrillas felt they were militarily ready, but they still had to locate the Nicaraguan equivalent of the Sierra Maestra. For this purpose, Fonseca and Santos López traveled through the northern Nicaraguan mountains in 1962 and decided on a remote area northeast of Matagalpa near the meeting of the Coco and Bocay rivers. "When we saw the miserable living conditions of the local population of Sumo Indians," Fonseca said shortly afterward, "we thought that this sector could support a struggle that favored their liberation." Looking back on the decision in 1970, Fonseca admitted that "there was a certain amount of guesswork involved," and that the area had various disadvantages: "isolation—the most isolated region of the northern part of the country—a population that was very sparse and backward, a primitive economy."[27]

The guerrilla operation known as Ríos Coco y Bocay or Raití-Bocay was not an invasion from Honduras. Fonseca had learned this lesson at El Chaparral. Nonetheless the logistical and political preparations all took place in Honduras: military training, arms purchases, selection of cadres, the drawing up of battle plans. In the course of 1962, several dozen men and a quantity of war matériel were introduced into the designated battle zone. A disastrous lack of coordination at one point resulted in the drowning of one combatant and the loss of a significant portion of the accumulated weapons and supplies. At its peak, this guerrilla "army" consisted of sixty-three men organized into three columns. Only half the soldiers carried firearms, most of them hunting rifles.[28]

The founders of the FSLN did not all agree on the organization's preparedness to launch a guerrilla struggle. In a statement to a Managua judge in July 1964, Fonseca said:

> I personally was extremely worried that our attempt would turn out to be an adventure that was unlikely to succeed, because not only was the Internal Front receiving little attention but also there was a problem of

indiscipline and a lack of seriousness in our activities in [Honduras]. . . . So what I did was continue to debate—sometimes patiently, sometimes not so patiently—what we were going to do about the problems we had run into since we conceived of the action in June [1962]. . . . Some compañeros painted a very rosy picture about the outcome, even seeing it leading to the development of an insurrection inside the country. I did not share this optimism. I had faith in the selflessness, the spirit of sacrifice, and the high morale of the compañeros who were in charge of work inside the country. But I was convinced that something more than high morale was necessary in order to be successful; it was also necessary to have some experience, which the compañeros inside the country did not have.[29]

While arguing against those he thought had overly optimistic views of the strength of the new movement, Fonseca found himself involved in the opposite debate with Noel Guerrero Santiago, the financial manager of the new organization and an influential voice. The politics of this particular dispute are shadowy: only charges and countercharges of organizational transgressions surfaced at the time, and Guerrero has since been written out of the official history of the FSLN. Apparently Guerrero retained some of the PSN's pessimism about the prospect for socialist revolution in Nicaragua and disagreed with the insurrectional strategy. In mid-1963 he left the FSLN and moved permanently to Mexico. The internal crisis produced by the conflict with Guerrero kept Fonseca from participating personally in the Ríos Coco y Bocay guerrilla operation as he had planned.[30]

Little or no advance work was done in the area chosen for the first guerrilla operation. The initial political work of the MNN and then FLN/FSLN inside the country was abandoned as energies were thrown into preparations for the military operation. The FSLN in late 1962 and early 1963 was virtually unknown inside Nicaragua—certainly unknown in the rain forest of the Atlantic Coast where the operation was based. Borge, who participated in the operation, later said that the guerrillas ended up in an area "where the population was politically and even economically primitive. . . . Many of them didn't know how to speak Spanish, and I don't think they ever understood very well who we were. They weren't sure whether we were National Guard or what we were. We were truly alien beings for them."[31] None of the guerrillas spoke either the Sumo or the Miskito language, although one twelve-year-old Sumo peasant did travel with the group.

In a 1979 interview, Borge admitted that "the truth is that the guerrillas couldn't possibly have been successful, because it was the most backward guerrilla operation you can imagine. We didn't know the territory, we had no supply lines, none of the things that could have made a guerrilla operation successful existed." Combatant Pedro Pablo Ríos later said that for the entire march from the Honduran border to the town of Raití, "We didn't have even a single friendly house to stay in, we had no social base and had to sleep in the wilderness."[32]

Often lost and almost always starving, wet, and cold, the guerrillas wandered through the mountains from May to August 1963, encountering the National Guard only by accident. They had somehow come up with the idea of rotating commanders every week. Certainly not anything learned from Che Guevara, the scheme had perhaps been carried over from the years they had spent as campus activists. In the life-and-death seriousness of guerrilla warfare, sharing the command turned out to be disastrous. The small bands into which the guerrillas were loosely organized were often separated from each other. In August one group was wiped out in a National Guard ambush, and the operation was abandoned. It took more than a month for the survivors, hungry and sick, finally to straggle back across the Honduran border.

Francisco Buitrago, Jorge Navarro, Iván Sánchez, Modesto Duarte, and Faustino Ruiz, all in their late teens or early twenties, were among those killed. According to peasant witnesses, they were taken alive and murdered by their captors. Only students under the influence of the FSLN protested when word got out about the killing of these well-known young rebels, a clear sign of the movement's isolation. "We should take note of the fact," Fonseca said later, "that there were no protests against this massacre by other forces in Nicaragua, neither the university leaders nor the church nor intellectuals."[33]

At the time of the Ríos Coco y Bocay operation, the members of the new FSLN knew very little about the political mood of Nicaraguan peasants. As Fonseca said a decade later, "It was an enormous obstacle not to have a single contact, even the most isolated, among the campesinos of the mountainous region, given the great weight we had correctly given to rural guerrilla warfare. We were still trying to work through opposition Conservative landowners, which was a complete waste of time."[34] Several of the young leaders of the FSLN, including Fonseca, had grown up in provincial towns or villages and were familiar with living conditions in the countryside, and a few, such as Faustino Ruiz and Germán Pomares, had rural backgrounds. But the organization did not really begin to do political work among small peasants and agricultural workers until after the 1963 defeat. The initiative then was taken by one of the Ríos Coco y Bocay guerrillas, Rigoberto Cruz (known by his pseudonym Pablo Ubeda), who remained in the northern mountains when the operation disbanded.

After the guerrilla defeat, Fonseca realized that he was the only person in a position to "take hold of what was left of our organization." But instead of returning to Nicaragua immediately to deal with the crisis, he decided to spend several more months in Honduras studying Nicaraguan and world history: "I spent," he said a few months later, "a rather lengthy period studying, in a very detailed way, the historical experience of the revolutionary movement in Nicaragua—as well as the lessons of the revolutionary struggles of other countries." Reports from Nicaragua made him wonder about the viability of the FSLN, but he did not return to see for himself until the end of May 1964. At that point, he said, "all my fears about the internal organization's lack of readiness to carry out combative actions were grievously confirmed."[35] Only a month after his return, Fonseca was arrested in Managua, together with another young FSLN activist, Mexican-born Víctor Tirado López.

When Fonseca was apprehended in the working-class Managua barrio of San Luís on 29 June 1964, he immediately began shouting as loud as he could, "I am Carlos Fonseca Amador, I am Carlos Fonseca Amador." By the time the jeep carrying the prisoners arrived at the police station, barrio residents had called local radio stations and the opposition newspaper La Prensa. Over the course of the 1960s and 1970s, a number of central leaders of the FSLN were captured alive, according to witnesses, and then reported by the National Guard as killed resisting arrest or attempting to escape. When Tomás Borge went on trial in August 1976, he made a public statement insisting that he had no intention of trying to flee custody or take his own life, and that he held the security forces responsible for anything that might happen to him. This statement, acknowledged by the judge and reprinted in full in La Prensa the next day, may have played a role in keeping him alive during his long imprisonment.[36]

June 1964 was the eighth and final time Fonseca was arrested inside Nicaragua. He was fortunate never to be captured in the late 1960s or 1970s, when his chances of being killed in custody would have been much greater. The political climate in Nicaragua in 1964 was not so conducive to the blatant mistreatment of prisoners, especially well-known ones such as Carlos Fonseca. A new Nicaraguan president, René Schick, had been elected in 1963. Anastasio Somoza was still head of the National Guard and Nicaraguans joked about the "big president" (Tachito) and the "little president," but Schick claimed to be opposed to the excesses of the past. The officer who arrested Fonseca and Tirado, one of the GN's most notorious torturers, beat his two prisoners on the way to jail. Fonseca suffered no torture while incarcerated, however. He was tried in open court on 9 July and released when his six-month sentence was over. His lawyer said that he had to "visit him constantly [in prison] and not leave him alone, in order to prevent the Guardia from killing him,"[37] but the danger of Fonseca's being killed during his 1964 imprisonment was probably quite small.

For several days after his arrest on 29 June, the government refused to confirm Carlos Fonseca's capture. The student movement did not wait, however, to launch a campaign of marches, strikes, building occupations, and news conferences. This time the protests were not confined to pro-FSLN students. Officers of the Conservative youth and the PLI youth group sent letters to the newspapers, and the president of the university led a protest march in León. On the evening of 30 June, a delegation of twenty-six students set out on foot from León to Managua (a distance of nearly sixty miles), leaving behind a sit-in by fasting students at an administration building decorated with banners reading "Stop the murder of students!" and "We demand freedom and respect for the life of our student compañero Carlos Fonseca!" Several departments at the León and Managua universities were closed by a student strike, and the Goyena Institute and a few other high schools saw solidarity actions. A new chant was heard: "What is it that brings us such delight? Carlos Fonseca and his guerrilla fight," adapted from an incantation of the Nicaraguan popular religious festival of Purísima. It was not the last time the youthful supporters of the FSLN would creatively appropriate and secularize existing religious idiom, much to the discomfort of the Catholic hierarchy.[38]

According to Fonseca's attorney, the news that he would be tried in open court "flew around Managua like dust, and more people showed up than could fit into the hall." Fonseca's *Declaración* of 9 July, reprinted in full in *La Prensa* the next day, was a spirited defense of the history and program of the FSLN. Like Fidel Castro's "History Will Absolve Me" speech of 1953 and Nelson Mandela's self-defense in the 1963 Rivonia Trial, Fonseca's courtroom speech became part of the basic programmatic literature of his movement.[39]

The rules for a judicial interrogation confined the prisoner to answering specific questions from the judge. In spite of these constraints, Fonseca managed to explain how and why the 1963 guerrilla operation was organized and to make an appeal for support for the FSLN. His 1964 *Declaración* was an early example of what became an important political tool for the Sandinistas. They tried to turn the unfortunate accident of arrest and imprisonment against their jailers and the Somoza government by using the courtroom itself to tell the FSLN's side of the story. Compared to some of the other propaganda vehicles used by the FSLN—mimeographed manifestos, wall posters, military communiqués, and interviews—the courtroom speeches quickly reached a relatively broad section of the public with information about the movement's activities and goals. Even when the content of the defense speeches was limited by judicial format, as was the case with Fonseca's 1964 *Declaración*, the trial context itself reinforced the image of the young rebels as standing up to the state and its police. That prisoners were charged with serious crimes also undermined the government's attempt to dismiss the revolutionaries as insignificant and ineffective.

The courtroom strategy proved most effective when the press reported defense speeches verbatim. Fidel Castro did not have this advantage when he delivered his "History Will Absolve Me" speech behind closed doors; he wrote it down from memory afterward and smuggled it out of the prison. In Nicaragua, with television controlled by the Somoza family, only *La Prensa* provided a voice for Sandinista defendants such as Carlos Fonseca and Tomás Borge. The newspaper was owned and managed by the Chamorro family, since the nineteenth century the most prominent family in Nicaraguan politics. Several Chamorros had been presidents of Nicaragua, and dozens had held key positions in a series of Conservative Party administrations. *La Prensa*'s society pages reported on the debutante balls and weddings of the wealthiest people in Nicaragua. But the daily was also the voice of the traditional anti-Somoza opposition, and Pedro Joaquín Chamorro, who had replaced his father as editor in the 1950s, had been jailed for his political activities. *La Prensa* covered the Sandinistas' activities, news conferences, and court hearings, even though it vehemently disagreed with their approach. The Schick administration may have been trying to discourage the Conservative newspaper from giving any more free publicity to the FSLN when in 1964 it charged Fonseca with, among other things, conspiring to burn down *La Prensa*'s offices.[40]

Despite *La Prensa*'s extensive coverage of Fonseca's 1964 arrest and trial, the language with which it described the prisoner differed little from that of the Somoza government. The presidential press secretary's news release on the arrest called Fonseca "the leftist leader and well-known foreign agent," and *La Prensa* referred to him as "a young terrorist" and "an agent of international communism" and urged parents to persuade their children "not to let themselves become instruments of International Communism with its maneuvers and slogans." Pedro Joaquín Chamorro ridiculed Fonseca in two signed editorials, one of which was entitled "What Should We Do with Him? Send Him Back to School!" The political stance of *La Prensa* came across clearly in the headline of one of its 2 July articles about the case: "Protests Demand Respect for Human Rights, Even for Communists." An editorial by Conservative Party intellectual Reynaldo Antonio Téfel introduced a theme *La Prensa* would sound throughout the 1960s and 1970s: that Somoza had created the "terrorist" problem by closing the door to the responsible opposition.[41]

By the time he went into court on 9 July, Fonseca had already composed his best-known prison writing, "From Jail, I Accuse the Dictatorship." Written with a stub of pencil donated by a common prisoner, Fonseca's *Yo acuso* was published as a pamphlet in León while he was in prison. In content and literary style it was similar to "History Will Absolve Me," which Fonseca might well have read. Like Castro, Fonseca said the dictatorship itself was guilty of all the crimes with which it was falsely charging him, including murder and theft.

In *Yo acuso*, Fonseca called for the formation of a Sandinista Party, "the party of the new generation," a party of action, not of "wasting time filling up Saturdays and Sundays with meaningless chatter." He criticized the "old generation" of Conservatives, Liberals, and Communists and addressed himself to "my own generation, to those who know me, who can understand me. . . . I speak for the youth of my downcast but not defeated generation . . . the generation of the 23rd of July." Referring to a political forum sponsored by the PSN and other opposition groups at the UNAN earlier in the year, Fonseca said it made him sad to see students waste their time with sterile debates.[42]

Víctor Tirado, interviewed in 1979, said Fonseca's call for a Sandinista Party in *Yo acuso* met with a less than enthusiastic response from other political tendencies. "Nobody paid any attention to it, in fact to the contrary some international revolutionary forces criticized it, and he ended up isolated and alone, and some compañeros even turned their backs on him." According to another observer, the pamphlet did meet some "receptive minds" in university and high school classrooms and labor circles, even though it was shunned by others, sometimes out of fear of government repression and "sometimes out of self-interest." Apparently even within the FSLN and circles friendly to it, there was not agreement with the call for a new political party. In September, Fonseca smuggled another manifesto out of prison: "This Is the Truth" defended the FSLN against government allegations of plans to assassinate members of the opposition (including Communists) and burn Conservative Party newspapers like *La Prensa*.[43]

Carlos Fonseca fell in love during this 1964 imprisonment. María Haydeé Terán, a young activist from León, took the bus to Managua to visit him almost every Sunday and Thursday, the prison's visiting days. Terán, two years younger than Fonseca, came from a well-known family of dissident Liberals. Her father and brother were leaders of the PLI, and the family owned a small opposition publishing house and bookstore in León, Editorial Antorcha. Although never enrolled at the university, María Haydeé met many student activists while staffing the Antorcha bookstore near campus, and she attended the 23 July 1959 student march. As she became more involved in anti-Somoza activities in the early 1960s, student members of the FSLN arranged for her to talk with an underground leader of the group. She only discovered she had met Carlos Fonseca himself when she later described this secret meeting to Octavio Robleto, whom she was dating at the time. She decided not to join the FSLN, but after the June 1964 arrest, she asked Robleto to accompany her to visit his old friend Carlos Fonseca in prison.[44]

The last time Maria Haydeé tried to visit Carlos in jail, in early January 1965, the guards told her he was gone and would give out no other information. Worried about Carlos's safety, María Haydeé bravely presented herself at the luxurious home of Fausto Amador and demanded he tell her whatever he knew about his son's whereabouts. Amador at first denied any knowledge but then admitted that the OSN had roused him from bed in the middle of the night and taken him to the airport, where he had spoken to Carlos and given him fifty American dollars before seeing him put on a military plane.

Fonseca's destination was Guatemala, the closest Latin American ally of Somocista Nicaragua. On this, his third deportation to Guatemala, he was imprisoned for several days in La Tigrera prison. "I spent several anxious days there," he wrote after his release. "Nobody in Guatemala knew where I was imprisoned, and I was afraid that under these circumstances something serious would happen to me." He was released without harm, however, and deported again to Mexico. María Haydeé came to Mexico City soon afterward, accompanied by her mother and brother. She and Carlos were married on 3 April in the home of Don Edelberto Torres.[45] For the next year or so, the newlyweds remained outside Nicaragua, Carlos physically distant and personally somewhat distracted as his underground organization grappled with a strategy for a changing Nicaraguan situation.

The Evolution of a Strategy, 1964–1968

Fonseca often used the word "clandestine" to describe his organizational efforts. Even before the formation of the FSLN, he called for a combination of rural guerrilla warfare and "clandestine activity, . . . such as illegal meetings on the fly, slogans painted on walls, subversive leaflets, and underground radio broadcasts." Of the preliminary organizing efforts of 1960, he said, "for the first time ever a group of revolutionaries had come together in Nicaragua to carry out something entirely new—organized clandestine activity that could start us down the road to armed struggle by the popular masses."[1] Using the term "clandestine" almost as a synonym for "revolutionary," Fonseca implied not only organizing in secret but also a level of moral commitment on the part of cadres, a strategy based on armed struggle rather than elections, and the goal of radical social transformation, not just a change of regime. Legal activity, while not rejected, was seen as playing a supporting role for underground and armed actions.

Nevertheless, from late 1964 to mid-1966, FSLN members participated almost exclusively in legal activities in coalition with the Communist Party and other opposition groups. Fonseca later analyzed this as a wrong turn, one that led the FSLN to the brink of disappearing as an independent revolutionary force. At the time, however, the movement seemed to be carrying out the perspective he had outlined in his July 1964 courtroom speech, when he said, "Now we need to concentrate on achieving unity with the other anti-Somocista and revolutionary forces, without excluding any of them." He acknowledged that the FSLN was too weak and isolated to lead an "armed popular struggle," which, he still insisted, was "the only way a revolutionary government could be won." Recent defeats, Fonseca said, "have taught us that we can't let ourselves be swept away by our desires and lose touch with reality."[2]

Coming out of the 1963 guerrilla defeat, the FSLN barely existed. According to Jacinto Suárez, who joined the FSLN in 1963 in Managua, the organization consisted of at most ten guerrillas in the mountains and perhaps twenty youths like himself in Managua and León. "Those were years," related Suárez, "in which we had nothing—we have to admit it—we had absolutely nothing! A wood frame for making silk-screen posters. One safe house. A box of colored markers. A few yards of cloth. Two pistols at the most. And plenty of desire to do something." Even learning of the existence of the FSLN could depend on where a person lived. Half a dozen young members of the movement, including the brothers Humberto and Daniel Ortega Saavedra, lived or worked within two blocks of Suárez's house in the San Antonio neighborhood of Managua.[3]

The opportunities for carrying out open political organizing in Nicaragua were greater than they had been for two decades. The 1960–62 upsurge in protests by students and intellectuals, combined with a slight increase in labor militancy, put pressure on the Nicaraguan government to allow the opposition more room to operate. At the same time, the U.S. government was using its Alliance for Progress program, which had a strong presence in Nicaragua, to press for cleaner elections and other reforms. The new Liberal president, René Schick, enjoyed a measure of democratic credibility, having been elected with more than 90 percent of the vote in 1963. Some participants in the Ríos Coco y Bocay guerrilla action took advantage of Schick's amnesty program to return to Nicaragua legally. One scholar has characterized this period as involving a significant expansion of civil society, with a flowering especially of middle-class and professional organizations that advanced the interests of their constituents within the context of overall support to the Somocista state. An influential organization of Liberal women, for example, won middle-class women increased access to political posts and professional jobs, in addition to turning out the vote for Somocista candidates. One indication of its success is that two-thirds of those who voted for Anastasio Somoza in 1974 were women.[4]

The economy was booming: from 1961 to 1967, Nicaragua's annual growth rate of over 7 percent was the highest in Latin America. The rate of growth in agriculture alone during the 1950s and 1960s averaged nearly 5 percent a year, one of the highest in the world. The explosion of cotton production starting in 1950 was joined in the next decade by a sharp increase in the export of beef, a traditional Nicaraguan product, and the beginning of large-scale commercial production of sugar, seafood, tobacco, and bananas for export. The new Central American Common Market led to a modest amount of industrialization, especially in first-stage processing of agricultural products and the packaging of insecticide and fertilizer. Alliance for Progress–sponsored programs created some public sector jobs in the civil service and education, and agricultural and industrial expansion led to a growth in managerial and commercial employment. U.S. economic aid in 1968 was twenty-seven times what it had been in 1960. A construction boom in the capital produced new middle-class neighborhoods. Downtown Managua acquired a real commercial district, with shops stocking U.S.-made goods for newly affluent consumers. The Nicaraguan middle class, still small even by Latin American standards, was culturally very much oriented to the United States.[5]

Most of the Nicaraguan population did not benefit from the economic boom. In the countryside, the distribution of wealth was more unequal than ever. In 1963, the top 0.1 percent of the rural population owned 20 percent of the land, and the bottom half made do with about 3 percent. Cotton was not a crop for small producers, and by the mid-1960s, 90 percent of cotton acreage was in the hands of large landowners. The growth of cotton production in the 1950s and 1960s was responsible for a greater degree of proletarianization of the peasantry than any previous crop. With the expansions of coffee production and cattle ranching in the nineteenth and early twentieth centuries, small landowners had tended to be pushed into tenant arrangements or displaced onto the agricultural frontier. It was not until the advent of cotton, the most profitable and highly mechanized crop in Nicaraguan history, that large numbers of peasants lost access to land altogether and, in many cases, migrated to the cities. Thousands poured into the *barrios orientales* on the east side of Managua, sprawling communities of new urbanites, many of whom traveled back to the cotton zone each year to work during the harvest season. The population of the capital doubled during the 1950s, to about 230,000, and then nearly doubled again in the course of the 1960s. Although the middle class was concentrated in the capital, the majority of the city's population was poor; in 1969 three-quarters of Managua households got by on less than $100 a month. By the end of the 1960s, nearly half the population of Nicaragua lived in urban areas, with Managua dwarfing all other cities and towns.[6]

The capital was the base of operations for the Republican Mobilization (Movilización Republicana, MR or PMR), a legal leftist coalition dominated by the PSN. The MR had been formed in 1958, with Carlos Fonseca—still associated with the PSN at the time—as one of the signers of its founding document. In 1964, following the defeat at Ríos Coco y Bocay, the young activists of the FSLN joined the MR, bringing a considerable infusion of energy to this somewhat sedate organization. Tomás Borge, who accurately described the group later as "an organization of the radical petit bourgeoisie," became a public leader of the MR and editor of its newspaper.[7]

The Republican Mobilization functioned as the left wing of the opposition movement. It provided a forum for those who thought the revolutionary perspective of the FSLN was too dangerous and unrealistic but who wanted to engage in anti-Somoza and pro-labor activity. The MR worked closely with the Conservatives, the PLI, and the Social Christians, and as the 1967 elections approached, it threw its support behind Conservative presidential candidate Fernando Agüero.

The FSLN was very much a junior partner in the MR. The politics of the Republican Mobilization were those of the PSN, which insisted that the road to change in Nicaragua was through reform, not revolution. The FSLN was competing with its coalition partner for the allegiance of radical youth, and the PSN offered numerous inducements the FSLN could not match, including a longer history, a working-class base, its own newspaper, free trips, and scholarships to study in the Soviet Union. The FSLN had little or no influence in the labor movement, and the PSN dominated important unions. The Communists were also a force in the peasant movement, organizing a conference and protest march of several hundred campesinos to Managua in mid-1965. When FSLN members entered the MR in 1964, according to one source, they agreed to stay out of rural areas and leave political work there to the PSN.[8]

The only arena in which the Sandinistas operated on an equal footing with their moderate MR allies was the student movement. Although few in number, FSLN supporters organized into the FER ran the university student governments in both Managua and León. Casimiro Sotelo, UCA student leader and secretary-general of the FER, edited the newspaper *El Estudiante*, which represented the revolutionary tendency at the two universities and a few high schools. Student leader Michelle Najlis explained later how a tiny team, including herself and Sotelo, "did everything" on the paper: "write the articles, find a printer, correct the proofs, sell the paper, collect the sales money and whatever we could get from the few people willing to place ads with us, or more likely hit up a few collaborators for voluntary donations."[9] Even in the student movement, however, the FSLN lost ground to more moderate forces in the mid-1960s. The 1965 student elections in León went to the Democratic Christian Front (Frente Democrático Cristiano, FDC). The following year, radicals lost control of the UCA student government in Managua as well, after the administration expelled their most popular leader, Casimiro Sotelo. In spite of a ten-day campaign by UCA students, including building takeovers, hunger strikes, and protest marches, the administration refused to allow Sotelo to return to campus. The FSLN's influence on campus was partly determined by the caliber of leaders it had available to work in the student milieu. Sotelo was expelled, some dynamic student agitators had to go into hiding because they were *quemado* ("burned," exposed to the authorities), and others were deliberately removed by the FSLN to work in the urban underground or fight in the mountains.

The student coalition that defeated the FER in 1965 to 1966 was linked to the Social Christian Party of Nicaragua (Partido Social Cristiano de Nicaragua, PSCN or PSC), a group that collaborated with, but was not part of, the MR. Made up largely of middle-class students and intellectuals, the PSCN advocated reforms to "uplift" the poor and improve living conditions of the majority. This movement blossomed in the relatively open environment of the mid-1960s, collecting 30,000 signatures in a short period to win official ballot status. The party offered financial scholarships for bright Nicaraguan students to study labor organizing and receive "ideological training" in Chile, Portugal, and Venezuela.[10]

During the FSLN's legal interlude from 1964 to 1966, the youthful Sandinistas concentrated on educational work and community organizing. They gave literacy classes to workers, using phrases like "Sandino was a great general" as their texts, and they campaigned to bring water and electricity to working-class barrios of Managua. Jacinto Suárez later admitted that he and the other students had trouble communicating with workers and that their organizing smacked of paternalistic social work: "The fact is that you go to the barrio but you don't live there, and you almost always go with a paternalistic attitude. This was a pretty general problem. . . . It was hard for us to really communicate with these people, partly because we had different vocabularies and partly because we didn't really understand the way they thought."[11]

The period of legal coalition work was supposed to give the FSLN time to "accumulate forces," to expand its influence and build up its tiny membership. The results, Fonseca said later, were exactly the opposite. "Reality taught us that this interlude lowered morale, destroyed the enthusiasm of our membership, and thus the only thing we 'accumulated' was powerlessness." In *Hora Cero,* written two years after the FSLN left the MR, Fonseca criticized the work of 1964 to 1966 as "extremely limited" and "marked with a reformist streak." He acknowledged the practical impossibility of continuing to organize armed actions in the period immediately following the defeat at Ríos Coco y Bocay but said the FSLN came very close to giving up on the strategy of insurrection and disappearing as an independent revolutionary force. The balance sheet he drew on work inside the MR was negative: a lower level of activity, the demoralization of cadres, the adoption of "the work habits and form of organization of the traditional petit bourgeoisie," and the loss of influence to "antirevolutionary elements that call themselves Christians" in the student movement and to the PSN in both the countryside and the cities.[12]

An examination of the weekly newsletter of the MR, *Movilización Republicana,* supports Fonseca's assessment that the FSLN gained little from its coalition activity. A mid-1965 issue of the newspaper, for example, never mentioned the name of the FSLN, even though the lead article described the funeral of Marvín Guerrero, killed by Somocista death squads. The article identified FSLN founder Guerrero only as an activist in the MR. Carlos Reyna, one of the FSLN's most important worker recruits, was listed as president of the MR's "Popular Civic Central Committee." Modesto Duarte, another founding member of the FSLN, was identified just as "a patriot killed at Bocay-Raití." A moderate "Message to Nicaraguan Youth" appeared with the byline "Silvio Mayorga, Cultural Secretary of the Republican Mobilization." Perhaps Mayorga and Reyna thought their political influence would be jeopardized by being publicly linked to a banned organization. But Guerrero and Duarte were, after all, dead. It is hard to avoid the conclusion that FSLN leaders inside the country deliberately decided not to publicize the organization's existence in a newspaper over which they had considerable influence.[13]

Fonseca's critique of the Sandinistas' activity in the mid-1960s was directed not toward their involvement in legal work per se but rather toward their failure to use the public arena to build the membership and influence of their own revolutionary current. He noted, for example, that the leaflets members distributed at the May Day demonstration in Managua in 1964 did not even mention the name of the FSLN. Sandinistas should have done more, Fonseca said, to distinguish themselves from the reform-oriented PSN. Instead, "the FSLN vacillated in putting forward a clearly Marxist-Leninist ideology," with the result that a strategy was advanced that "on the national level was rooted in compromise."[14]

The low point of the entire two decades for the FSLN's organizing on campus came during the 1966 to 1967 national election campaign. The CUUN in León worked closely with the Social Christians and the PSN to organize support for Fernando Agüero, the wealthy cattle rancher and perennial Conservative Party candidate who unsuccessfully challenged Tachito Somoza for the presidency. There were no student demonstrations in Nicaragua following the capture and murder of Che Guevara by the Bolivian army in October 1967. Student activism outside the electoral arena never completely disappeared, however. At the opening game of the 1966 baseball season, with Anastasio Somoza present in the stadium, some thirty Social Christian and Sandinista students suddenly unfurled—to cheers from the surprised crowd —a huge banner reading "No More Somoza!" The National Guard violently attacked the young protesters, killing several. When the GN killed FSLN member and former president of the law students at the UCA David Tejada in early 1968, students protested in León and Managua. They were outraged by reports that Tejada's body had been dropped from a helicopter into a live volcano.

Fonseca accepted full responsibility for the FSLN's decision to participate in Movilización Republicana. He was, however, out of the country for most or all of this period and did not have day-to-day responsibility for leading the FSLN's work. In comparison with later periods of exile, he paid little attention during the mid-1960s to organizational and political developments inside Nicaragua. He continued to be seen as the central leader of the FSLN and had already acquired superhuman qualities in the eyes of the youths attracted to the movement, but he seems to have been preoccupied with other matters during this period. After his marriage to María Haydeé Terán in April 1965, the couple lived together for a time in Mexico and then in Costa Rica. In San José, Fonseca returned to a literary project he had begun earlier with Edelberto Torres, researching the anti-imperialist poetry of nineteenth-century Nicaraguan poet Rubén Darío. There are almost no political writings by Fonseca between his release from jail at the beginning of 1965 and late 1966.

Several developments in 1966 played a role in ending the legal interlude of the FSLN and reasserting the principle of revolutionary clandestinity. The FSLN sent a delegation to the Tricontinental Conference in Havana in January 1966. The Sandinistas cheered when Fidel Castro attacked the conservative politics of Latin American Communist parties much like the PSN, and they later read Che Guevara's "Message to the Tricontinental" calling for "Two, Three, Many Vietnams." In mid-1966 Carlos Fonseca returned secretly to Nicaragua and began to participate in a more direct way in leading the FSLN. In August 1966 Anastasio Somoza announced his candidacy for president, President René Schick died of a heart attack, and the PSN-led Republican Mobilization threw all its energies into campaigning for the candidate of the bourgeois opposition. In November 1966, the central leadership of the FSLN published a manifesto repudiating the politics of the Republican Mobilization. Entitled "Sandino Yes, Somoza No, Revolution Yes, Electoral Farce No!" it was signed by Fonseca, Mayorga, Rigoberto Cruz, Oscar Turcios, and "Conchita Alday" (Doris Tijerino).[15]

The defining event of this period was a 22 January 1967 anti-Somoza rally called by the bourgeois opposition parties and the PSN. Like the 23 July 1959 student march in León, the 1967 march and rally ended with the National Guard shooting at fleeing unarmed demonstrators. More than 100 of the 50,000 demonstrators were killed.[16] Fonseca and the FSLN blamed the organizers of this demonstration almost as much as the National Guard for the massacre. They alleged that the Conservative, Liberal, and Communist opposition leaders had deliberately set up the disaster, believing it would provoke a split in the National Guard and the direct intervention of the United States, which would then supervise the upcoming elections or even install the opposition candidate Agüero. Although there is no evidence to support this charge, it is true that the leaders of the demonstration were all safely inside the Gran Hotel before the shooting started, and that the political perspective of these parties at the time and later was to look to the United States to bring down the Somoza regime.

The FSLN published a scathing attack on the electoralist opposition following the January demonstration, but its attention had turned to the northern mountains. Preparations for a second guerrilla operation began in mid-1966, at the same time that Che Guevara was making his way to Bolivia for what would turn out to be his final campaign. The Pancasán region chosen by the FSLN, although still remote, was closer to Matagalpa than the area where they had fought in 1963, and was inhabited by Spanish-speaking campesinos rather than Miskito Indians. The guerrillas were somewhat better prepared politically than they had been in 1963. Several leaders of the FSLN, including Carlos Fonseca, entered the region and began locating peasant families who would provide shelter and food. They met some veterans of Chale Haslam's guerrilla uprising of 1959 and even some old supporters of Sandino's movement. They were also able to learn some of the routines and informers of the National Guard in the area. Víctor Guillén, a local peasant guide, accompanied Fonseca in an area known as Fila Grande:

> Comandante Carlos worked night and day. I always accompanied him. This is the way it worked: we would approach a house and I would go up

first to make sure everything was all right and there were no visitors present. . . . The Comandante always insisted on being well organized. The campesinos didn't have any trouble understanding "Jesús," which was the name he went by there. . . . I remember that he always talked about the way the rich exploit us, the necessity of having land reform, and he emphasized the fact that the poor could never take power in Nicaragua if we weren't organized. The land in Fila Grande wasn't very good, it rained all the time. So the Comandante told the peasants that they were going to get better land to farm when the revolution triumphed. In order for this to happen it was necessary to get organized, to struggle for who knew how long. He always told everybody—don't think that this is going to be easy.[17]

The 1967 guerrilla operation, like that of 1963, was based in the remote mountains of north-central Nicaragua, a region the rebels called the *montaña*. This is an extremely sparsely populated and undeveloped area of some 10,000 square miles, stretching from near Matagalpa almost to the Honduran border on the north and the gold-mining enclaves of Siuna and Bonanza on the east. It varies in vegetation and altitude, encompassing dense humid jungle, pine forests, and brush-covered hillsides. In much of the region, it rains virtually every day from May through December, and the area is crisscrossed with rivers that must be forded on foot or by boat. In the 1960s and 1970s, the only town in the region with more than a thousand residents was Waslala. Most of the population lived in villages of 100 to 200 people and on widely scattered farms, without electricity, health services, and schools. There were no paved roads in the entire region, and the dirt roads linking villages were impassable for vehicles during the long rainy season. Covering 10 to 15 percent of the geographic area of Nicaragua, the region was home to less than 1 percent of the population. The FSLN's guerrilla region overlapped with Sandino's, but the range of Sandino's EDSN had stretched both further west and further east.

Most of the residents of the montaña were Spanish-speaking peasants of Indian descent, some of whom had been pushed off better and lower land by expanding coffee plantations in the nineteenth century and cotton plantations in the twentieth. Cattle ranchers began moving herds into the southern reaches of the montaña region in the 1960s. Most of the residents of the high jungle were subsistence farmers, growing corn, beans, and yucca for their own consumption and local sale. The lack of any transportation system except river canoes limited their possibilities for selling produce further afield. Groups of Miskito and Sumo-speaking Indians inhabited the farthest reaches of the guerrilla zone of operations, but the homelands of these Indian peoples were further north and east, downriver on the Río Coco and along the Atlantic shoreline.

The National Guard, headquartered in its Waslala *cuartel,* ruled the montaña through its village strongmen or *jueces de mesta.* The guerrillas depended on local peasants to hide them from the National Guard, as well as to provide them with food and guides. One of the first lessons the Sandinista guerrillas learned in the early 1960s, according to Fonseca, was the importance "of being extremely cautious every time we approached a new campesino." One reason for caution was that a large proportion of peasant families in the region had at least one relative in the National Guard. Since the 1930s, Somoza had implemented a policy of actively recruiting from the zone where Sandino's EDSN had been based. Fonseca often quoted Sandino's saying that *la montaña no entrega a nadie,* "the mountain never betrays anyone." He believed that peasants were morally stronger than urban collaborators, less likely to betray the rebels as a result of National Guard propaganda, bribes, or torture. Reality did little to substantiate this idea. The experience of the FSLN was that informers could come from any social class or region. There were poor peasants who ran to tell the Guard when they saw the Sandinistas, and there were members of wealthy urban families who deserted the guerrillas and told the authorities everything they knew about their former comrades.[18]

The FSLN could mobilize only about forty guerrillas for the Pancasán operation—two-thirds the number fielded four years before. But the combatants were slightly better trained, mostly in Cuba, and virtually all of them were armed. For the first time, a woman fought in the Sandinista ranks. Gladys Baez—at twenty-six, older than many of her fellow soldiers—came from a working-class family in Chontales and had been active in the PSN for ten years before joining the FSLN. Baez believes she was chosen because her peasant background and factory experience convinced the leaders of the FSLN that she could withstand the physical challenges of a guerrilla war. There were very few women in the FSLN at the time, perhaps no more than five or six, or about 10 percent of the membership; except for Baez, they were mostly student activists.

According to Baez, the central leaders—Fonseca, Mayorga, and Oscar Turcios—were committed to the idea of including women, but the rest of the guerrillas did not want her there. "Some said I would get them all killed, others that they were in favor of women's participation—but not now."

Three campesinos quit because of Baez, and Fonseca called the rest of the band together.

> It was 4 A.M. and freezing. Carlos said if people didn't want to fight to the end, they should leave and would not be considered traitors. Everyone was looking at me, and I wondered if I was expected to leave. Then we looked at Carlos—he had that piercing stare that looked right through you. And nobody left. They figured if the woman wasn't going to quit, then they couldn't either. They wanted to leave, but their machismo wouldn't let them.[19]

Baez perceived different motivations for including women, even among the guerrilla commanders. "Carlos understood how much women loved their children and parents, and the idea they would leave their families to join the struggle was something he had tremendous respect for." Mayorga was the most enthusiastic about women's participation, in her opinion. "Others were convinced it was necessary, but Silvio was excited about it. He thought women brought something special to the revolution because they learned to think of themselves in a new way." Gladys Baez's 1967 experience is a telling illustration of the attitudes toward women in the FSLN: general agreement in the abstract on the right of women to participate on an equal basis, combined with a tremendous unevenness among male Sandinistas in personal behavior and level of understanding of women's role in society.

The Pancasán guerrilla operation began in May 1967, with Carlos Fonseca —who celebrated his thirty-first birthday in the mountains—at the head of one of three guerrilla columns. Over the next few months, the guerrillas had several small clashes with the National Guard, which had concentrated 400 counterinsurgency troops in the area. On 27 August, a National Guard ambush wiped out Mayorga's entire column. Those killed included important leadership cadres of the FSLN: in addition to founder Mayorga, the organization lost Carlos Reyna, the Managua worker who represented the FSLN at the 1966 Tricontinental Conference in Havana, and Rigoberto Cruz, almost single-handedly responsible for developing contacts in the mountains after 1963. The guerrillas in the remaining two columns decided to call off the operation. More familiar with the territory than their predecessors had been in 1963, they retreated quickly to Honduras.

Militarily there seems to be little difference between the Ríos Coco y Bocay campaign of 1963 and Pancasán in 1967. But Fonseca and others in the FSLN always claimed that the Pancasán campaign represented a political victory, because it showed the whole country that the FSLN still existed and was capable of mounting an armed action, and because it represented a definitive break with the reform-oriented politics of the PSN and the Republican Mobilization. Fonseca probably exaggerated the extent to which Pancasán made the FSLN a household word in Nicaragua. American political scientist Thomas Walker, the author of some of the most widely read books on the Nicaraguan revolution, spent the summer of 1967 in Nicaragua doing research for a short book on the Christian Democratic movement. He got to know the young leaders of the legal opposition well, but his book does not mention the FSLN.[20]

Following Pancasán, Fonseca and the other survivors entered a period of intense discussion to figure out what had gone wrong. They decided that some of their tactics for organizing and recruiting peasants were counterproductive. In their preparations for Pancasán, for example, they had tried to win the confidence of peasants by providing economic help or arranging loans, a practice that they found "corrupted some peasants, who thought the money was for their personal use and ended up seeing the organization as a source of enrichment rather than something they would sacrifice for." Peasant recruits frequently deserted when called on to fight far from their homes. Noticing that these deserters later sometimes carried out antilandlord and anti-Guard actions in their own area, the FSLN drew the lesson that at least some of their peasant allies would provide logistical support or even participate in combat near their own land but not fight in other regions. It took time and experience, Fonseca said later, for the urban youth to learn how to tap into the natural rebelliousness of the Nicaraguan peasantry. "When we first made contact with the campesinos we didn't understand them as well as we should, and we weren't able to come up with the right forms of organization to bring them into the guerrilla ranks."[21] The communication gap that isolated Sandinista guerrillas from mountain dwellers in 1963 and 1967 and urban workers from 1964 to 1966 persisted well into the next decade.

The post-Pancasán discussion raised profound questions. October 1967 saw the capture and murder of Che Guevara in Bolivia. In country after country around Latin America, government armies crushed rural guerrilla movements, some of them much larger than the FSLN. Luis Turcios Lima, founder of the Revolutionary Armed Forces, was killed by the Guatemalan army, and guerrilla leaders Hector Béjar and Hugo Blanco were imprisoned in Peru. According to Jacinto Suárez, "In the midst of all this, a discussion began at the very center of the Frente Sandinista. What are we? A party? An armed group? A foco? What? We began to question the famous theory of foquismo and to try to define ourselves. OK, what is the Frente Sandinista anyway? Who are we? Where are we headed? What do we really want?"[22]

Henry Ruiz, who joined the FSLN during this period, has said that members interpreted the lessons of Pancasán in sharply divergent ways. Some wanted to maintain the focus on rural guerrilla warfare, and others favored abandoning the armed struggle to concentrate on political work in the student movement and urban barrios. Fonseca's role in these discussions was to try to find a course between the two extremes and counter the despair and even panic with which some militants responded to the movement's difficult situation. In a talk to FSLN members a few years later, he said the lesson to be drawn from Che's death was that the FSLN's difficulties represented a generalized problem and not something peculiar to Nicaragua. These were "normal problems," he insisted, that any organization experienced as it went through the intermediate stage between "the time when it had no revolutionary armed expression at all, and the coming phase in which the popular victory will be decided by the combat of revolutionary armies."[23]

Fonseca called his peasant guide Víctor Guillén to a meeting in a Managua safe house after the Pancasán defeat. He told Guillén to return to the area and look for any collaborators who had not been killed or captured. "We have to get ready to start over," Fonseca said, "because nobody can stop this struggle of ours."[24] At the same time, Oscar Turcios was sent to participate in the guerrilla struggle underway in Guatemala, both to aid that movement and to receive military training in action. Violent operations inside Nicaragua were largely restricted to the cities and consisted of isolated retaliation against symbols of the dictatorship and bank robberies. In October 1967, only a few months after the Pancasán defeat, the FSLN carried out an *ajusticiamento* (bringing to justice, i.e., execution) of one of Somoza's most hated torturers, Gonzalo Lacayo. A half-dozen attempts were made—some of them successful—to rob banks and corporation offices to raise funds for the FSLN. These urban armed actions were costly. More Sandinista militants were killed in the aftermath of the Gonzalo Lacayo execution and at shootouts during robberies than all those who had fallen at Pancasán.

In contrast to the period after the Ríos Coco y Bocay defeat, when they had retreated both politically and militarily, the FSLN went on the offensive politically after Pancasán. In the course of 1968, a series of short mimeographed manifestos sought to bring around new recruits and mobilize broader protests. These included a call to action on the thirty-fourth anniversary of Sandino's assassination in February, a May Day message supporting workers' struggles around concrete economic and social issues, a Mother's Day appeal highlighting the conditions faced by working-class and peasant women, a call for protests against a visit by U.S. President Johnson in July, a statement on the first anniversary of Che Guevara's death in October, and an antielectoralist manifesto on the anniversary of Casimiro Sotelo's murder in November. All of these were written by Fonseca. Although the FSLN now had a more formal leadership structure with a National Directorate, Carlos Fonseca was still almost single-handedly responsible for developing the group's political positions. In January 1968 he was named the political and military chief of the FSLN, and in February 1969 he became the secretary-general of the organization, a position he held until his death.[25]

The FSLN had fewer than a hundred members, but its propaganda in this period expressed a confidence that bore no relationship to its size, political influence, or military accomplishments. A typical mimeographed leaflet entitled "The Guerrilla Movement Is Invincible" showed no inclination to compromise with other opposition forces. In language that indicates it was written by Carlos Fonseca himself, the leaflet lashed out at "the false oppositionists, the false revolutionaries, the false Christians and the false Marxists, . . . all rubbing their hands with glee, thinking they can throw themselves into deal making, without any guerrillas getting in their way."[26]

This was the context in which Carlos Fonseca, in April 1968, wrote his "Message to Revolutionary Students," one of his most important writings on revolutionary strategy. In response to a new "Development Plan" issued by the UNAN with the support of both the Communists and the Social Christians, Fonseca's manifesto called on students who considered themselves revolutionary to "unmask" the "demagogues" of the PSC and the "false Marxists" of the PSN. Like his letter to Don Edelberto Torres in 1960 and his writings on guerrilla warfare in the 1970s, the central theme of Fonseca's 1968 *Mensaje* was the question of leadership.

Fonseca had harsh criticism for some of the antecedents of the student movement of the 1960s. He charged the Generation of '44 with raising "outdated Liberaloid demands" and "lacking any fire as a social movement" and said the proponents of university autonomy in the early 1950s "gazed thoughtfully down at the national condition from their intellectual Olympus." In a passage that would have been deeply offensive to prominent opposition intellectuals of the time, Fonseca called university autonomy a "farce" that was only made worse by "professors who call themselves democrats." Rather than a fake autonomy that gave the government a thousand ways to intervene, said Fonseca, the university needed to be tied to the interests of workers and peasants. "The university is maintained by the sweat of the working class. Culture is built on thousands of years of labor by the toiling masses."[27]

The same angry condemnation of middle-class intellectuals can be found in other writings by Fonseca during this era. In a 1968 letter to "R. C." requesting a financial donation, Fonseca wrote:

> Cultured people owe a huge debt to revolutionary combatants and the Nicaraguan masses these fighters defend. . . . When was the attitude of Nicaraguan intellectuals more contemptible? Was it when they were almost totally absorbed by the exploiting classes, from the martyrdom of Augusto César Sandino to the socialist victory in Cuba. . . ? Or was it perhaps during the last decade—from 1959 to 1968—when, although aware of the rottenness of the system, they do nothing but stand around with their arms folded?

He went on to demand C\$ 2,000 and warn that the FSLN had been "patient, excessively tolerant in the face of the indifference" of intellectuals. In another letter, Fonseca blasted "Dr. A. R." for not sending a promised contribution and said that such "insincere people" would be responsible if the movement failed. "If our isolation causes us to be defeated tomorrow," Fonseca went on, "we will go to our grave knowing that our spilled blood will be screaming loud enough to wake up deaf consciences."[28]

In his 1968 *Mensaje a los estudiantes revolucionarios,* Fonseca had harsh words for students who considered themselves revolutionaries, including those affiliated with the FSLN. While student guerrillas were dying in the mountains, he charged, "revolutionary students who have stayed behind in the classrooms have basically stood around with their arms folded doing nothing." The problem was not general student apathy. Fonseca insisted that the majority of students wanted to respond when leaders like Silvio Mayorga and Casimiro Sotelo were killed and were only waiting to be called into action when Che Guevara was murdered. The problem was a lack of leadership on the part of revolutionary students, whom Fonseca accused of "indiscipline" and of being influenced by "capitalist penetration of the universities."

Fonseca said revolutionary students often missed opportunities to mobilize their fellow students and to counterpose a broader political approach to the narrowly campus-focused campaigns of the moderate student organizations. He used the example of a campaign by reform-minded students to raise money for the UNAN by selling raffle tickets. It was not enough for revolutionary students to oppose such a collection, he wrote. "What they should have done is get together a mass student meeting, draw up informational materials explaining the government's hostility to the university, and reach out for broad popular support to try to force the government to increase the university budget and also spending on education in general."

The 1968 *Mensaje* picked up Fonseca's earlier theme that students had a special responsibility in a country such as Nicaragua, where only a privileged minority received a university or even a high school education. They had to be "standard-bearers for the masses" and learn their way around "the factories and barrios, the rural villages and plantations." Part of students' responsibility to the masses was to present a clear political alternative, an "unequivocally radical revolutionary ideology." Unfortunately, Fonseca charged, pressure from moderates had affected even students affiliated with the FSLN. The *Mensaje* pressed Sandinista students to be more aggressive in challenging the Social Christians' sermons on class harmony: "History teaches us that there cannot be peace between the rich and the poor, between millionaires and workers. Historical experience teaches that there are only two alternatives: either the rich exploit the poor or the poor free themselves by wiping out the wealth of the millionaires."

Fonseca urged young followers of the FSLN to study Marxism and be more open about their Marxist beliefs. He argued against those in parties like the PSCN and PSN who thought it possible to remove the Somoza dictatorship and win a greater measure of national self-determination for Nicaragua without a fundamental change in class relations. We in the revolutionary movement, said Fonseca,

> have to say as clearly as we can that our goal is to bring to an end a society divided into exploiters and exploited, a society divided into oppressors and oppressed. We say clearly that our main goal is to return to the workers and peasants, to all working people, the riches that have been violently ripped from them. National independence and the defeat of foreign imperialism are prerequisites for the building of a new world, one full of happiness. In our search for a new world, we are guided by the noble principles developed by Karl Marx. Modern history demonstrates that the principles of Marxism are the compass that orients the most resolute defenders of the poor, of the abused, of oppressed humanity.[29]

In 1970, when the Federation of Revolutionary Students regained control of the student government in León, its candidates won by openly declaring their affiliation with the FSLN. This was something new, according to FSLN activist Omar Cabezas, the student campaign manager for Edgard "the Cat" Munguía: "The Cat was the first president of the cuun elected by going from classroom to classroom, repeating over and over that he was a communist, that he was a Sandinista, that he was FER." For Fonseca and his followers, it was not necessary to be enrolled in school to qualify as a student leader, only to be young and politically active in the student milieu. Francisco Buitrago, for example, became a central leader of the cuun although he could never afford to register at the UNAN. He followed Carlos to León, as he had to Managua in 1956, to get involved in political activity.[30]

In his "Message to Revolutionary Students," Fonseca touched on a theme he would return to in his later writings on Sandino, warning that a national liberation struggle could not ultimately succeed if it did not go on to overturn capitalist property relations:

> There is the danger that an armed insurrection might not necessarily lead to a revolution, that is to the transformation of the social system that exists in the country. For this reason, we have the obligation to make sure that the Nicaraguan insurrection has a profound revolutionary content, that it involves radical social change. In the modern history of national liberation struggles, there have been cases when popular insurrections have actually won but haven't resulted in revolutionary governments taking power, cases in which the proletarian revolution has not been victorious.[31]

The revolutionary students of the FER and FSLN were fighting an uphill battle in the context of Nicaraguan politics in the late 1960s. The Nicaraguan case refutes the idea, found in the work of Mexican social scientist Jorge Castañeda and others, that the moderate Left in Latin America was pushed to the sidelines in the 1960s by euphoria over the Cuban revolution, that an electoralist Left favoring compromise rather than confrontation with the United States got a serious hearing only after the collapse of the Soviet Union in the late 1980s.[32] At the height of the 1960s, the nonrevolutionary opposition in Nicaragua was much stronger and more influential than the FSLN, with broader appeal, more prominent leaders, and the largest-circulation daily newspaper in the country. It was the FSLN, the only group in Nicaragua that identified with the Cuban revolution, that had to fight for a hearing, even among college and high school students.

Among the intellectuals who rejected the revolutionary option in the 1960s were some who later joined the FSLN, including Carlos Tunnerman,

Sergio Ramírez, and Ernesto Cardenal. When he became rector of the UNAN in 1964, Carlos Tunnerman said that university autonomy meant "a participatory university, not a politicized university invaded by shouts and passions from the street." In 1970 Tunnerman insisted that "there is no room in the University for politicos and rabble-rousing, but there is for politics, if what we mean by politics is studying and reflecting on the nation's fundamental problems."[33]

The political approach of the FSLN's reform-oriented competitors in the student movement comes across clearly in a manifesto signed by two dozen academics and intellectuals on the tenth anniversary of the 23 July 1959 student massacre. It emphasized the importance of the university community promoting the development of society as a whole, which the manifesto insisted had to be accomplished "through reason and not through force." Social progress was possible only "when intellectuals, scientists and highly trained technicians join together and put their talents into raising the general cultural level." After summarizing the extreme inequality of land ownership in Nicaragua, the intellectuals called for "reasonable" land distribution to "achieve mutual understanding and the peaceful living together of the elite and the masses." In addition to implementing this harmonious type of land reform, the government was urged to liberalize the import of capital goods, improve internal credit flow, encourage industrialization, stimulate education, and facilitate more efficient investment. The moderate academics concluded that the profound changes Nicaragua needed could only come "through the humanization of relations between employers and workers, which will put the economy and capital at the service of humanity."[34]

A comparison of Fonseca's 1968 "Message to Revolutionary Students" and the academics' 1969 "Document of the July 23 Generation" reveals the wide gap between the revolutionary and reform-oriented camps of the anti-Somoza student movement: armed struggle versus elections, the montaña versus the campus, class struggle versus class harmony, a leadership role assigned to workers and peasants versus one that looked to intellectuals and technicians, socialism versus capitalist development. It would be a mistake, however, to assume that the debates that took place in classrooms and student meetings were so clear or so sharply polarized. The two ideological camps existed, but many Nicaraguan students—probably the majority—did not agree completely with either one. The late 1960s and early 1970s were a period of intense political discussion and action by students in Nicaragua, as in many other countries around the world. Under the influence of world events, national politics, and their own family situations, individuals were always changing, some moving in a radical direction, and others becoming more conservative.

The competition between the FSLN and the Social Christians had more to do with politics than religion. The PSCN had no official relationship with the Catholic Church and included in principle and in fact "persons of different religions and even of none." But the fact that the party and its student affiliate identified themselves as "Christian" appealed to many of the young Nicaraguans of all classes who were morally outraged at the poverty, racism, and violence they saw around them. The relationship between Christianity and Marxism was hotly debated on college campuses, and Fonseca touched on this question in his *Mensaje*. "Being a convinced Marxist," wrote Fonseca, "does not exclude respecting the religious beliefs of the Nicaraguan people."[35] This straightforward democratic pledge of religious freedom is quite different from the idea that would be put forward a decade later that Christianity and Marxism are philosophically compatible, or even on some level identical. Catholic students did not have to renounce their religion to join the FSLN, but they did have to reject the idea that nonviolent methods could heal society's ills. Fonseca pointed to the example of Camilo Torres, a young Colombian priest from a wealthy family, who became an armed guerrilla and died fighting in the mountains in 1966.

Camilo Torres was a priest, but his political writings had more in common with Carlos Fonseca than with the Catholic intellectuals of the Nicaraguan PSC and Conservative Party. Only a few years before Fonseca, Torres wrote a "Message to Students" in which he accused university students of being non-conformist only so long as it did not prevent them from climbing the social ladder, and of having nothing to contribute at a time of real crisis except "blah-blah and good intentions." In language remarkably similar to Fonseca's, the Colombian cleric went on to charge that "when the working class demands students join its ranks with an effective, disciplined and responsible presence, the students answer with vague promises or with excuses."[36]

A recent comparative analysis of Third World revolutionary movements of the post–World War II period stresses the leading role of students educated in the United States and Western Europe.[37] In the case of Nicaragua, virtually none of the students who became leaders of the FSLN attended universities in the advanced industrialized countries. There were, however, two important groups of FSLN leaders educated outside Nicaragua, for whom their university experiences played an important role in the development of their political ideas. A handful of youths from wealthy Nicaraguan families studied in Chile during the Allende years and later became leaders of one of the tendencies in the FSLN. A more important experience was that of a slightly larger group of Nicaraguans who studied at Patrice Lumumba University in Moscow during the 1960s. The same debate about the revolutionary potential of Communist parties like the PSN that Fonseca was leading inside Nicaragua was taking place in Moscow. The PSN often gave scholarships for study in Moscow to members of its own youth group and other student leaders it sought to recruit. Gladys Baez, a young PSN member and union leader from a provincial working-class background, received such a scholarship in 1963. In a 1994 interview, she said that the first thing her Soviet hosts told her when she arrived was to stay away from Oscar Turcios, who would "fill her head with lies about Sandino." Baez instead searched out Turcios and was influenced by him before he returned to Nicaragua in 1964 to organize the FSLN underground. Other students recruited to the FSLN's political line in Moscow included Doris Tijerino, Henry Ruiz, Plutarco Hernández, Leticia Herrera, René Tejada, and José Valdivia.[38]

By 1968 the Central American students at Patrice Lumumba were divided into two factions: those who supported the guerrilla movements in Nicaragua and Guatemala and were critical of many aspects of Soviet foreign policy, and those who continued to support the pro-Moscow Communist parties. In October 1967 the pro-guerrilla group tried to organize a campus meeting to protest the murder of Che Guevara, which was broken up by orthodox Communist students from Argentina and Venezuela. After the August 1968 massacre at Tlatelolco in Mexico City, the more radical students at Patrice Lumumba organized a protest march, led by Mexican students, to the Mexican embassy in Moscow. To the students' surprise, police violently attacked the demonstration, which authorities feared might jeopardize the Kremlin's relationship with the Mexican government. Police also broke up a student march protesting the shah of Iran's visit to Moscow later the same year. Shortly afterward, the pro-FSLN students who had not already returned to Nicaragua were expelled from the Soviet Union.[39]

This ideological confrontation among students in Moscow coincided with Carlos Fonseca's 1968 condemnation of the conservative politics of the PSN. His "Message to Revolutionary Students" blamed the "opportunistic" politics of Communist parties like the PSN for the initial defeats suffered by "the insurrectional movement that arose in Latin America as a result of the victory of the patriotic Cuban revolution." For Fonseca, the death of Che

Guevara in 1967 represented the turning point between the false Marxism represented by the PSN and the genuine Marxism of the FSLN. As he told his student followers in 1968,

> the sacrifice of Ernesto Che Guevara, identified with Marxist ideals, teaches us that the era of the conformists who disguise themselves as Marxists is a thing of the past. Marxism is now the ideology of the most ardent defenders of Latin American humanity. It is high time for all revolutionary Nicaraguans to embrace the goal of proletarian liberation.[40]

The FSLN had, since its founding, drawn most of its recruits from the university, and it was not surprising that Fonseca's first lengthy writing on strategy was addressed to college and high school students. At the same time, Fonseca tried to reach out to intellectuals with a broad audience in Nicaragua, in the hope that they would speak out against human rights violations and publicize the issues around which the Sandinistas were struggling. It was not Fonseca's style to plead with these prominent intellectuals, appeal to their egos, or sometimes even to be polite. Ernesto Cardenal, already a well-known poet, met with Fonseca at various safe houses in and around Managua during 1967 and 1968. According to Cardenal,

> Carlos criticized me for not writing something that dealt directly with the guerrilla movement. I explained that I couldn't write poetry on demand, but the reality was that I wasn't ready to write the kind of things he wanted. But he kept after me, and eventually I was ready. When David Tejada was killed, I remember that Carlos wanted me to make a major *denuncia* about torture. So I went on the radio, and then I wrote something. I didn't want to promise him this, but he was very insistent, he wouldn't let me get out of it. He said if I didn't do something, I was defending torture.[41]

Fonseca also set up a secret meeting with Nicaragua's most prominent living poet, José Coronel Urtecho. The FSLN leader startled Coronel by accusing him of being "next to Somoza, the person with the greatest responsibility for the way things are in Nicaragua today." When, after several hours, Coronel said he had to leave to give a speech, Fonseca demanded he stay, saying "those folks can wait and anyway they aren't very important." Coronel's account of the meeting, like the Cardenal interview, illustrates Fonseca's characteristic abrasive attitude toward intellectuals, even those he respected. It also hints that Fonseca may have had a personal interest in these meetings, above and beyond the help he hoped the intellectuals would provide. According to Coronel Urtecho, "then we moved on to other subjects closer to both of our hearts, such as literary movements and Carlos's interest in poetry." Cardenal has also said that he and Fonseca spent many hours discussing philosophy, literature, and religion.[42]

To reach out beyond its own ranks to potential recruits and sympathetic intellectuals, the FSLN had to organize its own cadres more effectively. In June 1968 Fonseca circulated within the organization a paper entitled "What It Means for a Revolutionary Fighter to Be an Active Member of Our Organization." The document began:

> All too often, many members of the FSLN do not have ordinary tasks to do every single day. Most of the work our members do is sporadic. One serious consequence is that the movement's energies are wasted. The tendency to let all the weight of our work fall on a small number of compañeros has now become a habit. And without the participation of every single member, it is not possible for us to carry out all the tasks that are before the revolutionary movement.[43]

This document, addressed to militants in urban areas, dealt with such down-to-earth matters as the importance of preparing an agenda ahead of time, the right of every member to speak without being interrupted, and the need to keep meetings orderly. It urged members to become familiar with the local situation so that their leaflets and painted slogans could be very concrete, and not "make the mistake of calling on people to struggle against exploitation and oppression in the abstract." Fonseca seemed to be addressing criticisms previously raised by members when he stressed the importance of individual initiative and insisted that a meeting of the FSLN was not a talk shop for "those who talk and talk about revolution and in practice don't carry out actions in defense of the masses and the nation." Although Fonseca was a Marxist and thought everyone in the FSLN should study Marx and Lenin, his criterion for membership was always an individual's willingness to take revolutionary action, not his or her ideological preparedness. He had nothing but praise, for example, for two young poets who dedicated their lives to the revolutionary movement but did not consider themselves Marxists: Fernando Gordillo, who believed there was no proletariat and no real class struggle in Nicaragua and died just as he was about to join the guerrilla operation at Pancasán; and Leonel Rugama, who went to Mass every Sunday and died in a shootout with the National Guard in early 1970.

In parts of this document, Fonseca was clearly talking about his vision of the future, not the tiny and quite isolated group that the FSLN actually was in 1968. He called for

> organizing in every sector: construction workers, shoemakers, textile workers, furniture workers, drivers, mechanics, commercial workers, workers in big factories, stevedores and other port workers, students at all levels, poor campesinos, agricultural workers, etc. . . . The goal must be that in every barrio, every productive sector, every workplace, there is an active squad of the FSLN.

Fonseca referred to the 1965 uprising in the Dominican Republic and the building of barricades in Paris in mid-1968 as if these were activities the FSLN could emulate. These were ambitious goals indeed for an organization whose strength was probably fairly accurately reflected in a 1969 headline in the opposition weekly *Extra Semanal*, "28 Dead, 16 in Jail, and 12 Underground: Current Balance Sheet of the FSLN."[44]

Underground and Prison Life, 1968–1970

The FSLN's attention after the 1967 defeat at Pancasán turned to the urban underground. Over the next few years, an underground and prison culture took shape in urban safe houses and jail cells in Nicaragua, a culture with its own myths, values, secret language, gender relations, naming conventions, humor, and literature. Carlos Fonseca played a central role in the clandestine activity, acquiring a reputation as an underground warrior of superhuman proportions. FSLN member Hugo Torres has described his first meeting with Fonseca:

> There in front of us, with no posturing or pretense, without even introducing himself, was Carlos, the legend, Zorro, one of the Three Musketeers, Kadir the Arab, the Invisible Man, the one who escaped under the very nose of the Guardia, the one who mocked his jailers with his strength and his contempt for death, the one who entered his wife Haydeé's house in León without ever arousing the suspicions of the enemy standing guard outside, and even left her pregnant before escaping again, the one who died and came back to life, the one who just for the fun of it and as an example of popular creativity made Somoza and his cronies look like idiots, showing the superiority of the popular masses, which he personified, over their oppressors."[1]

The mythology surrounding Carlos Fonseca's personal participation in the urban underground has only a slight relationship with historical fact. María Haydeé Terán has said, for example, that Carlos never visited her in León a single time during the years he was being sought by police, never telephoned her, never sent her a letter by mail. The only contact she had with her husband came when FSLN messengers brought her a letter or took her to a safe house in another city. These visits were not frequent. Fonseca did not see his son Carlos Fonseca Terán—born in November 1966—until the baby was about ten months old. His daughter Tania de los Andes Fonseca Terán was born in January 1969, but when Fonseca was arrested in Costa Rica seven months later, he still had not seen her. The OSN, meanwhile, accumulated hundreds of pages of reports from a tap on Terán's phone, surveillance reports, and the interception of personal correspondence to and from her address.[2]

Fonseca's physical characteristics were hard to disguise. Over six feet tall, fair skinned and thin, with piercing light blue eyes, Fonseca looked quite different from most of his fellow Nicaraguans, especially in the countryside. He was nearly blind without his trademark eyeglasses. Benita Alvarado, a neighbor who watched for the police when Carlos came to visit his mother in Matagalpa in the 1960s, said that he came disguised as a charcoal seller. Although she heard stories of his visiting Matagalpa disguised as a nun, she never saw him in that guise; according to her, the rumors of Carlos attending his mother's funeral in a nun's habit were just "part of the legend." A friend of Fonseca's from the INN has said he recognized Carlos disguised as a woman on a Managua bus in the late 1960s. Fonseca was said to have deliberately gained about thirty pounds in Cuba in 1974 and 1975 so that he would look different when he returned to Nicaragua, and a young woman who shared a safe house with him in Managua in 1975 reported that he did facial exercises every day to enable him to change his appearance. This may be part of the mythology, however. As far as María Haydeé Terán knew, Carlos never used a female disguise or did face exercises. The weight he gained in Cuba, according to her, was the result of age and a more stable lifestyle.[3]

When he reentered Nicaragua for the last time in 1975, Fonseca used contact lenses and a mouthpiece that gave him heavy jowls, and he traveled under a fake passport that identified him as a businessman. Inside Nicaragua, Fonseca seems to have traveled from safe house to safe house with only a minimal disguise, such as changing his clothing or hairstyle or substituting contact lenses for glasses. There are several references to him "disguised" as a student, and Humberto Ortega has said that at their first meeting, in a working-class barrio of Managua, he found Fonseca "disguised" as a baseball player. These slight changes of appearance seem to have been enough to fool the Somoza police, who always turned out to be wrong when they claimed to have penetrated Fonseca's disguise. In 1973, for example, the Nicaraguan ambassador to Guatemala radioed Somoza that Fonseca had definitely been spotted dressed as a doctor in a Red Cross plane and that he was still working in Guatemala in that guise.[4] Fonseca was repeatedly placed inside Nicaragua during the years he spent in Havana in the early 1970s. Some of these reports may have started as popular rumors; even people who did not support the FSLN often believed the myth that Fonseca could pass under the Guard's nose without being seen. In other cases, members of the National Guard and government officials probably invented information about Fonseca to curry favor with superiors.

All the underground members of the FSLN and many of their collaborators had pseudonyms, and Fonseca himself used numerous false names. The FSLN's internal security regulations forbade using—or in many cases even knowing—a militant's real name. Sometimes new members were assigned pseudonyms by those who recruited them, in which case the underground name might be an affectionate nickname or diminutive, especially for very young recruits. More experienced members usually chose their own noms de guerre, and these names reveal a good deal about the culture of the underground movement. Luisa Amanda Espinoza, killed by the National Guard at the age of twenty-one, chose the name "Lidia" after Lidia Doce, a heroine of the Cuban Revolution. Doris Tijerino was known as "Conchita Alday" after a Nicaraguan peasant and Sandino collaborator killed by U.S. Marines in 1927. FSLN members often took the names of comrades killed in action. Fonseca frequently went by "David," which he assumed after the murder of student leader David Tejada. Fonseca named his own daughter Tania De Los Andes Fonseca Terán, after Tamara Bunke, or "Tania," who fought alongside Che in the Andean country of Bolivia. Dora María Tellez, a guerrilla commander in the late 1970s, adopted the names of people like herself, young women from well-to-do urban backgrounds, who had been killed fighting against the National Guard. "The pseudonym implied a commitment one was making to the martyr," she explained in a 1980 interview. "It was like picking up the torch she dropped. And at the same time it was like throwing a ghost in the enemy's face."[5]

Underground Sandinistas sometimes used each other's names, a practice that probably causes more problems for the historian than it did for the OSN. Ernesto Cardenal once loaned Carlos Fonseca a book about Gandhi, which was later returned with a letter commenting on the book. "He didn't want to get me in trouble for having a letter signed by Carlos Fonseca," explained Cardenal, "so he signed it with Tomás Borge's name, but he knew I would know who it was from."[6] Fonseca sometimes used the name Víctor in the mid-1960s when he was sharing a house in Mexico with Víctor Tirado.

The OSN kept extensive records on their efforts to uncover these secret names. A 1969 confidential report on "Names and Pseudonyms in letters sent and received by Carlos Fonseca Amador" gives at least one pseudonym each for more than a dozen FSLN members. Every OSN *historial*, or chronological record, on Fonseca contains information on the pseudonyms he used, as well as safe houses where he stayed. One pseudonym the OSN never discovered was "Jesús," used only during Fonseca's rural guerrilla campaigns.[7]

In the course of the 1960s, Fonseca and the other underground members of the FSLN built a network of safe houses in all the major cities of western Nicaragua. These houses, almost all in working-class neighborhoods or on small farms just outside town, were not just hiding places and transit points. They were also the places where the guerrillas recovered from their wounds, studied political books and wrote documents, held leadership meetings to discuss strategy, and carried out military training. Most of the safe houses were the family homes of collaborators of the FSLN, who jeopardized their own safety by providing sanctuary to the guerrillas. The Núñez family opened their small finca south of Managua to underground Sandinista organizers throughout the mid-1960s. After the 22 January 1967 demonstration and massacre, the entire family was jailed, including an eleven-year-old boy.[8]

Some of those who secretly housed the guerrillas were themselves the parents—especially the mothers—of revolutionaries. Fonseca often stayed at the house of Doña Teodorita Rubí, whom he called his adopted mother; her son, José Rubí, was one of the four students killed during the 23 July 1959 demonstration in León. When Fonseca was arrested in June 1964, he had been staying in the house of José Benito Éscobar's mother, Doña Irene. Fonseca often stayed with Róger Nuñez's mother, Doña Aurora Dávila, whom he called *mamita*, "little mother." Relatives of Jorge Navarro provided a safe house in a working-class neighborhood of Old Managua, and Carlos Reyna's family opened their home in a slum area near Lake Managua. Some of these families had to move more than once in order to continue providing sanctuary.[9]

Although some members of the FSLN came from middle-class and even bourgeois families, their safe houses were all in poor barrios, where they could come and go without drawing too much attention, and where the neighbors were more likely to offer protection. The Núñez farm outside Managua was little more than a shack with no electricity or running water. Doña Irene's house in Barrio San Luís was a rough, windowless wooden dwelling of only two or three rooms. When Fonseca and Víctor Tirado were arrested in June 1964, two blocks from Doña Irene's house, the response of the barrio was immediate. Residents called the press, and a young messenger took off across the city to where Doña Aurora was expecting Fonseca. Doña

Aurora threw all the FSLN papers in a suitcase and ran across the street to a neighbor as poor as she was. "Doña Zoilita," she begged, "keep this suitcase safe for me and I'll pay your rent this month." Although Aurora's house was searched, the suitcase stayed under Zoilita's bed until the FSLN was able to retrieve it.[10]

Omar Cabezas, a student leader and FSLN organizer in León, tried without much luck to convince prominent opposition figures in that city to provide refuge in their homes for underground revolutionaries. "The problem was that these guys were old, and I was just a kid then, in 1970 and 1971. . . . They were old, and they were used to taking part in old men's conspiracies, in the plots of Conservatives and Liberals, of old men who met to scheme in the aisles of movie theaters or in León's noble mansions." The problem was as much one of social class as of generational divide. Only a mile or so from these "noble mansions," in the indigenous barrio of Subtiava, Cabezas found an Indian worker and veteran community leader named Magnus Bervis, who turned his home into a safe house the Sandinistas respectfully called "The Fort."[11]

The task of keeping the safe houses clean, of feeding and nursing the fugitives, almost invariably fell to women. A few male Sandinistas, including Fonseca, were uncomfortable with this gender-based division of labor. A young woman who occupied the same Managua safe house as Fonseca in late 1975 said that the first time she asked for his dirty clothes he told her he would do his own laundry. He only agreed to let her continue when she reminded him that the house's security rules forbade his going outside to the laundry sink. Julio Buitrago, the head of the urban underground in the late 1960s, was in charge of a safe house that once received an unwelcome visitor in the middle of the weekly housecleaning. A description of the incident includes the following breakdown of tasks: Carlos was washing the walls, Róger mopping, Amanda sweeping, and Tamara cleaning the submachine guns.[12]

Even though female members of the underground were expected to do more than their share of the household tasks, they were treated equally when it came to military responsibilities. The fact that they were assigned weapons and taught to use them gave these young women a confidence that comes through clearly in some of the literature about underground life, as does the impact that this confidence had on their male comrades. A male FSLN member told writer Margaret Randall in 1980: "I remember once when Luisa Amanda was coming from the mountains and three guards stopped her. She was dressed as a nurse. They took her in and one of them wanted to rape her.

He took her down to the river and at first she played along with him. Then, right there by the side of that river, she killed him. That's the kind of strength Nicaraguan women have."

Carlos Guadamuz has described how two young women entered the urban underground and immediately began arms training. "We ended late, and even though it had been an exhausting day—at least for us guys, the girls were fresh as a daisy—they seemed to be ecstatic and satisfied with themselves and told us they couldn't wait to run into their first dog from Security to leave him flat as a postage stamp in the middle of the road."[13]

A variety of contradictory conventions and pressures affected relations between men and women in the underground. A patriarchal approach to family and social relations was deeply embedded in Nicaraguan culture. The ideal was that of a male head of household who provided for his family and dependents and made all decisions, and a wife who remained at home and took care of the children. Women's sphere was the home, and men's the larger world of politics and economic life. Only bourgeois families and sections of the middle class could afford to conform to this pattern. Working-class and peasant families were headed by women more often than not, and even when both parents were present, survival depended on the earnings of the mother and children. But as a cultural norm, the ideal of the stay-at-home wife and mother penetrated all layers of society. Even the young women and men who broke with social convention by joining an armed rebellion were affected by these deep-seated cultural expectations.

The underground FSLN also had its own conventions about the role of women, some related to security measures and some imposed by Carlos Fonseca. Perhaps because of his own upbringing, Fonseca had a rather traditional attitude toward monogamy and the inviolability of marriage ties. This could be hard on female as well as male Sandinistas. When a man and woman who were both members of the FSLN wanted to live together, they were required to get the permission of their organizational superior, or *responsable*. When Doris Tijerino and Ricardo Morales Avilés fell in love in the late 1960s, their ranks in the organization were such that they had to get the approval of Carlos Fonseca himself. Morales was legally married to another woman, and for four months, Fonseca refused to answer the couple's request. Tijerino described what happened when she decided they had waited long enough: "In the house where we were living there was an empty room, and I said OK, that is going to be Ricardo's and my room because we are setting up a relationship. And I remember that Carlos was furious and walked out in a huff without saying a word to me." Tijerino was living in

Cuba when Morales was killed in September 1973. Fonseca's behavior on that occasion infuriated her:

> When Ricardo was killed, Carlos took it on himself to write a letter to Ricardo's legal wife, who wasn't even in Nicaragua any more, she had moved to Mexico. He wrote expressing his condolences to *her* and didn't have even a kind word to say to me. He was the one who told me about Ricardo's death, but that was because I happened to be on guard duty when he got the news. After that his comportment was the way I've described—that she was his wife and not me. And that was just wrong.[14]

Fonseca could also be sharp with men who expressed backward attitudes toward women. In Havana in the early 1970s, according to one FSLN member,

> A bunch of us guys would get together sometimes and start talking about women—as is natural under those circumstances—and say this and that. And when Carlos came in, he would get very emphatic about the role women had to play, about their rights, about the exploitation of women, about the question of machismo. He couldn't stand it when men behaved in a crude way toward women—it was something he got furious about.[15]

Rigorous security measures were enforced in the urban underground. Militants had to memorize the procedures in a security manual they referred to as "the green book": passwords, false names, letters written in code, mail drops. A policy called "compartmentalization" was supposed to ensure that each member knew only the individual to whom he or she reported and a few other individuals—an impossible goal in an organization that in the late 1960s had only a few dozen members, some of whom had known each other since childhood. When a member or supporter was judged untrustworthy and deliberately excluded from the chain of information, that person was said to have been "compartmentalized." Guerrillas living in a safe house had to post guard twenty-four hours a day and sleep fully dressed so that they could escape quickly. Females were supposed to wear pants and not skirts for the same reason.

Letters between members of the underground were supposed to be written in code, but the examples that have survived suggest the meanings were quite transparent. In December 1965, for example, when René Schick was president of Nicaragua and most oppositionists considered Luis Somoza a lesser evil than his brother Anastasio, Fonseca wrote, in a letter supposedly encoded:

In terms of the possibility that Luis will take the position now held by Don René, I disagree with the idea many people are propagating that Luis's brother is the greater danger. This leads to many illusions that it would be a good thing if some new René were appointed. Whether it is a new René or Luis's brother, things will stay the same. Therefore the correct thing is to concentrate our fire on *continuismo,* whatever face it wears.[16]

Some of the guerrillas occasionally found humor in their security problems. On overnight guard duty at a Managua safe house, Carlos Guadamuz became suspicious about the driver of a car parked outside. After worrying for half an hour, Guadamuz finally woke Julio Buitrago, who looked at the car for a few seconds, said in a bored voice, "He's just jerking off," and went back to sleep. At that point, commented Guadamuz, "I realized there was a reason he was the head of the urban underground." Two leaders of the underground once gave a copy of the FSLN statutes to a student they were trying to recruit. At their next meeting, they asked what he thought of the material, and the student, proud of having grasped the importance of strict security measures, reported that he had read the statutes and burned them. "They called me to order," he confessed later, "because that was the only copy they had for the whole apparatus, but there was nothing to be done about it."[17]

For Carlos Fonseca, however, there could never be anything funny about security measures. He was known for his intolerance of the slightest lapse. In the early 1960s, Heriberto Rodríguez made an innocent error that made Fonseca so angry he could hardly speak. Fonseca often warned that friendship or family relationships were no excuse for militants to let down their guard when it came to security precautions. In a 1968 manifesto on norms of activity for members of the urban underground, he said, "We must do away with the bad habit many militants have of getting together in public when their revolutionary work doesn't require it, just because of some ill-conceived friendship. Problems need to be taken up seriously in clandestine meetings, not bantered about in street conversations." He tried to impose a semiclandestine lifestyle on FSLN exiles in Havana, as if they were in Honduras or Costa Rica or even in Nicaragua itself. This was very different from the policies followed in Havana by leftist exiles from other Latin American countries, and it was difficult to enforce, especially for the Nicaraguans with young children, who inevitably developed more open relationships with their Cuban friends and neighbors. In September 1973 the only two members of the FSLN National Directorate living inside Nicaragua, Ricardo Morales Avilés and Oscar Turcios, were captured outside a Managua safe house and killed by the National Guard. Fonseca wrote a twenty-page document spelling out the security transgressions that had led to this disaster.[18]

If an OSN document can be taken at face value, however, Carlos Fonseca himself committed one of the most serious security violations of the underground period. According to a secret police report dated 21 March 1967, Fausto Amador called the OSN on 18 March and then again on 21 March, each time reporting that he had just received a telephone call from his son Carlos Fonseca, warning him to stay away from the payroll office of the Central de Ingenios because it was going to be the target of an armed attack.[19]

Members of the underground and their collaborators lived with the constant danger of discovery and death. Over and over again through the course of the late 1960s, the National Guard tracked down known FSLN militants at their safe houses or on the streets and killed them. Sometimes the guerrillas were able to fire back, but they were usually outnumbered, and the death toll was extremely lopsided. On 4 November 1967, former student leader Casimiro Sotelo was killed, along with three other FSLN members. Sotelo had entered Nicaragua secretly less than a week earlier, after receiving military training in Cuba. On 15 January 1970, the poet Leonel Rugama was discovered in Managua and killed with two other FSLN members. Rugama's last words became an example of the culture of defiance, of almost laughing in the face of death, that became part of the mystique of the FSLN. When the National Guard called on those trapped in a safe house to come out and surrender, Rugama shouted back, "Tell your mother to surrender!" He was not quite twenty.[20]

The most famous example of resistance was Julio Buitrago, the head of the urban underground. Live television and radio coverage of his killing electrified the nation. On 15 July 1969, Buitrago's safe house in a working-class Managua neighborhood was discovered by the National Guard. Three other rebels, including Doris Tijerino, managed to get away under cover of gunfire from Buitrago. Over the next several hours, the National Guard moved in tanks and helicopters, as well as more than a hundred troops, to attack the modest two-story house, and they told reporters that the amount of firepower coming from inside proved they had found a nest of dozens of "communist terrorists." But when the firefight finally ended, there was only Buitrago's bullet-ridden body. He was twenty-three years old and weighed 114 pounds.[21]

An opposition weekly in Managua published excerpts from the diary found with Buitrago's body. Covering a three-week period in mid-1968, the diary entries reveal much about the problems of clandestinity and the state of the FSLN at the time. The picture they paint is one of real differences and debate among the central leaders about the immediate strategy and long-term perspectives of the organization. It was not danger that preoccupied Buitrago so much as boredom, frustration, and impatience with other members of the leadership, especially Fonseca. Buitrago noted at one point that he had not been out of his safe house for fifteen days, virtually paralyzed by the conditions of clandestinity. "The monotony is killing us," he complained, "and I think the only way to break it is with revolutionary action." He bemoaned the fact that the movement did not seem to be able to do anything but deal with the economic problems of subsistence. The anniversary of the 1959 student massacre passed, and "we did nothing; we didn't have the materials we needed to organize some protests." He got a discouraging report from a compañero code-named Eleven: "Some people have done absolutely nothing; he says they don't even come to meetings." Buitrago had several long discussions with Fonseca, whom Buitrago thought too conservative. "Sometimes I think he hasn't recovered from the recent defeat [at Pancasán], and that this has taken away his confidence."

"I just can't make myself believe," Buitrago wrote in his diary, "that it isn't possible right now, in addition to our political work, to carry out some military actions." The diary suggests that only respect for Fonseca was holding Buitrago back from a suicidal adventure. "I talked to Tere about what we would do if they kill David [Carlos Fonseca]. We decided we would launch an indiscriminate war to the death against our enemies."[22]

Buitrago's complaint that there was no money to buy paint or mimeo paper to commemorate the 1959 student massacre illustrates the FSLN's chronic financial problems. In a 1970 interview with the Chilean magazine *Punto Final*, Fonseca was asked what important actions the FSLN had carried out; he listed dozens of actions between 1963 and 1970, the majority of them *recuperaciones* (bank robberies). The first of these, carried out in Managua in May 1963, netted $10,000, but few others were as successful. The Sandinista guerrillas carried only small hunting arms during most of their urban and rural military operations, because that was all they could afford. Soliciting donations from middle-class oppositionists was an important enough task to be given to Fonseca himself at various times. In the OSN files there are copies (and occasionally originals) of handwritten letters from Fonseca demanding "a contribution that represents a real sacrifice" from individuals who "claim to support" the struggle against Somoza.[23]

For two decades, Somoza's Office of National Security kept every scrap of information it could get on Carlos Fonseca and his friends and contacts. Its voluminous file on Fonseca went from the childish letter he wrote Anastasio Somoza Debayle in 1956, demanding the return of confiscated books, to the little plastic-wrapped package of handwritten correspondence removed from his bloody corpse in November 1976. The only surviving copies of some of Fonseca's writings are those from the secret police archive, which passed into the hands of the FSLN when Somoza fled Nicaragua in 1979. The OSN files are important sources of information, but these documents have to be used with care. Documents written by other FSLN members are sometimes erroneously attributed to Fonseca.[24] It is possible that some OSN agents did not or could not read the documents they filed away; their reports and transcriptions reveal that some were barely literate.

There are a few documents in the OSN files that appear to be deliberate falsifications. There is a typed death sentence, for example, addressed to Prof. Eloy Canales Rodríguez and signed "Carlos Fonseca." The letter informed Canales that the FSLN had condemned him to death for "your contemptible behavior as an *oreja* ("ear," or spy) in the Instituto Ramírez Goyena" and "because of your wicked disrespect for the democratic elements who are risking their lives to liberate our country." Although the FSLN did occasionally execute Somocista agents, its targets were carefully chosen. The most famous ajusticiamento was the 1967 execution of hated National Guard torturer Gonzalo Lacayo, who had captured and beaten Victor Tirado and Carlos Fonseca in 1964. Canales Rodríguez, although several times elected to the Nicaraguan legislature as a member of Somoza's Liberal Party, was a popular educator with a reputation for honesty, and he had no connection to the National Guard or any other part of the repressive apparatus. In 1934 he was the first Nicaraguan legislator to support extending the vote to women.[25]

The file also contains a copy of a passionate love letter sent by Josefina Tijerino to "Víctor" in Mexico City in February 1965. An OSN clerk wrote "For Carlos Fonseca Amador" across the top. In the letter, Josefina, who was apparently a student, referred to spending time at school with her "beloved Víctor." This letter may have been put in Fonseca's file deliberately, in the hopes of using it to cause personal problems for the exiled revolutionary, who was about to marry María Haydeé Terán. More than thirty years earlier, a U.S. Marine captain had created a crisis for Augusto César Sandino by turning over to his wife Blanca Aráuz a letter—genuine, in this case—that Sandino had written to his mistress.[26]

Fonseca's 1968 *Militancia activa* and Julio Buitrago's diary from the same period make it clear that there were disagreements within the FSLN about its course and the pace with which it was moving. In his 1969 essay *Zero Hour*, Fonseca claimed that some members were "burned out" after the defeat at Pancasán and that it was time to regroup and politically orient a new cadre. It was in this context that Fonseca went to Costa Rica in early 1969, to draft a set of basic programmatic documents and prepare a general meeting of the FSLN leadership. Humberto Ortega described this episode as "a kind of pause, for the purpose of analyzing the rich experience we had had up to that point and improving upon this experience through analysis and study." Fonseca went to Costa Rica somewhat reluctantly, as he explained in a letter to Julio Buitrago from San José:

> It is painful for me to be here right now, which is almost like being on vacation. . . . I'm able to accomplish a certain task that is almost impossible in Nicaragua, namely composing a series of documents. I will do everything in my power to make this stay as short as possible and get back where I most want to be, at the side of those who are simply the best of the best.[27]

The desire to return quickly to Nicaragua would be a thread running through all Fonseca's exile writings.

In Costa Rica, Fonseca finished the essay *Hora Cero*, drawing a balance sheet of the legal interlude of the mid-1960s and guerrilla defeat of 1967, in the context of a brief social and economic analysis of Nicaragua. He then outlined a set of demands that was first published in 1969 as the "Sandinista Program" and has come to be known as the "Historic Program." His draft of the *Programa Histórico* was sent to Julio Buitrago in Managua and also smuggled to FSLN leaders imprisoned inside Nicaragua. In a letter written in the guise of business correspondence, six weeks before Buitrago was killed, Fonseca said he was sending his colleague another version of the "catalog" to circulate and comment on.

> I've already explained in other letters that our idea is that this material will be valid for a more extended period. This doesn't conflict with the need to put out more day-to-day materials on events as they occur. . . . The whole project has been modified according to suggestions made by

various associates. But I don't want to put out a final version until you [plural] have sent your comments. . . . The associates here are very enthusiastic, and some even think that this material is superior to that of other companies like ours in different countries around the region.[28]

In July or August 1969, almost all the central leaders and many of the members of the FSLN met in San José and adopted the Historic Program and a new set of organizational bylaws.

Hora Cero and the Programa Histórico represented an ideological breakthrough for the FSLN, the first time they put in writing the political approach they had been developing through action and debate for almost a decade. The Historic Program would be the program of demands under which the FSLN would lead a victorious revolution in 1979. *Hora Cero* was Fonseca's analysis of why a revolution was needed in Nicaragua, why the other opposition groups were incapable of leading a social and political transformation, and what the FSLN had done to begin to prepare for such a revolution. Fonseca argued that Nicaragua had been reduced to a "neocolony" of U.S. imperialism by three decades of rule by a "reactionary clique," which, in alliance with "the sector of capitalists who call themselves 'oppositionists,'" had imposed a backward and lopsided economic system on the country, exploiting and victimizing workers and peasants. *Hora Cero*'s analysis of the Nicaraguan state and economy led directly to the Programa Histórico's proposal for solutions. The Historic Program was published in the name of the FSLN, but it bore Carlos Fonseca's stamp as much as did *Hora Cero*. The Programa began with a short verse by Nicaraguan national poet Rubén Darío satirizing U.S. imperialism, followed by six or seven quotations from Fonseca's heroes, Augusto César Sandino and Ernesto Che Guevara.

The Historic Program called on the people of Nicaragua to mobilize around thirteen basic demands or tasks of the revolution. The heart of the document lay in its first two paragraphs, demanding the overthrow of the dictatorship and radical land reform. The first point promised the establishment of a revolutionary government that would guarantee basic democratic rights, expropriate the property of the Somoza family and its accomplices, and nationalize banking, foreign trade, and foreign-owned natural resources; this was reinforced by later points calling for an end to "Yankee" interference in internal Nicaraguan affairs, and pledging to abolish the National Guard and replace it with a "patriotic, revolutionary and people's army," and a people's militia. The second point called for immediate implementation of a far-reaching land reform, including a massive redistribution of land to those who worked it. The remaining points outlined social and economic programs focusing on the needs of the impoverished majority. They called for a revolution in culture and education, labor legislation and social security, a campaign to root out administrative corruption, the reincorporation of the Atlantic Coast and an end to the "odious discrimination" suffered there by Indians and blacks, the emancipation of women, respect for religious beliefs, unity among the Central American peoples, solidarity with anti-imperialist struggles around the world, and veneration of the Sandinista martyrs. The demands were largely democratic and nationalist in character, with a strong bias in favor of the needs of workers and peasants and an intransigent opposition to the entire Somoza apparatus.[29]

Articles dealing with the Atlantic Coast and women's liberation raised a series of concrete demands to begin to deal with the special oppression suffered by women and indigenous peoples. But the importance of these issues was not widely understood in the FSLN, and the organization never really advanced beyond the formal expression of these democratic ideals in the Historic Program. Indians and women were often viewed as nearly helpless victims of imperialist and capitalist exploitation rather than actors who could transform society. Fonseca himself provided little leadership on these important political questions, beyond strongly discouraging sexist behavior on the part of male Sandinistas. These political weaknesses, and especially the failure to grasp the importance of ethnic identity for sections of the Nicaraguan population, caused serious problems in the years after the 1979 revolution.

Once the Historic Program and new organizational statutes were adopted in mid-1969, Fonseca was anxious to return to Nicaragua to begin preparations for a new guerrilla operation. These plans were cut short when he was arrested by Costa Rican police on 29 August. When the international press interviewed him in jail a week later, many of their questions had to do with a bombshell news conference in Managua on 20 August, at which Fonseca's half brother Fausto Amador Arrieta, in the presence of their father, denounced the FSLN and urged Carlos to turn himself in and use legal methods to work for social change.[30]

Fonseca had been closer to his paternal brother Fausto, nine years his junior, than to any of his other siblings. In letters written in 1960 to his father and to his father's wife, he had extravagant praise for a speech by the young Fausto, which—as he told Lola Arrieta—"I have read over and over, and honestly it has made me feel proud to have such a brother." In the mid-1960s,

Carlos's young half brother was briefly a supporter or possibly a member of the FSLN.

Fausto junior told the media assembled at his family's palatial residence in Managua that the FSLN was carrying out "an absurd, pointless battle behind the back of the masses, that no one had any idea what it was doing," and that given "the rather deep friendship between Somoza and my father," Carlos could safely return to a legal life in Nicaragua.[31] Although other members of the FSLN followed a "foreign ideology," according to young Fausto, Carlos was no communist and personally favored a peaceful strategy. Both the Somocista daily *Novedades* and the opposition press played up Fausto Amador's physical resemblance to his brother (one said he had "the same blue eyes and was extraordinarily similar in voice and manners") and his advice to FSLN members to return to their families and apply themselves to their studies.[32]

Carlos's furious response, written only two days after Fausto's news conference, was entitled "Long Live the Brotherhood of Guerrilla Fighters." He blasted the use of the noble term *hermano* (brother) for "that cowardly deserter from our ranks whose declarations have been carried by the National Guard's radio stations and ill-reputed periodicals like *Novedades* and *La Prensa.*"[33]

> It isn't enough for the deserter to cover himself with mud. He also has to fling it at those who continue to stand up to the inevitable dangers that combat involves. The deserter charged that the author of these lines has only been following the guerrilla line because of pressure from foreigners. This is an outrageous and insulting lie. . . . The exploitation and oppression our people suffer cannot be wiped out with entreaties. This dirt can't be washed away with water, even holy water. Only blood can wipe out these stains. . . . This filthy deserter's response to the blows suffered by the guerrilla movement is to come out with his hands up.

Fonseca also defended his own belief in socialism, which, he said, "has more often than not responded to the hopes that history and the masses have placed in it." He contrasted his paternal brother's betrayal with the bravery of Julio Buitrago, killed only a month earlier, and of the imprisoned but defiant Doris Tijerino.

Carlos Fonseca never saw his father or brother again, and his only references to them were hostile. In 1973 Fausto Amador senior and René Fonseca deliberately misidentified the body of a slain FSLN guerrilla as that of Carlos

Fonseca. In an FSLN communiqué, Carlos charged that "Mister Amador . . . an individual tied personally to the Somoza family," had misidentified the body in order to demoralize Sandinista supporters and hand the dictatorship a propaganda coup.[34] He refused to acknowledge the more human and more likely motivation, that Amador and René Fonseca deceived the National Guard in the hopes it would give up its manhunt for their son and brother.

Fonseca's last and longest imprisonment took place in Costa Rica, a democracy that observed judicial norms that did not exist in Nicaragua. The president of Costa Rica was a longtime opponent of the Somoza dictatorship. The FSLN believed, however, that the Costa Rican police and prison apparatus had close links to the Nicaraguan National Guard and that Somoza would attempt either to extradite Fonseca or to have him assassinated in Costa Rica. An international campaign was launched against Fonseca's extradition to Nicaragua, which won the support of prominent individuals and received some media coverage in Europe and the United States. At the same time, the FSLN began preparing an attack on the jail to free its leader.

Fonseca played an active role in planning the escape, passing messages through Haydeé Terán, who also smuggled a pistol to him under her skirt during a conjugal visit. He helped choose the participants, including Humberto Ortega, twenty-two years old and already in exile in Costa Rica; Germán Pomares, a peasant veteran of the 1963 and 1967 campaigns; Rufo Marín, a young worker from the town of Estelí; and Costa Rican student Plutarco Hernández. In the attempted escape on 23 December 1969, Ortega was wounded, and a Costa Rican guard was killed. Fonseca and Ortega managed to flee in a getaway car driven by Rufo Marín, pursued, according to the Costa Rican press, by fifty-five police vehicles. As the car approached a police barricade, Fonseca gave the order to surrender because he was afraid Ortega, who was bleeding profusely, would die unless he received medical care right away.[35]

A Costa Rican judge sentenced Fonseca, Marín, and Ortega to long prison terms; Fonseca's was for eighteen years. Terán was charged with conspiring to help her husband escape and held for several months, after which she was released without trial, deported, and barred from reentering Costa Rica. Letters by Fonseca to the Costa Rican and Chilean press complained of the harsh conditions under which the prisoners were held after the escape attempt, and of the denial of adequate medical attention to Ortega.[36]

Fonseca still received books and newspapers, however, and journalists were allowed to interview him, even after the abortive escape attempt. Terán sent him a set of the journal *Revista Conservadora del Pensamiento Centro-americano,* which, according to Ortega, Fonseca "devoured." In late April, she mailed him seventeen requested books and magazines, including six volumes of Nicaraguan Central Bank statistics, half a dozen novels and books of poetry, and Stokely Carmichael's *Black Power.*

In a 1980 interview, Ortega said,

> Carlos kept himself to an incredibly disciplined regimen of study, analysis, and physical exercises. . . . There wasn't a single day in prison, even Sundays, when Carlos didn't go through the whole disciplined schedule he set for himself, devouring large numbers of books on the international situation and on the history of Nicaragua. He got up at dawn, did exercises, then read from eight in the morning until sometimes two or three the next morning, then at five was ready to begin his exercises again.

Fonseca, according to his fellow prisoner, followed events in Nicaragua and the rest of Central America through the daily papers—"even reading the social notes so that he would know the names of all the rich ruling-class families." He composed his first chronology of the anti-interventionist struggle in Nicaragua during this prison stay.[37]

Fonseca's writings do not indicate that he mellowed under prison conditions. If anything, he went on the offensive, not just against the Somoza dictatorship but also against the more moderate opposition groups. From his prison cell, he continued an angry debate with the editors of *La Prensa.* Before his arrest, Fonseca had fired off a letter entitled "An Answer for an Ideological Defender of Torture," in response to an article by anti-Somoza intellectual Jorge Eduardo Arellano. *La Prensa* did not print Fonseca's letter but answered it in a front-page unsigned article entitled "Fonseca's Letter: Fundamentally a Cry of Anguish for the Sad State of His Red Guerrillas." At the end of 1969, the imprisoned Fonseca dashed off a furious answer to an article by *La Prensa* coeditor Pablo Antonio Cuadra. Part of this letter ended up in the osn's file on Fonseca. Written in a nearly illegible slanted scrawl on both sides of a torn half sheet of brown paper, the letter's very appearance gives a sense of haste and extreme anger. Even in this state, however, Fonseca knew his country's history. He wrote, "1969 exists because first there was 1959, 1956, 1947, 1944, 1936, 1934, 1927, 1925, 1914, 1912, 1910, 1893, 1857, 1856, 1855, 1838, 1824, 1821, 1812 . . . 1743 . . . 1650 . . . 1531." Each of these numbers— written in larger and larger figures, in crooked lines climbing the page— represents a key date in Nicaraguan history.[38]

When interviewed by the Costa Rican and international press following his August 1969 arrest, Fonseca accused Conservative leader Pedro Joaquín Chamorro of organizing an ineffective opposition that only served Somoza's interests by enabling the dictator to pretend he tolerated dissent. Asked if he had reconsidered his refusal to support Fernando Agüero in the 1967 elections, Fonseca answered, "Multiply Pedro Joaquín's defects by a million, and you get Agüero." Chamorro tried to visit Fonseca in prison, saying that in spite of their differences, he considered it a common courtesy to visit an imprisoned fellow Nicaraguan. Fonseca refused to talk to him and—as Chamorro later told Ernesto Cardenal—"acted like a snake had come into his cell."[39]

In "We Are Honored by the Attacks of Costa Rica's Fake Revolutionaries," written in the San José Central Penitentiary on 26 March 1970, Fonseca sharply criticized the Costa Rican Communist Party. The PVP had ridiculed Fonseca and his movement in the 21 March issue of its newspaper *Libertad*.[40]

Although the international solidarity campaign succeeded in blocking Fonseca's extradition to Nicaragua, the prisoners and the FSLN feared an attempt on his life. A Nicaraguan prisoner nicknamed "Mamá Dolores" suddenly turned up as Fonseca's cellmate; this criminal had acquired a reputation at La Aviación prison in Managua for beating up political prisoners and for his close ties to the guards. There were rumors that the U.S. Central Intelligence Agency had mapped out a plan to have Fonseca killed during a fake escape attempt.[41]

Another direct attack on the prison to rescue Fonseca was out of the question, so the leadership of the FSLN decided to try to free him through a hostage exchange. On 21 October 1970, an FSLN commando group made up of three men and two women hijacked a Costa Rican commercial aircraft and took hostage two North American executives of the United Fruit Company. Carlos Agüero, the twenty-two-year-old chief of the operation, belonged to one of Nicaragua's wealthiest families and was the nephew of perennial Conservative Party presidential candidate Fernando Agüero. Again Carlos Fonseca participated directly in plans for the operation, including smuggling out instructions to treat the airplane passengers with respect. Agüero's squad offered to exchange the American businessmen and other passengers for Fonseca and his three fellow prisoners. The Costa Rican government approved the deal, and Fonseca, Ortega, Marín, and Hernández flew first to Mexico City and then to Havana.[42]

During the period Fonseca was in jail in Costa Rica, several dozen other Sandinistas were incarcerated in Nicaragua, and almost all the members of the FSLN in the 1960s and early 1970s spent some time in prison. Daniel Ortega and Jacinto Suárez, arrested in late 1967, spent over seven years behind bars. Ricardo Morales Avilés, Doris Tijerino, and Tomás Borge all were jailed repeatedly.

Under these circumstances, a prison culture and a prison literature emerged in Nicaragua. In his 1973 notes on the history of the FSLN, Fonseca singled out the prison writings as examples of a "rebirth of revolutionary culture" after 1956, which he contrasted to the earlier domination of intellectual life by Catholic rightists and fascist sympathizers.[43] The prison writings of Carlos Fonseca consisted of historical and political analysis, and other FSLN members produced poetry, *testimonios,* and drawings, usually with a political content. Daniel Ortega was famous for his prison poem "I Never Saw Managua When Miniskirts Were in Fashion." Carlos Guadamuz smuggled out of La Aviación prison the text of his political biography of Julio Buitrago, *And . . . the Houses Were Left Full of Smoke.* Ricardo Morales Avilés wrote almost daily love poems to Doris Tijerino in 1969; it took a network of cooperative guards and common prisoners to get them from his cell block to the women's prison. Tomás Borge composed his prose poem tribute to Carlos Fonseca in prison.

The material conditions under which this prison literature was produced were extremely difficult. Doris Tijerino explained in a 1973 taped interview by Carlos Fonseca that FSLN prisoners at La Aviación were forbidden to have paper or pencils and that all writing materials were removed from packages sent by relatives. The few books approved by prison censors were most useful for the blank pages on which letters and documents could be written. Sandinista prison literature was often written on tiny scraps of paper from cigarette boxes, with pencils contributed by the very young inmates (Tijerino used the word for children) whose job it was to clean up around the prison.[44]

The FSLN prisoners depended on common prisoners and their visitors, and on cooperative guards, to help them move their political and personal writings in and out of the prison. They had a policy of treating common prisoners and guards with respect, and when possible, they tried to involve nonpolitical fellow prisoners in discussions and classes. Humberto Ortega, jailed with Fonseca in Costa Rica in 1970, has said that common prisoners and even guards always called Fonseca "Don Carlos," as a sign of respect. According to Ortega, Carlos believed that getting to know who the common prisoners were, how they lived, and why they ended up in jail was important "in order to know one piece of our concrete reality."[45]

Sandinista women were sometimes jailed with prostitutes, whom they treated as political contacts and tried to convince to become informants for the FSLN. At the men's prison in Managua, the warden ran his own prostitution business on the side. The political prisoners refused to buy the sexual services of the women brought to the prison every Thursday, but they did try to recruit them as couriers.[46]

During her imprisonment in 1969, Doris Tijerino was in charge of organizing the circulation of secret correspondence inside the prison and with the outside world. She never had to pay guards and their family members to carry FSLN members' letters. In a series of interviews in 1994, Tijerino shared some of the hundreds of poems and political documents she received from Morales. Some were legible only to her—for example, a long political document written in impossibly cramped shorthand on a scrap of paper only a few inches square.[47]

Many political prisoners, including Fonseca, endured physical abuse, which sometimes included beatings, electric shocks, sexual torture, and being kept hooded for long periods. The beatings would often increase after FSLN urban or rural guerrillas outside had carried out a successful operation. René Nuñez was permanently disabled, and Gladys Baez required extensive medical treatment for injuries suffered behind bars. But a number of prisoners have said that the psychological torture to which they were subjected was worse than the physical. The first time Doris Tijerino was arrested, in early 1967, a lieutenant threatened to bring her sixteen-month-old son to the jail, "to see if he could survive one day in their hands."[48] Ricardo Morales Avilés was several times victim of a form of abuse called *pise y corre,* in which he was released only to be rearrested as he approached the prison gate. Guards and wardens tormented prisoners with the news that an FSLN member had been killed, especially when the victim was a central leader or the spouse or lover of one of the prisoners.

Female political prisoners were frequently raped by guards and subjected to other forms of sexual abuse. Even more than male prisoners, they were stripped, forced to do painful exercises naked, and subjected to electric shocks on their genitals. On the other hand, public pressure around the treatment of women prisoners, and occasionally the intervention of well-connected relatives, sometimes won better conditions for women than for their male comrades. Peasant women involved in struggles around land and union rights probably suffered even worse abuse than Sandinista women, because they did not have the same ability to get information to the public.[49]

When Doris Tijerino was jailed in 1967, about ten other inmates at the women's prison had been arrested for political activity. Of these ten, two were pregnant, and at least three were raped in prison. In addition to Tijerino and Gladys Baez, one other prisoner, who was pregnant and still in her teens, was a member of the FSLN. Another woman had been arrested because her boyfriend was suspected of being a member of the FSLN. In early 1969, at the age of twenty-five, Tijerino was arrested again and held for two years, during which time she was repeatedly subjected to sexual abuse. She was released only as a result of a campaign of news conferences, hunger strikes by supporters, and public protests outside the prison. The government's hatred for her comes across in the caption under a large picture of Tijerino in the 5 August 1969 issue of the Somoza-owned newspaper *Novedades:* "In order to keep uppermost in the public mind the interests of the Terrorist Front for Slavery, madam Doris Tijerino Haslam, a fanatical communist, was shameless enough to offer up details of an intimate feminine nature in her charges, the falsehood of which has been shown conclusively by a medical examination."[50]

Some of the worst abuse of female prisoners took place at the headquarters of the OSN near Somoza's bunker in central Managua. According to a 1972 article by Carlos Fonseca, witnesses there heard Anastasio Somoza Debayle himself order the torture of Sandinista women. Doris Tijerino has charged that Somoza participated in the rapes of female prisoners.[51]

Protest demonstrations in support of prisoners' rights linked the FSLN to a broader public. The student movement in particular mobilized around this issue. Again and again between Fonseca's 1964 arrest and the revolution of 1979, students organized demonstrations, held news conferences, went on hunger strikes, and took over churches and university buildings in support of freedom for political prisoners, for an end to physical abuse, and for more exercise, better food, and greater access to books inside the prisons. A 1971 protest campaign known as the "movement of the churches" because it involved primarily cathedral occupations won permission for a delegation of university authorities to visit the Sandinista prisoners and make sure they were alive.

Indigenous communities also lent support to protests around prisoners' rights, perhaps because Indians had long been victims of discriminatory arrests and brutality by police and prison guards. At the end of 1973 and beginning of 1974, public solidarity actions in response to a hunger strike by political prisoners included, in the city of León, "popular sectors from the municipality of Subtiava, who marched playing their traditional indigenous musical instruments called the *bombo* and the *caja*."[52]

Except for its student component, the public campaign in support of prisoners was overwhelmingly organized by women, especially by female relatives of those imprisoned. Gladys Baez, who first became involved in protest activities when her husband, a member of the PSN, was arrested in 1956, has said, "Wherever you have prisoners, you generally have the mothers, wives and daughters turning out every day." Men might give money, Baez noted, but the movement's "physical presence" came from the participation of women. Santos Buitrago became the central organizer of the prisoners' rights campaign after her son Julio was killed in 1969. Most of the women who demonstrated at the jails and visited the political prisoners came from working-class and peasant families, and some of them made long trips to the capital for Sunday visiting hours. Many of these mothers and other relatives were elderly, had never been involved in political activity, and were humiliated by the body searches and verbal abuse they endured from prison guards. They jeopardized their own safety and that of other family members by showing support for their imprisoned sons and daughters. Still they continued to come, even visiting other political prisoners after their own children were killed. Mothers of FSLN members sometimes brought food for the common prisoners as well, so that they would smuggle out letters and try to protect the political prisoners.[53] A few of the FSLN prisoners came from bourgeois families. Their parents, like Carlos Fonseca's father, occasionally intervened to get their own children released, but they never visited the prisons or demonstrated outside. When underground organizer Martha Cranshaw was arrested, her father, a minister in Somoza's government, publicly disowned her.

Fonseca took a personal interest in the campaign to build public solidarity with imprisoned Sandinistas. This human rights issue had broad support inside Nicaragua and internationally, and Fonseca believed that his own life and those of other prisoners had been saved by public pressure. His 1973 taped interview with Doris Tijerino was designed to be used as part of a broad international human rights campaign. In an interview with the Chilean magazine *Punto Final* in 1970, Fonseca—himself in prison—listed two dozen prisoners inside Nicaragua and the conditions under which they were held and urged readers to send messages to Nicaraguan officials and the media. Fonseca was the author of a pamphlet published in Havana in late 1972 calling for a worldwide campaign to win freedom for FSLN prisoners, some of whom had been behind bars since 1967. "We have to realize," he wrote, "that to be taken prisoner in Nicaragua is virtually a death sentence. Nevertheless, it is possible to stay the hand of the killer jailers and win freedom for the workers, students, and other Sandinistas in prison." He noted that the many years of campaigns for freedom and more humane conditions for prisoners were the best answer to charges from the regime and elements in the opposition that the FSLN was only interested in creating more martyrs for its cause.[54] The most spectacular actions of the FSLN in the 1970s—the December 1974 raid on the Castillo residence and the August 1978 National Palace takeover—were primarily designed to win the release of imprisoned leaders.

The 1960s were a decade of discovery and experimentation for Fonseca and the FSLN. It was a decade in which the FSLN became more and more Nicaraguan as its youthful cadres came to know the conditions of life in the remote montaña and in the urban working-class communities where their underground structure was based. They acquired a better understanding of all sectors of Nicaraguan society, sharing the daily life of workers and peasants and talking to common prisoners to learn "one piece of our concrete reality," but also reading society pages to learn about the rich and powerful. The culmination of this process was the Historic Program—a program not for some generic Latin American country that needed land reform and freedom from imperialist domination but for *Nicaragua*.

By 1963—even earlier in the case of Carlos Fonseca—the young rebels considered themselves followers of Augusto César Sandino. By the end of the decade, every analytical or programmatic document, including the *Programa Histórico* and the FSLN statutes, referred to the example of Sandino and his guerrilla army. The following decade and next stage of Fonseca's life would involve the systematic study of Sandino, the adaptation and refashioning of his image for the new reality of the 1970s.

Augusto César Sandino, 1895–1934.
Photograph courtesy of Instituto de
Historia de Nicaragua.

Carlos Fonseca Amador, 1936–1976.
Courtesy of Centro de Historia
Militar.

Fidel Castro addresses OLAS conference, Havana, 1967. Banner with Che Guevara's
picture reads "The duty of every revolutionary is to make the revolution." Photograph by Joseph Hansen, courtesy of *Militant*.

Matagalpa in the early 1950s. Postcard courtesy of Ramón Gutiérrez.

Anastasio Somoza Debayle, 1925–1980. Photograph courtesy of Instituto de Historia de Nicaragua.

Carlos with his mother, Augustina Fonseca, and younger brother René, about 1945. Photograph courtesy of Centro de Historia Militar.

Carlos Fonseca addresses the
Federation of Cuban Women,
Havana, 1961. Photograph courtesy
of Centro de Historia Militar.

Wedding of Carlos Fonseca and María
Haydeé Terán, Mexico, 1965. Photograph
courtesy of Centro de Historia Militar.

Left to right: Carlos Fonseca, Carlos
Agüero, and Humberto Ortega, Havana,
1970. Photograph courtesy of Centro de
Historia Militar.

Seated on right, Carlos Fonseca with
members of the December 1974
commando and released prisoners,
Havana. Photograph courtesy of
Centro de Historia Militar.

Fonseca disguised as a businessman
for his return to Nicaragua, 1975.
Photograph courtesy of Centro de
Historia Militar.

Funeral ceremony for Carlos Fonseca, 7 November 1979, Managua. Photograph by Fred Murphy, courtesy of *Militant*.

Tomás Borge and Daniel Ortega carrying Fonseca's casket, 7 November 1979. Photograph by Fred Murphy, courtesy of *Militant*.

FSLN National Directorate, 1979. *Left to right:* Luis Carrión, Víctor Tirado, Carlos Núñez, Humberto Ortega, Tomás Borge, Bayardo Arce, Jaime Wheelock, Henry Ruiz, Daniel Ortega. Photograph courtesy of Instituto de Historia de Nicaragua.

The author with Ramón Gutiérrez, Rivas, 1994.

Managua, September 1979. Photograph by Aníbal Yañez, courtesy of *Militant*.

Rally celebrating the first anniversary of the Nicaraguan revolution, 19 July 1980. Photograph by Fred Murphy, courtesy of *Militant*.

Nationalized shoe factory, Managua, 1981. Photograph by Arnold Weissberg, courtesy of *Militant*.

Campesinos who have just received land titles, Carazo, 1982. Photograph by Michael Baumann, courtesy of *Militant*.

The Sandino Writings, 1970–1974

In November 1970, only days after Carlos Fonseca was released from the San José penitentiary, he told journalists in Havana that he planned to return immediately to the mountains of Nicaragua to help prepare the population as a whole for the coming revolutionary war. He would in fact remain outside his country for five long years. Except for a six-month trip to North Korea for military training, he spent the entire half decade in Cuba. María Haydeé and the couple's two small children joined him in Havana in 1971, and for the first time the family was able to live a somewhat normal life together.

Fonseca would devote this longest exile to two projects designed to organize and mobilize the Nicaraguan people and his own organization for insurrectionary war. The first was researching and writing his analysis of Augusto César Sandino's role in the struggle for national identity and self-determination in Nicaragua. The second was participating in an intense debate on revolutionary strategy with other leaders of the FSLN.

By 1970, Fonseca had been studying Augusto César Sandino's war against the U.S. Marines for a decade. In the early 1960s, he had persuaded his fellow rebels to name their organization after Sandino. The image of the patriotic general of 1930, leading his campesino army against the Yankee invaders, was present in all Fonseca's major writings of the 1960s. Not until his long exile in Havana, however, could Fonseca systematically study Sandino's history and articulate in writing his own version of the events of 1926 to 1934.

Fonseca's historical writings all struck the same central political theme: the historic role of the FSLN was to carry out Sandino's unfinished tasks. According to Fonseca, Sandino tapped into a long tradition of resistance by the exploited masses of Nicaragua and brought this native rebelliousness to a new level with his military successes and his embryonic plan for social transformation. Circumstances beyond Sandino's control prevented him from going further. With Augusto Sandino as its inspiration and in new world conditions defined especially by the Cuban revolution, the FSLN could now lead Nicaraguan workers and peasants to a victory over U.S. imperialism and its local representatives impossible in Sandino's time.

Fonseca wrote five major texts on Sandino between the end of 1970 and the beginning of 1975. He completed *Sandino: Proletarian Guerrilla* before he left for the Far East in March 1971. This pamphlet, written for a mass audience, first appeared in the Cuban magazine *Tricontinental* in late 1971 and then in a clandestine edition in León in 1972. *The Political Ideology of General Sandino,* a selection of quotations from Sandino that Fonseca had been accumulating for almost a decade, was finished in the early 1970s and published in Cuba in 1977; mimeographed early versions circulated inside Nicaragua from the mid-1960s. The three longest writings in the Sandino collection, all finished in 1974 or early 1975, did not come to light until after the 1979 revolution. *Chronology of Sandinista Resistance* covered the period from the Monroe Doctrine of 1823 to the anti-imperialist Tricontinental Conference in 1966, with a focus on events during Sandino's lifetime (1895–1934). The book-length *Secret Chronicle: Augusto César Sandino Confronts His Betrayers* has never been published in its entirety. The long essay *Viva Sandino,* published in several editions after the revolution, represented Fonseca's final and most developed analysis of the lessons to be drawn from the history of Nicaragua's national hero.[1]

While he was writing these historical essays on Sandino, Fonseca also produced several short pieces on Rigoberto López Pérez, the Nicaraguan youth who assassinated Anastasio Somoza García in 1956. Two themes in particular link the articles on López Pérez, which have received little attention, to Fonseca's works on Sandino: the importance of individual commitment and self-sacrifice, and the political backwardness of Nicaragua before the Cuban revolution.[2]

Jaime Wheelock has described how Fonseca sent FSLN members to libraries and archives in Cuba, Mexico, Costa Rica, and Nicaragua to find documents and newspaper articles related to Sandino. They hunted down little-known books on Sandino, took notes on the international press coverage of events in Nicaragua during the 1920s and 1930s, and scoured the Cuban archives for U.S. naval records and copies of U.S. State Department cables. According to Wheelock, Fonseca gave the researchers a political orientation before they started:

Carlos told us that all these books were partial, some anecdotal, others saw Sandino as a type of folkloric campesino. He said some even claim Sandino was a man of little education, which wasn't true—in fact, he was well educated for his epoch. Besides, Carlos told us, the most important thing about Sandino was his action, what he did—this is what had to be collected.[3]

In addition to archival records and published accounts, some of the historical writings also cited Carlos Fonseca's personal experience or interviews he had done with veteran Sandinistas.[4]

There was nothing academic about Fonseca's interest in Sandino. Although he developed a unique Sandinista historiography for his country, he was not a historian. There is no indication that he deliberately falsified information about his subject, and most of his historical writings are carefully documented with extensive footnotes, but he had a definite purpose in mind when he selected and analyzed Sandino's ideas and campaigns.[5] He emphasized the class-oriented and nationalist content of his mentor's writings and ignored the religious mysticism he considered irrelevant to Sandino's political role. Fonseca wrote not for historians or for posterity in general but for his own and the next generation of Nicaraguan revolutionaries, those who he was convinced would overthrow the Somoza regime and restore Sandino to his proper place as the country's national hero. "Our greatest satisfaction," he wrote in *Viva Sandino*, "comes not from writing about our heroes but from following their example, whether in the rural trenches or in the catacomb of the city."[6] The purpose of studying the past, for Fonseca, was to change the present and the future.

In his writings on Sandino, Fonseca carried on a multilayered dialogue with others in the FSLN and with the broader Nicaraguan opposition, a discussion sometimes pedagogical and occasionally sharply polemical. On one level, he contrasted his own organization to the Conservative opposition, ridiculing the "posturing of Mr. P. J. Chamorro, who dares to display Sandino's portrait on his office wall."[7] The Conservative Party sometimes invoked the name and example of Sandino, but its belief that the U.S. government played a generally positive role in Nicaraguan history was dramatically different from the view of both Sandino and the FSLN. The historical writings also represented a continuation of Fonseca's long debate with the PSN, which presented a radical and "Marxist" critique of Sandino as a petit bourgeois adventurer while rejecting the prospect of socialist revolution in Nicaragua in the foreseeable future. Fonseca also sought to appeal to the students and campesinos who identified with Sandino as a fighter, his goal in this case being to politicize an already positive image of Sandino to bring these individuals closer to the FSLN. Finally, he used the Sandino writings to reinforce his arguments on strategic questions with other members of the FSLN leadership.

Some of Fonseca's books and essays also reveal a personal identification with his subject. The parallels in the family backgrounds of the two revolutionaries are quite striking. Both were the sons of poor unmarried women and prosperous businessmen, both suffered from the way their mothers were treated by employers and society, and both confronted their fathers and won some amount of support—more in Sandino's case than Fonseca's.

Fonseca wrote in a post–Cuban revolution world, and the historical writings again and again reveal the impact of that revolution on his political ideas. *Viva Sandino,* Fonseca's most important writing of the early 1970s, began and ended with the Cuban revolution. The essay opened with references to the Havana Tricontinental Conference of 1966, Che Guevara, and the First and Second Declarations of Havana, "two documents that, produced by the Cuban revolution, lay out the line of march for all fighters who defend the territory of Latin America." The essay closed with the impact of the Cuban revolution on "the Nicaraguan rebel spirit," and with the FSLN's embracing "the Marxism of Lenin, Fidel, Che, Ho Chi Minh." Fonseca's *Cronología* treated the anti-imperialist Tricontinental Conference as the culmination of a century and a half of Sandinista resistance. In *Viva Sandino,* Fonseca acknowledged that it was the Cuban revolution that caused him to begin his own serious study of Sandino: "We Nicaraguans would only begin to recover our sense of our own identity as a result of the explosion of a new battle for liberation whose first definitive victory came in a particular place: Cuba."[8]

Fonseca outlined his view of history and its relevance for the present in a public talk he gave in Havana in October 1973. In this speech, information about the past was presented as a revolutionary weapon, no less important than the other arms soldiers carried.

> Those of us who propose to wage a struggle to liberate our country and make freedom a reality must rescue our own traditions and put together the facts and figures we need in order to wage an ideological war against our enemy. This ideological war has to go step by step with the war we carry out arms in hand. I would even say that, to the same extent that we are able to use our rifles effectively, we will also be able to revive our

people's historical traditions, and to the same extent that we master our popular traditions, we will also find ourselves able to use our rifles successfully against the enemy.[9]

Like Che Guevara, Fonseca believed that history could serve the interest of the revolution only if it was presented truthfully. He once called a fellow guerrilla to order for substituting the word "pueblo" for "God" in reciting a famous poem by Rubén Darío, and he chastized the editor of the Cuban magazine *Bohemia* for asserting, without any evidence, that Sandino had read a certain letter by José Martí.[10] But he did not see his task as describing in full Sandino's eclectic philosophy, with all its contradictions, rather as selecting what was most useful for his own generation and then describing it truthfully. "The most important thing about Sandino was his action," Fonseca told his followers, and he used the same guide in choosing what to include in his historical writings.

The early 1970s saw growing protests against the Somoza regime, with student-led building occupations and hunger strikes in defense of political prisoners and militant strikes by teachers and construction workers. Opposition to the regime surged after a devastating earthquake struck Managua in December 1972, causing ten thousand deaths. Under these circumstances, the FSLN began to recruit new members and to influence a growing number of young people outside its own cadres. Fonseca's writings on Sandino sought to provide political education to these new militants and sympathizers, as well as to augment the leadership's knowledge about the revolutionary history of their own country. At a 1973 meeting, Fonseca stressed the urgency of publicizing Sandino's lessons and the FSLN's ideas to

> the layer of people in Nicaragua who will come to say "these folks are the ones with the good ideas, the ones who point the way forward, unlike that piece of shit *La Prensa*." Spontaneously these people will start to say "I've never seen such a clear explanation as these folks, who don't just talk and don't just write but who risk their lives in defense of the people—I thought this country had gone to hell, but now I see there are people who truly struggle for the interests of the masses."[11]

The Sandino writings were part of a collective effort to prepare for the armed popular insurrection Fonseca believed was on the horizon in Nicaragua. Early in 1973, Fonseca organized the Havana group into four task forces. He assigned Humberto Ortega's group to develop military strategy, a committee under Camilo Ortega to investigate Nicaraguan social and economic conditions, and a third group, led by Jaime Wheelock and Doris Tijerino, to draft organizational principles. Fonseca himself headed the task force on Sandino and also coordinated the project.[12] Although referred to as the task force on Sandino, Fonseca's committee had overall responsibility for political and programmatic questions.

Fonseca's historical writings on Sandino drew out the political lessons and parallels he thought were most important for the revolutionaries of his own time. He concentrated on six main themes: Sandino as a national and anti-imperialist symbol; the worker and peasant base of the movement; the moral stature of the guerrilla general; the bankruptcy of both bourgeois parties; Sandino's internationalism and relationship with the world Communist movement; and the reasons for the disintegration of Sandino's movement after his assassination.

Sandino's importance for Fonseca came first of all from the war he led against the United States Marines, who finally withdrew from Nicaragua at the beginning of 1933 after occupying the country off and on since 1912. Fonseca believed that U.S. imperialism politically and economically dominated his country and most of Latin America, and that genuine national independence could only be won by overthrowing the U.S.-backed Somoza regime.

Fonseca constantly stressed the military accomplishments of Sandino's EDSN, citing Marine Corps statistics on the number of encounters with guerrilla forces and claiming that even Gregorio Selser, whose book on Sandino Fonseca generally respected, underestimated the number of clashes that took place. In 1974 Fonseca wrote a long letter to the editor of the Cuban magazine *Bohemia* arguing that the EDSN had presented a more serious military challenge to the marines than implied in a recently published tribute to Sandino. Fonseca attributed the eventual withdrawal of U.S. troops largely to Sandinista military victories. His insistence that U.S. ambassador Bliss Lane had prior knowledge of Anastasio Somoza's plot to murder Sandino helped differentiate the FSLN from the Conservative opposition, which blamed only Somoza for the assassination. "A few decades after the crime of 1934," Fonseca wrote in *Viva Sandino*, "some aristocratic princes, heirs of the Nicaraguan oligarchy, who try to pass themselves off as patriots, have the audacity to absolve Yankee imperialism of its most criminal act, putting all the blame on the mercenary assassin."[13]

Fonseca hoped, through his description of the EDSN's war against the marines, to convince his own contemporaries that a war against U.S. imperialism was neither impossible nor crazy. When he emphasized the small number of poorly armed troops Sandino commanded and the EDSN's early defeats, he drew obvious parallels with the FSLN. When he wrote about the peasant guerrillas of the 1920s, "dressed in rags, with only banana leaves to protect them from the cold," Fonseca was describing his own comrades of 1963 and 1967 in the same chilly Segovia mountains. The military lessons Fonseca drew from Sandino's history were the tactics that could enable a small, poorly armed, rural band to deal blows to a much stronger army: ambush, homemade weapons, trickery, the ability to survive in the jungle.

Fonseca used the example of Sandino to inspire his own followers that they also could win, as long as, like Sandino, they had popular support and a leadership willing to fight. He frequently quoted Sandino's defiant responses to ultimatums received from the U.S. command, which became part of the FSLN liturgy. In 1927 Sandino had answered Navy Commander Hatfield: "I won't surrender and I am waiting for you; I want a free homeland or death." His response to Admiral Sellers the following year included the phrase "the sovereignty of a nation is not something to negotiate, it is something to defend arms in hand." In *Viva Sandino*, Fonseca quoted Sandino's San Albino Manifesto, written before he had won a single skirmish with the marines:

> Come on, you pack of drug fiends, come and murder us on our own land. I am waiting for you on my feet at the head of my patriotic soldiers, and I don't care how many of you there are. You should know that when this happens, the destruction of your mighty power will make the Capitol shake in Washington, and your blood will redden the white dome that crowns the famous White House where you plot your crimes.[14]

Adding to the folklore of popular resistance, Fonseca looked beyond Sandino's own writings for examples of more humble Sandinistas standing up to the United States. In *Viva Sandino* he told the story of the daughter of Sandino's most famous general as she was accosted on the road by a marine. "Aren't you Bandit Pete's daughter?" the soldier shouted at her, to which the young campesina retorted, "That's the daughter of *General* Pedro Altamirano to you, mister son-of-a-bitch tough-guy."[15]

Fonseca believed that Sandino's struggle—along with the tradition of resistance to Spanish colonialism—had given birth to the sovereign Nicaraguan nation, and that only those who identified with this struggle had the right to call themselves Nicaraguans. In a 1970 interview, he said of Anastasio Somoza García and Anastasio Somoza Debayle that "we cannot consider them Nicaraguan." In the *Ideario*, he quoted Sandino as saying the EDSN was not an army but rather an "armed citizenry."[16]

The true patriots, according to Fonseca, were those who fought arms in hand against foreign domination. As he said to his researchers when he sent them to the archives, "the most important thing about Sandino was his action, what he did." In words strikingly similar to Che Guevara's attack on "armchair revolutionaries," Fonseca wrote that even if Sandino's political program had shortcomings, those who criticized him had no right to do so.

> Don't these criticisms reflect a certain intellectual snobbery against San-
> dino the worker-peasant? Couldn't it be that these professors sitting at
> their desks inventing revolutionary theory don't think they can learn
> anything from simple campesinos in the Nicaraguan mountains, teach-
> ing a practical lesson on the usefulness of the tactic of guerrilla warfare
> for a serious struggle?[17]

No U.S. Marines occupied Nicaragua in the 1970s. The FSLN fought against a National Guard made up largely of Nicaraguan peasants, not foreign invaders. Yet Fonseca insisted that the National Guard was itself an instrument of U.S. domination. He believed that Sandino too considered the GN a threat to Nicaraguan national integrity but acknowledged that this idea was not widely accepted in 1934. By 1970, on the other hand, Nicaraguans had suffered through several decades of experience with the National Guard.

According to Fonseca, Sandino's war was not just a patriotic battle to end U.S. domination but also an uprising of the workers and peasants of Nicaragua against their oppressors. Sandino himself had pointed to the popular character of his movement and its leadership, but Fonseca went further in giving a class content to the struggle for national liberation. When he called his popular pamphlet on Sandino "Proletarian Guerrilla," he was referring at least as much to the class character of the nationalist movement as to the social origins of its leader. Fonseca counterposed the proletarian nationalism of Sandino and the FSLN to the bourgeois nationalism of the Conservative opposition, and he insisted that only the former could produce a serious struggle against foreign domination. Fonseca frequently quoted Sandino's 1927 San Albino Manifesto, which he said represented "not just the words of a patriot but also of a proletarian in arms."

In Nicaragua the word *proletario* refers not just to industrial wageworkers but also to artisans, market vendors, domestic servants, and their families. Carlos Fonseca used it to describe himself as well as Sandino. But the words Sandino generally used to describe himself were *plebeyo* or *artisano,* and he framed these terms in racial as well as class terms. In the San Albino Manifesto he wrote: "They will call me plebeian, those oligarchs who are like geese waddling through a bog. I don't care—my greatest honor is to have arisen from the bosom of the oppressed, who are the soul and nerve-center of the race."[18] For Sandino, the oppressed classes were the "soul and nerve-center" of the *raza indohispana*, and he also wrote of Indohispanic nations, governments, and peoples.

Fonseca believed that Sandino had been proletarianized by his work experience in Mexico and by his travels around Central America, when "like thousands of other Nicaraguans"—many, like Sandino, of campesino extraction—he left his country in search of work. He quoted Sandino in the *Ideario* as defending himself against charges that he was motivated by personal gain by saying, "I am perfectly capable of making a living and supporting my wife.... I am a mechanic and I could always go back to that trade if I needed to."[19]

Sandino worked as a mechanic at the Cerro Azul refinery in Veracruz, Mexico, and the Huasteca Petroleum Company in Tampico. When Fonseca referred to Sandino being proletarianized by his years in Mexico, however, he was talking as much about Sandino's exposure to new ideologies as about his occupation.

> The gusts of proletarian wind from the Bolshevik October—somewhat faint by the time they arrived at the distant American latitudes—reached Veracruz, the principal Atlantic port of Mexico. . . . We cannot say that October was the determining influence in the path Sandino chose, but it is undeniable that his sensitive worker-peasant heart was touched by the proletarian spirit that for the first time in history swept over the globe.

Fonseca also noted the influence of the Mexican revolution on Sandino, writing that "Mexico in the 1920s still smelled of the gunpowder fired by oppressed campesinos led by the guerrilla Emiliano Zapata." But when Fonseca referred to proletarian ideas, his reference was generally to faraway Russia, not to Mexico.

Fonseca believed that Nicaragua's long tradition of rebelliousness on the part of Indians, campesinos, and workers distinguished it from other Latin American countries—even on a continent with a proud history of insurgency. He found at least one example of popular resistance to oppression every single year for more than a century, from 1823, when the United States adopted the Monroe Doctrine, to 1926, when Sandino's uprising began. Fonseca traced this history to Indians' refusal to bow down to Spanish conquistadores and enslaved Africans' courageous escape to Nicaragua from slave ships and Caribbean plantations. Even when writing about sixteenth-century figures, Fonseca could not resist drawing class lines and pointing to twentieth-century political parallels. Of an Indian cacique who compromised with the Spanish, he said, "he suffered from utopian pacifism, which indisputably makes him the predecessor of the twentieth-century intellectuals who smoothed the way for the assassins who murdered Sandino."[20]

In his historical writings Fonseca stressed the working-class and peasant backgrounds of Sandino's assistants and generals, as well as of Sandino himself; *Crónica Secreta* contains short biographies of a half-dozen secondary figures. Fonseca thought the coming struggle in Nicaragua would also inevitably produce its own leaders from the oppressed classes. In 1973 he told other leaders of the FSLN—themselves mostly from a university background —that "we must have confidence that the popular masses include, by a law of nature, individuals of such caliber that they will take their places in the front ranks of the struggle."[21]

It was the support of the campesinos of the Segovias, according to Fonseca, that enabled Sandino to campaign through seven long years against a powerful enemy with only modest international support. The EDSN guerrillas knew the territory in which they were fighting, and a friendly population supplied them with crucial intelligence as well as food. It reached the point, Fonseca noted in *Guerrillero Proletario*, that simply being a campesino in the Sandinista zones became a crime in the eyes of the marines and National Guard.[22]

In several articles and interviews, Fonseca advanced the theory of intrinsic campesino rebelliousness, in comparison to other exploited layers of the population. "We believe," he told journalists in 1970, "that the Nicaraguan peasant is by his very nature a rebel." There was a certain tension between this romantic vision of the peasantry and Fonseca's Marxism, which was never resolved. He selected for his *Ideario* a quotation by Sandino that showed a strong distrust for the cities: "The city wears away at us and makes us smaller. [We prefer] the countryside: not to selfishly lock ourselves away there, but to advance on the city and make it better."[23] This statement was more antiurban than anything in Fonseca's own writings, but there were individuals in the FSLN who shared Sandino's view.

Fonseca's *Ideario* contains a section called "a program to resolve social problems," suggesting that Sandino advanced at least the rudiments of a program for social transformation. But he came up with very few quotations for this section, most of them involving a somewhat abstract identification with the interests of workers and peasants. Scouring all the works of Sandino available to him, Fonseca found nothing more concrete than a few comments favoring nationalization of the land and encouraging EDSN troops to fraternize with students. Fonseca also highlighted Sandino's goal of building agricultural cooperatives in the remote Atlantic Coast region, where dispossessed peasants from the western part of the country could produce foodstuffs to sustain, in Sandino's words, "the family of Nicaraguans in general."[24] Though favorable to such plans, Fonseca projected a more radical land reform in the Programa Histórico, one that would restore valuable land in the Pacific zone to the Indian and mestizo campesinos from whom it had been stolen, rather than simply moving dispossessed peasants to the Atlantic region. Fonseca never mentioned the problem that some of the land Sandino considered empty and available for colonization by landless campesinos was considered by Miskito and Sumo Indians to be *their* land, crucial for hunting the game and fish that were key elements of their diet and culture.

Sandino's appeal to Nicaraguan campesinos came in part from his reputation for humility and incorruptibility, which distinguished him from other politicians and military leaders. Unlike other generals in the war of 1926 to 1927 and all previous civil wars in Nicaraguan history, Sandino was no landowner who sent his peasants to do the fighting but rather a soldier who led his troops into battle. Like the plain-talking Fonseca, Sandino spoke to campesinos in words they could understand. In *Viva Sandino* Fonseca gives an example of Sandino's imagery: "If I don't live to see the victory over the invaders, the ants of the earth will find me where I am buried and tell me all about it." Fonseca almost never drank alcohol, and, according to him, neither did Sandino. Once when he was offered a drink, Sandino purportedly replied, "The clear water of the mountains is all I have drunk in recent years."[25]

Fonseca made liberal use of anecdotes to demonstrate Sandino's honesty and humanity and that of his army. In *Viva Sandino* he told the story of hungry and ragged EDSN troops finding gold relics in the knapsack of a captured Yankee soldier and returning them to the Yalí church from which they had been stolen. Fonseca claimed that one of Sandino's last statements, directed to the guardsmen who took his wallet just before killing him, was "There's no money in it, because I'm not one of those who steals from my country." The *Ideario* contains Sandino's account of his decision not to fire on houses in which marines were hiding, because of the pleas of the poor families who owned the houses: "That's why I forfeited a battle and let a whole bunch of those pigs go on living, because I put the interests of my fellow citizens ahead of the glory of my homeland."[26] Fonseca also frequently quoted Sandino's statements of sorrow when one of his officers or soldiers was killed; respect for the movement's martyrs was one of the principles of the FSLN as well as of the EDSN.

Fonseca personally identified with Sandino's high moral standards and tried to emulate them. He omitted from his portrayal of Sandino those aspects of his character that were at odds with the code of behavior Fonseca wanted his own troops to follow. He never mentioned, for example, the lover who accompanied Sandino in Mexico and the Segovias while his wife Blanca Aráuz stayed home in San Rafael del Norte. (Fonseca certainly knew about Teresa Villatoro, both from Somoza's book and from his own interviews with veteran Sandinistas such as Santos López.)

Both Sandino and Fonseca were critical of Nicaraguan landlords and capitalists and roundly detested by the ruling classes of their eras. Their criticisms were somewhat different, however. Sandino, whose focus was the struggle against foreign intervention, thought the Nicaraguan oligarchy's most serious crime was being *vendepatrias* (country sellers). Fonseca painted the Liberal and Conservative wings of the bourgeoisie as united not only in their slavish support for the United States but also in their hatred and fear of Nicaraguan workers and peasants. Of Sandino's assassination, Fonseca wrote:

> It was here in Nicaragua, where only the oligarchs know the secrets of political realism (which made them decide to sell themselves to the all-powerful dollar) that a humble man rose up to fight and defeat the invaders from the north. Once the invaders were expelled, the oligarchs in their frock coats were forced to sit down with the guerrilla in his simple country clothes. . . . Their unanimous support for the murder of our national hero reveals not only their foul submission to their imperialist master but also the hatred they feel for the oppressed and exploited of Nicaragua.[27]

Fonseca portrayed the war of 1926 to 1934 as not only an anti-imperialist guerrilla war with patriots on one side and vendepatrias on the other but also simultaneously and inevitably a class war between the workers and peasants of Nicaragua and the country's capitalists and landlords. He applied the same analysis to explain the behavior of intermediate layers. Describing the professionals who represented Sandino in negotiations to end the war, Fonseca wrote, "from the point of view of class, the illusions of these intellectuals can be understood as the expression of a petit bourgeoisie that is tired of struggling and desperately wants to turn to preserving and enjoying its own selfish interests."[28]

Fonseca used the history of Sandino to drive home his own opposition to both the Liberal and Conservative parties. When Sandino first took up arms in 1926, he fought as a Liberal general in an uprising against a U.S.-imposed Conservative government. This continued a century-old tradition of civil wars along Liberal and Conservative party lines in Nicaragua, and party loyalties had deep roots, including among the peasantry. On 4 May 1927, in the shade of an espino negro tree not far from Managua, all the Liberal generals except Sandino agreed to disband their armies in exchange for the promise of U.S.-supervised national elections. In *Guerrillero Proletario* Fonseca wrote: "Espino Negro showed that the Nicaraguan national bourgeoisie had once and for all joined hands with the feudal and reactionary class. Now more than ever, there was truth in the popular saying that 'five Conservative oligarchs plus five Liberal oligarchs adds up to ten bandits.'"[29]

Fonseca did not believe that the León-based Liberal Party, which represented the new coffee-growing bourgeoisie, was identical to the Conservative Party, based on the old cattle-ranching families of Granada. He insisted, however, that the two traditional parties would join forces to block any uprising of workers and peasants, and that neither could be counted on to fight for Nicaraguan sovereignty against U.S. domination. Fonseca spent several chapters of *Viva Sandino* tracing the historical development of this situation. He argued that in the context of aggressive United States interest in Nicaragua for its trans-isthmus canal potential, the Liberals were too weak to carry through "the bourgeois democratic social reforms that would otherwise have evolved naturally." Power passed to the outmoded Conservative oligarchy, and "Nicaragua began to lose its own identity."[30]

The 1927 pact of Espino Negro, according to Fonseca, "buried the Nicaraguan national bourgeoisie as a revolutionary class." He rejected the PSN's view that the Liberals, as the party of the national bourgeoisie, were more progressive than the oligarchical landowning Conservatives—a position the PSN itself abandoned in the 1960s, when it switched to supporting Conservative Party candidates. Even before 1927, Fonseca argued, neither party conformed to an ideal type, and isolated examples of willingness to stand up to U.S. pressure could come from inside the Conservative Party as well as from Liberals.[31]

By the time Fonseca wrote his histories of Sandino in the 1970s, the party alignment in Nicaragua was quite different than it had been in the late 1920s. A Liberal U.S.-backed regime led by Somoza now faced a Conservative Party in opposition. Although the Conservatives repeatedly entered into alliances with the regime,[32] they presented themselves at elections as the alternative to

Somoza, and the more anti-Somoza wing of the Conservative Party competed with the FSLN for the allegiance of students and intellectuals. Even though members of the FSLN sometimes referred to leading Conservative families as "oligarchs," they in practice considered both parties to represent the national bourgeoisie, and when Sandinistas talked about forming alliances with capitalist groups and parties to bring down Somoza, they were primarily referring to Conservative oppositionists like *La Prensa* editor Pedro Joaquín Chamorro.

In his rejection of either bourgeois party's right to govern Nicaragua, Fonseca went beyond the position of Sandino, who agreed in 1933 to respect the legitimacy of elected Liberal president Sacasa. "We are fighting," Sandino said, "not for the Liberals alone, but for Nicaraguans—in other words also for the Conservatives." Where Sandino saw his role as fighting for Nicaraguans who were both Liberal and Conservative, Fonseca saw the FSLN as fighting for the pueblo of Nicaragua against both the Liberal and Conservative parties. The need to remain independent of both traditional parties had been a theme of all Fonseca's political writings from the early 1960s. Toward the end of his life, Fonseca charged that the FSLN had become excessively cautious about attacking what he called the "pseudo-opposition," and that the time had come to step up the pressure, with the goal of "liquidating the influence of the traditional political caste" on the population.[33]

Fonseca had a particular dislike for Pedro Joaquín Chamorro. Ernesto Cardenal, a friend of both men, has said that Fonseca made much harsher public and private statements about Chamorro than the newspaper editor ever made about the younger rebel. "He even made a vicious attack on Pedro Joaquín because of his *father's* politics, something that was contrary to the principles of the FSLN—and after all, the politics of *Carlos's* father were much worse."[34]

Fonseca quoted extensively from Sandino's criticism of the "electoral farces" of 1928 and 1932, and his call for a boycott of both elections. Again, Fonseca went beyond anything by Sandino, who only condemned elections carried out "at the point of a Yankee bayonet."[35] Fonseca regarded all elections involving Conservatives and Liberals as "farces," whether or not they were overseen by the United States, and he maintained that real social change could never come in his country through elections.

Fonseca's insistence that Sandino recognized the bankruptcy of the two traditional parties led him to give credence to a rumor that the anti-imperialist general was moving in the direction of forming a party of his own and had already chosen a name, the Autonomist Party (Partido Autonomista). In early 1933, according to Fonseca, Sandino hoped to form "a new political party, which for the first time in Nicaraguan history would confront the two traditional parties that had monopolized public life throughout the entire existence of the nominal republic." In December of the same year, Sandino dropped—Fonseca used the term "corrected"—his proposal for a new party, a step that, according to Fonseca, "should not be in any sense taken to imply that he was rejecting the idea of starting an independent political movement." Sandino's decision not to form a new party, said Fonseca, "was just a change in the form through which he would realize his ongoing desire to set up an independent political movement to influence the direction the country was going. The thing we need to emphasize here is that Sandino broke completely the ties that before 4 May 1927, linked him to one of the traditional political groups."[36]

Sandino saw himself as an internationalist, fighting in the tradition of Simon Bolívar for the liberation of Latin America from foreign domination, and Fonseca called Sandino "the immediate precursor of the great internationalist of our own epoch, Ernesto 'Che' Guevara." Even beyond the rather obvious parallels between Sandino and Guevara, Fonseca drew out in his historical writings every possible connection between Sandino's struggle and events in Cuba, where a labor upsurge was under way in the early 1930s. He compared Sandino to José Martí, highlighted the contribution of Cuban Communist José Antonio Mella to the movement in solidarity with Sandino, quoted the 1935 diary of an unnamed Cuban revolutionary concerning Sandino's writings ("books like these can only come out of Cuba and Nicaragua"), and mentioned Cuban student Fidel Castro's enlistment in the "Sandino Battalion" organized to fight Dominican dictator Rafael Trujillo in 1947.[37]

Fonseca quoted Sandino on the decisive role of workers and peasants in forging Central American unity, and he agreed with Sandino that Nicaragua was one of six Central American and Caribbean "fallen republics that had already lost their independence and become colonies of Yankee imperialism." Fonseca's internationalism did not start with Central American unity, however, or even, like Sandino, with Latin American unity. For solidarity and inspiration he looked first to Cuba and then to Vietnam, Algeria, Korea, the Congo, China, and sometimes Colombia or Venezuela. In *Viva Sandino* Fonseca presented a very negative image of the other Central American countries when he wrote that "Marxist ideas . . . could not break through the seven borders (Guatemala, El Salvador, Honduras, Costa Rica, Panama, and two oceans) that like walls, seven walls, kept them from getting into a barricaded Nicaragua." In the next sentence, he contrasted the obstacle that Nicaragua's neighbors represented with the Cuban revolution, which, he said, broke through the walls and made it possible for Marxist ideas to reach "the Nicaraguan rebel spirit."[38]

Fonseca's idea that the Nicaraguan popular masses possessed a powerful tradition of rebelliousness contrasted sharply with the lack of revolutionary promise he saw in Costa Rica. As he wrote to his father in early 1960 from San José:

> The truth is that it doesn't even seem to be located next to Nicaragua—
> it is so totally different. . . . And even though this country is different
> from Nicaragua, and I am longing for a different Nicaragua, Costa Rica
> doesn't appeal to me, and I wouldn't want the Nicaragua of the future to
> be anything like Costa Rica. Here it seems like history has stopped and
> everything has been the same for a thousand years and will be the same
> for a thousand more. On the other hand, one can live peacefully here
> and it's the best vacation spot in the world. That's no good for me
> because I'm not looking for a peaceful life, and I'm not on vacation.[39]

In 1970, a journalist asked Fonseca about the danger the Costa Rican public would be alienated by the violent acts of groups like the FSLN. "It is possible that at some point we will face the problem of carrying out actions that frighten the public," Fonseca answered. "But looking frankly at the situation here in Costa Rica, who is carrying out actions that could frighten anyone? So why talk about a problem that doesn't exist? The danger that does exist is rather that of doing things that put people to sleep, that cause a tremendous lethargy."[40]

Fonseca devoted a considerable—even disproportionate—amount of his historical writing to the question of Sandino's relationship to the international Communist movement. While acknowledging that Sandino was not a Marxist, Fonseca stressed his openness to socialist and communist ideas, his close relationship with Salvadoran Communist Farabundo Martí, the presence of other Communists such as Venezuelan Carlos Aponte in his entourage, the solidarity of Cuban Communist José Antonio Mella, and reports of the "Internationale" being sung in EDSN camps. "Sandino identified with the world proletariat," Fonseca wrote in his *Cronología*. In general, Fonseca selected for his *Ideario* the most radical and class-conscious quotations he could find, such as Sandino's vision of a "proletarian explosion against the imperialists of the world," and his call on workers to join the Communist-led Latin American Union Federation. Some of these statements were atypical of Sandino's writings as a whole; a recent biographer attributes them to the influence of the Communist advisers in Sandino's camp.[41]

Although insisting on Sandino's openness to communist ideas, Fonseca also stressed the conflicts that developed between the Nicaraguan patriot and the organized Communist movement, in particular the Mexican Communist Party. The PCM and the "Hands Off Nicaragua" committee (Manos Fuera de Nicaragua, MAFUENIC) in which it played a leading role were Sandino's most important source of international solidarity in the early years of his rebellion. This changed abruptly in early 1929 when the PCM and MAFUENIC withdrew their support and began to accuse Sandino of being an agent of U.S. imperialism. In late 1929, *El Libertador,* the newspaper of the PCM-dominated "Anti-imperialist League of the Americas," published an article saying Sandino's war in Nicaragua was doomed and suggesting he go fight imperialism someplace else. In November 1930, the newspaper of the Communist Party U.S.A. said that the struggle in Nicaragua could be victorious only if it were led by the Nicaraguan Communist Party—an organization that would not be formed for another decade and a half. The shift in policy of the organized Communist movement severely hurt Sandino's struggle. Some of his most active solidarity groups became in effect anti-Sandino committees, and a number of his most prominent allies, including Farabundo Martí, deserted him.[42] Although Sandino himself attributed his diplomatic problems to the influence of "Yankee dollars," Fonseca blamed the Mexican Communist Party, and, to a lesser extent, APRA, and used the historical writings to criticize the Communist parties of his own day for their attacks on Sandino and their conservatism in abstaining from struggles for national liberation.

Sandino had been caught up in a policy shift on the part of the Soviet leadership that was completely beyond the Nicaraguan's control and unrelated to events in Central America. In 1928 the Stalin-led Third International or Comintern decided that a "Third Period" had opened in which socialist revolution was on the agenda in virtually every country. During this phase, which lasted until the mid-1930s, Communist parties everywhere adopted hostile attitudes toward social-democratic and nationalist movements. Their withdrawal of support for Sandino and strong condemnation of his appeal to the Mexican government for aid were consistent with this ultraleft and sectarian approach. For Sandino, who had no way of knowing about the international shift in policy, the sudden attack from former allies must have come as a terrible shock. In 1930 he called on workers to join the Latin American Union Federation (Confederación Sindical Latinoamericana or

Hispanoamericana, CSL), which he called "the only labor organization that defends workers' interests." The CSL had grown out of the Comintern's decision to build what they called "Red trade unions," separate labor organizations under Communist control; in other words, the CSL was a product of the same ultraleft international policy that led the Mexican and other Communist parties to turn against Sandino. It is more difficult to understand why Fonseca, more than forty years later, quoted Sandino's call to build the CSL with approval and called it evidence that Sandino "had some ideas bordering on socialism."[43] Fonseca either did not realize that the turn of 1929 was an international phenomenon or was reluctant to blame Moscow for the attack on Sandino. Even in his sharpest polemics with the pro-Moscow Communist parties of his own time, Fonseca traced the blame only as far as CPUSA secretary-general Earl Browder.

Fonseca's portrait of Sandino's relationship with the international Communist movement abounded with contradictions. On the one hand, he stressed Sandino's openness to communist ideas and brotherhood with Communists like Farabundo Martí, and on the other, he complained of back stabbing and historical falsification from the official Communist parties. Fonseca could identify with this paradoxical situation. He considered himself a Marxist-Leninist and a communist but had been attacked and ridiculed by parties like the PSN and PVP. In *Viva Sandino* he wrote of the need for a serious analysis of these contradictions: "There still has been no real analysis of the international revolutionary movement's attitude toward the Sandinista resistance. This analysis must be done, because it concerns an extremely interesting historical experience, whose lessons could help us avoid repeating old errors in a new period."[44] Fonseca never pursued this matter, however. He may still have been reluctant to trace the problem back to Moscow. Or perhaps he simply ran out of time.

Fonseca tried to explain in his historical writings, especially *Viva Sandino,* why the revolutionary nationalism of Sandino disintegrated after 1934, and why victory over the marines did not lead to a transformation of Nicaraguan society. The EDSN disappeared, according to Fonseca, because it was strictly a military organization without a political counterpart that could have built on the expulsion of the marines and continued the struggle against the Liberal government and the National Guard. Fonseca did not blame Sandino for the failure to build a political organization; rather he insisted that social and political conditions made it impossible for the struggle to go any further. Because Fonseca's goal was to lead a social revolution, he felt compelled to explain why the obstacles that blocked Sandino in the 1930s no longer existed in the 1970s.

In 1933, after the marines withdrew, Sandino negotiated a peace settlement in which he agreed to recognize the newly elected Liberal president Sacasa in exchange for being allowed to keep one hundred men under arms for at least a year. Fonseca defended Sandino's decision to negotiate with the Sacasa government. He pointed out in *Viva Sandino* that many workers and peasants still believed in the Liberal and Conservative parties, and that Sandino's enemies were waging an effective propaganda campaign charging that he did not really care about getting rid of the marines and just wanted personal power. The limits imposed on Sandino's movement flowed from material conditions inside the country and from the international situation. The Nicaraguan working class of the 1930s, said Fonseca, was small, largely artisanal in character, and lacking in class consciousness. The peasantry, in spite of its tradition of resistance, did not think of itself as a class or as a force for revolution. The pueblo, both workers and peasants, had a "rebelliousness bereft of any consciousness of itself as a class." The workers who accompanied Sandino were like the general himself: of campesino extraction, with no experience in the labor movement, their defining tradition was Nicaragua's history of popular rebellion.[45]

In a 1970 interview, Fonseca said Sandino's movement needed an infusion of revolutionary ideas from outside to be able to build on its popular traditions. There were fighters from other countries in Sandino's army, he pointed out, "but unhappily this internationalism was cut off once Sandino was assassinated, and the surviving Sandinista guerrillas, simple campesinos without any political training, lacked the kind of revolutionary orientation that revolutionaries from other countries could have given them."[46]

Sandino had to negotiate a compromise in 1933, Fonseca said, because of "the incredible political and ideological backwardness with which Nicaragua was flooded at the time, a period in which Marxism's entry into the country was still in the distant future." Sandino's most important contact with international Marxism was with the Mexican Communist Party, which ended up betraying him. By the 1970s, the international panorama was quite different: the FSLN looked not to the bureaucratic pro-Moscow Communist parties but to the example of the Cuban revolution.

A Fractured Movement, 1972–1975

The FSLN group in Havana during the early 1970s did not devote all its time to researching and writing the history of Sandino, on which there was general agreement. They spent at least an equal amount of effort debating the strategy and tactics of the ongoing revolutionary war in Nicaragua, a subject on which there was growing disagreement. Disputes arose over the relative weight of different social classes, the balance between political and military activity, the timing or pace of the struggle, the merits of urban versus rural warfare, vanguardism, and alliances with other parties and groups. By 1972, these differences led to the emergence of three political tendencies within the leadership, which eventually hardened into three public factions of the FSLN. Among the factors that aggravated the divisions within the FSLN and produced a de facto split were the inevitable problems associated with life in exile, the tradition of cliquism and personalism in Nicaraguan political culture, and special pressures that existed in Cuba in the early 1970s.

Fonseca's first message from Havana after his release from jail in Costa Rica said that a "crucial feature of the Nicaraguan drama" was "the bitterness of leaving the land of one's birth."[1] The pull of Nicaragua remained strong throughout his long exile. Life in Havana offered certain advantages: the possibility for collective discussion, access to historical sources unavailable in Nicaragua, and most of all security. But it also produced not just emotional but also serious political problems. Conflicts quickly developed between those who were carrying out revolutionary work inside Nicaragua and those who spent long periods in exile, often in the company of family and friends. Although the small Nicaraguan colony in Havana lived quite modestly in comparison to some of the other Latin American leftist exile groups, they certainly enjoyed greater comfort and security than the rural and urban guerrillas, prisoners, and even radical student leaders inside Somoza's Nicaragua.

The culture and economy of Nicaragua had long been dominated by a small number of wealthy families. Most prominent among the Conservatives were the Chamorro clan, the Cuadras, the Cardenals, and the Carrions. The biggest names among the Liberals were Sacasa and, in the twentieth century, Somoza. *Los abominables apellidos,* Fonseca called them. The "abominable surnames" controlled large numbers of dependents, poor relatives as well as campesinos and ranch hands, through ties that were personalistic as well as economic. The lack of any fundamental political differences between the Conservatives and Liberals did not prevent the great families from going to war against each other repeatedly in the course of the nineteenth and early twentieth century. Although Sandino's war against the U.S. Marines represented a break with this tradition in some ways, support for the EDSN was often influenced by personal loyalties, factionalism, and traditional family ties to a particular Conservative or Liberal strongman. For the Sandinistas of the early 1970s as well, personal relationships were sometimes as important as political doctrine in determining tendency allegiance. Individuals gravitated into the groupings of their brothers, lovers, those they fought alongside. There were several long-standing personality conflicts inside the leadership, such as those between Jaime Wheelock and Tomás Borge and between Carlos Fonseca and Oscar Turcios. Inside Nicaragua, young people were drawn toward the FSLN for political reasons, but they joined one of the three factions of the FSLN out of personal loyalty to the individual who recruited them. One guerrilla who fought in the montaña for many years heard mention of the split for the first time on the radio in 1978, "but all we knew for sure was that Comandante Ruiz was the chief of all of us."[2] All three tendencies had cliquish aspects, which helps explain why they continued to exist even though the political differences among them were sometimes minor and often obscure.

Political splits were commonplace in Nicaraguan political parties. The Conservative, Liberal, and Communist parties all went through more numerous, serious, and permanent ruptures than the FSLN. In the 1930s, Somoza split off the section of the Conservative Party most willing to work with him and lost the backing of a wing of his own Liberal Party, producing two new parties, the Nationalist Conservative Party (Partido Conservador Nacionalista, PCN) and the Constitutionalist Liberal Party (Partido Liberal Constitucionalista, PLC). A more serious split in the Liberal Party gave rise to the Independent Liberal Party, or PLI, in the 1940s, and in the early 1960s, most of the young members and a sizable component of the leadership of the

Conservative Party broke away and joined the Social Christian Party, itself formed in the 1950s by defectors from the Conservative and Liberal parties. In the 1970s, the Nicaraguan Socialist Party split into three distinct pro-Moscow Communist parties.

The political environment in Cuba was different in the early 1970s than it had been during the 1960s, and this put certain constraints on the activities of groups like the FSLN. Salvador Allende's election as president of Chile in 1970 seemed to prove that elections offered a more reliable and less costly road to socialism in Latin America than armed struggle. The journalists who interviewed Fonseca between 1970 and 1973 invariably asked him whether he believed that the Chilean nonviolent road to socialism was an option for Nicaragua. Soviet political and ideological influence was at its peak inside Cuba. Cuban universities stopped teaching courses on Che Guevara and removed Che's writings from their libraries. According to Jacinto Suárez, the only time during the entire two decades after 1959 that the Cubans refused to provide military training to the Nicaraguans was the years 1970 through 1973. The Sandinistas were something of an embarrassment to their Cuban hosts, many of whom agreed with their Soviet advisers that the guerrilla road had been superseded historically by events in the Southern Cone, if indeed it had ever had any validity. Fonseca seemed to be referring to these complications in a 1972 tribute to Cuban solidarity. "This solidarity is extended under delicate circumstances, and it is important to keep this in mind as we go through these difficult moments, or else we could lose heart and not give the struggle everything we have."[3]

Under these conditions of political and military pressure, communication difficulties, and geographic separation, three political tendencies, each with its own leadership, developed within the still-tiny revolutionary organization. The Prolonged People's War Tendency (Guerra Prolongada Popular, GPP) was the only tendency with its central leaders inside Nicaragua: Ricardo Morales Avilés and Oscar Turcios until their deaths in September 1973, and then Henry Ruiz and Tomás Borge. The central ideological leader of the Proletarian Tendency (Tendencia Proletaria, TP) was Jaime Wheelock Román, who lived in Chile until early 1973, when he moved to Havana. Humberto Ortega Saavedra, based in Havana, was the driving force behind the Insurrectional or Third Tendency (Tendencia Insurreccional, TI, or more commonly terceristas). Ortega's older brother Daniel played a secondary leadership role in the TI, but their younger brother Camilo Ortega apparently backed Fonseca in the tendency dispute.[4]

Carlos Fonseca's role in the tendency dispute has never been adequately explained. Insofar as scholars have tried to place him, they have assumed he was allied with the GPP.[5] In fact, Fonseca disagreed with all three tendencies on particular strategic questions: with the TI on the relationship between military and political struggle, with the GPP on the timing of the revolution, and with the TP on the role of rural guerrilla warfare. He counterposed to the somewhat abstract and country-less schemata of all three tendencies a vision of the coming insurrection that was specific to Nicaragua and deeply rooted in his nation's history.

The points of disagreement among the various FSLN tendencies could not easily be addressed in writings intended for public distribution such as the Sandino collection. Instead, they were debated in internal communiqués and meetings. Almost none of this material has ever been published, and most of it has been lost.[6] Surviving participants have consistently refused to discuss the factional battles. A few dozen of Fonseca's letters, manifestos, transcripts of speeches, and analytical essays still exist, however, in a closed archive at the Nicaraguan army's Military History Center (Centro de Historia Militar, CHM) in Managua. These documents show clearly that Fonseca intervened sharply and directly on all the political and tactical issues in dispute, and they reveal at least the general themes of his intervention. Furthermore, once these internal documents are considered, it is clear that Fonseca also addressed the controversial questions in his Sandino writings, albeit more obliquely.

In the years immediately preceding the 1979 revolution, international solidarity committees linked to the various tendencies published their programmatic and analytical statements.[7] These articles, on which scholars have had to rely for their analysis of the issues in dispute, come from a period when the tendencies were no longer talking to each other. The articles reveal nothing of the lively discussion and fluid situation of 1971 to 1976, with its interchange of ideas, attempts to persuade, sharp polemics, and appeals to authority and to reason. The tendency documents of 1977 and 1978, moreover, are written in impenetrable leftist jargon and at a level of abstraction that makes it difficult to perceive the real political differences. And of course they give no hint of Carlos Fonseca's role in the factional dispute.

The unpublished internal documents in the CHM archive show that differences over strategy appeared as early as 1971 and 1972, and that by mid-1973 all the important issues had surfaced and were being addressed in communications and leadership meetings. Without access to these writings, even the best-documented histories of the FSLN located the origins of the tendency fight in 1975 or even 1976.[8]

The differences expressed by the various tendencies of the FSLN from 1972 onward were debated within a single organization and with a common political framework. In other Latin American countries, the situation was quite different. In places where the Left had a longer history and the working class was stronger, it was not uncommon to have half a dozen different Marxist and quasi-Marxist groups, each representing a different international tendency, and each by itself larger than the FSLN. There were significant Trotskyist organizations in Bolivia, Peru, and Argentina, sizable pro-Moscow Communist parties almost everywhere, Maoist guerrilla movements in several South American countries, social-democratic parties calling themselves Marxist that held elected office and controlled large labor federations in a number of places, and, in Mexico and elsewhere, anarchist groups with roots going back to the nineteenth century. All these parties seemed constantly to be spinning off breakaway groups. Ecuador, for example, although not much larger than Nicaragua, had its own Maoist, Trotskyist, Left-social-democratic, and Stalinist groups. In Nicaragua, on the other hand, there were only the PSN, the FSLN, and some tiny sects that Fonseca called "micro-groups" and to which he advocated reaching out in a nonsectarian way.

The FSLN proved able to contain within a single (albeit fractured) movement the political differences that in other countries gave rise to completely separate and mutually hostile organizations. Some of the arguments raised by the proletarios were similar to those put forward by Trotskyist groups elsewhere; the GPP's position on rural guerrilla war had much in common with that of Maoist groups; and the terceristas advanced a political program that resembled the approach of social democrats in other countries. Fonseca often complained of the "political backwardness" of Nicaragua compared to other Latin American countries, but the FSLN may have benefited in one sense from this backwardness. With its late-developing student movement, small working class, and lack of any tradition of socialist electoral activity, Nicaragua did not provide fertile soil for a proliferation of Left groups.

It is difficult to draw sharp political lines demarcating the three tendencies of the FSLN, especially in the fluid situation from 1972 to 1976. No large ideological gulf separated them—comparable, for example, to the differences that existed at the time between the FSLN and the PSN, or the ideological chasm that separates the FSLN of the 1970s from the FSLN of the 1990s. All three tendencies described themselves as Marxist and Sandinista; they all insisted a revolution in Nicaragua had to involve armed struggle; none participated in elections or supported publicly any wing of the Liberal or Conservative parties; they all recognized Carlos Fonseca's authority on ideological and programmatic questions. Furthermore, the tendencies were internally heterogeneous and contradictory. The debate was kept within narrow leadership circles, and the ranks of the FSLN knew little about the political issues involved. A tercerista cadre inside Nicaragua could easily hold a position generally associated with the GPP, or a leader of a GPP-dominated student group could give a speech that sounded as if it came from a proletario. Even when the differences hardened after Fonseca's death, young people attracted to the FSLN often had only a hazy understanding of how their particular tendency differed from the others.

Leaders of the three tendencies paid little attention in their writings to concrete events in Nicaragua. "Concerning the Prolonged People's War, the Sandinista Cell, and Various Issues," a thirty-five-page GPP manifesto of 1975, contained virtually nothing about Nicaragua or anything that had ever happened there. Oscar Turcios's writings "Conditions for a Truly Revolutionary Organization" and "Concerning the Cells" float outside time and place. Fonseca's internal memorandums, on the other hand, almost always featured an update on events in Nicaragua: recent strikes and protests by Nicaraguan workers and youth, the latest electoral maneuvers of the traditional parties, the state of the economy. In 1973 he circulated a long summary of the highlights of recent publications by the Nicaraguan Central Bank and several research institutes: "Some of these figures are so important for revolutionary militants and cadres that every effort should be made to commit them to memory." The central purpose of his chronologies and historical writings on Sandino was to ground the FSLN's strategy in Nicaraguan reality. An internal communiqué Fonseca wrote in July 1974 said that for two years, "both in written documents and in meetings with cadres here [in Havana], the National Directorate has been stating very clearly that it is wrong to mechanically adopt this business of a 'prolonged war,' just copying an approach from books about experiences in other countries."[9]

Theoretically, the three tendencies agreed that Nicaragua was a dependent capitalist state and subscribed to the views Fonseca outlined in *Hora Cero* and a series of interviews and manifestos in the early 1970s. He stressed the contradictory nature of the Nicaraguan economy, with, on the one hand, a capitalist sector based on "the most absolute dependence on foreign capital," and, on the other, relations of production in the countryside that were "not in any way different from those that existed in feudal times." The national bourgeoisie, including the opposition to Somoza, was tied both to imperialism and to a serflike exploitation of the peasantry, leaving the only way out of the contradiction "a victorious social revolution."[10]

The Proletarian Tendency agreed that the Nicaraguan economy was based on agriculture but believed that production was fully capitalist, with no vestiges of precapitalist labor relations. They argued that the Nicaraguan peasantry had been proletarianized to a large degree and needed unions and wage increases more than land reform. The industrial proletariat in Nicaragua was very small, with fewer than 20,000 factory workers in Managua and only 75,000 in the whole country in the early 1970s.[11] The TP leaders argued that this sector would have an influence out of proportion to its size, and they also, with reason, included seasonal agricultural workers in their definition of proletariat. In practice, they concentrated on activity in the urban working-class communities, since they had little influence in the unions, which were still dominated by the PSN.

Fonseca criticized the TP for ignoring the needs of oppressed Nicaraguans who were not workers. He reminded TP leader Jaime Wheelock that Nicaraguans suffered national and ethnic oppression as well as exploitation as workers, complaining that a 1974 communication from Wheelock implied that the problem was just "superexploitation, without mentioning the other indispensable aspect, which is the extreme oppression." Fonseca pointed out that Wheelock's communication concentrated "exclusively on wageworkers—and only those in the Pacific region, without mentioning the North and the Atlantic Coast."[12]

The Proletarians claimed to be the most Marxist of the tendencies, and this characterization has been accepted by many scholars. Fonseca believed, however, that their orthodox Marxist language masked a conservative "economism." He was referring to the proletarios in 1975 when he wrote, "we have to be careful to avoid pseudo-Marxist verbiage, which tries to pass itself off as Marxism but is basically nothing but economic materialism, a caricature of Marxism."[13]

The GPP, on the other hand, emphasized the revolutionary nature of the peasantry and the continuation of feudal-like relations on the land. Its political work in the cities revolved around students and intellectuals, not workers. A 1973 GPP manifesto predicted that revolutionary struggle would be introduced into the working class from the outside: "From the barrios and villages, from the real bosom of our people, Sandinista cadres will penetrate the factories and workplaces and carry the revolutionary struggle to the furthest corner of the land." Fonseca repeatedly pushed the GPP to pay more attention to workers and try to increase the FSLN's influence in the workplace.[14]

The three tendencies had different views on whether revolutionary energies should be focused in the countryside or the cities, a debate in which Fonseca staked out his own position. The GPP, and later the TI, focused on rural guerrilla warfare, the montaña. "It will be from the countryside that we will advance on the cities and take them," said GPP leader Oscar Turcios. The Proletarian Tendency, on the other hand, emphasized work in the cities and was the only faction that never fielded its own rural guerrilla army. Fonseca warned that counterposing the cities to the remote jungle montaña left out the majority of Nicaragua and could lead to "*paralysis.*" He advocated paying more attention to what he called the *campo,* or countryside; that is, villages and towns of a few hundred to a few thousand people, and the nearby rural areas inhabited by families who worked on cotton and coffee plantations and on ranches. In several speeches and letters, he returned to the need to orient toward workers on the cotton plantations, the largest workforce in Nicaragua and a sector with which the FSLN had almost no experience.[15]

In November 1975, preparing to enter the montaña himself, Fonseca suggested extending guerrilla warfare from the remote mountains to the "rural areas on the periphery of certain urban locations." Even if such work could be carried out only sporadically and consisted at first of propaganda actions like posting red-and-black Sandinista flags, its importance was proved by the history of other revolutions. Guerrilla bands operating closer to town should "be made up almost entirely of people indigenous to the area, who were born or raised there and know the territory like the palm of their hand."[16]

In a 1973 discussion in Havana, Fonseca argued that too much emphasis on the strategic and military value of the montaña could turn into a political disability if the Sandinistas ignored more populated areas:

> We know that we have wonderful mountains, that our geographical situation is very useful for revolutionaries. But it is crucial that we don't just see the montaña as a place to hide but also a place to wage war. We should use the cover the mountains provide to carry out organizational tasks: to train cadres, to build up the combative spirit of our fighters, to link up military actions in the montaña with military operations in the Pacific zone, to make sure we have the flexibility to move smoothly from place to place.

On another occasion, he suggested inviting journalists or prominent individuals to interview the guerrillas in their mountain headquarters, as the Cubans had done with CBS film crews and *New York Times* reporter Herbert Matthews in the Sierra Maestra. "We could also consider holding some national gatherings there, of a political, economic, cultural or trade union character, not with the aim of keeping them secret, but on the contrary to use these events to reach out to public opinion."[17]

The clearest tactical differences among the three tendencies had to do with timing and the pace at which the revolution could be expected to develop. A related but more complex question, to which Fonseca devoted considerable attention, concerned the relationship between the military and political sides of the revolution. Both questions are addressed sharply in an internal document Fonseca circulated in 1972, long before the tendencies were officially declared. In the forty-seven numbered articles of "Notes on Some Current Problems," he criticized certain aspects of the strategic approaches of all three tendencies, in what was obviously already an ongoing discussion.

On the question of timing, he was concerned that some leaders were rationalizing long periods of inactivity by stressing the prolonged character of the struggle. The Prolonged People's War tendency, as its name implies, believed that the FSLN would gradually increase in size through the incremental growth of rural guerrilla units, partly through winning over peasants and partly through sending newly recruited students into the mountains, until at some point it could challenge the National Guard militarily. Fonseca warned the GPP against making a fetish out of the length of time they expected to remain in the mountains: "One thing needs to be made clear—there's no virtue in prolonging the struggle. As far as I am concerned, we should do everything we can to avoid prolonging the struggle too much." GPP leaders insisted that the task of the current stage was "propaganda," after which would come the job of "agitation," followed eventually by the opportunity to lead an insurrection. Fonseca, on the other hand, constantly warned his comrades to expect the unexpected. Opportunities for revolutionary action could develop suddenly, he said in 1973, and at an uneven pace around the country: "We can't have the idea that the struggle will move mechanically through a series of stages, one after the other. We can even have insurrectional actions at certain places in the country when the rest of the country is not at that stage. In some cases, we will see insurrectional uprisings followed by openings to do propaganda and agitational work." He proposed looking at countries "where revolutionary movements have gone through long and painful struggles to get to the stage where accelerated progress is possible, where in a relatively brief period of time the kind of growth occurs that wasn't possible in the whole long preceding period."[18]

It was clear in his 1972 "Notes" that Fonseca saw individuals in the leadership committing two opposite errors in terms of the relative importance of legal political work and underground military actions. He compared giving absolute priority to political work—which became the hallmark of the Proletarian Tendency—to the "pseudorevolutionary" practices of the PSN. "We have to make sure," Fonseca wrote, "that our political work is directed toward one clear objective: a revolutionary uprising." Fonseca then turned immediately to the opposite error of committing all the FSLN's energies to military actions: "We have to avoid," he insisted,

> the notion that revolutionary war could ever be an operation carried out by a small number of individuals with absolutely no ties to the masses. Before beginning a military campaign, the revolutionary nuclei . . . must have some kind of continuous relationship with a section of the population, have established some level of organization rooted in the masses. Their plans have to be drawn up on the basis of the real day-to-day lives of the workers and peasants.

It might seem simplistic, Fonseca admitted, to say that every action must be designed to sharpen the struggle between the exploited and the exploiters. "But it is justified, given the widespread tendency to recommend paramilitary operations that are not based on actions by the workers and peasants against their exploiters." In 1974 Fonseca rejected a proposal for an intensification of military operations because it was not based on concrete political accomplishments in terms of new members and increased influence. Fonseca demanded that the makers of the proposal send him as soon as possible a collection of the political propaganda they had issued over the last three years, including "leaflets targeting particular social sectors and material related to local or regional issues."[19]

In 1975 Fonseca used an internal class on the history of the FSLN to address some of the issues in dispute. He said "a certain involuntary militarism" was responsible for some of the setbacks of the early 1960s, attributing the exclusive focus on armed struggle to youthful enthusiasm, reaction against the conservatism of the PSN, and illusions about the recent Cuban victory. Young fighters were recruited, but "we have to admit that these compañeros were assigned exclusively military tasks, and we did not know how to take advantage of the experience some of them had in the class struggle. We never tried to incorporate their knowledge of social problems into any political analysis, and many of them were from farming regions where they had personally experienced exploitation by big landowners and other exploiters." Because they were just handed a gun and never given political work to do, Fonseca said, they left the movement as soon as it started losing battles in 1963.[20]

Fonseca's polemic against excessive "militarism" was directed primarily against the Insurrectional Tendency. A secret tercerista "plan of action" from the mid-1970s reveals a strategy that is extremely militant, even terrorist, in terms of armed actions, while deferring to the bourgeois opposition on political issues.[21] Most of the document consisted of a detailed list of economic targets for bombings and arson, and it closed with a list of the names of prominent Somocistas "who eventually could be liquidated." The "plan of action" warned that it was important to attack only those slaughterhouses, plantations, and factories most closely tied to Somoza, in order not to "create resentment among opponents of the regime, some of whom are even our sympathizers."

Both the GPP and the Proletarians were actively involved in the student movement at the time, with GPP members in the leadership of the FSLN's longtime student group, the FER. But the tercerista "plan of action" called the FER moribund and proposed instead working through a PLI-affiliated group, the Independent Liberal Student Vanguard. According to this document, the FSLN—by which it meant the TI faction—was working closely with one wing of the Conservative Party while holding meetings with the PLI and PSN about "a new reunification of the Left," in which the Frente's job would be to handle the armed struggle. Francisco Rivera, the commander of a tercerista guerrilla front in 1979, said he was warned by Humberto Ortega to report only military developments in his news releases and not include anything political, "because if we started to use radical language in our statements we could jeopardize all the complicated work they were doing of conciliating certain people and strengthening alliances."[22] This was a sharp departure from Fonseca's insistence throughout the last decade of his life that the FSLN had to project itself as the political vanguard of the revolution and make sure alliances strengthened rather than weakened the FSLN as an independent force.

Fonseca tried to suggest ways of combining military and political work to prepare the FSLN for a situation that would be qualitatively different from anything it had known before. It was not just a question of slow or rapid accumulation of forces along the lines experienced so far, he said, but a question of getting ready for a completely new reality.

> In many factories, in many barrios, in many villages, on many plantations, at the moment of the triumph of the revolution, and in the course

of the process leading up to this, there will be individuals who are sympathetic to and even come to identify with the FSLN's program, even though they have never had the opportunity to make contact with a member of the FSLN. . . . At a certain point the leadership must recognize . . . that the creativity, the initiative to stand up to the enemy, to stand up to the ruling classes, has become a mass phenomenon, and that many people who haven't been organized the way they should—because of the limitations of the Revolutionary Movement, the actions we have carried out, and, we have to admit, even of our propaganda—are fully capable of carrying out certain tasks on their own initiative.[23]

Although Fonseca did not live to see this phenomenon with his own eyes, it was a more accurate vision of what would actually happen in 1979 than the schematic views of all three tendencies.

The question of working with bourgeois political parties came to the fore in the social turmoil that followed a devastating earthquake that destroyed central Managua in December 1972. President Somoza appropriated much of the international relief aid for himself and loyal supporters in the Liberal Party and National Guard, and little was done to rebuild the capital. Under these circumstances, cracks began to appear in support for Somoza among some sectors of the Nicaraguan bourgeoisie. The Catholic establishment, under pressure from activists at the community level, broke with tradition and began to voice timid criticisms of human rights violations by the National Guard. The wealthy families still closed ranks behind the administration when faced with any challenge from below, however, as when they defeated a two-month-long, militantly anti-Somoza construction workers strike against the misuse of earthquake relief funds.

At Fonseca's initiative, the FSLN responded quickly to the earthquake, with a series of activities carried out in its own name. As part of a campaign to build international solidarity with the FSLN, Fonseca fired off letters to groups around the world requesting political support and donations. Especially interesting are the letters to "Afro-North-Americans" and to Native Americans (sent to various black and Indian groups in the United States), and to "Nicaraguans residing in the United States." The FSLN even published a call for an international scientific conference to study the earthquake faults under Managua and propose a new location for the country's capital—a bold attempt to present itself as a responsible future government at a time when it had fewer than a hundred members and most of its leaders were in exile. The FSLN inside Nicaragua was able to move its underground members around the country under cover of the hundreds of young earthquake victims, or *terremoteados,* being relocated to undamaged cities and towns. When construction workers went on strike in early 1973, FSLN members Bayardo Arce and Doris Tijerino organized a broad solidarity committee that provided more support to the workers than they were getting from their own PSN-led union. All these measures were consistent with the movement's approach since breaking with the Movilización Republicana in 1966: they projected the FSLN as the leadership of an anti-Somoza revolution and were oriented especially toward building support for the organization among workers and youth.[24]

Around this time, Fonseca spelled out the movement's approach to alliances in an internal memorandum entitled "Some Aspects of Mass Work." Organized political activity directed toward workers, he said,

> will give the Frente Sandinista our own mass base among the lower classes, made up of those who are committed to taking action along the lines set forward by our organization. In order to be able to carry out an independent revolutionary line, it is absolutely necessary to have our own mass base, composed of people who don't listen to any other organization, who are free of any bourgeois influence, who have no interests except those of the exploited.

Short-term alliances with bourgeois forces could be useful, Fonseca went on, but only if the FSLN clearly presented itself as the leadership of the struggle against Somoza and had its own independent mass base among the lower classes.[25]

Behind the scenes, however, a different approach was taking shape on the question of alliances with the bourgeois opposition. According to Doris Tijerino, she traveled to Havana in 1973 to make a proposal on behalf of the entire Prolonged People's War (GPP) leadership that the FSLN strike a deal with the Conservative opposition. The GPP thought Sandinista guerrillas could distract and neutralize the National Guard while the opposition carried out a coup to install Pedro Joaquín Chamorro as president. Tijerino claims she met personally with Chamorro to see if he would be willing to enter into such an arrangement, to which he responded that he needed time to think about it. When she met with Fonseca and Humberto Ortega in Havana, they summarily rejected the idea.[26] Although Ortega joined Fonseca in refusing to sanction the deal with Chamorro (perhaps because the proposal came from the GPP, which would have considerable influence over any alliance it initiated), he soon became the leading advocate of alliances with the bourgeois opposition. The Proletarian Tendency's alliance strategy was similar. Influenced by their years in Chile, they foresaw the development of something like Allende's Unidad Popular coalition, with the FSLN playing the role of the Movement of the Revolutionary Left, or MIR, and the PSN substituting for its Chilean counterpart, the Communist Party.

The differences on alliances were related to different concepts about what it meant to be a vanguard organization or party. As with all the issues of the tendency struggle, unanimity at a certain level of abstraction masked sharp differences on tactical implementation and day-to-day political orientation. Everyone in the FSLN considered the organization a political vanguard that would play a necessary role in organizing and leading a massive popular insurrection to topple Somoza. But the FSLN leaders had a variety of ideas about what the vanguard should be doing to prepare for the coming insurrection, of how their small movement could concretely reach out, recruit, and influence Nicaraguan public opinion. Fonseca had a particularly inclusive definition of the FSLN as vanguard: "Whatever differences there may be among Nicaraguans, everyone belongs in the ranks of the Frente Sandinista. This is the way a vanguard that identifies with the working class and the peasantry, that is guided in action by the philosophy of scientific socialism, must be." In the same 1970 statement, he singled out the importance of "true revolutionaries and true Christians" joining forces in the ranks of the FSLN.[27] The FSLN leader most closely identified with Fonseca on this question was GPP leader Ricardo Morales Avilés, who was killed in 1973.

Even with an inclusive approach to recruitment, not everyone who wanted to fight against Somoza would join the FSLN. In a 1973 talk, Fonseca said: "It is impossible for the revolutionary movement to act and carry out the struggle just with the activity of its members. We are the vanguard, but the term vanguard implies that there are intermediate forces and rear guard forces— without them, there is no such thing as a vanguard." He urged the other leaders of the FSLN always to be looking not just for recruits but for sympathizers and collaborators. "There are also people who can give a minimal level of cooperation, who we need to pay attention to, even though they can't maintain the level of activity necessary to be a member. There may be people like this who only participate on one occasion, but it is at the moment that is decisive for the revolutionary movement taking power."

In the early 1970s, Fonseca perceived in other FSLN leaders signs of the same social-work mentality they had taken into the barrios of Managua a decade before. He warned them not to think of the vanguard as something closed and elitist. The job of a vanguard, Fonseca insisted, was not to substitute for the working class or patronize workers. "We have to say," he wrote, "that every worker is a real living encyclopedia of knowledge, to which the Frente Sandinista has to pay the closest attention." In the same internal circular, he said, "It is important for us to understand that, even if we don't know anything about it, simple but real signs of protest by workers are going on every day and in workplaces everywhere."[28]

Fonseca urged FSLN leaders to learn from "the wisdom of the popular masses, a wisdom the masses acquire not in some university or research institute, but through their own experience and their labor."

> Our people is one that has great historical experience, even greater, we have to say, than most folks now believe. We have to be on the lookout for signs of discontent among sections of the population. We have to know how to take every single sign of resistance seriously and pay careful attention to it. Because it is only insofar as we pay attention to our masses, our workers, our campesinos, that we will ever make a revolution in Nicaragua. . . . We have to be alert to these spontaneous forms of struggle, because often the masses create with their wisdom, with their creativity, formidable methods of struggle.

He cited the example of an Indian community's successful collective defense of a member who had killed a thieving and abusive landlord:

> I mention this example to give more reality to this question of the spontaneous struggles waged by the people of Nicaragua. We have to pay attention to this, compañeros, where there are exploited, there is class struggle. And if we don't understand there is class struggle going on, it's not because it isn't happening, but rather because we ourselves haven't had enough contact with workers, because we haven't developed the kind of relationship we should with the exploited.[29]

If there was theoretical agreement on the vanguard role of the FSLN, there was not even theoretical agreement on the related question of whether the FSLN was—or should be—a revolutionary party. (When Latin American armed groups of the 1970s, including the FSLN, debated the "party question," they were talking not about an electoral political party but about a combat party modeled at least to some extent on the Bolshevik Party of Lenin.) In a 1973 talk to the FSLN leadership, Fonseca said:

> This question of the party has been debated among Latin American revolutionaries because of the Cuban revolution; some have gone to the

extreme of arguing that in Cuba they, in practice, waged a successful guerrilla war without ever having a party of their own. In my opinion some people have gone too far along these lines. What's involved here, in my opinion, is the need for us to recognize the important role a political organization plays in the whole insurrectional process. I believe that in Cuba—like in Russia, like in Vietnam, like in other places where it has been possible to carry out a successful revolution—that all these places have in common the fact that the insurrectional movement was able to count on a team of experienced cadres who were familiar with revolutionary principles, with the principles of revolutionary philosophy.

Fonseca feared that both the GPP and the TI made precisely the error of misreading the lesson of the Cuban revolution and underestimating the importance of a disciplined political organization. The GPP and the TI had different ideas about how long the military side of the struggle against Somoza would last, but they both thought the formation of a party could be postponed until the military balance of forces was more favorable, or even until after the revolution. This question would not be resolved during Fonseca's lifetime—or even afterward. He returned to it in the final section of his last major political work.

Every bona fide revolutionary party has been born in combat, and if Cuba is the case we are most familiar with, that does not mean it was the first case. In Russia, Vietnam, China, Korea, Algeria—there too the parties grew out of struggle. . . . If [in Nicaragua today] it is not realistic to talk about a party with a central committee, congresses, newspapers, theoretical magazines, it is definitely necessary to carry out some of the tasks of a party: more systematic study of our national conditions (especially in the combat zones); a better combination of military and political analysis; building links with the exploited masses, wherever we might find them, to involve them in the revolutionary war; steeling ourselves against ideological sectarianism; prioritizing political work without doing anything to hurt our military operations; strengthening the political communications among various sectors of the movement (in which there have been problems caused by a certain haphazardness); taking measures to make sure we are doing the most to maximize everyone's potential for struggle, etc.[30]

Fonseca conceded that it might be "premature" to use the word *party* to describe a group that accomplished "all these modest tasks," but he was clearly setting forth his political priorities for the FSLN. And his list of "modest tasks" included precisely those strategic issues around which the organization was split.

Some of Fonseca's unpublished writings dealt with problems of internal discipline and organization. All the leaders and members of the FSLN agreed in theory with the concept of building a democratic centralist organization, where the personal preferences of individual members were subordinated to the goals of the movement as a whole, and where all members—especially leaders—were under the discipline of the leading bodies. In the case of the FSLN, the leadership structure involved the jefe, or chief, of a cell; the responsable, or director, of a city or region (sometimes working as part of a regional committee); and the National Directorate (Dirección Nacional, DN), made up generally of three to five full members and one or two alternates. The DN, the highest authority in the FSLN, was established in the late 1960s, replacing a looser leadership committee called "the Executive." The DN was not an elected body. At first Carlos Fonseca simply appointed individuals who were taking on increasing responsibility such as Julio Buitrago or Doris Tijerino. (Tijerino, placed temporarily on the DN by Fonseca in late 1966, was the only woman to serve until the 1990s.) In the 1970s the DN itself chose replacements for members who had been killed by the National Guard. Members rarely left the DN unless they died, although at least two, Efraín Sánchez Sancho and Plutarco Hernández, were either expelled or asked to resign. During the tendency disputes there were differences of opinion on who was a bona fide member of the National Directorate.

The issue of democratic centralism was brought to the fore in September 1973, when disaster struck the leadership of the FSLN. The only two full members of the DN inside Nicaragua, Oscar Turcios and Ricardo Morales Avilés, were captured in the town of Nandaime, not far from Managua, and killed by the National Guard. Fonseca and Humberto Ortega assigned DN alternate member Pedro Aráuz to inform Henry Ruiz that he, Ruiz, was now in charge of all the FSLN's political and military work inside the country. Aráuz refused to do so, claiming that Oscar Turcios had named him successor in the event of Turcios's death. Fonseca explained his decision to remove Aráuz from the DN but allow him to remain in the organization as follows: "This is a sign of our desire not to show off our authority. Compañero Federico [Pedro Aráuz] is being given the chance to remain a member of the Organization even though his insubordination represents a crime which could—although we are not proposing to do this—be justification for his execution, expulsion, or suspension." On another occasion, Fonseca sharply criticized two members of the DN living in Havana, Humberto Ortega and Eduardo Contreras, for refusing to return to Nicaragua and for violating discipline by discussing political differences with individuals who were not members of the leading body.[31]

Some of Fonseca's points about the responsibilities of a disciplined member of the FSLN were general enough to appear in the public writings. In *Viva Sandino,* he said that even with their political differences, it was inexcusable for the Communist parties and APRA not to send their cadres to fight in a disciplined way under Sandino's command. As the factional conflict escalated within his own organization, Fonseca wrote: "The reason I am pointing this out is because a revolutionary has every right to express his opinion about a situation according to what his own political perspective is, but this opinion should never be used as an excuse for refusing to take his place in the trenches." The *Cronología* described a 1930 letter in which Sandino, according to Fonseca, "refers in a critical tone to the hair-splitting complaints of certain elements who stay permanently outside the country, and he mentions that help is not coming into Nicaragua from outside." In the same writing, Fonseca used the example of Sandino to make the argument that revolutionaries, whatever their quarrels, had to present a united face to their enemies. Fonseca quoted a 1931 message in which Sandino said it was crucial to demonstrate "that we are one united Army, and that the isolated groups the enemy talks about do not exist."[32]

The disputes of the early 1970s sometimes raised moral issues. Fonseca believed that a Sandinista fighter had to be willing to risk personal danger and if necessary to die for the sake of the revolution, and he pointed to Che Guevara, as well as to Sandino, as examples of the kind of total dedication that was necessary. In language reminiscent of Che, Fonseca told a journalist in 1970, "You can't have a revolutionary movement unless you have revolutionaries, and you can't have revolutionaries unless you have people who are willing to dedicate their entire life, full time, their dreams and their waking hours, to the suffering of the people." The lesson he drew from Guevara's defeat in Bolivia in 1967 was not that the campaign had been a mistake but that Latin America needed *more* Che Guevaras. Fonseca saw shortcomings in the level of revolutionary commitment shown by individual representatives of all three tendencies. Proletarian Tendency leaders, influenced by their years in Chile and by their antirural orientation, considered some— perhaps all—of the FSLN's military actions to be adventures that only led to stepped-up government repression. They thought the organization should conserve its cadres until the organized labor movement was ready to be led into an insurrection, and they accused some of the other leaders and cadres of the FSLN of having a "death wish." The GPP, although based in the countryside and organized militarily, also put considerable emphasis on conserving cadres and avoided encounters with the National Guard as much as possible. Fonseca was addressing both groups when he said: "It is true that during a certain stage it is important to conserve one's strength. But a movement that is always primarily concerned with saving its strength and only slightly concerned with eliminating the enemy is a movement that is never going to take power."[33]

A few years later, Fonseca said the refusal of TI leader Humberto Ortega and DN member Eduardo Contreras to return to Nicaragua was "unconscionable" and a certain sign of their "despair." It was understandable, Fonseca said, for them to think that certain leadership cadres should be kept in reserve outside the country and not exposed to the dangers of underground life. "But it is wrong for them to decide *they* should be the ones to be kept in reserve, without even consulting the other compañeros of the DN." If the leadership as a whole had a chance to discuss the question, Fonseca went on, it might choose to bring out some comrades who had been fighting inside the country and assign them to be the "reserve."[34] Humberto Ortega had been outside Nicaragua since 1967 except for a brief visit in 1972, and he did not move back to the country until the FSLN took power. Eduardo Contreras had been in Havana only a little more than a year; he returned to Nicaragua in mid-1976 and was killed by the National Guard a few months later.

Fonseca believed there was a class character to moral qualities. "Proletarianization," he told other FSLN leaders in 1972, "isn't just a question of ideological identification with the interests of the proletariat, but also of the membership adopting a proletarian spirit: industriousness, humility, self-sacrifice, honesty." Sandino's selflessness, loyalty, discipline, and modesty were all related, in Fonseca's mind, to the fact he was a "proletarian." A middle-class upbringing, Fonseca thought, tended to produce selfish behavior, a lack of self-discipline, arrogance, an attachment to property and consumer goods, and even sexual promiscuity. He pointed to the middle-class leaders of Latin American revolutionary movements who had ended up compromising with reactionary regimes or with imperialism to save their own lives and property. On several occasions, Fonseca recommended that certain leaders of the Proletarian Tendency, who came from some of the wealthiest families in Nicaragua, find ways to "proletarianize" their daily lives. Although he was opposed to assigning militants to the rural guerrilla operation against their will, Fonseca agreed with leaders of the GPP such as

Henry Ruiz that the montaña could be a proletarianizing experience in a moral sense.[35]

Although the content of his own remarks was often sharp, Fonseca tried to keep the tone of the tendency debate civil. Personal attacks were out of order, he said in 1973: "In our struggle to confront various problems, in our struggle against certain weaknesses . . . we have to avoid this being turned into a struggle against certain individuals . . . because it is crucial that our cadres and militants develop their ability to think for themselves. Nothing is easier than just saying—'it's all so-and-so's fault, he's a slacker.'" He criticized leaders of the various tendencies for using epithets like "Menshevik" to characterize their opponents, instead of carrying out their debate in more fraternal language. One of the themes of Fonseca's writing, especially his polemical writing, was that words, including terms of address, were important. In both his Sandino collection and internal writings, he drew out the implications of the fact that Sandino's followers addressed each other as hermano, or brother.[36]

Differences became sharper and more personal in character, however, following the FSLN's December 1974 raid on a party honoring the U.S. ambassador at the home of wealthy Somocista businessman José María "Chema" Castillo. Fifteen guerrillas, including three women, waited until Ambassador Thomas Shelton had gone home and then occupied the residence, taking hostages who included President Somoza's brother-in-law and the minister of defense.[37] This operation, carried out by GPP members and terceristas, led to the release from prison of more than a dozen FSLN leaders, some of whom had been behind bars for seven years, as well as the payment of a $1 million ransom and the broadcast of two FSLN communiqués on radio and television. Members of the GPP in particular hailed the action as "breaking the silence," but the Proletarians called it an adventure that only gave the Somoza dictatorship an excuse to unleash repression against student and labor activists.[38]

Tensions between Sandinistas inside the country and those in exile became more acute around the same time. In October 1974 the Nicaragua-based members of the National Directorate passed a motion saying that except for Carlos Fonseca, no one outside the country could speak in the name of the leading body. Humberto Ortega, and perhaps others, angrily rejected the internal DN's right to pass such a motion.[39]

There are indications that at least two of the tendencies tried to relegate Carlos Fonseca to a kind of "emeritus" status as an elder statesman without day-to-day responsibility for making military and political decisions. Fonseca fought angrily against every suggestion that he was out of touch in Havana. In 1973 he defended himself against doubts voiced by members of both the GPP and TP concerning his ability to lead the practical work of the movement:

> You have to remember that we have stayed in constant communication with the compañeros inside the country, in this way staying up to the minute with the results of our work and with the activities our Organization is carrying out inside the country. You also have to keep in mind that the compañeros who come here from Nicaragua have given us detailed reports that have enabled us to understand the milieu they are working in, and the tasks they undertake, and make it possible for us to give advice in each and every case.[40]

This issue would not die, however. A year later, Fonseca again passionately defended his intimate knowledge of the movement's activities inside Nicaragua. He reminded the GPP leadership of his many years of underground experience and pointed out that in exile he had been visited regularly by FSLN members who gave him "detailed reports on the methods of work, on the political, military, and underground activity under way, on the ways contact is being made with the masses, on the personal experiences of these members, the social milieu they come from, etc." He implied he got better information from rank-and-file members than from the leadership, citing the case of a militant who had been involved in a strike of a thousand people and came to Havana to report first to Fonseca. When Jaime Wheelock complained about a lack of political direction, Fonseca accused the TP leader of ignoring "the political demands laid out in the correspondence from members of the Directorate in exile to those inside the country, and also the orientation sessions that militants have had in Havana." According to Víctor Tirado, members of the TI had also started to hint that Fonseca had been out of the country so long that he no longer had a grasp of the situation.[41]

Surviving documents from this period give a picture of Carlos Fonseca the student of Sandino and political strategist, but of Carlos Fonseca the man they reveal almost nothing. An extremely private person, Fonseca never kept any kind of journal. Except for a few letters to his father and to Don Edelberto Torres during the 1960s, his extant correspondence is strictly political in nature. Unlike Che Guevara, who wrote dozens of humorous, affectionate, sometimes angry or worried letters to his parents and aunt, Fonseca left no correspondence revealing his inner self. Although it is possible he wrote more intimate letters to his mother or wife, the fact that not a single example of such correspondence was ever intercepted by the National Guard suggests that he did not. In Havana, Fonseca spent most of his time at the Miramar office and residence of the FSLN that they all called Cuarenta because it was on Fortieth Street. Haydeé Terán has described her husband's life in Havana as disciplined and devoted largely to politics: up early to run three kilometers and do his exercises, days spent in meetings at the Cuarenta house, often returning there after dinner at home in the family's modest second-story apartment in nearby Buena Vista. Fonseca's son Carlos remembers that his father sometimes took him to the FSLN office, but that his little sister Tania never went along, "because she was too rambunctious."[42]

The American-born writer Margaret Randall, one of Fonseca's few friends in Havana outside the small community of Nicaraguan exiles, wrote in 1994:

> I remember Carlos Fonseca so clearly, as vividly as the intense clarity of his blue eyes. He had one of those stares that literally ate you up. He was almost always serious, at least at the time I knew him (Havana, early seventies). He would come to visit, sometimes bringing his children— who were quite young then, about the ages of my youngest. He would sit on our living room couch and we'd talk . . . about all sorts of things. He struck me as extremely committed, dedicated, perhaps single-tracked with regard to Nicaragua. Almost anything that came up in a conversation, he would invariably use as a lead-in to talk about that issue or that thing as it related to his country. He obviously loved Nicaragua more than life itself.[43]

Young Carlos Fonseca Terán was nine years old when his father left Havana. Interviewed years later, he remembered Fonseca as a "homebody" (*hogareño*) who took the children to the park and beach, sometimes to movies, and who liked to sing them songs he made up himself and recite poetry. But he could also be strict. Carlitos called his father "one of those old guys who was set in his ways. Super austere, very disciplined, methodical, cautious. He didn't drink or smoke. In fact, he used to tell us not to let my mother smoke."[44]

Fonseca was not the only FSLN leader who was becoming quite settled in Havana. Several, including Plutarco Hernández, had married Cuban women. Jaime Wheelock brought his Chilean wife to Havana, where she worked to build international solidarity with the FSLN. Humberto Ortega was married to a Costa Rican and raising a family. Doris Tijerino brought her young son with her to Havana and gave birth to Ricardo Morales Avilés's daughter shortly after she arrived.

Citing the examples of Sandino and Che Guevara, Fonseca often said that a revolutionary leader belonged on the front lines. Sometime in the first half of 1975, he decided to return to Nicaragua. He rejected the warnings of at least some FSLN leaders inside the country that the movement was too weak to guarantee the safety of a leader who was so well known and physically so distinctive.

Prolonged life in exile had created both ideological and practical problems. On an ideological level, while Fonseca and his followers sought to learn from other revolutions and use the tools of the international Marxist movement, they also wanted to be rooted in Nicaraguan history and reality. This was why Fonseca spent his Havana years studying Sandino. In a practical sense, although they could study, discuss, and learn military skills outside the country, they could only build a combat organization and test it in action inside Nicaragua.

Three years of discussion and debate in Havana had failed to resolve the differences on strategic and tactical issues. By 1975 the tendencies were further apart than ever. Fonseca was convinced that the only possibility of bringing the three factions together lay in his returning to the country to lead the movement in action as well as in theory. Disguised as a businessman, he made his way back to Honduras, and from there overland through the mountains to Nicaragua, arriving in October or November 1975.

The Montaña and the Death of Fonseca, 1975–1976

As Fonseca made his tortuous underground journey back to Nicaragua in 1975, the fight among the three tendencies reached a dangerous new level. In October 1975, the National Directorate, largely at the initiative of Tomás Borge of the GPP, expelled from the FSLN the principal leaders of the Proletarian Tendency, Jaime Wheelock, Luis Carrión, and Roberto Huembes. Around the same time and also acting in the name of the National Directorate, Plutarco Hernández of the terceristas organized an internal trial of longtime FSLN militant and peasant leader Chicho Zepeda. Convicted of "treason," Zepeda was executed by his own comrades. Fonseca later expressed his personal disagreement with both measures while accepting responsibility for them as a member of the National Directorate. The internal crisis was now so severe that the three tendencies did not even agree on who was a member of the DN, beyond Carlos Fonseca himself and perhaps Henry Ruiz deep in the jungle.[1]

The widening split within the FSLN compromised its work among different sectors of the population and hobbled its still-modest military capacity. One of the expelled proletarios, Roberto Huembes, had been in charge of the underground work of the FSLN in Managua, and another, Luis Carrión, had built a base for the movement among radical-minded Christian youth. The guerrilla component of the FSLN was reduced by late 1975 to a few dozen fighters, increasingly isolated from both their urban support networks and their peasant collaborators, and hotly pursued by the National Guard.

Fonseca went back to Nicaragua in the hopes of reaching consensus on a united effort to reinforce the guerrilla army and prepare for a new offensive against the Somoza government, which he planned personally to command. In late 1970 he had told two Cuban journalists of his immediate plan to "return to the montaña." Nearly five years later, he was finally on his way to the Segovias.

He first entered the urban underground for a series of meetings to discuss the political and strategic differences. From December 1975 until February 1976, he hid in a safe house twenty kilometers outside Managua on the road to Masaya. With him were Pedro Aráuz, Carlos Agüero, Claudia Chamorro, and Luz Marina Acosta. Aráuz was the head of the urban underground, having been reincorporated into the leadership after his 1973 demotion for indiscipline. Agüero had been the commander of the 1970 skyjacking that freed Fonseca from jail in Costa Rica and was now Henry Ruiz's second in command in the mountains. Acosta and Aráuz pretended to be a middle-class couple renting the house, and two elderly peasant collaborators posed as gardeners. In order not to arouse the suspicions of neighbors or National Guard patrols, the house was decorated with Christmas ornaments in December, making all the residents—including Carlos Fonseca—homesick for their families.

Security at the safe house was extremely tight. Fonseca almost never left the building. On New Year's Eve the entire household suddenly had to evacuate the premises and retreat to a house nearby because of a false report their hideout had been discovered. Luz Acosta, the only resident of this safe house who survived until 1979, has left an account of the holiday that reveals a good deal about Carlos Fonseca's reserve and the emotional distance he placed between himself and his comrades—especially female comrades. It also shows how this distance was sometimes impossible to maintain given the intimate conditions of underground life and the youth of many of the guerrillas. Acosta was still in her teens at the end of 1975.

Shortly before midnight New Year's Eve, the guerrillas sat on the floor in a darkened room, listening to low music on a radio. Fonseca tried to reassure Acosta that the holiday meal she had spent all day cooking would be waiting for them the next day.

> "That's fine," I said to the Comandante, "Tomorrow we'll eat our feast, but tonight we dance." His eyes almost popped out of his head when he saw how determined I was to make him dance. I was already swaying with the music, and I reached out my hand to make him get up. He didn't have any choice, he pushed himself up and stood there, but without moving. . . . I grabbed his arms and moved them from one side to the other. When I let go of his hands, they dropped heavily to his side. . . . I finally said, "no, that's not it, this is the way you do it." I put

one hand on his shoulder and with my other grabbed his hand, and that way forced him to dance. He took two steps and then stopped and said, "OK, there, we danced." But I wouldn't give up. "None of that," I said, "not until the end of the song." When it ended, he tried to sit down again, but Elena [Claudia Chamorro] wouldn't let him, she had already turned the radio dial and found the same song. He danced with her too. That morning I slept well, happy about my little mischief in the midst of all that tension. I made Carlos Fonseca dance.

According to Acosta, people came and went from the house in great secrecy and closeted themselves with Fonseca, Agüero, and Aráuz in meetings that sometimes lasted from before dawn to the next night. Not all Fonseca's meetings involved central leaders of the FSLN. He also met with the brothers Ernesto and Fernando Cardenal, priests who were among the most prominent intellectuals supporting the Frente. At least one meeting was organized in León, in spite of the danger associated with travel from one place to another. There the rendezvous had to be changed at the last minute because Carlos noticed his sister, Estela Fonseca, tending a shop across the street. Henry Ruiz, in charge of the FSLN's work in the mountains since 1971, was not among those who came to the Kilometer Twenty safe house. Ruiz, known by the nom de guerre Modesto, remained with the Pablo Ubeda Brigade in the most remote region of the montaña.

Since the defeat at Pancasán eight years before, not much progress had been made in reestablishing a guerrilla presence in the northern mountains. The first attempt after 1967 was a small-scale operation near Zinica in 1970, but it was quickly quashed. When combatants entered the montaña again in the spring of 1971, they came planning to stay a long time. During their preparations in 1962 and 1966, the guerrillas' perspective had been to train and accumulate supplies for an uprising to start in a matter of months. In 1971, however, the goal of the guerrillas was to stay out of the National Guard's reach for a protracted period, patiently building up contacts and learning the territory, in preparation for a military campaign at some indefinite point in the future. José Valdivia, one of the original eight who entered the mountains during Holy Week of 1971, described the group's accomplishments in a 1980 interview: "For three years we were never detected, and we were never forced to enter into combat a single time. It seems that the jueces de mesta in the area did inform the Guard that people were going by at night, that they had seen lights, but the Guard never bothered to do anything."[2]

Henry Ruiz outlined his philosophy of guerrilla warfare in a 1980 interview in which he called the montaña "a crucible in which the best revolutionaries were forged." Ruiz explained that guerrillas were never able to integrate themselves into the campesino population until "we arrived in the montaña with the idea of staying the rest of our lives," prepared to share the rough homes and work of the population, to become just another family member. He worked through family networks, winning the trust, if not the political agreement, of heads of households who could put the newcomers in touch with relatives. Peasant support made it possible, according to Ruiz, for guerrilla leader Víctor Tirado to sustain his small group "for nine months with just five córdobas in his pocket," and for Ruiz himself to keep his band in the mountains with little or no financial support from the cities. "With the campesinos providing our food and the city sending only a little clothing and our boots, we were able to survive." Ruiz, like the majority of the guerrilla nucleus of the early 1970s, was of urban working-class background, but he learned to be a farmer. "We even reached the point of having to grow and harvest our own food in the montaña." Several of the guerrilla leaders, including Ruiz, Tirado, and René Tejada, developed long-term relationships with peasant women, who bore their children in the mountains.[3]

Although the guerrilla band could survive indefinitely this way without losing any members in combat, it could hardly be regarded as waging revolutionary war. Fonseca later called the groups in the mountains between 1971 and 1974 "pre-*guerrilla* nuclei." Ruiz's evaluation of the guerrillas' accomplishments was more positive: by 1972, he boasted, "we had discovered the secret of organizing campesinos," and "we had the general panorama all ready." But some of the guerrillas had begun to complain that they never brought down a single enemy soldier, and to suspect that the reason the Guardia did not bother following up on reports of guerrilla activity was that they did not consider the rebels much of a threat. As early as 1973, Carlos Fonseca made reference to this frustration—which fed the factional infighting of the early 1970s—and acknowledged that the unit in the mountains was accomplishing very little.

The FSLN's successful hostage-taking raid in Managua in December 1974 produced a spurt of military actions in the montaña. In January 1975 a squad led by Carlos Agüero attacked the Waslala cuartel. The FSLN suffered no casualties in this, its most ambitious military operation ever in the mountains, and about ten guardsmen were killed, most or all of them by their own comrades in the confusion of the surprise attack. Shortly afterward, the town of Río Blanco was briefly occupied by Sandinista forces. But the euphoria was short-lived. By the spring of 1975, the military situation of the

FSLN and its peasant supporters was deteriorating. The National Guard increased its presence in the area and launched a wave of repression, carrying out bombing raids against villages suspected of collaboration with the guerrillas. Several hundred peasants, including many women and children, were killed during this period. Many of these civilian casualties had never had any contact with the guerrillas. In September 1975, in an effort to show that it was not completely unable to defend its supporters, the FSLN organized an ambush of a National Guard patrol and managed to kill a dozen Guardia. In the immediate aftermath of this ambush, however, two of the most experienced guerrilla leaders were captured and killed. By the end of 1975, according to a survivor, the guerrilla contingent "was absolutely incapable of taking any offensive action . . . and all we could do was flee and flee, and they killed a lot of us that way." By the first months of 1976, according to another guerrilla:

> The Guard began to realize that we were running away from combat, they began to pick up war matériel we left behind—knapsacks containing money and food and radios. And they began to emerge from their barracks and set up a strategic circle around us, starting by cutting off our access to our supply routes, and establishing control over the zones leading into the montaña.[4]

Fonseca, like GPP leader Henry Ruiz, had a somewhat romantic view of the innate rebelliousness of the Nicaraguan campesino. The Sandinistas even took a racist and derogatory term that landowners used for Indian peasants and turned it into a term of proud self-identification for themselves and an affectionate description of their favorite collaborators.[5] Fonseca believed that "the combative traditions of the Nicaraguan people . . . are more alive in the campo and the montaña than they are in the city. The campesino is less exposed to the influence of the ruling ideology." Equally important, whereas Sandino represented history for city dwellers, he was "a living presence in the campo, and even more so in the montaña."[6]

Fonseca's approach to the peasantry was, however, more political than that of the GPP, and he did not share that tendency's view that the coming Sandinista revolution would be fundamentally a peasant revolution. Fonseca told an interviewer in 1970 that the Sandinistas were

> convinced that the campesino of Nicaragua is by his very nature a rebel. But what is absolutely crucial is that we learn how to convert this rebellious spirit into action. All our years of struggle have taught us that just because a campesino is rebellious doesn't mean he is ready to stand

up to the dictatorship, for that he needs to master the art of turning this rebelliousness into action.

It had taken the Sandinistas some time, Fonseca continued, to learn that they could not just arrive from outside and impose "artificial methods" on peasants. The key was organizing campesinos to fight on their own behalf, he insisted, not just convincing them to support what the guerrillas were doing. "Just because campesinos support us, that doesn't mean the guerrillas are going to win. It is crucial to know how to advance and organize this support. *And even more, we have to carry out overall political work to get the masses in general ready to wage a war.*"[7]

It was more important for the FSLN to have its eyes on *todo el pueblo*, "the masses in general," than to strive for the support of the entire peasantry. "We don't believe there has to be unanimous support for us among the campesinos in order to initiate the next stage of the struggle. We think some may be lukewarm toward the struggle, and there will even be others who are confused or downright hostile." In the final analysis, it was the working class, not the peasantry, that would lead the Nicaraguan revolution, according to Fonseca, "because the revolutionary virtues of the peasants of our villages and mountains will just be passive qualities, without the presence of the proletarian guerrillero who has worked in one of the major capitalist enterprises, and of the student who comes from a working-class background or has been sufficiently proletarianized."[8]

The guerrillas got their best response from peasant contacts on the issue of land reform. Omar Cabezas, who entered the montaña in 1974, started conversations by asking campesinos who owned the land they were working, and he found that nearly every peasant could tell the story of how his grandfather or great-grandfather had lost the family land to a rancher or plantation owner. According to Cabezas, the Sandinistas talked to peasants about the class struggle and tried to "awaken in them their dream about the land."

"But we never promised the campesinos a land reform," he went on emphatically. "Never! What we did was urge the campesinos to struggle—we told them they would only get land reform by fighting for it." This was in the tradition of Carlos Fonseca, who, according to his guide in 1966 and 1967, never told peasants the FSLN would give them land, but rather that it would take a "long, hard, and bloody struggle," in which "some would go into the mountains to fight and others would stay at home, organizing unions to struggle for the rights of campesinos."[9]

Most peasants the Sandinistas met in the remote montaña could not read or write. Infant mortality was high, and the guerrillas frequently came upon a family mourning a dead baby. Building schools and clinics in the mountains was almost as important as the land issue for the FSLN and its peasant contacts. Fonseca once saw Tomás Borge and Germán Pomares teaching a group of young peasants to load and break down weapons, and told them to "also teach them to read." Pomares, a guerrilla leader from a peasant family, learned to read in the ranks of the FSLN. The FSLN organized reading classes for illiterate peasant and worker recruits, giving lessons in urban safe houses, in the mountains, and even in prison. Marlene López, a fifteen-year-old *guerrillera* in the mountains near Zinica in 1976, received lessons from Fonseca himself. "And Carlos was the one who finished teaching me to read, because he always made sure that those of us who were campesinos had to learn how to read and write."[10]

At one point, Fonseca even sent a student to teach a single peasant family to read and write. Leopoldo Ochoa Pérez, a longtime peasant collaborator, involved his whole family in protecting the rebels from the National Guard. His children learned to make rough brooms for sweeping away guerrilla tracks and to lead farm animals over the paths the guerrillas had taken. On discovering that none of the children could read, Fonseca promised to send a teacher, and according to Ochoa, ten days later, "a young kid with plenty of book-learning" arrived at the house.[11] But Fonseca did not see this as the solution to illiteracy in the countryside, and he may have sent the student to live with the Ochoa family as much for what he would learn as for what he would teach. Two decades had passed since the young editor of *Segovia* had urged his fellow students in Matagalpa to go into the fields to teach reading to peasants and coffee pickers. As Fonseca wrote in his 1968 "Message to Revolutionary Students," and as the FSLN guerrillas explained to campesinos, only the state could provide schools and clinics in the countryside, and it would never be done by a government that represented the rich landowners. Like land reform, health and education could only be won through a "long, hard and bloody struggle" on the part of campesinos themselves, as part of a nationwide uprising of todo el pueblo.

The relationship of the Nicaraguan peasantry to the church varied greatly. Especially in the remote regions, peasants rarely saw a priest, and many had never been inside a church. Most couples were not officially married, and few infants were baptized. At the same time, most rural people considered themselves Catholic, or, in the eastern regions, Moravian, and the traditions of these religions played an important role in popular festivals. The FSLN guerrillas met some deeply religious peasants who refused to help because their priests and pastors had warned them against the rebels. Sometimes the Sandinistas argued against church doctrines that discouraged peasants from fighting to change their lives. One longtime collaborator summarized what he had learned from Fonseca as follows: "Carlos taught us that if we were poor it was not because it was God's will but rather because in this world there are oppressed people and there are oppressors." Leonel Espinosa, who operated between the northern town of Ocotal and the montaña proper, has said that the guerrillas learned to expect different responses from different religious denominations. The Franciscan-organized Delegates of the Word, for example, tended to see the world as divided into rich and poor and would often carry messages for the guerrillas, but nothing but hostility could be expected from the Jehovah's Witnesses. In a 1969 letter, Fonseca referred to Dominican clergy as "our close brothers." Some guerrillas found that "the most conscious" of their peasant contacts "looked for religious solutions during dead times, when there was nothing going on politically. But when they find out the Frente is coming, they throw away their Bibles." And not all peasants were religious, even during "dead times." According to Espinosa, "In the same zone there were campesinos who were really advanced; who would ask us, 'So, what's going on in Cuba? Tell me what it's really like there, don't come talking to me about stupid things.'"[12]

By October 1976, Fonseca had his own experience with the network of peasant collaborators built up by the FSLN guerrillas in the montaña. In his last major writing, he called for a more political approach to peasant contacts, highlighting shortcomings that, he said, "it will be fatal for us to ignore." He complained about alleged collaborators who "don't even know the name of our organization," who thought the guerrillas were "some kind of left-wing Conservatives," and who "mix their sympathy for our combatants with illusions in the traditional politicians of the bourgeois opposition." He pointed out that the FSLN had not been involved in any mass mobilizations in the countryside since 1964, and that winning the collaboration of individual peasants "must never be confused in any way with the mobilization of thousands of campesinos."[13]

Fonseca, following Che Guevara, believed that the struggle itself transformed men and women into better human beings as they acquired a higher level of consciousness and discipline. Both thought that a "new man" and "new woman" would begin to emerge as the old oppressive structures were swept away. Although similar in some ways to religious concepts of self-sacrifice and individual fulfillment, Fonseca's view of the "new man" had more to do with patriotism and social class than with theology.

Nicaragua cannot be saved by politicians who represent the exploiting classes, nor by landlords, large merchants, industrial magnates, or the press that defends them all. The new world cannot be created by those who make men into beasts of burden. The new world can only be created by those who try to make every man a brother. Such were Augusto César Sandino, Karl Marx, Ernesto "Che" Guevara.[14]

For Fonseca, more than for Guevara, approximating the "new man" implied strict standards of personal and sexual behavior and the avoidance of "indulgences" such as drinking and smoking. Photographs of Fonseca and Guevara project a very different image: only one picture of Fonseca shows him smiling, and there are none of him enjoying a cigar.

Strict norms of personal behavior were imposed in the Nicaraguan underground for security reasons as well as ideological ones. In mid-1969, the clandestine structure was nearly destroyed when a member of the DN, Efraín Sánchez Sancho, broke every security rule in his pursuit of a young woman. Stalking the compañera for romantic reasons, he tangled with and killed an OSN officer who had her under political surveillance. Several known Sandinistas had to take refuge in foreign embassies or go underground, at a time when the FSLN was desperately trying to rebuild its shattered apparatus after the killing of Julio Buitrago.

Even before this incident, Sánchez had a reputation as a womanizer and drinker, problems Fonseca addressed in a letter written from San José, Costa Rica.

> Benito tells me you have committed some personal error that has led you to ignore your political duties, and he is right to be concerned. . . . I just want to remind you of one thing. It is that we must learn how to become new men in a full sense. It is not easy. In the times we are going through, our personal conduct is extremely important. We have to understand the simplicity and honesty of the masses. The great helmsman [Sandino] was right in taking as a model the purity of the campesino. . . . I think a guideline that can help us get through moments of confusion is to think about whether certain personal attitudes are going to help resolve the problems we face. We have to avoid doing things that just give us pleasure as individuals but do not benefit our collective self.

This short letter reveals several different aspects of Fonseca's view on morality: security considerations, the collective good over selfish pleasure, the class basis of ethics and especially the ideal of the pure campesino, and the examples set by Che and Sandino. In other writings, he raised an additional factor: high moral standards were part of the debt revolutionaries owed to the movement's martyrs.[15]

Revolutionary ethics were considered crucial for the urban fighter, as shown by the negative example of Efraín Sánchez. For both Fonseca and Guevara, however, the "new man" was forged in the most accelerated way in the rural guerrilla band. Fonseca sometimes used a different word to describe this process—he said the montaña "proletarianized" the guerrilla fighter. The mountains taught recruits discipline, tested their level of political commitment, and forged the kind of human solidarity that came from risking one's life to help comrades. The best demonstration of what the FSLN had accomplished in fifteen years of struggle, Fonseca said in the mid-1970s, was that "we have been able to field a column of combatants made of steel." One of the advantages of the montaña, he went on, was that

> the difficult material conditions put to the test in a matter of days a combatant's humanity and revolutionary fiber, something that often took much longer in the city. And in addition, the montaña makes it possible for those who have the necessary moral and revolutionary qualities to strengthen these attributes.[16]

That the montaña could "proletarianize" new recruits did not mean, according to Fonseca, that commanders should be indifferent to the class and ethnic origins of their soldiers. In 1976 Fonseca noted "with concern and even alarm the fact that the guerrilla units in the mountains do not include representatives of the exploited from the various regions of the country and from the different productive sectors where the workers are exploited to the very marrow of their bones."[17] Fonseca's admission of "alarm" suggests that the class composition of the rebel army was not just of theoretical importance but had more immediate military implications. His complaint about "the various regions of the country" could refer to the fact that the Afro-Nicaraguans and Miskito Indians of the Atlantic Coast were virtually absent from the guerrilla bands.

Many recruits to the guerrilla ranks came from the university. One of the first things that students, especially those from middle-class backgrounds, learned in the mountains was humility. "I arrived in the mountains from the city accustomed to giving orders," explained student leader Omar Cabezas.

> I was used to being in charge, and they put a campesino—who was illiterate no less!—in charge of *me*. . . . The way I looked at it, here I was,

having read all there was to read about dialectical materialism, mastered the Latin American school of sociology, etc.—and I get to the mountain and the first thing they do is send me to collect firewood. And I had never held a machete in my life!

Bayardo Arce was another student with a reputation as a powerful orator:

I was used to speeches that lasted hours, but I found out that all a campesino would give me was ten minutes to explain everything. And at the end I would ask, "So, what do you say?" And he would answer, "Fine, there will be a little tortilla here for you whenever you come by." Period. I felt like my whole scheme of things had just collapsed.

At first Arce did not even know what to wear in the countryside—he started out dressed like the kind of campesino "who only exists in folklore."[18]

New recruits—workers and peasants as well as students—went through a month or more of hard physical and military training when they first entered the mountains. They carried heavy packs up and down steep hills, forded rivers, and learned to keep ammunition and reading material dry in a downpour. Francisco Rivera, an instructor in the mid-1970s, said that most of his charges were male peasants in their teens, but that in several courses he trained "women of various ages, who were not inferior to the men in any way and turned out to be fantastic students."[19]

Although the guerrilla units always tried to organize classes on Marxism and Nicaraguan history, life in the mountains was overwhelmingly taken up with basic survival. The search for food and water consumed an enormous amount of time and energy and often determined the guerrilla band's movements. "Our worst enemy was hunger," a campesino guide said of the 1963 Ríos Coco y Bocay operation. "We went entire days without eating anything, until we managed to hunt a tapir or wild boar or monkey or come upon a small palm called a *maquenque* or find honey in a bees' nest."[20] The guerrillas tried to store food in their supply caches, or *buzones,* and to persuade friendly peasants to sell them food, but when high rivers or National Guard patrols cut the guerrillas off from these sources, they survived on what they found in the wilderness.

Under these conditions, sharing and showing self-restraint with food became a measure of a guerrilla's ethical stature. Dora María Tellez, who commanded a guerrilla unit in the late 1970s, explained:

It got so that it was a serious problem if somebody would eat a half teaspoon more sugar than someone else . . . and a crime of enormous proportions if someone took two extra swallows of water from a canteen that had to do for a whole squad. . . . Every little weakness you have comes out under these circumstances: either you think about the collective good, or else you eat that half-teaspoon of sugar. The montaña forces you to overcome your personal weaknesses, or else you leave.[21]

A guerrilla commander got the same rations as anyone else, and Carlos Fonseca, like Che Guevara, often tried to give away part of his allotment.

The only guerrillas who received extra food were those who were sick or wounded. The most debilitating guerrilla diseases were diarrhea and a skin disorder known as "mountain leprosy." Seriously disabled combatants were taken to a collaborator's house to recuperate or sometimes evacuated from the mountains to receive medical care. Juan de Dios Muñoz, a young worker once described as "someone who didn't belong to our era, someone who represented the future," refused to leave the montaña for treatment in Cuba or the Soviet Union, even after he had lost one eye to a National Guard bullet while trying to cover his retreating comrades.[22]

Carlos Fonseca did not suffer from chronic health problems like the asthma that sometimes left Che Guevara unable to walk during the Congo and Bolivia guerrilla campaigns. Fonseca had toughened up considerably in the years since the chiefs of the El Chaparral operation thought him too weak to participate. His eyesight had continued to deteriorate, however, and he was nearly blind in dim light or darkness. Hugo Torres, who crossed the river from Honduras into Nicaragua with Fonseca in the fall of 1975, was concerned about his commander's poor vision.

> Carlos had serious problems with his eyesight. Serious problems! Very serious! He was nearly blind. In the montaña he had to walk holding on to the shoulder of the compañero in front of him. I really don't think they had considered this question of his myopia when they asked him to go up into the montaña. Especially since in the mountain good eyesight is crucial. Absolutely crucial![23]

The guerrillas were human beings, not just fighting machines, and they celebrated birthdays and Christmas in the mountains with special food. Except when communications were completely broken, the FSLN network in the cities tried to send a Christmas packet into the mountains for each guerrilla unit, containing at least some cookies and Kool-Aid, and when possible a bottle of rum. Especially after military defeats, despair sometimes overcame the guerrillas—many of whom were still in their teens. One combatant, who served under Fonseca in his last campaign, paraphrased the commander's attempts to lift their spirits:

> Listen, guys, when you are sad, discouraged, demoralized, when you want to run off and get away from it all, when you feel like crying, just remember that nobody forced you to get involved in this, that we are all here voluntarily. And think about the thousands of children who are out there begging, barefoot and half naked, think about the injustice of poverty, think about how the bosses aren't going to give up because they feel like it, and about how we are the only alternative for the despised and exploited, the only hope they have in the world.[24]

In the harsh material conditions of the montaña, where the life of a guerrilla literally depended on the watchfulness and support of his or her comrades, strong personal bonds developed. Che Guevara was especially close to two or three individuals who fought at his side first in the Sierra Maestra, then a few years later in the Congo, and then again in Bolivia.[25] Although Fonseca appears never to have developed this kind of strong personal relationship with any of his fellow combatants, choosing instead to maintain a certain aloofness, close bonds did develop among some of the Sandinista guerrillas. Cabezas has described his friendship with his first instructor in the mountains, René Tejada, and his anguish at Tejada's death in battle. In the case of Tejada and Cabezas, this special relationship involved two young men from similar backgrounds. But Francisco Rivera, the youngest of ten children of an Estelí washerwoman, developed the same kind of trust and respect for Claudia Chamorro, whose aristocratic background had initially led Rivera to dismiss her as "una niña high life." Cut off from the rest of the troop in late 1976, Rivera and Chamorro wandered through the mountains for two months, hungry, hotly pursued by the National Guard, and forced to depend on each other in ways they had never anticipated. Rivera recalled later:

> She had a terrible time with her menstrual periods and bled very heavily, and she ran out of the supplies she had brought into the mountains with her. . . . What we did was get some old rags from some campesinos . . . and when they were bloody, she would wash them in the river and dry them on branches. We would have to wait until they were dry and she could put them on again, before we could resume our march. She would take care of this, and I would stand guard, with my gun cocked, a little ways off so as not to embarrass her. Once, when she was washing out the

rags, the National Guard came upon us. I stood them off, while she collected her things, and we both got away safely.

On 9 January 1977, Chamorro was killed in a shootout with the National Guard, shouting for Rivera to retreat while she covered him. She was twenty-four years old. Rivera in his testimonio described her as "braver in combat and in death than many men I have known—and I have known quite a few."[26]

The number of guerrilleras had grown slowly since Gladys Baez first joined the Pancasán operation in 1967. By the mid 1970s, the guerrilla bands commonly contained one or possibly two female combatants, mostly from peasant backgrounds.[27] Recruiting peasant women as soldiers and collaborators involved breaking down obstacles, both practical and psychological, that male supporters did not face. Isabel Loáisiga, an activist from La Tronca in the mountains above Matagalpa, explained in a 1986 interview how Carlos Fonseca persuaded her to get involved:

> He talked to us about cooperatives and said that when we won the war we were going to be able to return the land to the campesinos, and that the children of workers and peasants would go to school and would become professors and doctors, that it would not be only the children of the bourgeoisie who would go to university but also the children of us campesinos. He was very gentle with us. Don't get the idea that bringing us into the movement was something brusque—I don't think any of us would have gone along with that. One step at a time, he explained the importance of campesinos getting ourselves organized.

Loáisiga said Fonseca told peasant women, "The most important thing is for the campesinas to understand that they have to participate, that they have to free themselves from this mistaken idea their husbands have planted in their heads, which keeps them from working in the organizations and understanding they have the same rights. These are things we have to change."

Fonseca invited Loáisiga to join the guerrillas, but when she raised the problem of her small children, he agreed that she could remain in her village and work as a collaborator. The work the young woman carried out for the FSLN, smuggling weapons to combatants and distributing revolutionary propaganda, was probably as dangerous for her and her children as if she had become a guerrilla. She hid bullets in her children's clothes, and once, when the National Guard started to search the passengers of a bus on which she was traveling, she hid a pistol under her baby daughter's bottom, in diapers "nicely loaded with shit."[28]

Fonseca's attitude toward women fighters was contradictory. On the one hand, he tried to give female recruits, especially campesinas, confidence in their ability and right to participate in the struggle. On the other, he thought the presence of unmarried young women in the guerrilla band could cause problems of morale and security, and he had a very traditional attitude toward sexual relations outside of marriage. A revealing incident in the montaña during the last months of Fonseca's life is described in the testimonio of guerrilla Francisco Rivera. Celestina López, an attractive young campesina fighter with the nom de guerre of Mayra, entered the mountains with Fonseca in March 1976. Fonseca was disturbed about the attention she received from some of the male guerrillas, and at one point Mayra mentioned to him that she had been involved in a romantic relationship with Rivera the year before.

According to Rivera, Fonseca—"who was a very upright guy in matters of the heart"—asked him his intentions regarding Mayra and instructed him to talk to the young woman "and let me know what you decide." When Rivera came back and reported the two had decided to "live together," Fonseca said, "These things are very serious, especially when they involve Sandinista militants. So if the two of you have come to an agreement, let's go ahead and formalize the marriage." Then, continued Rivera, "he sat us down in front of him, and spent about two hours explaining the meaning of marriage for the guerrilla, how revolutionaries should treat women, and he urged us to reflect on what we were doing and think it over, because once we got married we always had to respect each other, that she had to respect me and that I also had to respect her." The rest of the guerrillas were assembled, and Fonseca, holding the bride and groom by the hands, "declared us man and wife by the laws of the revolution."

In spite of his sermon about mutual respect, Fonseca in his capacity as guerrilla commander did not treat the new couple on an equal basis. Rivera explained:

> From that time on, whenever she was supposed to go out on a mission with other compañeros, Carlos would always check with me first and only order her to go if I agreed. And even though I always said that she was my companion but before she was ever my companion she was a militant of the FSLN, he still went on asking me every time, because that's just the way he was, very formal and respectful.[29]

Fonseca did not, however, ask López's permission before sending her new husband on a mission.

Fonseca's mentor on questions related to guerrilla warfare, and especially the moral qualities of the guerrilla fighter, was Che Guevara. But his approach to matrimony in the mountains—or anywhere else—did not come from Che. An interview with the first female to fight under Guevara's command appeared in the Cuban magazine *Bohemia* in 1967. Like Loáisiga and López, Oniria Gutiérrez was a teenager when she joined the guerrilla army, and she came from a peasant family. Guevara was reluctant to admit her and did so only after she argued strenuously with him. After the first few days, he ordered her to stop washing and mending her male comrades' clothes, as she had started doing on her own initiative. All this behavior would have been completely in character for Fonseca. But he would never have responded the way Che did when Gutiérrez later mentioned she was about to get married. Guevara exploded, "What do you mean get married?! What you have to do is study so that you can do something useful!"[30]

Fonseca believed that the tie of matrimony was almost as serious as the commitment revolutionaries made when they joined the FSLN. According to an FSLN leader who knew him in the underground and in exile, "Carlos always insisted that it was possible to be completely devoted to the Revolution and still find a way to fulfill one's duty to family and children."[31] But it was easier for Fonseca to be "completely devoted to the Revolution" than it was for other Sandinista militants who were parents, especially those who were single mothers. He had a wife who was not involved in politics, and she took care of their children.

When Carlos Fonseca entered the montaña in March 1976, the military situation for the guerrillas was extremely grave. The Somoza government had just launched a counterinsurgency offensive called Aguila Sexta, involving troops from other Central American countries and supported by advisers from the U.S. military. National Guard presence in the guerrilla zone was reinforced with six hundred additional troops, organized into squads of fifteen to eighteen men, with helicopter support to enable them to close in rapidly when rebels were sighted. Through the late spring and early summer of 1976, the Guardia moved eastward from Matagalpa province in a combing operation, following roughly the same route as Fonseca's small band had traveled in March.

Before Aguila Sexta, the guerrillas had noticed that guardsmen would track them for a certain distance and then give up. But at the end of April 1976, the National Guard followed a small guerrilla band deep into the forest, killing a longtime leader of the FSLN who had entered the mountains only a few days before. In the attack, the guerrillas lost "twelve backpacks full of ammunition and special food for the wounded, and—the worst thing of all—the security of our route leading to the Iyás River." Around the same time, guerrilla Roberto "Tito" Chamorro—Claudia's brother—was taken out to Matagalpa because he claimed to be sick. He surrendered to the National Guard and revealed everything he knew about the FSLN in the mountains, including routes, names of collaborators, caches of supplies, and pseudonyms.[32] Chamorro had been escorted to Matagalpa by Edgard "the Cat" Munguía, the famous student activist who recruited Omar Cabezas and was the first FSLN member elected president of the CUUN. Munguía was ambushed and killed after he returned to the mountains.

Roberto Chamorro could not reveal, because he did not know, that Carlos Fonseca was already in the mountains, on his way to join the group Chamorro had just left. By the end of March, the FSLN leader had reached the rural township, or *comarca,* of El Chile, south of Waslala, having made his way eastward from the Matagalpa area without being detected. In May he joined the main guerrilla band in the area, consisting of just over a dozen combatants, and took over the command from Francisco Rivera.

For seven months, from the end of March until early November, Fonseca and his followers moved around a relatively small area between El Chile and the Zinica hill—a distance of perhaps twenty-five miles. Despite their desperate efforts to avoid the hundreds of National Guard in the area, the rebels' camp was discovered in late August. A shootout ensued, in which Fonseca was slightly wounded in the foot, but no guerrillas died.

The National Guard had circulated posters bearing Fonseca's picture throughout the region of guerrilla activity. Under these circumstances, his physical distinctiveness represented a serious liability. Henry Ruiz, describing his own years as a guerrilla, said that he became so well known that he could travel only at night: "It was enough for somebody to see a fair-skinned guy pass by, a 'whitey' whose color stuck out, and it would be reported to the Guard, who would start to terrorize the campesinos, asking from house to house, following my tracks, etc." But Ruiz, although fair skinned, is short and stocky, with dark hair and eyes. If it was difficult for him to blend in with the population of the area, it was infinitely more so for Carlos Fonseca, over six feet tall, with pale skin, light blue eyes, and his trademark thick glasses. Traveling after dark was no solution for Fonseca, because of his night blindness. The campesino who led Fonseca into the mountains worried about the noise his charge made as he stumbled and fell in the darkness.[33] Fonseca, who turned forty in June 1976, was also getting a little old for the conditions of life in the mountains.

Fonseca remained in this extremely dangerous area for seven months, because an important meeting was scheduled to take place on 15 November on the banks of the Iyás River. Henry Ruiz was supposed to come down from his Puyús Mountain base camp, and other leaders ascend from the cities for a summit, presided over by Fonseca himself, to address the issues of the split in the movement. It does not seem that other leaders of the FSLN gave this meeting the same importance Fonseca did. At the end of July, he dispatched a small group of guerrillas to remind the FSLN leaders in the cities of the urgency of the meeting, but the squad fell into a National Guard ambush, and there is no evidence the urban leaders ever set out for the mountains. In October an experienced fighter, sent across the Iyás River to make sure Ruiz was starting his descent, brought back a report that Modesto had not begun his journey.[34]

During the first week of November 1976, Fonseca's band of ten men and two women was camped near Zinica. As commander—and over the objections of the others—Fonseca divided the guerrilla unit into four small groups. He sent one northward to try to open up a new route into the region from Honduras, and another west to meet the urban leaders expected to attend the 15 November meeting. Both parties left camp on 5 November. Fonseca assigned a third group, including Rivera and Claudia Chamorro, to remain in Zinica, and Fonseca declared that he would begin the five-day march to the Iyás meeting spot, accompanied only by Cresencio Aguilar, a sixteen-year-old campesino recruited to the FSLN the year before, and Benito Carvajal, a teenage worker from León who had spent just six months in the mountains.

Fonseca carried a packet of four letters from other guerrillas, wrapped in plastic for protection from rivers and rain. These letters, seized after Fonseca's death and transcribed by the National Guard in Waslala, give a sad picture of the state of the war in the montaña. One was a report on a series of misadventures—missed appointments, bad passwords, and security snafus. The letter writer was frustrated and angry about the death of guerrilla Edgar Munguia: "This shows we have to give the Guardia what it deserves. I hope we can do it soon, and we'll show those sons of bitches what we are made of. I hope my language doesn't offend you and that you hear what I'm saying, because it is high time we teach them a lesson." The other three letters were all semiliterate, written in a peasant vernacular, with additional errors in spelling and grammar introduced by the National Guard transcribers. All the letters plead for items urgently needed by the FSLN guerrillas, including plastic sheeting, underwear, powdered soup for the sick, and, in every letter, medicine for the wounded and disabled.[35]

On Sunday, 7 November, at about seven in the evening, Fonseca and his teenage companions set out in the darkness and pouring rain. Although the band in the mountains did not know it, two important leaders of the FSLN had already been killed by the National Guard that day in separate incidents in Managua. Dead were National Directorate member Eduardo Contreras, the commander of the December 1974 raid on the Castillo house, and underground organizer Roberto Huembes of the Proletarian Tendency.

Just a few hours after he left camp and only a mile or so away, Fonseca fell into a National Guard ambush.[36] A peasant informer known as "El Pinto" had reported guerrillas moving through the area. The Guard set up an ambush near the house of a peasant named Matías López Maldonado. Forced to wait in a back room, López heard a gunfight lasting an hour or more. Fonseca and Carvajal were shot in the firefight. Aguilar escaped but was tracked down and killed two days later.

When López emerged from his house the morning of Monday, 8 November, he saw two bodies on the ground and watched the guardsmen shoot them again. The Guard ordered several campesinos, including López, to retrieve the bodies and take them on muleback to a nearby chapel. The peasants all said later that they believed Carlos Fonseca had been alive until morning. His body, unlike Carvajal's, was still warm, and fresh blood flowed from the wound in his chest, but the blood around his massive leg wound was dry. At the chapel, the guardsmen cut off Fonseca's hands to send to Managua for identification. They also removed C$ 10,000 from his pack and divided it up among themselves. Covering his chest wound with a black plastic sheet, they took the photographs that were later released to the press. The Guard then ordered López and the other campesinos to take the bodies away for burial.

Sometime in the course of the day on Monday, the authorities identified Fonseca's corpse. President Somoza was at the symphony in Managua that night when a high-ranking National Guard officer rushed in and told him, "General, the communist Carlos Fonseca is dead. I swear to you that this time he's dead, if we are wrong again, you can kill us." According to an observer, the president jumped up, grabbed the messenger by the shoulders, demanded, "Say it again! Say it again!" and rushed out of the theater.[37]

In his prose poem *Carlos, the Dawn Is No Longer beyond Our Reach*, Tomás Borge remembers the jubilant commander of Tipitapa prison coming personally to his cell to tell him the leader of the FSLN was dead. "You are wrong, colonel," Borge says he answered, "Carlos Fonseca is one of the dead who never die." The colonel left muttering, "You guys are something else." On 11 November, at a meeting in Havana, the FSLN officially confirmed Fonseca's death.[38]

The Revolution of 1979

10

Many Nicaraguans did not believe the Somoza government's news release on 10 November 1976 claiming that Carlos Fonseca was dead. For one thing, this announcement had been made several times before. For another, in the popular imagination, Fonseca had acquired superhuman powers, and some people believed that he could not be killed or that he had the ability to make himself invisible or to change into a parrot or a monkey. Even after the FSLN confirmed the news of Fonseca's death a few days later, some refused to accept it.

The jubilant Somoza government had no doubts the FSLN would perish without its principal leader. The press office set out bottles of whiskey and vodka at the news conference announcing Fonseca's death, and GN colonels pressed journalists to join them in toast after toast, in spite of the early morning hour. The National Guard declared that Fonseca and Contreras' deaths reduced to about one hundred its list of "subversives"—including those already in custody—and confidently predicted the quick capture of those still at large.[1]

The FSLN cadres in the mountains and urban underground were devastated by the news of Fonseca's death. As 1976 came to a close and 1977 wore on, it began to seem as if the FSLN truly would not survive the loss. Other longtime leaders were killed: Carlos Agüero in the mountains in April, National Directorate member Pedro Aráuz near Managua in October. Henry Ruiz has described 1977 as the most difficult in the entire history of the FSLN; for more than a year, he was completely cut off from any contact with supporters outside the montaña. By the end of that year, the entire rural guerrilla "army" numbered only eleven.[2]

The factional divisions in the FSLN hardened. For two years after Fonseca died, the leaders of the three tendencies never came together for discussion, never attempted to resolve political disputes. The Prolonged People's War tendency (GPP) and the Insurrectional Tendency (TI, or terceristas) each had its own small guerrilla group: the first, led by Ruiz, was trying to avoid the National Guard in the deep montaña, and the second, led by Víctor Tirado, retreated across the Honduran border to reorganize. The GPP and the Proletarian Tendency (TP) each had its own student affiliate, its own network of Christian activists, its own farmworker and peasant allies. Each tendency had its own solidarity groups outside the country, in cities such as San Francisco, Mexico City, Havana, and San José.

Although all three tendencies identified themselves as followers of Carlos Fonseca, all were moving away from the program and strategy hammered out under Fonseca's leadership in the late 1960s and early 1970s. The Insurrectional Tendency took this process the furthest and merits the closest attention, because its program has been viewed by scholars as the program of the FSLN as a whole. The TI is generally assumed to have become the largest tendency in the FSLN in the period following Fonseca's death, although it is possible that the GPP or TP may have had more members and supporters active inside Nicaragua at certain points. Where the TI did have a clear majority was on the National Directorate. With the death of several GPP leaders and Carlos Fonseca and the isolation of Henry Ruiz, the functioning DN after 1976 consisted of Humberto Ortega, Daniel Ortega, and Víctor Tirado. The policy statements of these three tercerista leaders were always issued in the name of the FSLN National Directorate, although only Humberto had been a full member of the DN during Fonseca's lifetime.

The political approach underlying tercerista documents in 1977 and 1978 had much in common with the GPP proposal rejected by Humberto Ortega and Carlos Fonseca in 1973. The FSLN would concentrate its energies on the military task of defeating the National Guard, with the expectation that the bourgeois opposition would dominate the post-Somoza government but allow some FSLN representation. This kind of division of labor was alien to Fonseca's view of a "Sandinista popular revolution" of mobilized workers and peasants led by the FSLN. If the removal of Somoza left the traditional parties in power, Fonseca had warned over and over, the Nicaraguan masses would be once again, as in the time of Sandino, denied their revolutionary victory.

Although strongly committed to armed struggle, the tercerista program resembled the politics of the PSN and other pro-Moscow Communist parties in its policy of broad multiclass alliances and its "two-stage" theory of revolution. According to this theory, the first stage of revolution in an underdeveloped country like Nicaragua would be led by the national bourgeoisie and win independence from imperialism or dictatorial rule, which would then open up the possibility of a second socialist stage in which the working class would play the dominant role. Carlos Fonseca had subscribed to this theory when he belonged to the PSN, but he had argued strenuously against it since at least the mid-1960s. In *Hora Cero,* written in 1969, he said only the support of "broad popular layers" for the FSLN would be able to "prevent the opposition capitalist forces, which have proven their subservience to Yankee imperialism, from taking advantage of the chain of events unleashed by guerrilla warfare in order to grab political power for themselves."[3]

Perhaps this explains why Fonseca spent so much time polemicizing against the PSN in his last major contribution to the tendency debate before he left Cuba in 1975. The PSN was seriously weakened by this time and represented less competition to the FSLN than ever before. Yet Fonseca devoted much of a long lecture on the early history of the FSLN (the transcript runs to ninety pages) to explaining the political weakness of the PSN.[4]

Fonseca foresaw a time when "temporary or even momentary" alliances with opposition bourgeois groups might "advance the cause of building national anti-Somoza unity under the leadership of the exploited classes." But before the Sandinistas could consider entering into such alliances, he insisted, "it is absolutely necessary to have our own mass base, composed of people who don't listen to any other organization, who are free of any bourgeois influence, who have no interests except those of the exploited." Otherwise the revolutionaries risked ending up "nothing more than appendixes of the traditional political forces."[5]

In May 1977, the rump National Directorate of the Ortega brothers plus Tirado issued a sixty-page document called the "General Political-Military Platform of the FSLN," authored by Humberto Ortega and, according to the text, in preparation for a year. Although a picture of Carlos Fonseca appeared on the cover (after photos of Sandino and Rigoberto López Pérez), the document mentioned Fonseca only once, toward the end of a list of a dozen or so men who contributed to developing the program of the FSLN in the 1960s. A lengthy section on the history of the Nicaraguan revolutionary movement, starting with Sandino, never mentioned the Cuban revolution. Fonseca's sharp focus on mobilizing the working class and peasantry against Somoza and his refusal to concede a leading role to the bourgeois opposition was absent from the vision of the *Platforma General:*

The formidable force that will overthrow somocismo and install a revolutionary democratic popular government will consist of the workers, peasants, middle class, intellectuals, Christians, patriotic members of the military, professionals, small and medium-sized landowners and businessmen in the countryside and cities, the bourgeois opposition, patriotic and progressive individuals from the middle and upper classes, students, women, children, the elderly, Indians, blacks, whites and mestizos.[6]

Even more revealing is a revised version of the Historic Program published by the tercerista DN in 1978. Like Fonseca's 1969 version, it was called "Programa Sandinista," some of the enumerated points bore identical titles, and it used some of the same language. But a close reading shows the 1978 document to vary enough from the 1969 original to represent a different and substantially more moderate strategy. It dropped the word "Revolutionary" from its call for a "Democratic and Popular Government," promised only to nationalize property belonging to the Somoza family, and proposed a limited and vague land reform. Where the 1969 program demanded the immediate abolition of the National Guard and formation of a "Revolutionary, Patriotic and Popular Army" and armed popular militias, the tercerista program simply called for putting together a new army that would include some elements of the GN. The Historic Program pledged solidarity with Third World peoples struggling against U.S. imperialism, supported demands for withdrawal of U.S. military bases around the world, and championed the struggles of North American blacks against racism. The TI version never mentioned U.S. imperialism and said merely that postrevolution Nicaragua would "have relations with all the nations in the world." The terceristas' plank on development of the Atlantic Coast dropped the Historic Program's reference to the "odious discrimination" suffered by Miskito and Sumo Indians and blacks. Several sections of the 1978 tercerista program amounted to little more than liberal platitudes, such as the ideas that teachers and civil servants should be "treated better" and that water and power companies needed "honest and well-trained managers."[7] Although some scholars assume it represented the program of the Nicaraguan insurrection, it is likely that the TI's "Programa Sandinista" was virtually unknown inside Nicaragua, both before and after the 1979 revolution. The only place it can be found is in a book published in Colombia. The program published—and widely circulated—by the FSLN after the revolution was Fonseca's Historic Program of 1969.

The tendency led by Humberto Ortega was contradictory in nature, as it had been during Fonseca's lifetime. Politically it was the most moderate of the three groups—and far more conservative than Carlos Fonseca—but militarily it was the most aggressive. Fonseca had called this combination "militarism" and polemicized against it as a dangerous imbalance and lack of attention to political work directed toward the workers and peasants. But Fonseca was not against taking bold military action when it was politically justified, and he had also sharply criticized the GPP and Proletarian Tendency for their lack of military initiative.

The tendencies did not turn on each other with the kind of violence and constant public attacks that ripped apart other leftist movements around Latin America, but they did not collaborate, either. When tercerista commandos attacked three National Guard cuarteles in mid-October 1977, both the GPP and the TP condemned the actions; the proletarios calling them "*golpista* adventures . . . in the purest tradition of bourgeois military coups." The divisions among the three tendencies distressed and mystified rank-and-file members and contacts of the FSLN inside Nicaragua. The second volume of Omar Cabezas's testimonio describes the confusion and pain he suffered, torn between his loyalty to Ruiz and the GPP and his admiration for the tercerista guerrillas who were beginning to carry out military operations.[8]

By late 1977, recruitment to all three tendencies was accelerating in urban areas, although not in the montaña. The total membership of the Frente reached perhaps 150 to 200, and its influence and reputation were growing much faster than its size.[9] The growth of the revolutionary movement was a reflection—and also a cause—of a deepening political and social crisis for the Somoza dictatorship.

The origins of this crisis are often traced to the 1972 earthquake in Managua and Somoza's theft and misuse of relief aid. Several books about the Nicaraguan revolution begin with dramatic descriptions of the quake or otherwise suggest Somoza's fate was sealed when he denied other sections of the bourgeoisie their "fair" share of the reconstruction spoils.[10] Conservative and dissident Liberal politicians were increasingly vocal in their opposition to Somoza during the year or two after the quake, and the Catholic hierarchy took steps to end its decades-long support for the regime. The years 1973 and 1974 also saw increased activity by workers and students: strikes by construction and health care workers and by teachers, and building occupations and hunger strikes in support of political prisoners. In 1974, following Anastasio Somoza Debayle's election as president for an unprecedented seven-year term, several Conservative and dissident Liberal groups joined forces with the PSN and Social Christian Party in an opposition coalition called the Democratic Union of Liberation (Unión Democrática de Liberación, UDEL).

The idea that the 1972 earthquake represented the main turning point in the effort to remove Somoza from power flows from an overestimation of the role played by bourgeois and middle-class forces in the dictator's fall. The aftermath of the earthquake did exacerbate real economic and political conflicts between the Somoza family and other sections of the Nicaraguan bourgeoisie (although these tensions were somewhat calmed by a minor economic boom based on a rise in world market prices for Nicaraguan exports from 1974 to 1977, which benefited agro-export and commercial capital as a whole).[11] These interelite conflicts could conceivably have brought down the Somoza dictatorship, either through the election of a Conservative challenger in 1981, or—perhaps more likely—through a relatively bloodless coup by the bourgeois opposition and sections of the National Guard, with the tacit approval of the United States. Either of these developments would have had broad popular support. But neither happened. Instead Somoza was driven out of power by a massive popular insurrection that for a time called into question the future of capitalism in Nicaragua. The Nicaraguan revolution of 1979 cannot be understood by starting with the resentment of the non-Somocista bourgeoisie. It can only be understood by looking at the FSLN and its relationship to the Nicaraguan masses.

December 1974 represented as much of a turning point as December 1972 in the history of the Nicaraguan revolution. The FSLN's dramatic and successful hostage-taking raid of 27 December marked the reappearance of Sandinista guerrillas after several years of relative quiescence. As had been the case with the 1972 earthquake, it was Somoza's response to the 1974 raid, not the event itself, that produced a new political climate. The government immediately declared a state of siege and launched a wave of repression that resulted in an estimated three thousand deaths. The first targets were radical students, workers, and Catholic activists in the cities, but the majority of victims were campesinos suspected of aiding the guerrillas. The massive counterinsurgency drive in the countryside that succeeded in killing Carlos Fonseca also involved dropping bombs and napalm on settlements, burning peasant homes and fields, and disappearances, rapes, and incarceration in concentration camps. As news of this terror reached the cities, the desire to rid the nation of Somoza acquired new urgency, especially among the lower classes who were the principal targets of the repression, but also among middle-class Nicaraguans. Neither Tachito nor Tacho Somoza had ruled exclusively by violence; both had generally been able to convince significant sections of the population of their right to rule, through a combination of power sharing, economic policies that benefited the bourgeoisie as a whole, and populist appeals to workers. The repression of 1975 and 1976 seriously undermined the idea that Somoza had a moral right to govern Nicaragua or that he could continue to do so with any measure of stability. The increasing visibility of the FSLN, in spite of the repression, gave the bourgeois opposition yet another reason to hate Somoza. That government terror was spawning revolutionaries was at least as objectionable to them as Somoza's use of political power for unfair economic advantage.

The regime's crisis deepened, although not at a steady rate. In September 1977 Somoza lifted the state of siege imposed in December 1974, partly because he felt more secure in light of the economic recovery and near-annihilation of the rural guerrillas, but also in response to growing public pressure. New protest organizations sprang up, often with links to the FSLN. Sandinista women took the initiative in forming an organization called the Association of Women Confronting the National Problem (Asociación de mujeres ante la problemática nacional, AMPRONAC); everyone knew the "national problem" was Somoza. The association organized demonstrations against human rights violations, with a special focus on the abuse of peasant women by the Guardia and of female political prisoners in Somoza's jails. Christian activists in the Proletarian Tendency played a leading role in a dynamic new organization of agricultural labor, the Association of Rural Workers (Asociación de Trabajadores del Campo, ATC). The bourgeois opposition continued to look to the electoral arena. Pedro Joaquín Chamorro announced his intention to run for president in 1981 against a Liberal candidate already projected to be yet another Anastasio Somoza, the son of Tachito and grandson of Tacho.

The pace of events picked up dramatically in 1978, partly because of repressive actions by Somoza, partly because of FSLN initiatives, and partly because of semispontaneous mass actions. The bourgeois opposition was left trying to catch up with, and bring under its control, a rapidly radicalizing situation. It tried to carve out some space for itself in the political center, but in the increasingly polarized atmosphere of 1978 and 1979, which at times approached civil war, there was little ground to stand on in the center. On 10 January 1978, UDEL leader Pedro Joaquín Chamorro was assassinated on his way to work at *La Prensa*. Chamorro was the best-known oppositionist in the country and had been a prominent leader of the Conservative opposition for more than three decades. Protest demonstrations swept the country following his murder, and on 23 January the opposition business groups called a national protest strike. Initially projected to last "until Somoza resigns," the strike was instead called off abruptly in less than two weeks, after workers ignored the employers' strike slogan of "Don't Leave Your Homes" and instead organized militant street actions.

Sporadic protests continued in cities and towns around western Nicaragua in the aftermath of the Chamorro assassination. New forms of popular struggle took shape, became generalized over the course of the next year, and came to symbolize the Nicaraguan insurrection: raging street bonfires of smelly rubber tires, homemade Molotov cocktails and contact bombs, and cobblestone barricades to protect poor neighborhoods from GN tanks. Hundreds and then thousands of walls sprouted revolutionary slogans, sometimes signed by the FSLN-GPP or FSLN-TP. In February 1978, an anti-Somoza uprising organized by none of the three tendencies erupted in the indigenous community of Monimbó, located in the city of Masaya, only twenty miles from Managua.

In April a student strike closed Nicaragua's universities and 80 percent of its public and private high schools. In July crowds of cheering supporters gathered in several cities to greet members of Los Doce (The Twelve), a San-José–based group of pro-FSLN businessmen, intellectuals, and religious leaders, organized by the terceristas. The same month, popular Sandinista organizations, mostly influenced by the TP, coalesced to form the United People's Movement (Movimiento Pueblo Unido, MPU).

On 22 August 1978, two dozen tercerista guerrillas disguised as National Guard captured the National Palace in Managua, holding hostage 3,500 politicians and businessmen until Somoza agreed to release all fifty-nine FSLN members in prison. The daring action captured public and media attention, and the operation's "Commander Two" became an instant legend: "Dora María Tellez / twenty years old, / slight and pale / in her boots, her black beret, / her enemy uniform / a size too large. . . . Dora Maria / young warrior woman / who caused the tyrant's heart / to tremble in rage."[12] As the school bus carrying FSLN guerrillas and freed prisoners passed through working-class neighborhoods on its way to the airport, tens of thousands of residents came out to cheer them, some chanting, "Down with Somoza" and "Somoza to the gallows!"

Almost as challenging to the dictatorship was a semispontaneous uprising that erupted in Matagalpa at the end of August, because it represented a pattern that would be repeated in city after city over the next year. About five hundred high school students, supported by older residents, took control of much of the city, fighting the National Guard for five days before their rebellion was crushed by aerial bombing and the introduction of several thousand crack antiriot troops.[13] The insurgents wore red-and-black bandannas and chanted Sandinista slogans, but the uprising caught the FSLN by surprise. There was not a single FSLN cadre in the city of Matagalpa until some guerrillas who were nearby rushed into town to support the students.

During the second week of September 1978, FSLN guerrillas organized uprisings in a series of cities north and south of the capital, including Masaya, Chinandega, Diriamba, León, Jinotepe, and Estelí. The TI leadership initiated the September actions, which it called the "final offensive" against Somoza, but youths associated with all three tendencies fought and died in the rebellions, and most participants in the street battles were not affiliated to any tendency. Somoza responded with aerial bombing and artillery attacks, killing an estimated five thousand people.[14] Social and economic conditions reached desperate proportions following the crushing of the September uprisings. About fifty thousand refugees fled to neighboring Costa Rica, Honduras, and El Salvador. Food shortages were reported in several cities, and there was widespread unemployment—unusual for the harvest season— and sharp inflation.

In these conditions of fierce repression and social crisis, growing numbers of Nicaraguans came to see the FSLN as their organization and as the legitimate leadership of the fight against Somoza. Both the bourgeois opposition and the United States government were afraid that more moderate voices in the opposition would be swept aside and that the FSLN would end up with a leading role in the post-Somoza government. After years of dismissing the Sandinistas as an insignificant group of terrorists, irrelevant to Nicaraguan politics, the Conservatives and Social Christians suddenly found *themselves* considered less and less relevant. The moderate oppositionists had organized a new coalition, the Broad Opposition Front (Frente Amplio Opositor, FAO). But the legitimacy of the FAO came more from the presence of the pro-FSLN Los Doce than from the collection of Conservative, dissident Liberal, Social Christian, and Communist organizations. The other two FSLN tendencies belonged to a different coalition, the United People's Movement, or MPU, but the terceristas, who had a closer relationship with the bourgeois opposition, had assigned Los Doce to work in the more moderate FAO. (Los Doce functioned as the public face of the tercerista FSLN. Although it presented itself as an independent pro-FSLN group, its most prominent spokespeople were secretly members of the FSLN, and several others were fathers of FSLN militants.)

Carlos Fonseca had always warned the FSLN that the United States would try to block a revolution in Nicaragua, and he had criticized the bourgeois opposition for counting on the United States to help remove Somoza. Although Somoza still had his loyal supporters in the U.S. Congress—sometimes called "The Dirty Thirty"—by 1978 the administration of U.S. president Jimmy Carter wanted to see Somoza eased out of office and replaced by a democratic, nonrevolutionary government. Early in October 1978, the Carter administration formed an Organization of American States mediation committee called the Commission of Friendly Cooperation and Conciliation to try to defuse what the U.S. embassy in Nicaragua called a "dangerously polarized situation." The commission, made up of representatives of the United States, Guatemala, and the Dominican Republic, held a series of meetings with the moderate FAO and agreed on a proposal that Somoza relinquish the presidency to a successor he would name, with the National Guard to be kept intact and legislative power shared between the bourgeois opposition parties and Somoza's PLN. The plan included no role at all for the FSLN. The FSLN's Los Doce walked out of the FAO in protest and shortly afterward joined the MPU and others in a new coalition, the National Patriotic Front (Frente Patriótico Nacional, FPN).

The Carter administration had hoped to strengthen the FAO and reduce the influence of the Sandinistas, but the imposition on the FAO of a proposal that no wing of the FSLN could possibly accept had exactly the opposite effect. The departure of Los Doce stripped the FAO of its claim to represent the leadership of the anti-Somoza movement. Instead of a stronger FAO, there was a new radical coalition that represented all three wings of the FSLN plus the PLI and a splinter Social Christian party that had left the FAO with Los Doce. At the urging of the United States, FAO leader Alfonso Robelo attempted direct negotiations with Somoza after the collapse of the OAS mediation effort, which produced no results except the further discrediting of the bourgeois opposition.[15]

In his arguments with the GPP in the early 1970s, Fonseca had urged his comrades to be prepared for a situation in which the prospects for revolutionary action could change dramatically almost overnight. As 1979 began, even the FSLN did not realize how quickly pro-revolution sentiment had spread. The GPP and TP leaderships still believed that victory was years—not months—away. The terceristas thought victory was closer, but they envisioned only the first, nationalist stage of a revolution, producing a post-Somoza government dominated by the bourgeois opposition.

After the crushing of the September 1978 uprisings, violent government repression had let up slightly, but with the departure of the OAS commission in January 1979, attacks on activists and youth escalated again. *La Prensa* reported almost daily murders and disappearances by the National Guard and right-wing paramilitary groups like the Mano Blanca (White Hand). Armed skirmishes increased between the National Guard and FSLN guerrillas in the countryside. Cities, towns, and villages saw a sharp rise in the incidence of protest activities of all sorts: strikes of students and workers, land seizures, religious marches and funerals that turned into mass demonstrations, building occupations, and attacks on National Guard barracks. Civil Defense Committees (Comites de Defensa Civil), first seen in Estelí during the September 1978 rebellion, sprang up in other cities and towns. Within a few months, a full-scale insurrection was under way. One scholar has described the final stage of this uprising as

> so massive, so popular, that the thousands of *milicianos* with their red and black kerchiefs and assorted pistols, shotguns, rifles, Molotov cocktails and contact bombs were never fully organized by Frente cadres or always led by known Sandinistas. In fact, in the hour of victory, anyone who had built a barricade, thrown a bomb, fired a gun, carried a message, or cared for the wounded had earned the right—at least temporarily—to call himself or herself a Sandinist.[16]

The tens of thousands of mostly young Nicaraguans who threw themselves into the fight against Somoza changed Nicaraguan politics, and they also changed the FSLN. The entry of these masses into action pushed the FSLN to the left, not only in terms of speeding up the war against Somoza but also in terms of the radicalism of the revolution's goals. This pushed all three tendencies back toward Carlos Fonseca, toward his vision of a Sandinista revolution that would initiate a process of radical social transformation.

The first result of the fact that revolutionary sandinismo had become a mass phenomenon was the reunification of the FSLN. The new recruits of 1978 and 1979 were attracted to the FSLN because they wanted to fight against Somoza, not because they wanted to debate the fine points of strategy with other revolutionaries. Young men and women associated with the three tendencies all joined in action in the urban uprisings, and all responded in a similar way to the rapidly changing political situation. Growing numbers of Nicaraguans who identified with the FSLN started in practice simply to ignore the tendency divisions, which they had never liked or understood anyway. The same pressure did not exist in solidarity networks based outside

Nicaragua, where the fact that each tendency had its own newspaper, financial backers, political allies, and eventually even friendly publishers and celebrity supporters gave them all a reason to exist as separate entities.

On 7 March 1979, the three FSLN tendencies announced their unification and the establishment of a joint National Directorate made up of three men from each tendency, with the rank of *comandante de la revolución* (commander of the revolution). This Dirección Nacional would remain virtually the same for an entire decade: Daniel Ortega, Humberto Ortega and Víctor Tirado from the TI; Tomás Borge, Bayardo Arce, and Henry Ruiz from the GPP; Jaime Wheelock, Luis Carrión, and Carlos Núñez from the TP.[17] Twenty-seven fighters were awarded the rank of *comandante guerrillero* (guerrilla commander), with nine chosen by each tendency. Only three were women, Dora María Tellez and Leticia Herrera from the TI and Mónica Baltodano from the GPP.

The long-awaited reunification of the FSLN opened the final insurrectionary period. In early April, FSLN guerrillas carried out a harassing action against the National Guard in Estelí, which, to the Sandinistas' surprise, sparked a general uprising that put control of the town in rebel hands for ten days. By the middle of April, there were almost daily clashes between guardsmen and red-and-black kerchiefed youth in cities throughout the country, including, for the first time, the building of barricades in working-class neighborhoods of Managua.[18]

Outside the cities and towns, five guerrilla fronts of varying sizes operated under a joint command set up by the newly reunified FSLN. The Southern Front, commanded by Humberto Ortega from a camp in Costa Rica, was by far the largest—perhaps as big as the other four together—and practiced the most conventional type of warfare. In late May the seven hundred soldiers and ten armored vehicles of the Southern Front launched another "final offensive" with attacks on National Guard posts near the border. They got bogged down in fixed-position warfare for more than a month and suffered heavy losses. The schema that guerrilla armies would advance on the cities and "liberate" them had nothing to do with what actually happened in Nicaragua in 1979. By and large, the cities liberated themselves, although the Western Front, commanded by Dora María Tellez and practicing guerrilla rather than conventional warfare, played an important role in driving the National Guard out of León. By the time the Pablo Ubeda Brigade came to conquer the mining towns of Siuna and Bonanza and the coastal city of Puerto Cabezas, the National Guard had already given up. This was lucky, because the BPU, eight years in the mountains, was down to fewer than five guerrillas.[19]

On 4 June the unified DN called an insurrectionary general strike, to last until Somoza fell. A few days later, it launched a full-scale uprising in the city of Managua. By mid-June the National Guard had abandoned León and Matagalpa, the second- and third-largest cities in the country, as well as a half-dozen smaller towns. By the end of the month, the FSLN controlled more than twenty towns and cities throughout the Pacific zone, in some of which it had set up local government structures and food distribution systems.[20]

These urban insurrections were overwhelmingly working-class in character, as Fonseca had anticipated. A pro-revolution sociologist has examined the records on all those who died in the insurrection who were later vouched for by the FSLN as "combatants," some 6,000 individuals. Fifty-four percent of the dead were workers. Another 29 percent were college and high school students, most of whom came from working-class families. Another indication of their class background is that more than half the 6,000 were born out of wedlock; very few middle-class and bourgeois women in Nicaragua are unmarried mothers. Three-quarters of the fighters in this survey were between fifteen and twenty-four years old when they were killed, and 93 percent were male. Less than 5 percent were identified as peasants. A human face can be put on these statistics by examining the photographs and biographies assembled in many towns after the revolution by the Committees of Heroes and Martyrs. The committee's museum in a modest house in León, for example, contains several hundred revealing pictures and short biographies. The fifty-four "FSLN combatants" killed in the midsize town of Jinotepe in 1978 and 1979 were described in a locally produced booklet: more than three-quarters were younger than twenty-five when they died, and most of the pictures appear to have been taken at school graduations or confirmations. A majority of those killed in Jinotepe had finished primary school, but fewer than half graduated from high school, and fewer than a fifth started college. Three were women—a journalist, age twenty-seven; a Catholic student activist, twenty-one; and a fourteen-year-old student and street fighter. Several of the older combatants had some experience in the PSN. Most of the entries do not specify social class; those that do, through occupation or phrases like "mother poor," indicate a working-class background.[21]

Almost all the urban fighting took place in working-class and poor barrios, another indication of the class dynamic of the insurrection. Virtually every newspaper report on the uprisings located them in the "urban slums."

The FSLN's Frente Interno, after drawing up detailed logistical plans for the final offensive in both the eastern and western barrios of Managua, decided to concentrate on the east because "political conditions were more favorable there." The western neighborhoods—heavily working-class but with middle-class residential pockets—had "better physical conditions," more concrete buildings, and a few two-story houses where lookouts could be posted. The wood shacks of the eastern barrios offered less protection; they burned easily, and a whole block could be pierced by a single National Guard rocket. But the eastern zone, an unbroken string of *barrios populares,* was a Sandinista stronghold, outweighing its physical limitations. The eastern neighborhoods responded quickly to the 8 June call for an insurrectionary general strike in the capital. Within a few days, "not a single shop was open, not a bank, not an office. No petrol stations, no public transport, no buses out of the city. No supermarkets, no grocers. Everything shut. Nothing working . . . absolutely nothing."[22]

Somoza's bombing and rocket attacks everywhere targeted the poorest barrios. In some of the smaller cities and towns, neighborhoods were not so clearly defined, but in Managua whole working-class communities were obliterated while most middle-class areas went completely untouched. Somoza ordered his air force to "bomb everything that moves" on the east side of Managua. As the *Washington Post* reported from Managua on 25 June, "As residents of the middle-class suburbs in the hills around Managua watched in awe, government helicopters hovered over low-lying slum areas of guerrilla concentrations . . . dropping bombs that exploded with a vibration that shook windows three miles away." The factories destroyed by aerial bombing were targeted because they sat in the middle of workers' neighborhoods, not because they were the property of wealthy oppositionists. Some of the bombed factories, in fact, belonged to Somoza.

The tens of thousands who participated in the urban uprisings of 1979, and the hundreds of thousands who wanted them to win, had different motives for getting involved and different ideas of what the revolution would bring. The greatest number simply wanted the repression to stop and saw the Frente as the only organization capable of ending the rule of "the Beast" Somoza. Many were also struggling around class demands: for land, year-round employment, decent housing and health care, an end to abuse by employers and landlords. For some the most important thing was the right of Nicaraguans to run their own country, free of U.S. interference. Others were drawn in by a particular event that happened in their own town or neighborhood, like the GN slaughter of patients and doctors at an Estelí hospital or attacks on schools or religious services. Many women initially became part of the Sandinista barrio support networks for family reasons, to protect their children or their children's friends. On the Atlantic Coast and in Indian neighborhoods such as Subtiava and Monimbó, a desire for greater autonomy and an end to racist abuse fueled support for the revolution. Although most of them had never read it, they were all fighting for different pieces of Carlos Fonseca's Historic Program of 1969, and the success of the FSLN lay in bringing these different struggles together into a unified movement that increasingly posed a serious threat to the dictatorship.

The FSLN had to scramble to catch up with the uprisings that broke out almost spontaneously in 1978 and 1979. But it did catch up. By the spring of 1979, committed and experienced FSLN cadres (who might have been in the organization only a few months) were leading the day-to-day activity of the revolution, distributing the limited number of weapons available, training milicianos, organizing community support, food supplies, and care of the wounded, deciding when and where to strike and when to retreat, and in the process recruiting and training new leaders.

It looked more and more as if there were only two sides in Nicaragua—the FSLN and the increasingly Sandinista masses on one, and Somoza and the National Guard on the other. Under these circumstances, significant sections of the bourgeois opposition became willing to negotiate with the FSLN and concede the Sandinistas a role in the post-Somoza government. On 16 June the FSLN announced in San José the formation of a provisional revolutionary government made up of three FSLN members (Daniel Ortega, Moisés Hassán of the MPU, and Sergio Ramírez of Los Doce), millionaire industrialist and FAO leader Alfonso Robelo, and Violeta Chamorro, the widow of slain Pedro Joaquín Chamorro. The FSLN leaders in San José—primarily terceristas but with the backing of the unified DN—had also agreed to hold elections soon after Somoza's departure for a new legislative body in which the bourgeois parties would be guaranteed a controlling role. It is difficult to say whether either side was negotiating in good faith. The terceristas might have been—the plan was consistent with their 1977 Platforma General. The bourgeois opposition probably was not. As one capitalist described their attitude just before the revolution: "The businessmen thought of the Sandinistas as their peons. They thought they could put [the Sandinistas] in the field to take care of the guard. Then they would step in and take over when Somoza fell. If there was a problem, the United States would stop the Sandinistas from taking power."[23]

The five-person junta did become the government of Nicaragua with the overthrow of Somoza. But it would be a mistake to see Chamorro and Robelo as the capitalist minority in a government that represented a real coalition of different classes. Political power rested with the FSLN, especially with the nine-man Dirección Nacional. Chamorro and Robelo held their seats on the governmental junta at the invitation of the FSLN, and their legitimacy came from their identification with the Sandinista revolution. Alfonso Robelo normally did business in a suit, but when he spoke to a mass rally in Cuba on 26 July 1979, he put on a black T-shirt, tied a large red-and-black bandanna around his neck, and gave a rousing Sandinista speech. The projected post-Somoza legislature did not take office until May 1980, at which time it was dominated by the FSLN and a collection of pro-FSLN organizations created during the insurrection, representing workers, women, youths, peasants, and community activists.

The United States government continued until the end to try to prevent the FSLN from coming to power. Washington's proposal in late June 1979 to send an OAS "peace-keeping force" to Nicaragua was widely understood to be a desperate attempt to disarm the FSLN; only Somoza's representative voted in favor of the motion. On 8 July, with virtually the entire Pacific zone in a state of war, a *Washington Post* interview with Somoza created an uproar in Nicaragua. In it Somoza revealed that he had offered to resign but the U.S. government was delaying his departure until a new command structure for the National Guard could be put in place. That same week, the Red Cross released a report that 50,000 civilians, including 9,000 in Managua alone, had been killed by government forces in the months of war.[24]

On 16 July Somoza named his presidential successor, Liberal congressman Francisco Urcuyo, and a new National Guard commander, Colonel Federico Mejía. Shortly after midnight on the morning of 17 July, Somoza presented his resignation to a hastily convened meeting of the National Assembly at the Intercontinental Hotel in Managua and fled to Miami.[25] President Urcuyo and GN chief Mejía soon followed him. On 18 July three members of the new revolutionary government flew to León, which had been declared the provisional capital of Nicaragua. The National Guard disintegrated. An official of the traffic police was left with the job of surrendering on behalf of the National Guard, which he initially refused to do because the FSLN commander to whom he had to surrender was a woman.

On 19 July 1979, FSLN guerrilla columns entered Managua. The next day, when members of the governing junta and FSLN National Directorate addressed cheering crowds in the capital, the square was decorated with two large banners bearing the portraits of Augusto César Sandino and Carlos

Fonseca Amador. Crowds chanted, "Carlos Fonseca, *¡Presente!*" The influ-ence of Carlos Fonseca was indeed present: in the ideology of Nicaraguan nationalism and anti-imperialism, in the organizational strategy symbolized by the guerrilla tanks and uniforms, in the overwhelming support of Nicara-guan workers and peasants for the insurrection, and as a symbol of the "new man." The crowds could also have chanted—as they did on other occasions—"Augusto César Sandino, *¡Presente!*" Ernesto Che Guevara, *¡Presente!*"

Epilogue

In February 1990, after a tumultuous decade in power, the FSLN was voted out of office when Conservative leader Violeta Chamorro narrowly beat Daniel Ortega in the presidential race. The FSLN's loss came as a tremendous shock to nearly everyone. The FSLN and its supporters around the world had celebrations planned; the Nicaraguan and international press all predicted an FSLN victory, perhaps a landslide; and even the coalition backing Chamorro viewed the campaign more as an opportunity to score propaganda points against the Sandinista revolution than a chance to get its candidate elected. The FSLN campaign was crafted in tone and content to reassure and reach out to middle-class Nicaraguans, but perhaps not surprisingly, the middle class voted overwhelmingly for Chamorro. What is harder to explain is that a significant number of Nicaraguan workers and peasants, the shock troops of the 1979 insurrection and the base of support for revolutionary measures during the 1980s, also voted against the FSLN.

Part of the explanation can be found in the FSLN leadership's gradual distancing itself from the ideas and example of Carlos Fonseca. The process developed unevenly, by fits and starts, but by the end of the decade, the FSLN had changed. Still paying homage to the revolutionary icon of a safely dead and saintly Carlos, the FSLN was no longer in philosophy or practice the party of Carlos Fonseca. Some of the costly mistakes of the FSLN in the 1980s are presaged by debates that took place a decade or more earlier, in which Fonseca warned of precisely these errors and advocated a different course. Although the subject of this book is not the evolution of the FSLN following 1979, I want to close by briefly suggesting a few of the ways in which policies of the National Directorate moved away from the ideas of Fonseca and the Historic Program.

In the first months and years of the revolution, the Sandinista government, supported, and sometimes nudged forward, by a mobilized population, made rapid progress on some of the changes promised in the Historic Program. The agricultural and industrial holdings of Somoza and his closest cronies were confiscated and turned into state property. High school and college students were inspired and organized to carry out a massive literacy campaign in the countryside; one of the slogans of the drive was "En cada alfabetizador, un Carlos Fonseca Amador" [A Carlos Fonseca in every literacy teacher]. With the assistance of Cuban doctors and rapidly trained new Nicaraguan health workers, basic free medical care was extended to rural areas throughout the country, with a special emphasis on the health needs of women and children.

Less progress was made on the crucial issue of land reform. The new minister of land reform, Jaime Wheelock, believed that Nicaraguan peasants had been almost completely proletarianized and needed workers' rights, not land—a theory Fonseca had argued against when Wheelock led the Proletarian Tendency of the 1970s. It was not until the second anniversary of the revolution, after repeated peasant demonstrations in the capital and land occupations in the countryside, that the first hesitant agrarian reform measure was announced, one that granted land titles only to peasants organized into cooperatives. Large-scale distribution of land to individual peasant families did occur in the mid-1980s, but it was driven by military necessity rather than principle. When the war emergency ended in 1987, Wheelock announced that the land reform was over, even though tens of thousands of peasant families were still waiting for land.

The radical measures of the first years of the revolution quickly produced a sharp class polarization inside Nicaragua and the active hostility of the United States government under President Ronald Reagan. Five years of bloody war, financed and organized by Washington, supported by much of the Nicaraguan bourgeoisie and middle class, and spearheaded by former National Guard counterrevolutionaries, or contras, failed to overthrow the Nicaraguan revolution or remove the FSLN from power. The Nicaraguan people paid a terrible price for their victory over the contras, in economic devastation and fifty thousand deaths. And the FSLN paid a political price because of the way the war effort was managed by minister of defense and DN member Humberto Ortega. Carlos Fonseca had polemicized in the early 1970s against Ortega's "militarism," his reliance on military force rather than political organizing. A revolutionary army's strength, insisted Fonseca, came from the commitment of its fighters, not from its sheer numbers or military hardware. Although young men and women volunteered in large numbers for the units organized in 1982 to combat the first contra raids, Ortega and the rest of the DN quickly opted for a draft to raise a huge conventional army. The popular militias that had started to organize in neighborhoods and workplaces were abandoned. Middle-class Nicaraguans with teenage sons (even some who were members of the FSLN) simply moved their families to Miami to avoid the draft, and forced conscription was used almost exclusively against working-class and peasant youth, sometimes against boys who were not yet draft age. The army of the mid-1980s, with its heavy armament, conventional warfare, and strict military hierarchy, resembled the Soviet army more than Sandino's. The Nicaraguan people defeated the contras, just as they had defeated the National Guard in 1979. In both cases, I would argue, they won in spite of Humberto Ortega's military strategy, not because of it.

As Fonseca had predicted, new mass leaders developed in the course of the 1979 insurrection, overwhelmingly young and mostly from poor families. Following the victory, some of them found outlets for their organizing talents and revolutionary zeal in the Popular Sandinista Army and Sandinista Police or the new community associations, unions, and organizations of farmworkers, women, and youth. Fonseca had warned that the FSLN, if it wanted to be considered the "vanguard," needed a constant infusion of new cadres from the working class and peasantry, needed to learn from "the wisdom of the popular masses, a wisdom the masses acquire not in some university or research institute, but through their own experience and their labor." But the FSLN after 1979 recruited few of these new leaders into its ranks and none onto its leading bodies. The nine-man National Directorate, which remained virtually the same throughout the entire decade, made all important decisions. Meetings were held in secret, and a strict internal discipline meant differences were never revealed. The FSLN claimed—with some justice in the early years—to be governing in the interests of workers and peasants. But in the absence of internal democracy or any effort to bring new leaders from oppressed social layers into positions of responsibility, this claim deteriorated into the paternalistic idea that the FSLN knew what was best for Nicaraguan workers and peasants.

The refusal of the DN to admit a single female member during the eleven years of FSLN rule was a particularly glaring example of the way it closed itself off. The prerevolution FSLN was very uneven in its understanding of women's role in society and in revolutionary change. Carlos Fonseca did not provide the same kind of leadership on the issue of women's rights that he did on anti-imperialism or the conflict between classes. But there were women fighters inside the FSLN who were more than capable of leading on this issue after 1979 if they had been allowed to do so.

The relationship between ethnic identity and revolutionary politics was much more complicated than Fonseca or anyone else in the FSLN understood before 1979. But at least the Historic Program recognized the "odious discrimination" suffered by the indigenous peoples and blacks of the Atlantic Coast and promised to respect the distinct cultural values of the region. It was not until the mid-1980s that this began to be implemented in what was called the autonomy process. Autonomy, like the large-scale distribution of land to peasants, was instituted out of military necessity.

Fonseca always pointed to the political example of the Cuban revolution. He frequently paired Augusto César Sandino and Che Guevara as the FSLN's guides and inspiration. Members of the DN of the 1980s rarely mentioned Cuba except to acknowledge its generous financial aid and the indispensable contribution of Cuban doctors and teachers. Only Tomás Borge talked about the inspiration of the Cuban socialist revolution, and he did so less and less frequently as the decade wore on. Sandino and sandinismo were increasingly *counterposed* to Che and Marxism.

Fonseca constantly argued against relying on the traditional opposition or any other sector of the Nicaraguan bourgeoisie to solve the problems of poverty, inequality, and economic and cultural backwardness. Conflicts between peasants and landlords, workers and capitalists, were inevitable, he said, and revolutionaries had to take the side of the oppressed. The economic and social policies implemented by the FSLN government in the late 1980s did just the opposite. Their solution to the economic devastation of the contra war was to adopt tax, credit, and labor policies designed to encourage private enterprise. In a policy known as *concertación* or national unity, the factory owners and growers for whom Fonseca had such scorn were rechristened "patriotic producers." Agricultural and industrial workers, who had put aside their own economic and social struggles during the war, were told they had to continue to sacrifice in order for their employers to regain their peace of mind and profitability. Because the austerity policies came from the FSLN and because the DN was united in support of concertación, most workers went along with the new directives. But the policies brought confusion and demoralization.

Although the FSLN did not merge with the Nicaraguan Communist Party or any of its offshoots, the political approach and electoral orientation of the FSLN by the late 1980s had much in common with the conservative positions

Fonseca had attacked in the PSN and other pro-Moscow parties. The privileged lifestyle of many FSLN leaders resembled that enjoyed by Soviet bureaucrats. The collapse of the Soviet Union seemed to some FSLN leaders to rule out any possibility that a country like Nicaragua could move toward socialism. But the goal of a social transformation in Nicaragua had never been predicated on economic or political support from the Soviet Union; rather, it was born in ideological combat with the Kremlin and the parties it influenced.

The sum of the FSLN's policies coming out of the contra war represented a rightward shift, away from Carlos Fonseca, away from the workers and peasants of Nicaragua, away from the example of Cuba. This shift was somewhat obscured by the fact that the FSLN was still to the left of the other party in the 1990 elections, especially on the issue of self-determination. The United States aggressively backed the Chamorro candidacy with financial support, propaganda, and promises of future aid. The strategy of the FSLN campaign was to push ahead with its pro-business economic policies and soften its revolutionary image as much as possible. Ortega's campaign slogan was "Everything Will Be Better," and attempts were made to popularize his appeal through crude sexual jokes and songs that were deeply offensive to many women.

The party once known for the personal austerity and high moral standards of its central leader was rocked by sexual and financial scandals in the late 1980s and early 1990s. In a "piñata" of self-enrichment during the few months interregnum between the election and Chamorro's inauguration, FSLN politicians and officials appropriated hundreds of houses and farms that had been nationalized following the 1979 revolution. The privatization of state property during the Chamorro years made Humberto Ortega (who remained commander of the army until 1995) one of the richest men in the country.

Over the course of more than a decade, the FSLN progressively abandoned its own revolutionary tradition. This evolution was symbolized by the decision around 1986 to stop publishing the works of Carlos Fonseca and by the formal repeal of the Historic Program and substitution of a moderate electoral platform in 1989. The decomposition of the FSLN accelerated in the mid-1990s as members split to form competing organizations or simply drifted away. In 1996, with Daniel Ortega again the FSLN standard bearer, a Somocista Liberal named Arnoldo Alemán was elected president of Nicaragua.

For leaders of the FSLN, the lesson of the 1990 electoral defeat is that a social revolution can never succeed in a region the United States regards as its backyard. Faced with the growing hostility and violence of both Washington and the Nicaraguan bourgeoisie, the Sandinista revolution was, according to the FSLN leadership, doomed to fail. But the defeat of 1990 was no more inevitable than the victory of 1979. At both times decisions were made, mistakes corrected or deepened, trust won or lost. The FSLN of Carlos Fonseca did not look to the United States or the bourgeois parties to overthrow Somoza or expect these forces to be neutral in the face of a successful popular revolution. Fonseca said the FSLN learned from watching the Cuban leadership's "growing identification with the ideology of the proletariat in the course of 1961" that "the best way to defend a successful revolution against attacks by reactionary forces and by imperialism was through identification with the exploited classes." The people of Nicaragua—especially young men and women from the working class and peasantry—overthrew Somoza and defeated at tremendous cost a military attack by U.S.-backed contras, only to have the FSLN turn its back on them in the late 1980s. They deserved better.

Notes

Introduction

1 *Barricada* (Managua), 6–8 November 1979; *La Prensa* (Managua), 7–8 November 1979; *Intercontinental Press* (New York), 3 Dec. 1979; all translations by author unless otherwise indicated.

2 Carlos Fonseca Amador, *Síntesis de algunos problemas actuales,* in *Obras,* vol. 1 (Managua: Editorial Nueva Nicaragua, 1982), 98–99; italics in original.

3 Earl Browder was the general secretary of the Communist Party in the United States from 1930 to 1944.

4 The most extreme form of this thesis is found in the work of Cancino, who starts with the premise that Marxism is fundamentally incompatible with nationalism and that "there is no way to integrate elements of nationalist discourse with marxist-leninist discourse"; see Hugo Cancino Troncoso, *Las raíces históricas e ideológicas del movimiento sandinista: Antecedentes de la revolución popular nicaragüense, 1927–79* (Odense: Odense University Press, 1984), 140.

5 Carlos Fonseca Amador to Compañero Denis, 17 Sept. 1960, IES Archive.

6 I was in Cuba for most of July 1979 and attended the 26 July rally. Thousands of Cubans had turned out at the airport to greet the expected delegation of two or three Nicaraguans. It was a moment of high drama as the young fatigue-clad guerrillas slowly emerged from the airplane one after another, in a seemingly endless line.

7 See, for example, George Black, *Triumph of the People: The Sandinista Revolution in Nicaragua* (London: Zed Press, 1981); John A. Booth, *The End and the Beginning: The Nicaraguan Revolution* (Boulder: Westview, 1982); Julio López C., Orlando Núñez S., and Carlos Fernando Chamorro B., *La caída del somocismo y la lucha sandinista en Nicaragua* (San José: EDUCA, 1979); Manlio Tirado, *La revolución sandinista* (México, D.F.: Editorial Nuestro Tiempo, 1983); Thomas W. Walker, *Nicaragua in Revolution* (New York: Praeger, 1982). None of these scholars goes as far as a recent book claiming that the Cuban revolution had little impact anywhere in Central America outside of Guatemala; see Thomas C. Wright, *Latin America in the Era of the Cuban Revolution* (Westport: Praeger, 1991), 178. Two studies of Nicaragua that give greater emphasis to

the role of Cuba (the first generally supportive of the Sandinistas and the second hostile) are Harry E. Vanden and Gary Prevost, *Democracy and Socialism in Sandinista Nicaragua* (Boulder: L. Rienner, 1993); and David Nolan, *The Ideology of the Sandinistas and the Nicaraguan Revolution* (Coral Gables: Institute of Interamerican Studies, 1984).

8 Peter Finley Dunne, *Mr. Dooley on Ivrything and Ivrybody* (New York: Dover Publications, 1963), 203.

Chapter 1 Matagalpa: The Early Years, 1936–1950

1 CHM reg. 18698, caja 1, "documentos personales" folder.

2 Jesús Miguel Blandón, *Entre Sandino y Fonseca Amador* (Managua: DEPEP, 1981), 181, 183.

3 Blanca Aráuz was only three years older than Augustina Fonseca, and the two tall, fair-skinned girls even resembled each other. (Sandino once introduced his wife as "95% Spanish"; see Volker Wunderich, *Sandino: Biografía Política* [Managua: Instituto de Historia de Nicaragua, 1995], 70.) They would almost certainly have known each other in the small town of San Rafael del Norte.

4 Benita Alvarado, interview by author, Matagalpa, 20 Feb. 1996; José Ramón Gutiérrez Castro, interview by author, Rivas, 24 Feb. 1996. A picture of Lt. Pennington appeared frequently in anti-intervention newspapers in Mexico and the United States in the 1930s. He looks very young, and in his right hand he is holding, by the hair, the decapitated head of Sandinista guerrilla Silvino Herrera. In a grisly coincidence, the Cuban newspaper *Granma* put this photo next to an article by Carlos Fonseca on 20 Feb. 1971.

5 During the 1980s, this residence, known as the *casa cuna* (cradle house), was made into a museum dedicated to Carlos Fonseca's life.

6 Benita Alvarado, interview by author, Matagalpa, 20 Feb. 1996; María Haydeé Terán, interview by author, León, 2 July 1994; Nelly Arrieta de Vilches, interview by author, Matagalpa, 10 June 1995; Reynaldo Guido, interview by author, Rivas, 27 May 1995.

7 Blandón, *Entre Sandino,* 185.

8 Benita Alvarado, interview by author, Matagalpa, 20 Feb. 1996; María Haydeé Terán, interview by author, León, 2 July 1994; Doris Tijerino, interview by author, Managua, 28 June 1994; see also Carlos Fonseca Amador, "Declaración, 1964," in *Obras,* vol. 1, 182.

9 José Ramón Gutiérrez Castro, interview by author, Rivas, 26 June 1994; "CARFONA" [Carlos Fonseca Amador], "Está bién, pero está mal," *Segovia* 2 (Sept. 1954); Blandón, *Entre Sandino,* 220.

10 Guillermo Rothschuh Tablada, "Tres fichas universitarias de Carlos Fonseca Amador," *Ventana,* 25 Apr. 1981.

11 Carlos Fonseca Amador, San José, to "Querido papá," Managua, 11 Apr. 1960, CHM folder "cartas familiares," caja 3. Fonseca often referred to Isaura and Victoria Ubeda as his aunts although they were actually his great-aunts. At the time C$ 100 was worth about $15.

12 CHM reg. 19887, caja 3(18).

13 Jeffrey L. Gould, "El café, el trabajo y la comunidad indígena de Matagalpa, 1880–1925," in *Tierra, café y sociedad: Ensayos sobre la historia agraria centroamericana,* ed. Héctor Pérez Brignoli and Mario Samper (San José: Programa Costa Rica, FLACSO, 1994), 332–34; "Fausto Amador hijo explota con tierras," *El Nuevo Diario,* 25 Feb. 1996; Nelly Arrieta de Vilches, interview by author, Matagalpa, 10 June 1995. Because of his close association with Somoza, Fausto Amador's property was confiscated shortly after the 1979 revolution. It was returned in the 1990s.

14 José Ramón Gutiérrez Castro, interview by author, Rivas, 26 June 1994; Carlos Fonseca Amador, "16 versos del molendero," *Segovia* 6–7 (Jan.–Feb. 1955); Octavio Robleto, interview by author, Managua, 9 June 1995.

15 Blandón, *Entre Sandino,* 191–92; CHM, reg. 00535, caja 1.

16 Benita Alvarado, interview by author, Matagalpa, 20 Feb. 1996; José Ramón Gutiérrez Castro, interview by author, Rivas, 26 June 1994.

17 Nelly Arrieta de Vilches, interview by author, Matagalpa, 10 June 1995; Carlos Fonseca Amador, San José, to "doña Lolita," Managua, 10 June 1960, CHM reg. 00332, caja 3.

18 See, for example, Sahily Tabares Hernández, "Carlos Fonseca Amador: Continuador de Sandino," *Barricada,* 13 Aug. 1979; Jacinto Suárez, "En cada militante está presente la labor de Carlos," *Nicaráuac* 13 (Nov.–Dec. 1986); Humberto Ortega Saavedra, "Estrategia triunfante fue obra de todos bajo la orientación de Carlos," *Barricada,* 7 Nov. 1979. Fonseca himself fostered this idea, telling a journalist in 1970, "For family reasons I had ties both to the exploiting classes and to the exploited classes, but, as I became more conscious about the world, I decided to break all ties with the exploiters." See Carlos Fonseca Amador, "La lucha armada en Nicaragua [interview by Hernán Uribe Ortega]," *Punto Final* (Santiago) 129 (27 Aug. 1971).

19 Carlos Fonseca Amador, San José, to "Querido papá," Managua, 15 Jan. 1960, IHN Archive, also CHM reg. 00326, caja 3. Six months earlier, Fausto had visited his wounded son in a Honduras hospital, a visit Carlos said "strengthened my soul and filled it with happiness."

20 Carlos Fonseca Amador, San José, to "Papá, queridisimo papá," Managua, 12 June 1967 [68?—last digit illegible], CHM reg. 00350, caja 3, folder "cartas familiares."

21 "Carlos Fonseca visto por María Haydeé Terán," *Barricada,* 9 Nov. 1979; Benita Alvarado, interview by author, Matagalpa, 20 Feb. 1996; Octavio Robleto, interview by author, Managua, 27 Feb. 1996. Tomás Borge, in a 1982 speech, referred to "those letters full of tenderness that Carlos used to write to Doña Justina, sharing with her his joys and his discoveries," but there is no evidence of these letters anywhere. See Tomás Borge, "Fieles a Carlos y a su sagrada herencia," *El Nuevo Diario,* 25 June 1982.

22 Carlos Fonseca Amador, "Mensaje del FSLN a las madres de los Mártires nicaragüenses," 30 May 1968, CHM reg. 00299, caja 5; Benita Alvarado, interview by author, Matagalpa, 20 Feb. 1996; Blandón, *Entre Sandino,* 214. Fonseca—like most Nicaraguans—used the term "proletarian" to refer not just to industrial wageworkers but to a broader social layer including domestic servants, market vendors, craftspeople, workshop owners, and sometimes even small landowners.

23 Gould, "El café," 303; Alberto Vogl Baldizón, *Nicaragua con amor y humor* (Managua: Ministerio de Cultura, [1985?]), 328. (1 manzana equals 1.7 acres.)

24 Vogl, *Nicaragua,* 330, 340; see also advertisements in *Rumores* and *Segovia.* A 1930 National Guard report on the twenty-four families with the largest coffee properties in Matagalpa lists nine North Americans, seven Nicaraguans (including an Amador, who was Carlos Fonseca's uncle), three Germans, three British, one Italian, and one Swiss; see Gould, "El café," 366–72.

25 Ernesto Centeno M., "Matagalpa," *Segovia* 5 (Dec. 1954).

26 The leading exponent of this view is Jaime Wheelock Román; see his *Las raíces indígenas de la lucha anticolonial en Nicaragua* (México, D.F.: Siglo XXI, 1975). Carlos Fonseca Amador, *Viva Sandino,* in *Obras,* vol. 2 (Managua: Editorial Nueva Nicaragua, 1982), 34. In this passage Fonseca also called the War of 1881 "a symbol of the decomposition of the feudal system in Nicaragua," and a transmission belt between earlier "secular rebellions by campesinos of indigenous origin" and Augusto César Sandino's "colossal guerrilla war" a half century later.

27 Josefina Arnesto, *Breves apuntes de la historia de Matagalpa* (Matagalpa: n.d.), 4–8; Ramón Gutiérrez Castro, *Breve historia de Matagalpa: La guerra de los indios de 1881* (Managua: Tipografía Villalta, 1954); Vogl, *Nicaragua,* 215; Guillermo McEwan, *El interior es lo de afuera* (Managua: Editorial Vanguardia, 1994), 110; Reynaldo Guido, interview by author, Rivas, 27 May 1995.

28 Gould, "El café," 238; Jeffrey L. Gould, " '¡Vana Ilusión!' The Highlands Indians and the Myth of Nicaragua Mestiza, 1880–1925," *Hispanic American Historical Review* 73 (Aug. 1993), 423, 427–29; see also Jeffrey L. Gould, *To Die in This Way: Nicaraguan Indians and the Myth of Mestizaje, 1880–1965* (Durham: Duke University Press, 1998), for the impact of the discourse of a mestizo Nicaragua on Indians in various parts of the country.

29 Jaime M. Biderman, "Class Structure, the State, and Capitalist Development in Nicaraguan Agriculture" (Ph.D. diss., University of California, Berkeley, 1982), 61–63; Laura J. Enríquez, *Harvesting Change: Labor and Agrarian Reform in Nicaragua, 1979–1990* (Chapel Hill and London: University of North Carolina Press, 1991), 29–30; Gould, "El café," 327.

30 Knut Walter, *The Regime of Anastasio Somoza García and State Formation in Nicaragua, 1936–1956* (Chapel Hill: University of North Carolina Press, 1987), 236, 238; Biderman, "Class Structure," 18; Amalia Chamorro, "Estado y hegemonía durante el somocismo," in *Economía y sociedad en la construcción del estado en Nicaragua,* ed. Alberto Lanuza et al. (San José: ICAP, 1983), 241–76; Jeffrey L. Gould, "For an Organized Nicaragua: Somoza and the Labour Movement, 1944–1948," *Journal of Latin American Studies* 19 (Nov. 1987), 353–87.

31 See Richard Millett, *Guardians of the Dynasty* (Maryknoll, N.Y.: Orbis Books, [1977?]); Eduardo Crawley, *Dictators Never Die: Nicaragua and the Somoza Family Dynasty* (New York: St. Martin's Press, 1979); Timothy P. Wickham-Crowley, *Guerrillas and Revolution in Latin America: A Comparative Study of Insurgents and Regimes since 1956* (Princeton: Princeton University Press, 1992), 269–70.

32 Walter, *Regime,* 129–34.

33 Miguel Ángel Herrera, "Carlos Fonseca: El anhelo de servir a la patria," MS, Managua, n.d., 3. Baldizón was killed at the age of twenty-two, fighting alongside Carlos Fonseca at the battle of El Chaparral.

34 Doris Tijerino, *Inside the Nicaraguan Revolution* (Vancouver: New Star Books, 1983).

35 Except in El Salvador, the pro-Moscow Communist parties of Central America and the Caribbean had by World War II adopted names that did not include the word *communist:* in Cuba after 1944, the Communist Party was officially named the Partido Socialista Popular (PSP), in Costa Rica the Partido Vanguardia Popular (PVP), in Guatemala the Partido Guatemalteco del Trabajo (PGT), and so on.

36 I cannot agree with Jeffrey Gould's conclusion that the PSN "did not derive their qualified support of Somoza from ideological postulates, but rather from a careful reading of an extremely complex conjuncture" (Gould, "Organized Nicaragua," 383). The PSN's support to Somoza was in line with the policies adopted by pro-Moscow parties around the world in two fundamental ways: first, they backed a ruler associated with the Allied powers in World War II; and second, they operated within the electoral framework of the traditional capitalist parties.

Chapter 2   A Rebellious Student, 1950–1958

1 Benita Alvarado, interview by author, Matagalpa, 20 Feb. 1996; Blandón, *Entre Sandino,* 194; José Ramón Gutiérrez Castro, "Nuestro Instituto Nacional del Norte celebró el 2 de marzo acto de clausura," *Segovia* 6–7 (Jan.–Feb. 1955).

2 *Vanguardia Juvenil,* 7 Dec. 1946.

3 Ramón Gutiérrez Castro, Rivas, to author, Managua, 7 June 1995; IES, "Cronología Básica de Carlos Fonseca," in Carlos Fonseca Amador, *Obras,* vol. 1, 431.

4 Carlos Fonseca Amador, "Declaración, 1957," in *Obras,* vol. 1, 166–67.

5 Ernesto Cardenal, interview by author, Managua, 27 June 1994; Denis Lynn Daly Heyck, *Life Stories of the Nicaraguan Revolution* (New York: Routledge, 1990), 24.

6 IES, "Cronología Básica," 433; a shorter version, published for popular consumption a few years later, does not mention Fonseca's membership in the Communist Party, see IES, *Carlos: El eslabón vital* (Managua: ENIEC, 1985); Guillermo Rothschuh Tablada, *Los guerrilleros vencen a los generales: Homenaje a Carlos Fonseca Amador* (Managua: Ediciones Distribuidora Cultural, 1983), 2; Fonseca, "Declaración 1957," 170. This denial is not credible, both because it is inconsistent with other statements by Fonseca and because it was the policy of the PSN and of similar organizations around the world for its members to deny affiliation when questioned.

7 José Ramón Gutiérrez Castro, interview by author, Rivas, 26 June 1994; Tomás Pravia Reyes ("Colocho"), interview by author, Matagalpa, 20 Feb. 1996.

8 Blandón, *Entre Sandino,* 197; Tomás Pravia Reyes ("Colocho"), interview by author, Matagalpa, 20 Feb. 1996. The PSN newspaper was called *Unidad* and *Orientación Popular* at different times during this period.

9 Tomás Pravia Reyes ("Colocho"), interview by author, Matagalpa, 20 Feb. 1996; Walter, *Regime,* 226, 282.

10 Jeffrey Gould, "Nicaragua," in *Latin America between the Second World War and the Cold War, 1944–1948,* ed. Leslie Bethell and Ian Roxborough (Cambridge and New York: Cambridge University Press, 1992), 263; Blandón, *Entre Sandino,* 193; Gould, "For an Organized Nicaragua," 353–87.

11 Tomás Pravia Reyes ("Colocho"), interview by author, Matagalpa, 20 Feb. 1996; José

Ramón Gutiérrez Castro, interview by author, Rivas, 26 June 1994. It should be noted that both these interviews took place four decades after the disputed events.

12 Juan Aburto, "Recuerdos de Carlos Fonseca," *Ventana,* 8 Nov. 1986.

13 Tomás Borge, *La Paciente Impaciencia* (Managua: Editorial Vanguardia, 1989), 97; José Ramón Gutiérrez Castro, interview by author, Rivas, 26 June 1994. Buitrago became an early leader of the FSLN and was killed in action in 1963; Gutiérrez never joined the FSLN and is the only one of the three friends who has survived. The school year in Nicaragua ran from May or June through February; Carlos's final year at the INN began in May 1954.

14 José Ramón Gutiérrez Castro, interview by author, Rivas, 26 June 1994.

15 The only exceptions are Werner Mackenbach, "El problema de la nación en el pensamiento juvenil de Carlos Fonseca," MS, 1995; and Blandón, *Entre Sandino.* A few of the cultural articles were reprinted years later in a Cuban magazine; see "Carlos Fonseca en Segovia," *Casa de las Americas* (Havana) 174 (1989): 3–11.

16 Bertha Z. Prado, "Carlos, un gran lector," *Barricada,* 9 Nov. 1980.

17 Carlos Fonseca Amador, "Editorial: La juventud intelectual matagalpina necesita ponerse en contacto para orientarse bién y poder triunfar," *Segovia* 6–7 (Jan.–Feb. 1955).

18 Francisco Buitrago Castillo, "Pensares de un estudiante Segoviano," *Segovia* 1 (Aug. 1954); *Segovia* 10 (n.d., early 1956); Francisco Buitrago C., "Estudiantes: hacia un verdadero estudiantado," *Segovia* 3 (Oct. 1954); Carlos Fonseca Amador, "Carta al Sr. Ministro de Educación Pública en la que se Sugiere utilizar las Barberías como Bibliotecas populares," *Segovia* 11 (Feb. 1956).

19 Carlos Fonseca Amador, "Editorialoide," *Segovia* 2 (Sept. 1954); "Editorial," *Segovia* 10 (n.d., early 1956).

20 Carlos Fonseca Amador, "Futuro," *Segovia* 1 (Aug. 1954).

21 Carlos Fonseca Amador, "El voto de la mujer," *Segovia* 9 (Dec. 1955).

22 Carlos Fonseca Amador, "Editorialoide," *Segovia* 2 (Sept. 1954).

23 The geographic term *Segovia* refers to the five northern provinces of Matagalpa, Jinotega, Estelí, Madriz, and Nueva Segovia; it is a hilly region bounded by the Pacific coastal plain to the west, the Honduran border to the north, and the mountains of the Atlantic Coast region to the east.

24 The PSN did not exist when Sandino was assassinated in 1934, but the newspaper of its Costa Rican counterpart contained the following note a few days after the guerrilla general was killed: "Sandino, the son of campesinos and a campesino himself, had all the characteristics of the class he came from: he was individualistic, of limited mentality, with a fetishistic respect for private property, and unable to assimilate a revolutionary social doctrine that could chart a firm course for the struggle." In a similar vein, *El Machete,* the newspaper of the Mexican Communist Party, made the following comment on Sandino's death: "Sandino wanted so much to become President of Nicaragua that he betrayed the struggle against imperialism. But the only thing he accomplished was to die like a poor devil" (see *La Prensa,* 18 May 1995, 12).

25 Gutiérrez, "Nuestro INN celebró," in *Segovia* 6–7 (Jan.–Feb. 1955); Carlos Fonseca Amador, "El Capital y el Trabajo: Examen de Bachillerato, INN," Matagalpa, 27 Feb. 1955, CHM reg. 00398, caja 2. A photocopy of the handwritten original was found in

the files of the Office of National Security (Oficina de Seguridad Nacional, OSN), apparently the earliest writing by Carlos Fonseca that was saved by Somoza's secret police.

26 "Colaboradoes de Carlos en SEGOVIA," *Segovia* (Managua) 1 (July 1985).

27 Humberto López, "No era igual a nosotros: 57 años del natalicio de Carlos Fonseca," *Barricada,* 23 June 1993; Roberto Sánchez Ramírez, "Carlos Fonseca Amador, Bibliotecario," *El Nuevo Diario,* 5 Nov. 1981; Carlos Fonseca Amador, "Notas y experiencias revolucionarias (transcripción de charla)," 1975, CHM reg. 09466, caja 2B.

28 Sánchez, "Carlos, Bibliotecario," *El Nuevo Diario,* 5 Nov. 1981.

29 Ignacio Briones Torres, "Bajo las banderas de Sandino," *Barricada,* 23 June 1980. Cleto Ordóñez resisted the annexation of Nicaragua by self-declared "Emperor of Mexico" Augustín de Iturbide following independence from Spain in 1821.

30 Sánchez, "Carlos, Bibliotecario," *El Nuevo Diario,* 5 Nov. 1981.

31 Guillermo Rothschuh Tablada, "El carácter pedagógico de Carlos Fonseca," *El Nuevo Diario,* 23 June 1983; Guillermo Rothschuh Tablada, "Carlos, gran bibliotecario y gran lector," part 1, *El Nuevo Diario,* 10 Nov. 1982.

32 José Ramón Gutiérrez Castro, interviews by author, Rivas, 26 June 1994 and 27 May 1995.

33 Sánchez, "Carlos, Bibliotecario," *El Nuevo Diario,* 5 Nov. 1981; Tomás Borge, "Historia político-militar del FSLN," *Encuentro* (Managua) 15 (Sept. 1979); Sergio Ramírez Mercado, "La generación del 23 de julio, una generación decisiva," in *Las armas del futuro* (Managua: Editorial Nueva Nicaragua, 1987), 106.

34 In a single boom year during the 1950s, several hundred cotton pickers in Chinandega province died from inhaling pesticide fumes. See Jeffrey L. Gould, *To Lead as Equals: Rural Protest and Political Consciousness in Chinandega, Nicaragua* (Chapel Hill: University of North Carolina Press, 1990), 164.

35 Rolando Avendaña Sandino, *Masacre estudiantil: 23 de Julio de 1959, León, Nicaragua* ([Managua?]: Tipográfico América, 1960), 30; Marcia Traña Galeano, Xiomara Avendaño Rojas, and Roger Norori Gutiérrez, "Historia del movimiento estudiantil universitario (1944–1979)," MS, Managua, 1985, n.p.

36 Blandón, *Entre Sandino,* 201; Octavio Robleto, interview by author, Managua, 9 June 1995.

37 Carlos Fonseca Amador, *Un Nicaragüense en Moscú,* in *Obras,* vol. 1, 281.

38 Fonseca, "Notas y experiencias revolucionarias [1975]"; José Ramón Gutiérrez Castro, interview by author, Rivas, 26 June 1994.

39 Carlos Fonseca Amador, *Notas sobre la carta-testamento de Rigoberto López Pérez,* in *Obras,* vol. 1, 396.

40 Carlos Fonseca Amador, Matagalpa, to "Coronel," 11 Dec. 1956, CHM reg. 00346, caja 3.

41 CHM reg. 00535, caja 1; all punctuation and spelling are from the original.

42 Rothschuh, *Los guerrilleros,* 118.

43 Fonseca, *Un Nicaragüense en Moscú,* 281, 283; CHM reg. 00698, caja 1(8). Fonseca's original delegate card ended up in the OSN file.

44 Fonseca, *Un Nicaragüense en Moscú,* 208, 310–11, 306, 325.

45 Ibid., 316–17.

46 Ibid., 322.

47 Articles in the Nicaraguan press, to the contrary, all treat *Un Nicaragüense en Moscú* as just an early example of a consistent body of work. See, for example, Jorge Eduardo Arellano, "Carlos y su amistad con Manolo," *Ventana*, 28 Nov. 1987; Fidel Coloma, "La prosa juvenil de Carlos Fonseca Amador," *La Prensa Literaria*, 11 Nov. 1979; Carlos F. Chamorro B., "En torno a Un Nicaragüense en Moscú," *Segovia* (Managua), 26 July 1985; David Gutiérrez López, "Con Carlos Fonseca en la URSS," *Nicaráuac*, 13 (Nov.– Dec. 1986).

48 Carlos Fonseca Amador, "Mensaje de Carlos Fonseca con el seudónimo de Pablo Cáceres en el IV Congreso Sindical Mundial, RDA," CHM reg. 07193, caja 5.

49 Rodolfo Romero, interview by author, Granada, 24 June 1994; Clara Mayo, "'Fue una noche de junio cuando conocí a Che,' Entrevista a Rodolfo Romero," *Juventud Rebelde* (Havana), 7 June 1988, 8; Jon Lee Anderson, *Che Guevara, a Revolutionary Life* (New York: Grove Press, 1997), 394, 396.

50 Rafael René Corea, "Breve imagen de Carlos Fonseca," *El Nuevo Diario*, 7 Nov. 1991; Nelly Arrieta de Vilches, interview by author, Matagalpa, 10 June 1995; Blandón, *Entre Sandino*, 202; Ignacio Briones Torres, "La primera guerrilla de Carlos Fonseca (Apuntes para una biografía)," *El Nuevo Diario*, 28 Oct 1982; Carlos Fonseca Amador, [León?], to Gen. Anastasio Somoza, Managua, 21 May 1958, CHM reg. 00348, caja 3.

51 Carlos Fonseca Amador, "Acerca de la lucha del FSLN: breve cronología," 1972, CHM reg. 00244, caja 2A.

52 Folder: "Cartas de Carlos Fonseca como Secretario de Relaciones del CUUN," CHM reg. 00376, caja 3.

53 Carlos Fonseca Amador, León, to Mariano Fiallos Gil, León, 25 Nov. 1958, CHM reg. 00376, caja 3; Corea, "Breve imagen," *El Nuevo Diario*, 7 Nov. 1991; Arias, *Nicaragua*, 22. Ignacio Briones Torres, who has written numerous articles about Fonseca, was also a delegate to the high school conference; see CHM reg. 00376, caja 3.

54 Rodolfo Romero, interview by author, Granada, 24 June 1994; Jeffrey L. Gould, "'La raza rebelde': Las luchas de la comunidad indígena de Subtiava, Nicaragua (1900– 1960)," *Revista de Historia* (San José) 21–22 (Jan.–Dec. 1990): 104–7.

Chapter 3   The Cuban Revolution, 1958–1961

1 *La Prensa*, 3, 7, 8, and 10 Jan. 1959.

2 Víctor Tirado López, "La historia dió la razón a Carlos Fonseca," in *Habla la vanguardia* (Managua, 1982), 92; Blandón, *Entre Sandino* 158, 169, 61. In a 1970 interview, Fonseca said the rebirth of Nicaraguan guerrilla activity was "rooted in the Cuban revolution. And even when they were still fighting in the Sierra in Cuba, that struggle was already beginning to have repercussions in Nicaragua." See Carlos Fonseca Amador, "Retornar a las montañas," *Verde Olivo* (Havana), 46 (15 Nov. 1970): 54.

3 I want to thank Michael Schroeder for bringing to my attention the documents on Raudales's 1948 guerrilla uprising.

4 Blandón, *Entre Sandino*, 69, 79, 101, 203, 102. Unfortunately for Lacayo, a plane in which he was traveling had to make an emergency landing in Havana, where he was arrested, tried, and executed.

5 Ibid., 86.

6   María Luísa Lafita, interview by Eloise Linger, Havana, June 1991. I want to thank Linger for sharing her tapes of these interviews with me.

7   Anderson, *Che Guevara*, 396–97; Rodolfo Romero, interview by author, Granada, 24 June 1994. Romero's description to me of his 1959 conversation with Che is consistent with what he told Jon Anderson's interviewer. Nevertheless, I believe he was mistaken in remembering as his own firm opinions of early 1959 political judgments concerning the PSN that he (together with Fonseca) actually reached later in 1959 or even in early 1960.

8   Blandón, *Entre Sandino*, 109, 65, 107, 108.

9   Ignacio Briones Torres, "La primera guerrilla de Carlos Fonseca," *El Nuevo Diario*, 28 Oct. 1982, 7–9 Nov. 1982.

10 Carlos Fonseca Amador, Tegucigalpa, to "Recordada Estelita" [Estela Escobar], Guatemala, 15 July 1959, CHM reg. 19086, caja 3; emphasis in original.

11 Carlos Fonseca Amador, San José, to Prof. Edelberto Torres, Mexico City, 8 June 1960, IHN Archive.

12 Fonseca, "Notas y experiencias [1975]."

13 Rodolfo Romero, interview by author, Granada, 24 June 1994.

14 Blandón, *Entre Sandino*, 204.

15 Simon Delgado, "Versión de un testigo del combate de 'El Chaparral,'" *El Nuevo Diario*, 9 Nov. 1980; Simon Delgado, "Carlos, un humanista," *El Nuevo Diario*, 28 Nov. 1982.

16 Fernando Gordillo, *Obra* (Managua: Editorial Nueva Nicaragua, 1989), 297, 295.

17 Avedaña, *Masacre estudiantil*, 90; Ramírez, "La generación del 23 de julio," 106; Traña et al., *Movimiento estudiantil*.

18 Avedaña, *Masacre estudiantil*, 47–49.

19 Briones, "La primera guerrilla de Carlos Fonseca," *El Nuevo Diario*, 9 Nov. 1982; Emilio Surí Quesada, *Y nadie se cansa de pelear* (Managua: Editorial Vanguardia, 1987), 179.

20 Anastasio Somoza García, *El verdadero Sandino, o, el calvario de las Segovias*, 2d ed. (Managua: Editorial San José, 1976).

21 For a variety of interpretations, see Steven Palmer, "Carlos Fonseca and the Construction of Sandinismo in Nicaragua," *Latin American Research Review* 23 (1988): 91–109; Bruce E. Wright, *Theory in the Practice of the Nicaraguan Revolution* (Athens: Ohio University Center for International Studies, 1995), 55–66; Donald Hodges, *Intellectual Foundations of the Nicaraguan Revolution* (Austin: University of Texas Press, 1986); Cancino, *Las raíces históricas*.

22 Tomás Borge, *Carlos, the Dawn Is No Longer beyond Our Reach* (Vancouver: New Star Books, 1984), 20–22; Vanden and Prevost, *Democracy and Socialism*, 35; Dennis Gilbert, *Sandinistas* (New York and Oxford: Basil Blackwell, 1988), 5. On the twentieth anniversary of Fonseca's death, the FSLN newspaper *Barricada*, edited by Borge, ran a special feature that had more to do with Tomás Borge than Carlos Fonseca.

23 Hodges, *Intellectual Foundations*, 167–72.

24 Wall poster: "Manifiesto del Centro Universitario al Pueblo de Nicaragua '23 de Julio 1960'" (León: Editorial Antorcha, 1960), CHM reg. 03258, caja 5; John M. Kirk, "From Apóstol to Revolutionary: The Changing Image of Jose Martí," *NorthSouth* 4, no. 7: 88–106; Carlos Fonseca Amador, "Discurso en acto de solidaridad," Havana, 6 Sept.

1974, CHM reg. 19729, caja 5; Carlos Fonseca Amador, letter to Angel Guerra, editor of *Bohemia,* Havana, 16 Feb. 1974, CHM reg. 00379, caja 3.

25 *Combate* (Havana), 10 June 1960. The Frente Unitario Nicaragüense (FUN) was a loose coalition of anti-Somoza exiles in Venezuela, Mexico, and a few other countries.

26 Miguel Ángel Herrera, "Carlos Fonseca: A treinta años de El Chaparral," *Barricada,* 25 June 1989 (Dalton was a member of the Communist Party of El Salvador at the time); Blandón, *Entre Sandino,* 214.

27 Wall poster: "Manifiesto '23 de Julio 1960.'"

28 Fonseca, "Notas y experiencias [1975]," 77–80; Blandón, *Entre Sandino,* 69, 80.

29 Fonseca, "Notas y experiencias [1975]," 24, 46, 57; Carlos Fonseca Amador, *Nicaragua Hora Cero,* in *Obras,* vol. 1, 86–87.

30 Carlos Fonseca Amador, "Bajo la sombre de Sandino [interview by Víctor Rico Galan]," *Siempre* (Mexico) 542 (13 Nov. 1963): 31. Between the analytical essays and personal correspondence of the first half of 1960 and this interview more than three years later, only one document attributed to Fonseca has survived, and its authorship is doubtful.

31 Carlos Fonseca Amador, "Charla del Co. Carlos Fonseca en la Conmemoración del 4 de Octubre," Havana, 4 Oct. 1973, CHM reg. 00248, caja 6 (1); Fonseca, "Notas y experiencias [1975]," 34, 81.

32 Fonseca, "La lucha armada en Nicaragua," 19 (this interview from *Punto Final* is reprinted as "Una entrevista a Carlos Fonseca," in the 23 June 1983 *Barricada,* but the *Barricada* version omits everything in the quoted passage after the words "Frente Sandinista"); the 1961 quote from Fonseca appeared in a later article about his 1964 arrest, *La Prensa,* 2 July 1964; Carlos Fonseca Amador, "Entrevista, 1970" [interview by Ernesto González Bermejo], in *Obras,* vol. 1, 227; Carlos Fonseca Amador, "Mensaje del FSLN con motivo del 150 aniversario del rompimiento del yugo colonial español," 21 Sept. 1971, CHM reg. 00317, caja 5.

33 In his 1970 *Punto Final* interview, "La lucha armada en Nicaragua," Fonseca said that mid-1958 saw a break with the "obscurantist tradition of the past, which was especially strong in Nicaragua for a variety of reasons, among them the fact that the country did not receive any at all of the late-nineteenth-century immigration of European workers who brought with them socialist ideas"; this passage is omitted from the version reprinted in *Barricada,* 23 June 1983. The same point is made in Fonseca, "Entrevista, 1970," 220, and Fonseca, *Viva Sandino,* 35.

34 Carlos Fonseca Amador, "Militancia activa del combatiente revolucionario," 6 June 1968, CHM reg. 00269, caja 2A.

35 Fonseca, "Notas y experiencias [1975]," 27.

36 Carlos Fonseca Amador, "Retornar a las montañas"; Fonseca, "Entrevista, 1970," 217, 219. See also Carlos Fonseca Amador, "Notas sobre la situación actual de Nicaragua," 21 June 1972, 20, CHM reg. 00247, caja 2A (15); and Fonseca, *Viva Sandino,* 35.

Chapter 4   Founding the FSLN, 1960–1964

1 Carlos Fonseca Amador, "La lucha por la transformación de Nicaragua, [1960]," in *Obras,* vol. 1, 28.

2 Ibid., 27.

3 Blandón, *Entre Sandino*, 206; Carlos Fonseca Amador, "Antecedentes del FSLN," *Ventana*, 6 July 1985. No copies of *Juventud Revolucionaria* are known to exist.

4 Carlos Fonseca Amador, "Breve análisis de la lucha popular nicaragüense contra la dictadura de Somoza," in *Obras*, vol. 1, 39–54; see also Frente Unitaria Nicaragüense, *Intervención Sangrienta: Nicaragua y su pueblo* (Caracas: FUN, 1961). Fonseca felt somewhat guilty about attending this conference because his mother had just arrived in Costa Rica to visit him, bringing his eight-year-old sister Estela.

5 See "Principios de la Juventud Patriótica Nicaragüense" and "El porque, para que, y como del JPN," in IHN, Colección Hacia el Sol de la Libertad.

6 Fonseca said the organizers of the JPN represented an "improvised" leadership thrown up by the mass movement at a time when the Nicaraguan masses had not yet found their "historic leadership." He considered it a leadership that "in general, almost without exception, showed itself not to be equal to the responsibilities history put in its hands." See Fonseca, "Antecedentes del FSLN"; Fonseca, "Notas y experiencias [1975]," 53.

7 CUUN, "Unámonos en la Liberación Nacional," León, 1960, in Traña et al., *Movimiento estudiantil*; Gould, "For an Organized Nicaragua," 368–75.

8 Fonseca, "Breve análisis [1960]," 48–49; Fonseca, "La lucha por la transformación [1960]," 29–30.

9 See Arias, *Nicaragua*, 26; Fonseca, "Lucha guerrillera," 16; "El Coronel Santos López en los primeros pasos del FSLN," *Barricada*, 28 Feb. 1984. Santos López died of natural causes in 1965.

10 "Comunicado del FSLN: Al combate, pueblo de Nicaragua," n.d., but OSN date stamp on file document says 26 Sept. 1963, CHM reg. 25076, caja 5; Frente Sandinista de Liberación Nacional, "Juramos vengar a los mártires del Rio Bocay," Managua, 10 Oct. 1963, CHM reg. 25077, caja 5; Fonseca, "Antecedentes del FSLN"; Fonseca, "Bajo la sombra de Sandino," 30.

11 Fonseca, "La lucha por la transformación [1960]," 37–38; Carlos Fonseca Amador, "Nicaragua, tierra amarga," *Nuevo Amanecer Cultural*, 21 July 1990; see also the wall poster "Manifiesto '23 de julio 1960.'"

12 Borge, *Paciente Impaciencia*, 121, 184, 187. This is the same conversation Borge placed in 1955 or 1956 in his prison writing *Carlos, the Dawn*. In the autobiographical *Paciente Impaciencia*, Borge is imprecise about the date, but he does say Guerrero was the main opponent of naming the organization after Sandino in the early 1960s.

13 Fonseca, "Antecedentes del FSLN"; Fonseca, *Yo acuso*, 236.

14 Heriberto Rodríguez Marín, interview by author, Managua, 14 Feb. 1996; see also the interview with Rodríguez in Manuel Eugarrios, "Carlos: Revolucionario ejemplar," *El Nuevo Diario*, 8 Nov. 1986; "Gabriel" (Germán Gaitán), Managua, to "Julián" (Carlos Fonseca), Tegucigalpa, 2 Aug. 1961, CHM reg. 00392, caja 3, folder "cartas."

15 Fonseca, "Declaración, 1964," 183, 188.

16 "El Frente de Liberación Nacional (Sus Fines)," *Trinchera*, Jan. 1963, in IHN, Colección Hacia el Sol de la Libertad.

17 Buitrago, nineteen years old in 1963 and from a working-class Managua family, later became head of the urban underground. All three of these UCA leaders were killed by

the National Guard between 1967 and 1969. CEUCA, "Los estudiantes de la UCA manifiestan . . . ," in Traña et al., *Movimiento estudiantil.*

18 See, for example, Borge, *Carlos, the Dawn,* 33; Black, *Triumph,* 75; Lisa Gross, *Handbook of Leftist Guerrilla Groups in Latin America and the Caribbean* (Boulder, Colo.: Westview Press, 1995), 126.

19 "And in 1961—here's an odd fact we haven't noticed before—on the 19th of July, 1961, the FSLN was founded. (We have been in such a state of shock that I'm only now, at this very moment, noticing the coincidence.)"; Borge, "Historia Político-militar del FSLN," *Encuentro* 15 (Sept. 1979), 41.

20 Rodolfo Romero, interview by author, Granada, 24 June 1994. At the time of this interview, Romero was an active rank-and-file member of the FSLN.

21 Fonseca, "Notas y experiencias [1975]," 65.

22 Blandón, *Entre Sandino,* 214–16; Paco Ignacio Taibo II, *Guevara, Also Known as Che* (New York: St. Martin's Press, 1997), 357–59; "Entrevista a Carlos Fonseca Amador por Elena A. Ferrada," Radio Habana, Cuba, 30 Oct. 1970, transcription in CHM reg. 24807, caja 6, italics in original.

23 Claribel Alegría and D. J. Flakoll, *Nicaragua: La revolución sandinista* (México: Ediciones Era, 1982), 192–93.

24 Regis Debray, *Revolution in the Revolution?* (New York: Grove Press, 1967); see also Matt D. Childs, "A Historical Critique of the Emergence and Evolution of Ernesto Che Guevara's *Foco* Theory," *Journal of Latin American Studies* 27 (Oct. 1995): 593–624.

25 Fonseca, "Notas y experiencias [1975]," 58–60. Ríos Coco y Bocay was the name given to the guerrilla operation of 1963.

26 Mayo, "Fue una noche de junio," *Juventud Rebelde,* 7 June 1988, 8; Anderson, *Che Guevara,* 394, 396; IES, Colección Dirección Nacional Histórica, "Silvio Mayorga."

27 Fonseca, "Declaración, 1964," 184; Fonseca, "Entrevista, 1970," 222.

28 Gabriela Selser, "La primera guerrilla del Frente Sandinista," *Barricada Edición especial,* 7 Nov. 1986.

29 Fonseca, "Declaración, 1964," 184–85. *Frente interno* referred to the underground organization inside the country, especially in the cities.

30 In a 1979 speech, Borge referred to Guerrero as "a Nicaraguan guy who lived many years in Mexico and whose name I don't want to mention" (Borge, "Historia Político-militar del FSLN"). Fonseca must have been talking about Guerrero when he said that the leadership group of 1962 lacked cohesion because of the decisive weight of "elements with pacifistic bad habits, who in any case soon afterward abandoned and deserted the revolutionary movement" (Carlos Fonseca Amador, "Notas sobre la lucha popular contra la tiranía somocista," 1973, CHM reg. 00253, caja 2B). See also Tomás Borge, "Carlos y la fundación del FSLN," *Barricada,* 8 Nov. 1980.

31 Borge, "Historia Político-militar del FSLN," *Encuentro* 15 (Sept. 1979), 43.

32 Arias, *Nicaragua,* 28; Selser, "La primera guerrilla," *Barricada,* 7 Nov. 1986.

33 Fonseca, "Bajo la sombra de Sandino," 30; Fonseca, "Notas sobre la lucha popular [1973]."

34 Ibid.

35 Fonseca, "Declaración, 1964," 187–88.

36 Gabriela Selser, "En algun lugar de Nicaragua," *Barricada Edición especial,* 7 Nov. 1986; *La Prensa,* 17 Aug. 1976.

37 Roberto Fonseca López, "Carlos en la cárcel hace 25 años," *Barricada,* 23 June 1989.

38 *La Prensa,* 2 July 1964. "Quién causa tanta alegría? Carlos Fonseca con su guerrilla" was adapted from "Quién causa tanta alegría? La Concepción de María." See Suárez, "En cada militante," *Nicaráuac* 13 (Nov.–Dec. 1986).

39 *La Prensa,* 1, 2 July 1964; Roberto Fonseca López, "Carlos en la cárcel hace 25 años," *Barricada,* 23 June 1989; Fidel Castro, "History Will Absolve Me," in *Fidel Castro's Political Strategy: From Moncada to Victory,* by Marta Harnecker and Fidel Castro (New York: Pathfinder Press, 1987); Nelson Mandela, *The Struggle Is My Life* (New York: Pathfinder Press, 1986).

40 The newspaper's hostility to Fonseca became much sharper after the founding of the FSLN and continued at the editorial level until the end of his life. Before 1963, *La Prensa* sometimes published favorable articles about Fonseca's opposition activity and even an affectionate, although more than a little patronizing, poem: "Muchachito / A Carlos Fonseca A. / Muchachito de barrio / muchachito sin menú / muchachito de una sola camisa" (*La Prensa,* 17 July 1960). The relationship between *La Prensa* and the FSLN took on a new dynamic in the mid-1970s, when many reporters became sympathetic to the organization and some became members. Less than a year after the 1979 revolution, the newspaper split, with the pro-FSLN reporters and editors setting up a new daily newspaper called *El Nuevo Diario,* and the anti-FSLN faction in firm control of *La Prensa.* The Chamorro family itself split: *La Prensa, El Nuevo Diario,* and the new FSLN daily *Barricada* were all edited by children or siblings of Pedro Joaquín Chamorro.

41 *La Prensa,* 1, 2, 3 July 1964; Reynaldo Antonio Téfel, "El caso Fonseca Amador, Los Somozas, y el Comunismo," *La Prensa,* 19 July 1964.

42 Carlos Fonseca Amador, *Desde la cárcel yo acuso a la dictadura,* in *Obras,* vol. 1, 231–38.

43 Marcio Vargas and Filadelfo Alemán, "A pesar de todo . . . vacío," *La Prensa,* 8 Nov. 1979; Arnando Ñurinda, "El 'Yo acuso' de Carlos Fonseca," *El Nuevo Diario,* 22 June 1985; Carlos Fonseca Amador, *Esta es la verdad,* in *Obras,* vol. 1, 239–42. English translations of *Yo acuso* and *Esta es la verdad* appear in Tomás Borge, *The Patient Impatience* (Willimantic, Conn.: Curbstone Press, 1992), 190–98.

44 Years later Carlos told Haydeé that he remembered meeting her for the first time in the late 1950s, when he knocked on her family's door collecting signatures on a protest petition (María Haydeé Terán, interview by author, León, 2 July 1994). Robleto soon realized that an emotional bond was developing between Fonseca and Terán. When there were other visitors and the guards would only allow two people at a time to visit Fonseca, Haydeé went to talk to Carlos, and Octavio passed the time with Víctor Tirado (Octavio Robleto, interview by author, Managua, 9 June 1995). María Haydeé Terán never joined the FSLN.

45 María Haydeé Terán, interview by author, León, 2 July 1994. Carlos Fonseca, Tapachula, Mexico, to Rodolfo Tapia Molina, director, Radio Informaciones, Managua, 16 Jan. 1965, CHM reg. 00333, caja 5; "Carlos Fonseca visto por María Haydeé Terán," *Barricada,* 9 Nov. 1979.

Chapter 5   The Evolution of a Strategy, 1964–1968

1   Fonseca, "La lucha por la transformación [1960]," 30; Fonseca, "Lucha armada en Nicaragua"; Fonseca, "Notas sobre la lucha popular [1973]."

2   Fonseca, "Declaración, 1964," 191.

3   Arias, *Nicaragua,* 33, 35, 26.

4   One wing of the Conservative Party backed Schick while the other called for a boycott after its candidate, Fernando Agüero, was not allowed to campaign freely; see Alegría and Flakoll, *Nicaragua,* 173; Chamorro, "Estado y hegemonia," 260–66; Victoria Gonzalez, "Somocista Women, Right-Wing Politics, and Feminism in Nicaragua, 1936–1979," paper presented at Latin American Studies Association Conference, Chicago, 24–26 Sept. 1998.

5   Thomas W. Walker, *The Christian Democratic Movement in Nicaragua* (Tucson: University of Arizona, Institute of Government Research, 1970), 9, 17; Enríquez, *Harvesting Change,* 37–38, 41–43.

6   Amaru Barahona, *Estudio sobre la historia de Nicaragua del auge cafetalero al triunfo de la revolución* (Managua: Instituto Nicaragüense de Investigaciones Económicas y Sociales, 1989); Enríquez, *Harvesting Change,* 37–47; Biderman, "Class Structure"; Cancino, *Las raíces históricas,* 109; *Extra* (Managua), Suplemento 72 (25 Dec. 1969).

7   Tomás Borge, "Historia político-militar del FSLN," *Encuentro* 15 (Sept. 1979).

8   *La Prensa,* 13 Aug. 1976, quoting Tomás Borge.

9   IES Archive: Colección Dirección Nacional Histórica, "Casimiro Sotelo."

10 Walker, *Christian Democratic Movement,* 37, 45.

11 Arias, *Nicaragua,* 36–37.

12 Fonseca, "Entrevista, 1970," 222–23; Fonseca, *Hora Cero,* 87–88; Fonseca, "Notas sobre la lucha popular [1973]."

13 *Movilización Republicana* (Managua), no. 114 (5 Aug. 1965). Only a few issues of *Movilización Republicana* have been located; the others (from 1964 and 1965) are similar.

14 Fonseca, "Notas sobre la lucha popular [1973]"; Fonseca, *Hora Cero,* 88.

15 Ernesto Che Guevara, "Vietnam and the Struggle for Freedom (Message to the Tricontinental)," in *Che Guevara and the Cuban Revolution* (New York: Pathfinder Press, 1987), 347–60; Carlos Fonseca Amador et al., "Sandino sí, Somoza no; revolución sí, farsa electoral no!" in *Obras,* vol. 1, 243–47.

16 Alegria and Flakoll, *Nicaragua,* 178; Walker, *Christian Democratic Movement,* 17.

17 Herrera, *Carlos Fonseca: El anhelo,* 32–35; Víctor Guillén, "A partir de abril del 66," *Nicaráuac,* 13 (Nov.–Dec. 1986): 121.

18 Fonseca, *Viva Sandino,* 52; Michael J. Schroeder, " 'To Defend Our Nation's Honor': Toward a Social and Cultural History of the Sandino Rebellion in Nicaragua, 1927–1934" (Ph.D. diss., University of Michigan, 1993); Fonseca, "Notas sobre la lucha popular [1973]"; Arias, *Nicaragua,* 96.

19 Gladys Baez, interview by author, León, 1 July 1994; see also Randall, *Sandino's Daughters,* 175–77.

20 Walker, *Christian Democratic Movement.*

21 Fonseca, "Notas sobre la lucha popular [1973]"; Fonseca, "Entrevista, 1970," 224; Fonseca, "Retornar a las montañas."

22 Arias, *Nicaragua,* 46.

23 Fonseca, "Notas sobre la lucha popular [1973]," part 7.

24 Guillén, "A partir de abril," 124.

25 Carlos Fonseca Amador, "Mensaje del FSLN en el 34 aniversario del asesinato de A. C. Sandino: Continuámos combatiendo!" 21 Feb. 1968, CHM reg. 25299, caja 5; Carlos Fonseca Amador ["for the FSLN"], "Mensaje del FSLN en ocasión del 1° de Mayo," 1 May 1968, CHM reg. 25300, caja 5; Carlos Fonseca Amador, "Mensaje del FSLN a las madres de los Mártires nicaragüenses," 30 May 1968, CHM reg. 00299, caja 5; Carlos Fonseca Amador, "Yanqui Johnson: Go Home," in *Obras,* vol. 1, 251–53; Carlos Fonseca Amador, "En el primer aniversario de la inmolación del 'Che' juramos ser leales a su ejemplo," 8 Oct. 1968, CHM reg. 25281, caja 5; Carlos Fonseca Amador, "Los mártires del FSLN son el honor de la Nicaragua de hoy," 4 Nov. 1968, CHM reg. 25090, caja 5.

26 "En las montañas de Yaosca combaten nuestros compañeros; el movimiento guerrillero es invencible," 28 Feb. 1969, signed with pseudonym "Juan Pablo," CHM reg. 18859, caja 5.

27 Carlos Fonseca Amador, *Mensaje del Frente Sandinista de Liberación Nacional, FSLN, a los estudiantes revolucionarios,* in *Obras,* vol. 1, 55–74. The next year, Fonseca would insert into the Historic Program of the FSLN a sharp attack on self-centered academics: "The university must stop being a breeding ground for bureaucratic egotists."

28 Carlos Fonseca, to "Lic. R. C." [Raul Castellon], 28 June 1968, CHM reg. 00354, caja 3(6); the original of Fonseca's handwritten letter was found in an OSN file, along with a photocopy with the margin note "delivered by messenger," suggesting the recipient turned it over to the police; Carlos Fonseca to "Dr. A. R.," 22 Mar. 1968, CHM reg. 00363, caja 3(6).

29 Fonseca, *Mensaje,* 57, 64, 59.

30 Omar Cabezas, *La montaña es algo mas que una inmensa estepa verde* (Mexico: Siglo XXI, 1982), 38; Blandón, *Entre Sandino,* 205.

31 Fonseca, *Mensaje,* 67, 68.

32 See Jorge G. Castañeda, *Utopia Unarmed: The Latin American Left after the Cold War* (New York: Alfred A. Knopf, 1993).

33 Carlos Tunnerman Bernheim, *La Universidad: Búsqueda permanente* (León: Editorial Universitaria de la UNAN, 1971), 23, 36.

34 Dr. Alejandro Serrano C. et al., *Frente a la situación nacional: Documento de la generación del 23 de Julio* (León: Editorial Antorcha, 1969).

35 Walker, *Christian Democratic Movement,* 52; Fonseca, *Mensaje,* 67.

36 Camilo Torres, "Mensaje a los Estudiantes," *Revista Conservadora del Pensamiento Centroamericano* 105 (June 1969): 6.

37 Forrest D. Colburn, *The Vogue of Revolution in Poor Countries* (Princeton: Princeton University Press, 1994).

38 Gladys Baez, interview by author, León, 1 July 1994; Heyck, *Life Stories,* 93–94.

39 Plutarco Hernández, *El FSLN por dentro* (San José: Talleres Gráficos de Trejos Hermanos, 1982), 29–33.

40 Fonseca, *Mensaje*, 67.

41 Ernesto Cardenal, interview by author, Managua, 27 June 1994. David Tejada was killed in mid-1968.

42 José Coronel Urtecho, "Carlos Resucitó a Sandino," *Nuevo Amanecer Cultural*, 8 Nov. 1986; see also Beltrán Morales, "Carlos fue el centro, el alma del Frente en realidad," *Nuevo Amanecer Cultural*, 7 Nov. 1982.

43 Fonseca, "Militancia activa," 1.

44 "28 muertos, 16 en la cárcel y 12 en la clandestinidad: Saldo del FSLN," *Extra Semanal*, 27 July 1969.

Chapter 6   Underground and Prison Life, 1968–1970

1 Hugo Torres, "Semblanza de una leyenda llamada Carlos," *Barricada*, 8 Nov. 1988.

2 María Haydeé Terán, interviews by author, León, 2 July 1994 and 27 Jan. 1996; "Carlos Fonseca Amador: Es patrióta no ladrón" [interview with María Haydeé Terán and Sergio Ardón], *El Universitario* (San José), Sept. 1969; folders "OSN: Informes de vigilancia a M. H. Terán" and "OSN: Telefonemas interceptados a M. H. Terán," in CHM caja 1A.

3 Benita Alvarado, interview by author, Matagalpa, 20 Feb. 1996; Dona Bütching, interview by author, Matagalpa, 10 June 1995; Luz Marina Acosta, "Km. 20, Testimonio sobre Carlos Fonseca," *Nuevo Amanecer Cultural*, 8 Nov. 1986; María Haydeé Terán, interview by author, León, 27 Jan. 1996.

4 Ortega, "Estrategia triunfante," *Barricada*, 7 Nov. 1979; Carlos Manuel Pérez Alonso, Guatemala, to Excelentísimo General Don Anastasio Somoza Debayle, Jefe Supremo de las Fuerzas Armadas, Managua, 29 Jan. 1973, CHM reg. 00529, caja 1.

5 Espinoza, whose mother worked as a washerwoman in León to support her large family, was the first female FSLN member killed by the National Guard (Randall, *Sandino's Daughters*, 33); Fonseca knew Burke in Cuba in the early 1960s (Suárez, "En cada militante," *Nicaráuac* 13 [Nov.–Dec. 1986], 134; Marta Rojas Rodríguez, *Tania, la guerrillera inolvidable* [Havana: Instituto del Libro, 1970], 149); Arias, *Nicaragua*, 126.

6 Ernesto Cardenal, interview by author, Managua, 27 June 1994.

7 CHM reg. 00533, caja 1, folder "OSN: Documentos personales"; CHM reg. 00536–00538 and 00540–00542, caja 1.

8 Humberto Fonseca Linares, "Las casas de seguridad de Carlos," *El Nuevo Diario*, 7 Nov. 1982; Selser, "En algun lugar," *Barricada*, 7 Nov. 1986; Yolanda Núñez, interview by author, Managua, 22 Jan. 1996.

9 Fonseca Linares, "Las casas de seguridad," *El Nuevo Diario*, 7 Nov. 1982.

10 Selser, "En algún lugar," *Barricada*, 7 Nov. 1986.

11 Cabezas, *La montaña*, 50–51, 53–55; Arias, *Nicaragua*, 72.

12 Acosta, "Km. 20," *Nuevo Amanecer Cultural*, 8 Nov. 1986. Carlos José Guadamuz, *Y . . . las casas quedaron llenas de humo* (Managua: Editorial Nueva Nicaragua, 1982), 50. "Amanda" was Olga López Avilez, and "Tamara" was Fátima Avilez; the two male guerrillas were Carlos Guadamuz and Róger Núñez.

13 Randall, *Sandino's Daughters*, 30; Guadamuz, *Y . . . las casas*, 36.

14 Doris Tijerino, interview by author, Managua, 28 June 1994. See also Randall, *San-*

dino's Daughters Revisited, 132–34, for Milú Vargas's story of how her application to join the FSLN was held up for four years because the man with whom she was living (a member of the FSLN National Directorate) was officially married to someone else.

15 "Para la generación del 60: Carlos Fonseca es como los pinos del Norte," *Barricada,* 8 Nov. 1987.

16 "Abraham" [Carlos Fonseca], San José, to "Angel" [Julio Buitrago?], Managua, 14 Dec. 1965; CHM folder "cartas a Julio Buitrago," reg. 00343, caja 3. Although this document is in a folder entitled "letters to Julio Buitrago," it was probably directed to some other underground leader; Buitrago was living on the Atlantic Coast in December 1965.

17 Guadamuz, *Y . . . Las casas,* 43; "Para la generación del 60," *Barricada,* 8 Nov. 1987.

18 Heriberto Rodríguez Marín, interview by author, Managua, 14 Feb. 1996; Fonseca, "Militancia activa"; Blandón, *Entre Sandino,* 207; Doris Tijerino, interview by author, Managua, 28 June 1994; María Haydeé Terán, interview by author, León, 2 July 1994; Carlos Fonseca Amador, "Análisis Sucesos de Nandaime," 20 Oct. 1973, CHM reg. 00254, caja 2B.

19 CHM reg. 00535(8), caja 1, folder "OSN: Documentos personales." Although this file appears to be genuine, I am personally skeptical because the behavior was so out of character for Carlos Fonseca. Fausto Amador could have invented the warning to demonstrate his loyalty to Somoza. The OSN could have planted false information in its own files, as it did on other occasions. The report could have resulted from misinformation or confusion.

20 See Alegría and Flakoll, *Nicaragua,* 197. "¡Que se rinda tu madre!" was seen everywhere on posters and banners during mobilizations against the contra war of the 1980s.

21 Carlos Fonseca Amador, "Lucha guerrillera en Nicaragua," *Punto Final* (Santiago), no. 110 (4 Aug. 1970): 17; Borge, *Carlos, the Dawn,* 57. (Typically, Fonseca says 200 troops and two hours, whereas Borge says more than three hours and more than 400 troops.) "El Diario de Julio Buitrago," *Extra Semanal* (Managua), no. 51 (27 July 1969).

22 "El Diario de Julio Buitrago."

23 Fonseca, "Lucha guerrillera," 15–17; letters to Dr. A. R., Dr. A. P. A., Dr. R. C. M., Lic. R. C., Mar.–June 1968, CHM regs. 00363, 00352, 00355, 00534, caja 3.

24 Carlos Fonseca Amador, León, to Coronel Anastasio Somoza Debayle, Managua, 11 Dec. 1956, CHM reg. 00346, caja 3; folder "cartas a Agatón," CHM regs. 00390–00395, caja 3(5); CHM reg. 00567, caja 1B; "Jorge" [Jaime Wheelock], Santiago, Chile, to "Compañero Cardenal," Managua, 10 Apr. 1973, CHM reg. 00033, caja 3. The files had been moved from the OSN headquarters to Somoza's heavily fortified bunker in Managua, where they were discovered by Rodolfo Romero and Guerrilla Commander Hugo Torres on 19 July 1979. "We still don't understand how they could have left all those documents there for us to find," Romero said in 1994. "All the secrets were there, the secret police plans going back to 1968, the list of the informers they had infiltrated into various organizations." The files were in a room with Somoza's huge collection of pornographic films. See Rodolfo Romero, interview by author, Granada, 24 June 1994.

25 CHM reg. 00362, caja 3(6); Julián Guerrero Castillo and Lola Soriano de Guerrero, *100 Biografías Centroamericanas*, vol. 1 (Managua: Imprenta Nacional, 1971, 1973), 360–63.

26 Josefina Tijerina, to Víctor, Mexico, 20 Feb. 1965, CHM reg. 00386, caja 3(6); Wunderich, *Sandino*, 110.

27 Fonseca, *Hora Cero*, 93; Humberto Ortega Saavedra, "Carlos usó la cárcel para ser más grande de lo que era," á *Barricada*, 23 Oct. 1980; "Salvador" [Carlos Fonseca], San José, 28 May 1969, to "Hermano" [Julio Buitrago], Managua, CHM reg. 00357, caja 3, folder "cartas a Julio Buitrago."

28 Ibid.

29 FSLN, *El Programa Histórico del FSLN* (Managua: DEPEP, 1981). An English translation can be found in Bruce Marcus, ed., *Sandinistas Speak* (New York: Pathfinder Press, 1982), 13–22. The original 1969 version, "Programa Sandinista," is reproduced in Dennis Gilbert and David Block, eds., *Sandinistas: Key Documents/Documentos Claves* (Ithaca, N.Y.: Cornell University, Latin American Studies Program, 1990), 3–21.

30 *La Prensa*, 4 Sept. 1969.

31 Carlos Fonseca Amador, San José, 10 June 1960, to "Recordada doña Lolita," Matagalpa; Carlos Fonseca Amador, San José, 11 Apr. 1960, to "Querido papá," Managua; Fausto Amador, "How I Came to Be a Trotskyist," *Intercontinental Press* (New York), 27 June 1977, 743.

32 "La entrega de Fausto Jr," *Extra Semanal*, 24 Aug. 1969; "Carlos Fonseca A.: Nacido para la insurrección. El más completo reportaje sobre el hombe No. 1 del FSLN," *Extra Semanal*, 7 Sept. 1969; *Novedades*, 21 Aug. 1969, 1 Sept 1969.

33 Carlos Fonseca Amador, "Viva la Fraternidad Guerrillera," 22 Aug. 1969, in CHM reg. 00313, caja 5. A substantially edited version of this statement, with all references to Fausto Amador deleted, appears as Carlos Fonseca Amador, "Proclama del FSLN," in *Obras*, vol. 1, 267–69.

34 Carlos Fonseca Amador, "Algunos puntos sobre la situación de Nicaragua," Havana, 12 Nov. 1973, 4, CHM reg. 00247, caja 2A.

35 Carlos F. Chamorro B., "La última cárcel de Carlos Fonseca," *Barricada*, 24 June 1989; Fonseca, "Retornar a las montañas," 54. Rufo Marín was the name of a famous Sandinista fighter killed at the battle of Ocotal in July 1927; this could be a pseudonym, or the Marín of 1970 could be a descendant.

36 See Carlos Fonseca, San José penitentiary, to *Punto Final*, Santiago, Chile, 23 Mar. 1970, CHM reg. 00363, caja 5. Humberto Ortega was permanently disabled in the right arm as a result of his wounds.

37 Chamorro, "La última cárcel," *Barricada*, 24 June 1989. CHM caja 1A, folder OSN: Vigilancia a María Haydeé Terán; Carlos Fonseca Amador, "No Hay Islas" [Interview by Marco Altamirano], Oct. 1970, CHM reg. 00322, caja 6; Fonseca, "Lucha guerrillera," 15–18; Humberto Ortega Saavedra, "Conductor integral de la vanguardia," *Barricada*, 8 Nov. 1980; Ortega, "Estrategia triunfante," *Barricada*, 7 Nov. 1979.

38 Carlos Fonseca Amador, "Respuesta a un ideólogo de la tortura: Carta a Sr. Jorge Eduardo Arellano, Diario La Prensa," 15 Jan. 1969, CHM reg. 00356, caja 2A; *La Prensa*, 2 Feb. 1969; Carlos Fonseca Amador, Alajuela Prison, San José, to Pablo Antonio Cuadra, Managua, 2 Dec. 1969, CHM reg. 00306, caja 3 (ellipses in original).

39 "Carlos Fonseca A.: Nacido para la insurrección," *Extra Semanal,* 7 Sept 1969; Ernesto Cardenal, interview by author, Managua, 27 June 1994. See also Joaquín Sanson Arguello, "P.J.Ch.: Mi visita a Fonseca Amador fue humanitaria," in *Extra Semanal,* 21 Feb. 1971; "Seremos implacables y vendrá más dureza en la lucha anuncia Fonseca Amador," *Extra Semanal,* 14 Feb. 1971 (unsigned but author is William Ramírez).

40 Carlos Fonseca Amador, "Los ataques de los falsos revolucionarios de Costa Rica nos honran," *COPAN, Revista Teórica* (San José), nos. 2–3 (Aug. 1984): 94–105.

41 Rolando Angulo, "Carlos Fonseca, gran problema para Presidente Figueres," *Extra Semanal,* 16 Aug. 1970; Ortega, "Carlos usó la cárcel," *Barricada,* 23 Oct. 1980.

42 Oscar L. Montalbán, "Carlos Fonseca Amador, Pedro Joaquín Chamorro, y Fernando Agüero," *Extra Semanal,* 14 Sept. 1969; Wm. Ramírez, "Sobrino de Agüero Guerrillero FSLN," *Extra Semanal,* 31 Jan 1971; "Pueblo tico apoyó rescate de Carlos," *Barricada,* 21 Oct. 1980.

43 Fonseca, "Notas sobre la lucha popular [1973]."

44 Carlos Fonseca Amador, "Charla con una compañera (sobre la cárcel)," 28 Sept. 1973, CHM reg. 00324, caja 6(2).

45 Chamorro, "La última cárcel," *Barricada,* 24 June 1989; Ortega, "Conductor integral," *Barricada,* 8 Nov. 1980.

46 Fonseca, "Charla con una compañera"; Roberto Fonseca López, "Audacia, rebeldia y coraje en las cárceles del tirano," *Barricada,* 25 June 1989. See also Margaret Randall, *Sandino's Daughters* (Vancouver: New Star Books, 1980), 208, for the story of a working prostitute recruited to be an FSLN messenger.

47 Doris Tijerino, interviews by author, Managua, 28 June and 11 July 1994; Fonseca, "Charla con una compañera."

48 Tijerino, *Inside the Nicaraguan Revolution,* 75.

49 See Randall, *Sandino's Daughters,* 80.

50 Tijerino, *Inside the Nicaraguan Revolution,* 79–80; *Novedades,* 5 Aug. 1969.

51 Carlos Fonseca Amador, "Mensaje del FSLN con motivo del XVI aniversario del 21 de Septiembre," 15 Aug. 1972, CHM reg. 25288, caja 5 (also published in Havana as a small pamphlet entitled *La Tierra de Sandino clama Solidaridad*); Tijerino, *Inside the Nicaraguan Revolution,* 79.

52 Declaración de la Dirección del Frente Sandinista de Liberación Nacional (FSLN), 8 Jan. 1974, CHM reg. 00318, caja 5.

53 Randall, *Sandino's Daughters,* 166, 70; Fonseca, "Charla con una compañera"; Heyck, *Life Stories,* 248–49.

54 Fonseca, "Lucha guerrillera"; Fonseca, "Mensaje . . . 21 de Septiembre."

Chapter 7   The Sandino Writings, 1970–1974

1 Carlos Fonseca Amador, *Sandino: Guerrillero proletario,* in *Obras,* vol. 1, 368–84; Carlos Fonseca Amador, *Ideario político del general Sandino,* in *Obras,* vol. 2, 169–99; Carlos Fonseca Amador, *Cronología de la resistencia sandinista,* in *Obras,* vol. 2, 89–167; Carlos Fonseca Amador, *Crónica Secreta: Augusto César Sandino ante sus verdugos,* MS prepared in 1995 by Instituto de Historia de Nicaragua (extracts previously

published in *Obras,* vol. 1, 412–27, and *Barricada Edición especial,* 7 Nov. 1986); Fonseca, *Viva Sandino,* in *Obras,* vol. 2, 19–86. All page references are to these editions.

2   Carlos Fonseca Amador, "16 aniversario de la muerte del héroe nacional, Rigoberto López Pérez" [1972], CHM reg. 00623, caja 2A; Carlos Fonseca Amador, "Rigoberto López Pérez en la lucha por la Liberación," Havana, 1972, CHM reg. 00262, caja 2A; Carlos Fonseca Amador, "Notas sobre la carta-testamento de Rigoberto López Pérez," in *Obras,* vol. 1, 393–406.

3   Marcio Vargas, "La Historia de 'Viva Sandino,' " *Barricada,* 5 Nov. 1982.

4   See especially Fonseca, *Cronología,* 166–67.

5   The politicization of Sandino by Fonseca has been criticized by some recent historians who have tried to rescue Sandino a second time, now not from oblivion but from the vision of him created by Fonseca. See, for example, Wunderich, *Sandino,* and Michael J. Schroeder, "Horse Thieves to Rebels to Dogs: Political Gang Violence and the State in the Western Segovias, Nicaragua, in the Time of Sandino, 1926–1934," *Journal of Latin American Studies* 28 (May 1996): 383–434. They have had to untangle some of the "myth of Sandino" to do justice to the contextual framework of the late 1920s and early 1930s. But my own purpose is to do justice to the political reality of the late 1960s and early 1970s. Setting aside the more politicized aspects of Fonseca's historical writings may be useful to achieve a rounded portrait of Sandino, but it makes it impossible to understand Carlos Fonseca and the world he lived in.

6   Fonseca, *Viva Sandino,* 23.

7   Fonseca, *Síntesis,* 100.

8   Fonseca, *Viva Sandino,* 21, 85, 22; Fonseca, *Cronología,* 167.

9   Fonseca, "Charla en la Conmemoración del 4 de Octubre." Two Nicaraguans that Fonseca considered symbols of the fight against U.S.-imposed regimes fell in battle on 4 October: Liberal general Benjamín Zeladón in 1912 and veteran Sandinista Ramón Raudales in 1958.

10   Borge, *Paciente Impaciencia*; Fonseca, letter to Angel Guerra, Havana, 16 Feb. 1974. Fonseca was right, and the *Bohemia* author wrong; Martí's 1895 letter condemning the United States was suppressed until the 1959 revolution, so Sandino could not have read it.

11   Carlos Fonseca Amador, "Charla del Comp. Carlos Fonseca" (10 Sept. 1973), 6, CHM reg. 00292, caja 6. This document is a long transcript of Fonseca's remarks over a two-day period, with each day paginated separately.

12   Jaime Wheelock, "Presentación," in Carlos Fonseca Amador, *Obras,* vol. 2, 16; Borge, *Paciente Impaciencia,* 563.

13   Fonseca, *Guerrillero Proletario,* 375; Fonseca, *Viva Sandino,* 51, 56; Fonseca to Ángel Guerra, Havana, 16 Feb. 1974 (*Bohemia* did not publish this letter); Fonseca, *Viva Sandino,* 82; see also Fonseca, "Los ataques de los falsos revolucionarios," 96.

14   Fonseca, *Guerrillero Proletario,* 374, 372, 377; Fonseca, *Viva Sandino,* 63.

15   Fonseca, *Viva Sandino,* 50, 58.

16   Fonseca, "Lucha guerrillera," 18; Fonseca, *Ideario,* 174.

17   Fonseca, *Viva Sandino,* 73.

18 Ibid., 49, 50; Fonseca, *Ideario,* 176–77.

19 Fonseca, *Guerrillero Proletario,* 368; Fonseca, *Ideario,* 173.

20 Fonseca, *Viva Sandino,* 43; Fonseca, *Cronología;* Carlos Fonseca Amador, "Cronología histórica de Nicaragua," in *Obras,* vol. 1, 347–62; Carlos Fonseca Amador, "Reseña de la secular intervención norteamericana en Nicaragua," in *Obras,* vol. 1, 368–84; Fonseca, *Viva Sandino,* 24. The chronologies were long lists of historical events, focusing on foreign interventions and the local opposition to them.

21 Fonseca, "Charla del Comp. Carlos Fonseca" (10 Sept. 1973), 2.

22 Fonseca, *Guerrillero Proletario,* 373.

23 Fonseca, "Retornar a las montañas," 56; Fonseca, *Ideario,* 178.

24 Fonseca, *Ideario,* 178.

25 *Viva Sandino,* 64. The theme of Sandino's honesty and simplicity comes across repeatedly in the interviews with elderly veterans and peasants collected in IES, *Ahora sé que Sandino manda* (Managua: Editorial Nueva Nicaragua, 1986).

26 Fonseca, *Guerrillero Proletario,* 383; Fonseca, *Ideario,* 197.

27 Fonseca, *Viva Sandino,* 83.

28 Ibid., 74–75.

29 Fonseca, *Guerrillero Proletario,* 371.

30 Fonseca, *Viva Sandino,* 34–40.

31 Ibid., 47; Fonseca, "Los ataques de los falsos revolucionarios," 101–2.

32 In 1971 a pact between Somoza and Fernando Agüero formalized the latest power-sharing arrangement between the two parties; from 1972 to 1974, the country was run by a triumvirate made up of two Somocista Liberals, and Conservative Agüero—called by the Sandinistas the "junta of the three little pigs."

33 Fonseca, *Ideario,* 179; Fonseca, *Síntesis,* 101–2.

34 Ernesto Cardenal, interview by author, Managua, 27 June 1994.

35 Fonseca, *Ideario,* 180. In both 1928 and 1932, the U.S. military officer who was president of the Electoral Council virtually ran Nicaragua. See Walter, *Regime,* 13.

36 Fonseca, *Viva Sandino,* 79, 80; Fonseca, *Guerrillero Proletario,* 382.

37 Fonseca, "Lucha guerrillera," 18; Fonseca, *Cronología,* 110, 125, 161.

38 Ibid., 127; Fonseca, *Ideario,* 188–89; Fonseca, *Viva Sandino,* 85. This theme is developed in Matilde Zimmermann, "La Conexión Centroamericana: Ideologías revolucionarias entre 1959 y 1979," paper presented at the Tercer Congreso Centroamericano de Historia, San José, Costa Rica, 18 July 1996.

39 Carlos Fonseca, San José, to "Querido Papá," Managua, 15 Jan. 1960, IHN Archive.

40 Carlos Fonseca Amador, "No Hay Islas" [1970 interview by Marco Altomirano], in *Obras,* vol. 1, 202.

41 Fonseca, *Viva Sandino,* 70, Fonseca, *Ideario,* 182, 185; Fonseca, *Cronología,* 110, 130; Fonseca, *Guerrillero Proletario,* 378; Wunderich, *Sandino,* 221.

42 Wunderich, *Sandino,* 189, 208.

43 Fonseca, *Ideario,* 185; Fonseca, *Viva Sandino,* 68.

44 Ibid., 71.

45 Ibid., 77, 47, 45.

46 Fonseca, "Lucha guerrillera," 18.

1   Carlos Fonseca Amador, "Mensaje de Carlos Fonseca, dirigente del Frente Sandinista de Liberación Nacional," Havana, 7 Nov. 1970, IHN, Colección Hacia el Sol de la Libertad.

2   Fonseca, "Mensaje con motivo del 150 aniversario" [1971]; Borge, *Paciente Impaciencia*, 303, 356; Doris Tijerino, interview by author, Managua, 28 June 1994; Heyck, *Life Stories*, 117.

3   Jacinto Suárez, interview by author, Managua, 8 July 1994; Carlos Fonseca Amador for DN of FSLN, "Acerca de la solidaridad," 12 June 1972, CHM reg. 00272, caja 5.

4   Camilo, for example, turned over to Fonseca a personal letter from his brother in which Humberto revealed his political differences with the rest of the DN. See Carlos Fonseca Amador, "Nota sobre algunos problemas de hoy," Mar. 1976; in author's files, unpaginated MS, point 9.

5   Hodges, *Intellectual Foundations*, 245; Nolan, *Ideology of the Sandinistas*, 57, 144.

6   Only two of Fonseca's many contributions to the tendency debate have been published, *Síntesis de algunos problemas actuales,* written in Managua in November 1975, and *Notas sobre la montaña y algunos otros temas,* written in October 1976, shortly before Fonseca's death. In the latter article, he promises to "deal as carefully as I can with any questions that are subject to differences of opinion." Historical speeches and articles by surviving FSLN leaders pass quickly over the tendency dispute and never acknowledge any involvement of Fonseca except that he "favored unity." See, for example, Tomás Borge, "Carlos, el constructor revolucionario," *El Nuevo Diario,* 22 Nov. 1982.

7   See, for example, FSLN [TI], "La situacion general del FSLN [April 1978]," reprinted in Gabriel García Márquez et al., *Los Sandinistas* (Bogotá: La Oveja Negra, 1980), 188–223; FSLNTP, *La Crisis Interna y Las Tendencias* (Los Angeles: Sandinistas por el Socialismo en Nicaragua, 1978); *Gaceta Sandinista* (Havana) was one of the periodicals reflecting the views of the GPP; *Lucha Sandinista* (San José) identified itself as "the organ of the Exterior Commission of the FSLN," and was published by the terceristas.

8   See Black, *Triumph,* 91; Booth, *The End and the Beginning,* 143; Gilbert, *Sandinistas,* 8.

9   FSLN, "Sobre la Guerra Popular Prolongada, La Celula Sandinista y Algunos Problemas," Aug. 1975, IHN, Colección Hacia el Sol de la Libertad; Oscar Turcios, "Condiciones para una organización verdaderamente Revolucionaria," and "Acerca de las celulas," in IES, Colección Dirección Nacional Histórica, 113–16; Carlos Fonseca Amador, "El Enemigo Confiesa," 1973, CHM reg. 00275, caja 2A; Carlos Fonseca Amador, "Carta a compañeros de la parroquia," 31 July 1974, point 7, CHM reg. 00367, caja 2B (44).

10 Carlos Fonseca Amador, "Análisis sobre la situación nacional, el Programa Sandinista, en ocasión del Primero de Mayo de 1970," CHM reg. 25279, caja 2B.

11 Cancino, *Las raices históricas,* 110.

12 Carlos Fonseca Amador and Humberto Ortega, "Notas sobre comunicación 'Questiones urgentes para la organización,'" 30 Apr. 1974, CHM reg. 00282, caja 2B.

13 Fonseca, *Síntesis,* 110.

14 "Acerca del trabajo revolucionario en barrios y comunidades," 1973, IHN, Colección Hacia el Sol de la Libertad; Fonseca, "Charla del Comp. Carlos Fonseca" (10 Sept. 1973), 11, 4.

15 "Oscar Turcios Chavarria," in IES, Colección Dirección Nacional Histórica; Fonseca, "Notas sobre algunos problemas actuales," 1972; CHM reg. 00247, caja 2A, unpaginated MS, point 14, italics in original; Fonseca, "Charla del Comp. Carlos Fonseca" (11 Sept. 1973), 11.

16 Fonseca, *Síntesis*, 120.

17 Ruiz, "La montaña," 14; Fonseca, "Notas sobre la lucha popular [1973]," section 8; Fonseca, *Síntesis*, 120.

18 Carlos Fonseca Amador, "Respuesta a las Cuestiones que Plantean los Compañeros en los Textos que Elaboraron con Motivo de los Documentos que les Fueron Suministrados," CHM reg. 00289, caja 2B (37), n.p., part 4; Fonseca, "Charla del Comp. Carlos Fonseca" (10 Sept. 1973), 18; Fonseca, "Notas sobre algunos problemas actuales [1972]," point 42.

19 Fonseca, "Notas sobre algunos problemas actuales [1972]," points 20, 22, 23, 41; Fonseca, "Carta a compañeros de la parroquia [1974]," point 21.

20 Fonseca, "Notas y experiencias [1975]," 76, 60, 65.

21 FSLN, "Lineas y criterios que entrarán en el plan de acción militar," CHM reg. 00266, caja 2A(13). The CHM inventory dates this document to 1973, but internal evidence suggests it was written after mid-1975. That it was issued in the name of the FSLN with a political approach so different from Fonseca's suggests that the FSLN leader was either in the mountains or already dead.

22 Francisco Rivera, *La Marca del Zorro* (Managua: Editorial Nueva Nicaragua, 1989), 211.

23 Fonseca, "Charla del Comp. Carlos Fonseca" (10 Sept. 1973), 6.

24 Carlos Fonseca Amador, "Carta a los nicaragüenses residentes en Estados Unidos" [30 Jan. 1973], in *Obras*, vol. 1, 154–55; Carlos Fonseca Amador, letter to "Hermano Afronorteamericano" [30 Jan. 1973], *Barricada*, 5 Nov. 1985; Carlos Fonseca Amador, letter to "Hermanos Indios de los Estados Unidos" [30 Jan. 1973], in author's files; Carlos Fonseca Amador, "Llamamiento del Comité de Nicaragüenses en el exterior pro damnificados," Havana, 1973, CHM reg. 00303, caja 5.

25 Carlos Fonseca Amador for FSLN, "Algunos aspectos del trabajo entre las masas" [text says 1971, but internally dated to post–Dec. 1972 earthquake], IHN, Colección Hacia el Sol de la Libertad, unpaginated MS, points 41, 42.

26 Doris Tijerino, interview by author, Managua, 11 July 1994.

27 Fonseca, "Mensaje de Carlos Fonseca [1970].

28 Fonseca, "Algunos aspectos del trabajo [1973?]," points 40, 35.

29 Fonseca, "Charla del Comp. Carlos Fonseca" (10 Sept. 1973), 9, 15; (11 Sept. 1973), 15.

30 Fonseca, *Notas sobre la montaña*, 140–41.

31 Carlos Fonseca Amador, "Reunión general para informar sobre problemas de la organización," Havana, 14 Nov. 1973, CHM reg. 00293, caja 2B; Fonseca, "Nota sobre algunos problemas de hoy [1976]," points 5–12.

32 Fonseca, *Viva Sandino*, 74; Fonseca, *Cronología*, 123–24, 133. The chant "¡Un Solo Ejército!" became a code word for FSLN and Nicaraguan unity in the early 1980s.

Michael J. Schroeder has shown, however, that Sandino's EDSN was at least as riven with factionalism as the FSLN; see Schroeder, "Horse Thieves"; Schroeder, "To Defend Our Nation's Honor."

33 Fonseca, "No Hay Islas," 201; Fonseca, "Charla del Comp. Carlos Fonseca" (11 Sept. 1973), 10. As he was speaking, the Allende government was being overthrown in Chile, but the FSLN leaders in Havana did not learn about this until the end of their meeting. A few months earlier, Fonseca had ordered the small FSLN nucleus in Santiago to leave Chile because he feared a military confrontation was coming on which they could have no impact.

34 Fonseca, "Nota sobre algunos problemas de hoy [1976]," point 16.

35 Fonseca, "Notas sobre algunos problemas [1972]," point 30; see, for example, "Abraham" [Carlos Fonseca], San José, to "Ángel" [Julio Buitrago?], Managua, 14 Dec. 1965, CHM folder "cartas a Julio Buitrago," reg. 00343, caja 3; Fonseca, "Los ataques de los falsos revolucionarios"; see especially Fonseca, "Notas sobre algunos problemas actuales, [1972]," point 30; and Fonseca, "Nota sobre algunos problemas de hoy [1976]," point 26.

36 Fonseca, "Charla del Comp. Carlos Fonseca" (10 Sept. 1973), 17; Fonseca, Síntesis, 109; Fonseca, Viva Sandino, 53; Fonseca, "Viva la Fraternidad Guerrillera."

37 Frente Sandinista, Diciembre Victorioso (Mexico: Editorial Diógenes, 1979); DEPEP (FSLN), Y se rompió el silencio (Managua: Editorial Nueva Nicaragua, 1981); Gabriel García Márquez, El Asalto: El operativo con que el FSLN se lanzó al mundo (Managua: Editorial Nueva Nicaragua, 1982).

38 See FSLNTP, La Crisis Interna y Las Tendencias, 2.

39 Hernández, El FSLN por dentro, 74.

40 Fonseca, "Reunión general [1973]."

41 Fonseca, "Carta a compañeros de la parroquia [1974]," point 27; Fonseca and H. Ortega, "Notas sobre comunicación 'Questiones urgentes' [1974]"; Vargas and Alemán, "A pesar de todo," La Prensa, 8 Nov. 1979.

42 María Haydeé Terán, interview by author, León, 2 July 1994; Borge, Paciente Impaciencia, 280; Noel Irías and María Haydeé Terán: "Era muy cariñoso," Barricada, 8 Nov. 1992.

43 Margaret Randall, Albuquerque, letter to author, 26 May 1994.

44 Irías and Terán, "Era muy cariñoso," Barricada, 8 Nov. 1992.

Chapter 9   The Montaña and the Death of Fonseca, 1975–1976

1 Luis Carrión Montoya, La ruta del comandante Pancho (Managua: Editorial Nueva Nicaragua, 1992), 50–52 (the author is Luis Carrión's father); Rivera, La Marca del Zorro, 115; Fonseca, "Nota sobre algunos problemas de hoy [1976]," point 26. At the beginning of 1976, Fonseca was trying to set up a DN executive committee consisting of himself and Ruiz; see La Prensa, 15 Aug. 1976, quoting Tomás Borge.

2 Acosta, "Km. 20," El Nuevo Diario, 8 Nov. 1986; Arias, Nicaragua, 81.

3 Henry Ruiz, "La montaña era como un crisol donde se forjaban los mejores cuadros," Nicaráuac 1 (1980): 14–16, 22; Rivera, La Marca del Zorro, 113, 139; Heyck, Life Stories,

97. For the strategy of working through family patriarchs see Arias, *Nicaragua,* 96, and Cabezas, *La montaña,* 272.

4 Rivera, *La Marca del Zorro,* 107; José Valdivia Hidalgo, "Testimonio sobre los mártires del 7 y 8 de noviembre de 1976," *Nuevo Amanecer Cultural,* 5 Nov. 1983; Arias, *Nicaragua,* 114, 117–18.

5 The word *chapioyo* or *chapiollo* refers to an inferior breed of cattle and by extension anything of poor quality. See Arias, *Nicaragua,* 71, 222–23; Joaquím Rabella and Chantal Pallais, *Vocabulario Popular Nicaragüense* (Managua: Imprenta El Amanecer, 1994), 69.

6 Fonseca, *Notas sobre la montaña,* 137.

7 Fonseca, "Retornar a las montañas," 56; italics in original.

8 Ibid., 56; Fonseca, *Notas sobre la montaña,* 137.

9 Cabezas, *La montaña,* 275; Guillén, "A partir de abril," *Nicaráuac* no. 13 (Nov.–Dec. 1986): 121.

10 Borge, *Carlos, the Dawn,* 76; Marlene López Dávila, "Carlos me enseñó a leer y a pelear," *Barricada,* 1 Nov. 1982. "También enséñenles a leer" and "En cada alfabetizador, Carlos Fonseca Amador," became the slogans of a massive literacy drive after the revolution and were commemorated on numerous posters and murals.

11 Juan Ramón Huerta, "Los amigos de montaña de Carlos Fonseca," *Barricada,* 23 June 1986.

12 Ibid.; Arias, *Nicaragua,* 97–98; Carlos Fonseca Amador, "Carta a Efraín Sánchez en relación a errores incurridos," 2 July 1969, CHM reg. 18839, caja 3 (6).

13 Fonseca, *Notas sobre la montaña,* 132–33.

14 Carlos Fonseca Amador, "Los mártires del FSLN son el honor de la Nicaragua de hoy," Algun lugar de Nicaragua, 4 Nov. 1968, CHM reg. 25090, caja 5.

15 Fonseca, "Carta a Efraín Sánchez." On reverence for martyrs, see Fonseca, "Viva la Fraternidad Guerrillera [1969]"; Fonseca, "Los mártires del FSLN [1968]."

16 Fonseca, *Notas sobre la montaña,* 128, 133.

17 Ibid., 139–40.

18 Arias, *Nicaragua,* 103–4, 92.

19 Rivera, *La Marca del Zorro,* 93.

20 Selser, "La primera guerrilla," *Barricada,* 7 Nov. 1986.

21 Arias, *Nicaragua,* 126.

22 Ibid., 99–100.

23 Ibid., 115.

24 Rivera, *La Marca del Zorro,* 130, 126.

25 See especially the relationships with Harry Villegas ("Pombo"), José María Martínez ("Ricardo"), and Carlos Coello ("Tuma"), described in Ernesto Che Guevara, *Bolivian Diary* (New York: Pathfinder Press, 1994).

26 Rivera, *La Marca del Zorro,* 129–31.

27 The figure that is generally given for the percentage of women in the FSLN guerrilla armies at the time of the victory of the revolution is 30 percent, which seems high even for 1979. (It first appeared in Margaret Randall's 1981 introduction to *Sandino's Daughters.*)

28 Huerta, "Los amigos de montaña de Carlos Fonseca," *Barricada,* 23 June 1986.

29 Rivera, *La Marca del Zorro,* 113–14.

30 "I argued that women too could fight." *Militant* (New York), 19 Feb. 1996, translated from *Bohemia* (Havana), 20 Oct. 1967.

31 Lenín Cerna, "¡Cómo lo admirábamos, cómo lo queríamos! El perfil humano de Carlos," *Nicaráuac,* no. 13 (Nov.–Dec. 1986): 141–42.

32 "Los últimos que vieron a Carlos Fonseca," *Barricada Edición especial,* 7 Nov. 1986; Arias, *Nicaragua,* 117.

33 Ruiz, "La montaña," 19; "Los últimos que vieron a Carlos Fonseca," *Barricada,* 7 Nov. 1986.

34 Rivera, *La Marca del Zorro,* 118. In a 1982 speech, Ruiz mentioned that he was in his camp on Puyús Mountain when he heard the radio report of Fonseca's death; see Henry Ruiz, "Permiso para informar, Comandante Carlos: Tu pueblo, tu Frente Sandinista, nosotros, tu Dirección Nacional, agradecemos infinitamente tu enseñanza," *Barricada,* 8 Nov. 1982.

35 OSN folder "cartas a Agatón," CHM reg. 00390–00395, caja 3 (5).

36 The exact circumstances of Fonseca's death have been a matter of some dispute. The following picture emerges by combining Francisco Rivera's account with published interviews by several FSLN combatants, a National Guardsman, the peasant who lived closest to the shootout, and other peasants ordered by the Guard to retrieve and bury Fonseca's body. Rivera, *La Marca del Zorro,* 120–23; "Los últimos que vieron a Carlos Fonseca," *Barricada,* 7 Nov. 1986; "El último combate de Carlos Fonseca," *Barricada,* 23 June 1980; Ernesto Aburto M., "El nunca murió," *La Prensa,* 7 Nov. 1979.

37 Silvio Mora, "El sueño de Carlos Fonseca," *El Nuevo Diario,* 8 Nov. 1988. Two days later, when the National Guard announced Fonseca's death to the nation, they said he had been killed in a shootout that started at seven o'clock on the evening of Monday, 8 November. The gunfight actually occurred on Sunday night, and the bodies were retrieved Monday morning. The 8 November issue of *La Prensa,* an afternoon newspaper, already contained a report on the death of two unidentified guerrillas and the escape of a third in a battle in the northern mountains.

38 Borge, *Carlos, the Dawn,* 87; *La Prensa,* 12 Nov. 1976.

Chapter 10   The Revolution of 1979

1 Mora, "El sueño," *El Nuevo Diario,* 8 Nov. 1988; *La Prensa,* 11 Nov. 1976.

2 Ruiz, "La montaña," 21–22; Heyck, *Life Stories,* 116.

3 Fonseca, *Hora Cero,* 93–94. Although I agree with much of Dennis Gilbert's analysis of the Marxism of the FSLN, I think he is wrong in saying the Sandinistas always saw their task in terms of a two-stage revolution. He cites a 1957 statement by Carlos Fonseca—at the time a member of the PSN—and the 1977 General Platform of the terceristas, but both are quite inconsistent with the political approach of the FSLN during the intervening decades; see Gilbert, *Sandinistas,* 36.

4 Fonseca, "Notas y experiencias [1975]."

5 Fonseca, "Algunos aspectos del trabajo entre las masas [1973?]," points 41, 42.

6 Gilbert and Block, *Sandinistas: Key Documents*, 56. The entire *Plataforma General* is reproduced in this volume.

7 García Márquez et al., *Los Sandinistas*, 243–57.

8 Black, *Triumph*, 104; Omar Cabezas, *Canción de amor para los hombres* (Managua: Editorial Nueva Nicaragua, 1989).

9 Heyck, *Life Stories*, 13; Gould, *To Lead as Equals*, 302.

10 See, for example, Gilbert, *Sandinistas*; Booth, *The End and the Beginning*; Rose J. Spalding, *Capitalists and Revolution in Nicaragua: Opposition and Accommodation, 1979–1993* (Chapel Hill: University of North Carolina Press, 1994).

11 The most thorough examination of the conflicts between the Somoza family and other capitalists is in Spaulding, *Capitalists and Revolution*. For the political impact of the temporary economic boom, see DEPEP (FSLN), *Carlos Fonseca frente a su tiempo* (Managua: Colección "El Chipote," 1982), 6; Managua newspapers reported record retail sales during the 1975 to 1976 Christmas season.

12 Daisy Zamora, "Commander Two," Margaret Randall, in *Sandino's Daughters Revisited: Feminism in Nicaragua* (New Brunswick, N.J.: Rutgers University Press, 1994), 231–32.

13 *Washington Post*, 25 Aug. 1978; *Washington Post*, 1 Sept. 1978; *El Diario* (New York), 31 Aug. 1978. The special GN units called EEBI (Escuela de Entrenamiento Básico de Infantria, Basic Infantry Training School) were commanded by Anastasio Somoza Portocarrero, known as El Chigüín ("The Punk"), widely believed to be even more vicious and corrupt than his father and grandfather.

14 Black, *Triumph*, 132.

15 Shirley Christian, *Nicaragua: Revolution in the Family* (New York: Random House, 1985), 71. The OAS commission disbanded without results in early January 1979. The following month, the Carter administration terminated all military agreements with Nicaragua. (U.S. representatives did, however, vote for an IMF grant of $66 million to the Somoza government three months later, on 14 May 1979.)

16 Richard R. Fagen, *The Nicaraguan Revolution. A Personal Report* (Washington: Institute for Policy Studies, 1981), 8.

17 Sergio Ramírez was added to the DN in the late 1980s, and Carlos Núñez, its youngest member, died of a heart attack in 1990. By 1999 more than half the members of the 1980s National Directorate had resigned from the FSLN, and only two, Daniel Ortega and Tomás Borge, were still on the DN.

18 Published accounts of the insurrectionary period by rebel leaders include Arqueles Morales, *Con el corazón en el disparador: Las batallas del Frente Interno* (Managua: Editorial Vanguardia, 1986); and Carlos Nuñez Tellez, *Un pueblo en armas* (Managua: Colección Juan de Dios Muñoz, 1981). For the travails of the U.S. ambassador assigned to negotiate the resignation of Somoza (and a surprisingly sympathetic description of the insurrection in Managua), see Lawrence Pezzullo and Ralph Pezzullo, *At the Fall of Somoza* (Pittsburgh: University of Pittsburgh Press, 1993). The most complete secondary source on the insurrection and final offensive is Black, *Triumph*, 142–81.

19 Heyck, *Life Stories*, 119–20.

20 Walker, *Nicaragua in Revolution*, 37.

21 Carlos M. Vilas, *Sandinista Revolution* (New York: Monthly Review Press, 1986), 108–12; Vilas calls them "the rank-and-file of the revolution" and recognizes that the vast majority were not actual members of the FSLN; *New York Times*, 27 June 1979; Comité de Dirección Zonal de Jinotepe, *Por la memoria de nuestros héroes y mártires, cumpliremos con la patria*, n.d.

22 Morales, *Corazón*, 51; Black, *Triumph*, 157.

23 Spaulding, *Capitalists and Revolution*, 61.

24 Pezzullo and Pezzullo, *At the Fall of Somoza*, 180.

25 In September 1980, Anastasio Somoza Debayle was killed in Paraguay by a squad of Argentine guerrillas. See Claribel Alegría and D. J. Flakoll, *Somoza: Expediente cerrado* (Managua: Editorial El Gato Negro, [1993?]).

Glossary of Organizations

AMPRONAC Asociación de mujeres ante la problematica nacional, Association of Women Confronting the National Problem

ATC Asociación de Trabajadores del Campo, Association of Rural Workers

CUUN Consejo Universitario de la Universidad Nacional, Student Council of the National University

DN Dirección Nacional, National Directorate

EDSN Ejército Defensor de la Soberanía Nacional, Defending Army of National Sovereignty

EEBI Escuela de Entrenamiento Básico de Infantria, Basic Infantry Training School

FDC Frente Democrático Cristiano, Democratic Christian Front

FER Federación de Estudiantes Revolucionarios, Federation of Revolutionary Students

FSLN Frente Sandinista de Liberación Nacional, Sandinista National Liberation Front

FUN Frente Unitario Nicaragüense, Nicaraguan United Front

GN Guardia Nacional, National Guard

GPP Guerra Popular Prolongada, Prolonged People's War Tendency

INN Instituto Nacional del Norte, National Institute of the North

JDN Juventud Democrática Nicaragüense, Democratic Nicaraguan Youth

JPN Juventud Patriótica Nicaragüense, Patriotic Nicaraguan Youth

JRN Juventud Revolucionaria Nicaragüense, Revolutionary Nicaraguan Youth

MAFUENIC	Manos Fuera de Nicaragua, "Hands Off Nicaragua" Committee
MPU	Movimiento Pueblo Unido, United People's Movement
MR or MRP	Movilización Republicana, Republican Mobilization
OSN	Oficina de Seguridad Nacional, Office of National Security
PGT	Partido Guatemalteco del Trabajo, Guatemalan Workers' Party
PLI	Partido Liberal Independiente, Independent Liberal Party
PLN	Partido Liberal Nacionalista, Nationalist Liberal Party
PSCN or PSC	Partido Social Cristiano de Nicaragua, Social Christian Party of Nicaragua
PSN	Partido Socialista de Nicaragua, Socialist (Communist) Party of Nicaragua
PSP	Partido Socialista Popular, Popular Socialist Party (Cuba)
PVP	Partido Vanguardia Popular, Popular Vanguard Party (Costa Rica)
TI	Tendencia Insurreccionalista, Insurrectionalist Tendency, "terceristas"
TP	Tendencia Proletaria, Proletarian Tendency
UCA	Universidad Centroamericana, Central American University
UDEL	Unión Democrática de Liberación, Democratic Liberation Union
UNAN	Universidad Nacional Autónoma de Nicaragua, National Autonomous University of Nicaragua
UNAP	Unión Nacional de Acción Popular, National Union of Popular Action

Bibliography

Archives

CHM   Centro de Historia Militar, Ejército de Nicaragua, Managua
IES   Instituto de Estudio del Sandinismo, Managua
IHN   Instituto de Historia de Nicaragua, Managua

Newspapers and Magazines

Barricada, Managua
Bohemia, Havana
Nicaráuac, Managua
Novedades, Managua
El Nuevo Diario, Managua
Patria Libre, Managua
La Prensa, Managua
Segovia, Managua
Segovia, Matagalpa
Verde Olivo, Havana
Tricontinental, Havana

Writings of Carlos Fonseca

Hereafter is a list of all known extant writings of Carlos Fonseca, published and unpublished, arranged chronologically in the order they were written. All were consulted for this book.

1954

"Editorial." *Segovia* (Matagalpa) 1 (Aug. 1954).
"Futuro." *Segovia* 1 (Aug. 1954).
"Editorialoide." *Segovia* 2 (Sept. 1954).

"Está bién, pero está mal" [by "CARFONA" (Carlos Fonseca Amador)]. *Segovia* 2 (Sept. 1954).

"C.A.F.A.TERIAS." *Segovia* 2 (Sept. 1954).

"Editorial." *Segovia* 4 (Nov. 1954).

"C.A.F.A.TERIAS." *Segovia* 4 (Nov. 1954).

"Editorial." *Segovia* 5 (Dec. 1954).

1955

"16 versos del molendero." *Segovia* 6–7 (Jan.–Feb. 1955).

"Editorial: La juventud intelectual matagalpina necesita ponerse en contacto para orientarse bién y poder triunfar." *Segovia* 6–7 (Jan.–Feb. 1955).

"El capital y el trabajo." Final exam, Instituto Nacional del Norte, Matagalpa, 27 Feb. 1955, CHM reg. 00397, caja 2.

"El voto de la mujer." *Segovia* 9 (Dec. 1955).

1956

"Carta al Sr. Ministro de Educación Pública en la que se Sugiere utilizar las Barberías como Bibliotecas populares." *Segovia* 11 (Feb. 1956).

"Editorial: Significado patriótica de la lucha estudiantil." León, 1956, CHM reg. 18942, caja 2A.

Letter to "Coronel" [Somoza], Matagalpa, 11 Dec. 1956, CHM reg. 00346, caja 3.

1957

"Mensaje de Carlos Fonseca con el seudonimo de Pablo Cáceres en el IV Congreso Sindical Mundial, RDA." Oct. 1957, CHM reg. 07193, caja 5.

"Declaración, 1957." In *Obras,* vol. 1, 159–81.

1958

Un nicaragüense en Moscú. In *Obras,* vol. 1, 277–344.

Letter to Gen. Anastasio Somoza, Managua, 21 May 1958, CHM reg. 00348, caja 3.

Various letters from Carlos Fonseca as Secretario de Relaciones del CUUN, León, 1958, CHM reg. 00376, caja 3.

1959

Letter to "Querido Papá," Guatemala, 22 Apr. 1959, in *Obras,* vol. 1, 148–50.

Letter to "Recordada Estelita," Tegucigalpa, 15 July 1959, CHM reg. 19086, caja 3.

1960

Letter to "Querido papá," San José, 15 Jan. 1960, IHN Archive.

"La lucha por la transformación de Nicaragua." In *Obras,* vol. 1, 25–38.

"Breve análisis de la lucha popular nicaragüense contra la dictadura de Somoza." In *Obras,* vol. 1, 39–54.

"Nicaragua, tierra amarga." *Nuevo Amanecer Cultural,* 21 July 1990 [internally dated to after Feb. 1960, first published in *Mella* (Havana), 10 Jan. 1961].

Letter to "Querido papá," San José, 11 Apr. 1960, CHM folder "cartas familiares," caja 3.

Letter to Prof. Edelberto Torres, San José, 8 June, 1960, IHN Archive.

Letter to "doña Lolita," San José, 10 June 1960, CHM reg. 00332, caja 3.

Wall poster: "Manifiesto del Centro Universitario al Pueblo de Nicaragua '23 de Julio 1960.'" León: Editorial Antorcha, 23 July 1960 [edited by Fonseca], CHM reg. 03258, caja 5.

Letter to Sr. Narciso Báldizon Caldera, Guatemala, 5 Sept. 1960, CHM reg. 00330, caja 3.

Letter to "Compañero Denis," Guatemala, 17 Sept. 1960, IES Archive.

1962

"En que forma ha penetrado en Nicaragua la llamada 'Alianza Para el Progreso' de Kennedy," CHM reg. 07030, caja 2A [authorship questionable].

1963

"Bajo la sombre de Sandino [interview by Víctor Rico Galan]." *Siempre* (Mexico) 542 (13 Nov. 1963): 30–31.

1964

Desde la cárcel yo acuso a la dictadura [La Aviación prison, 8 July 1964]. In *Obras,* vol. 1, 88–97.

"Declaración, 1964." In *Obras,* vol. 1, 182–93.

"Esta es la verdad." In *Obras,* vol. 1, 239–42.

1965

Letter to Sr. Rodolfo Tapia Molina, Tapachula prison, Guatemala, 16 Jan. 1965, CHM reg. 00333, caja 5.

Series of letters in code to "Querido hermano," San José, Oct.–Dec. 1965, CHM regs. 00341, 00338, 00342, 00343, caja 3.

Letter to "Querida mamita," Mexico, 13 Apr. 1965, CHM reg. 00334, caja 3.

1966

"¡Sandino sí, Somoza no; revolución sí, farsa electoral no! [Managua, 25 Nov. 1966]." In *Obras,* vol. 1, 243–47.

1967

Letter to Don José Moreno and Sra Estrela de Moreno, Managua, 19 Mar. 1967, CHM reg. 00349, caja 3.

Letter to "Papá, queridisimo papá," San José, 12 June 1967 [possibly 1968, last digit illegible], CHM reg. 00350, folder "cartas familiares."

1968

"Mensaje del FSLN en el 34 aniversario del asesinato de A. C. Sandino: Continuamos combatiendo!" 21 Feb. 1968, CHM reg. 25299, caja 5.

Mensaje del Frente Sandinista de Liberación Nacional, FSLN, a los estudiantes revolucionarios [Apr. 1968]. In *Obras,* vol. 1, 55–74.

"Mensaje del FSLN (en ocasión del 1º de Mayo)," 1 May 1968, CHM reg. 25300, caja 5.

Series of letters to Dr. A.R., Dr. A.P.A., Dr. R.C.M., Lic. R.C., Mar.–June 1968, CHM regs. 00363, 00352, 00355, 00534, caja 3.

"Mensaje del FSLN a las madres de los Mártires nicaragüenses," 30 May 1968, CHM reg. 00299, caja 5.

"Militancia activa del combatiente revolucionario," 6 June 1968, CHM reg. 00269, caja 2A.

"Yanqui Johnson: Go Home" [5 July 1968]. In *Obras*, vol. 1, 251–53.

"En el primer aniversario de la inmolación del 'Che' juramos ser leales a su ejemplo," 8 Oct. 1968, CHM reg. 25281, caja 5.

"Bajo las banderas de Sandino." In *Obras*, vol. 1, 248–50.

"Los mártires del FSLN son el honor de la Nicaragua de hoy," 4 Nov. 1968, CHM reg. 25090, caja 5.

1969

"Respuesta a un ideólogo de la tortura," San José, 15 Jan. 1969, CHM reg. 00356, caja 2A.

"Por un primero de mayo guerrillero y victorioso," 1 May 1969, CHM reg. 25086, caja 5.

Series of letters from Fonseca to Julio Buitrago, San José, May–June 1969, CHM regs. 00357, 00358, 00359, caja 3, folder "cartas a Julio Buitrago."

"Viva el combate revolucionario de los Estudiantes de América Latina," 1 June 1969, CHM reg. 29270, caja 5.

"Carta a Efraín Sánchez en relación a errores incurridos, San José," 2 July 1969, CHM reg. 18839, caja 3.

"Con la sangre de nuestro mártires construiremos un futuro feliz" [17 July 1969]. In *Obras*, vol. 1, 257–58.

"En el X aniversario de la masacre estudiantil" [23 July 1969]. In *Obras*, vol. 1, 259–60.

"El FSLN es la mas generosa creación de la nueva generación de Nicaragua," 31 July 1969, CHM reg. 25079, caja 5.

"Juramos cobrar implacable venganza por la sangre de Julio Buitrago, Marco Rivera, Aníbal Castrillo y Alesio Blandón" [15 Aug. 1969]. In *Obras*, vol. 1, 263–65.

"Proclama del FSLN." In *Obras*, vol. 1, 267–69.

"Viva la Fraternidad Guerrillera," San José, 22 Aug. 1969, CHM regs. 00313 and 25177, caja 5.

"Continuemos el ejemplo del inmortal Ho Chi Min" [Sept. 1969, text incomplete]. In *Obras*, vol. 1, 266.

Letter to *Punto Final*, CHM reg. 24809, caja 7.

Nicaragua Hora Cero. In *Obras*, vol. 1, 75–95.

El Programa Histórico del FSLN. Managua: DEPEP, 1984.

Declaration to Special Commission appointed by Costa Rican Legislature, Alajuela prison, 7 Oct. 1969, CHM reg. 00526, caja 1; extensive extracts in "Entrevista," in *Obras*, vol. 1, 206–13.

Letter to Pedro Antonio Cuadra, Alajuela prison, 2 Dec. 1969, CHM, reg. 00306, caja 3.

1970

"Los ataques de los falsos revolucionarios de Costa Rica nos honran" [San José penitentiary, 26 Mar. 1970]. *COPAN, Revista Teórica* (San José) 2–3 (Aug. 1984): 94–105.

"Análisis sobre la situación nacional, el Programa Sandinista, en ocasión del Primero de Mayo de 1970," San José penitentiary, 1 May 1970, CHM reg. 25279, caja 2B, and reg. 00276, caja 5.

"Carta a los lectores de *Punto Final*," CHM reg. 00363, caja 5.

Letter to Sr. Guido Pernandez, editor of *La Nación*, San José penitentiary, CHM reg. 00368, caja 3.

"Lucha guerrillera en Nicaragua." Interview in San José penitentiary, *Punto Final* (Santiago) 110 (4 Aug. 1970): 16–19.

"La lucha armada en Nicaragua." Interview by Hernán Uribe Ortega, Havana, *Punto Final* (Santiago) 129 (27 Aug. 1971); reprinted with some omissions in *Barricada*, 23 June 1983.

"Mensaje de Carlos Fonseca, dirigente del Frente Sandinista de Liberación Nacional," Havana, 7 Nov. 1970, IHN, Colección Hacia el Sol de la Libertad.

"No Hay Islas." Interview by Marco Altamirano, San José penitentiary, Oct. 1970, CHM reg. 00322, caja 6.

"Entrevista, 1970" [by Ernesto González Bermejo]. In *Obras*, vol. 1, 214–27.

1971

"Heroismo y martirio de Sandino." *Granma*, 20 Feb. 1971.

"Sandino, el combatiente insobordable." *Verde Olivo*, 28 Feb. 1971, 58–59.

Letter to "Camarada Ko," Havana, 23 Apr. 1971, CHM reg. 03595.

Sandino: Guerrillero proletario. In *Obras*, vol. 1, 368–84.

"Mensaje del FSLN con motivo del 150 aniversario del rompimiento del yugo colonial español," 21 Sept. 1971, CHM reg. 00317, caja 5; a shortened version appeared as "El Frente Sandinista de Liberación Nacional," *Bohemia* (Havana), no. 40 (1 Oct. 1971): 94–97; reprinted in *Obras*, vol. 1, 363–67.

1972

Breve chronología de la historia de Nicaragua, 8 Mar. 1972, CHM reg. 00245, caja 4.

"Reseña de la secular intervención norteamericana en Nicaragua" [Mar. 1972]. In *Obras*, vol. 1, 385–92.

"Saludo de la representación del FSLN al II congreso de la Unión de Jóvenes Comunistas," Havana, 29 Mar. 1972, CHM reg. 24849, caja 5.

"Respuesta a la posición de un grupo de compañeros," 6 Apr. 1971, CHM reg. 00285, caja 2B.

"Respuesta a las notas del compañero M.," 6 Apr. 1972, CHM reg. 00283, caja 2B.

"Respuesta a las notas del compañero A.," 7 Apr. 1972, CHM reg. 00284, caja 2B.

"Declaración del FSLN con motivo del 4 de mayo," 4 May 1972, CHM reg. 24831, caja 5.

"Acerca de la solidaridad," 12 June 1972, CHM reg. 00272, caja 5.

"Notas sobre la situación actual de Nicaragua," 21 June 1972, CHM reg. 00247, caja 2A.

"Nicaragua, from Sandino to the Frente Nacional Sandinista: An Interview with Carlos Fonseca Amador by Margaret Randall and Robert Cohen," 28 June 1972, Havana, MS, trans. Margaret Randall; Spanish original in CHM reg. 00320, caja 6.

"Plan de instrucción local,"10 July 1972, CHM reg. 00271, caja 2B.

"Mensaje del FSLN con motivo del XVI aniversario del 21 de Septiembre," 15 Aug. 1972, CHM reg. 25288, caja 5; also known as "La Tierra de Sandino clama Solidaridad."

"Notas sobre la carta-testamento de Rigoberto López Pérez." In *Obras*, vol. 1, 393–406.

"16 aniversario de la muerte del héroe nacional, Rigoberto López Pérez," CHM reg. 00623, caja 2A; same as "Rigoberto López Pérez en la lucha por la Liberación," CHM reg. 00262, caja 2A.

"Observaciones sobre los informes organizativos," 12 Dec. 1972, CHM reg. 00288, caja 2B.

"Acerca de la lucha del FSLN: breve cronología," CHM reg. 00244, caja 2A.

"Notas sobre algunos problemas actuales," CHM reg. 00295, caja 2B.

Ideario político del general Sandino. In *Obras*, vol. 2, 169–99.

1973

"Carta a los nicaragüenses residentes en Estados Unidos" [30 Jan. 1973]. In *Obras*, vol. 1, 154–55.

Letter to "Hermano Afronorteamericano" [30 Jan. 1973]. *Barricada*, 5 Nov. 1985.

Letter to "Hermanas y Hermanos Norteamericanos" [30 Jan. 1973]. *Barricada*, 6 Nov. 1985.

Letter to "Hermanos Indios de los Estados Unidos" [30 Jan. 1973], from files of Vernon Bellecourt.

"Llamamiento del Comité de Nicaragüenses en el exterior pro damnificados," Havana, Jan.–Feb. 1973, CHM reg. 00303, caja 5.

"Algunos aspectos del trabajo entre las masas" [1973?], IHN, Colección Hacia el sol de la libertad.

"Charla del Comp. Carlos Fonseca," 10 Sept. and 11 Sept. 1973, CHM reg. 00292, caja 6.

"Charla con una compañera (sobre la cárcel)," 28 Sept. 1973, CHM reg. 00324, caja 6.

"Charla del compañero Carlos Fonseca en la conmemoración del 4 de octubre," Havana, 4 Oct. 1973, CHM reg. 00248, caja 6.

"Análisis Sucesos de Nandaime," 20 Oct. 1973, CHM reg. 00254, caja 2B.

"Algunos puntos sobre la situación de Nicaragua," Havana, 12 Nov. 1973, CHM reg. 00247, caja 2A.

"Reunión general para informar sobre problemas de la organización," Havana, 14 Nov. 1973, CHM reg. 00293, caja 2B.

"El enemigo confiesa," CHM reg. 00275, caja 2A.

"Opinión sobre algunos problemas y tareas," CHM reg. 00294, caja 2B.

"Notas sobre la lucha popular contra la tiranía somocista," CHM reg. 00253, caja 2B.

1974

"Presentación al documento 'Refutación a las afirmaciones del presidente Taft'" [Jan.–Feb. 1974]. In *Obras*, vol. 1, 409–27.

Letter to Angel Guerra, editor of *Bohemia*, Havana, 16 Feb. 1974, CHM reg. 00379, caja 3.

"Con motivo del 40 aniversario del asesinato de Sandino, el FSLN demanda solidaridad hacia el pueblo de Nicaragua," Havana, 21 Feb. 1974, CHM reg. 24794, caja 5.

"La dominación yanqui en Nicaragua" [13 Apr. 1974]. *Barricada*, 8 Nov. 1983.

"Notas sobre comunicación 'Questiones urgentes para la organización,'" 30 Apr. 1974, CHM reg. 00282, caja 2B.

"Manifiesto: 23 de julio—símbolo de tradición estudiantil nicaragüense," 23 July 1974, CHM reg. 00251, caja 5.

"Carta a compañeros de la parroquia," 31 July 1974, CHM reg. 00367, caja 2B.

"Discurso en acto de solidaridad," Havana, 6 Sept. 1974, CHM reg. 19729, caja 5.

"Problemas estratégicos de la lucha revolucionaria nicaragüense," 30 Sept. 1974, CHM reg. 00281, caja 2B.

"Por una correcta linea de masas," Dec. 1974, CHM reg. 02396, caja 2A [authorship questionable].

Cronología de la resistencia sandinista, in *Obras*, vol. 2, 89–167.

"Crónica Secreta: Augusto César Sandino ante sus verdugos." MS prepared in 1995 by Instituto de Historia de Nicaragua (extracts previously published in *Obras*, vol. 1, 412–27; and *Barricada Edición especial*, 7 Nov. 1986).

1975

Viva Sandino. In *Obras*, vol. 2, 19–86.

"Notas y experiencias revolucionarias (transcripción de charla)," CHM reg. 09466, caja 2B.

Síntesis de algunos problemas actuales [3 Nov. 1975]. In *Obras*, vol. 1, 96–121.

"Sobre la actual represión en Nicaragua," CHM reg. 00250, caja 5.

1976

Nota sobre algunos problemas de hoy, Feb.–Mar. 1976, in author's files; also known as "El último documento/testamento de Carlos Fonseca."

"Tomás Borge: Un sandinista," from files of Tomás Borge.

Notas sobre la montaña y algunos otros temas [8 Oct. 1976]. In *Obras*, vol. 1, 122–41.

Undated (Arranged Alphabetically)

"Antecedentes del FSLN." *Ventana*, 6 July 1985; appears to have been written around 1973.

"Aspectos de la estrategia y organización en algunas experiencias," CHM reg. 00279, caja 2B.

Cronología de la intervención norteamericana de 1909 a 1910, CHM reg. 00258, caja 4.

Cronología de la resistencia de 1912, CHM reg. 00260, caja 4.

"Lucha de masas y guerra revolucionaria," CHM reg. 00287, caja 2B.

"Noticia sobre Darío y Gorki." In *Obras*, vol. 1, 407–8.

"Respuesta a las cuestiones que plantean los compañeros en los textos que elaboraron con motivo de los documentos que les fueron suministrados," CHM reg. 00289, caja 2B.

"Sobre la situación de Costa Rica," CHM reg. 00296, caja 2A.

"¿Que es un Sandinista?" *Barricada*, 9 Nov. 1980.

Selected Books and Articles

Alegría, Claribel, and D. J. Flakoll. *Nicaragua: La revolución sandinista*. México: Ediciones Era, 1982.

——. *Somoza: Expediente cerrado*. Managua: Editorial El Gato Negro, [1993?].

Anderson, Jon Lee. *Che Guevara: A Revolutionary Life*. New York: Grove Press, 1997.

Arias, Pilar. *Nicaragua: Revolución. Relatos de combatientes del frente sandinista.* México: Siglo XXI, 1980.

Avendaña Sandino, Rolando. *Masacre estudiantil: 23 de Julio de 1959, León, Nicaragua.* [Managua?]: Tipográfico América, 1960.

Barahona, Amaru. *Estudio sobre la historia de Nicaragua del auge cafetalero al triunfo de la revolución.* Managua: Instituto Nicaragüense de Investigaciones Económicas y Sociales, 1989.

Biderman, Jaime M. "Class Structure, the State, and Capitalist Development in Nicaraguan Agriculture." Ph.D. diss., University of California at Berkeley, 1982.

Black, George. *Triumph of the People: The Sandinista Revolution in Nicaragua.* London: Zed Press, 1981.

Blandón, Jesús Miguel. *Entre Sandino y Fonseca Amador.* Managua: DEPEP, 1981.

Booth, John A. *The End and the Beginning: The Nicaraguan Revolution.* Boulder: Westview, 1982.

Borge, Tomás. *Carlos, the Dawn Is No Longer beyond Our Reach.* Vancouver: New Star Books, 1984.

——. "The FSLN and the Nicaraguan Revolution." *New International* 3 (spring–summer 1984): 133–53.

——. *La paciente impaciencia.* Managua: Editorial Vanguardia, 1989.

——. *The Patient Impatience.* Willimantic, Conn.: Curbstone Press, 1992.

Cabezas, Omar. *La montaña es algo más que una inmensa estepa verde.* México: Siglo XXI, 1982.

——. *Canzión de amor para los hombres.* Managua: Editorial Nueva Nicaragua, 1989.

Camejo, Pedro, and Fred Murphy. *The Nicaraguan Revolution.* New York: Pathfinder Press, 1979.

Cancino Troncoso, Hugo. *Las raíces históricas e ideológicas del movimiento sandinista: Antecedentes de la revolución popular nicaragüense, 1927–79.* Odense: Odense University Press, 1984.

Carmona, Fernando, ed. *Nicaragua: La estrategia de la victoria.* México: Editorial Nuestro Tiempo, 1980.

Carrión Montoya, Luis. *La ruta del comandante Pancho.* Managua: Editorial Nueva Nicaragua, 1992.

Castañeda, Jorge G. *Utopia Unarmed: The Latin American Left after the Cold War.* New York: Alfred A. Knopf, 1993.

Castro, Fidel. *Second Declaration of Havana.* New York: Pathfinder Press, 1984.

Colburn, Forrest D. *The Vogue of Revolution in Poor Countries.* Princeton: Princeton University Press, 1994.

Crawley, Eduardo. *Dictators Never Die: Nicaragua and the Somoza Family Dynasty.* New York: St. Martin's Press, 1979.

Departamento de Propaganda y Educación Política (DEPEP), FSLN. *Habla la Dirección de la vanguardia.* Managua, 1981.

——. *Y se rompió el silencio.* Managua: Editorial Nueva Nicaragua, 1981.

——. *Carlos Fonseca siempre.* Managua: Centro de Publicaciones Silvio Mayorga, 1982.

Fagen, Richard R. *The Nicaraguan Revolution: A Personal Report.* Washington: Institute for Policy Studies, 1981.

Fonseca Amador, Carlos. "Los ataques de los falsos revolucionarios de Costa Rica nos honran" [San José penitentiary, 26 March 1970]. *COPAN, Revista Teórica* (San José) 2–3 (Aug. 1984): 94–105.

———. *Obras.* Vol. 1, *Bajo la bandera del sandinismo.* Vol. 2, *Viva Sandino.* Managua: Editorial Nueva Nicaragua, 1982.

———. *El Programa Histórico del FSLN.* Managua: DEPEP, 1984.

Frente Sandinista de Liberación Nacional (FSLN). *Diciembre Victorioso.* México: Editorial Diógenes, 1979.

———. "Unity Statement." *Latin American Perspectives* (winter 1979): 108–13.

———. *La revolución a través de nuestra dirección nacional.* Managua: SNPEP, 1980.

García Márquez, Gabriel, et al. *Los Sandinistas.* 3d ed. Bogotá: La Oveja Negra, 1980.

Gilbert, Dennis. *Sandinistas: The Party and the Revolution.* New York: Blackwell, 1988.

Gilbert, Dennis, and David Block, eds. *Sandinistas: Key Documents/Documentos Claves.* Ithaca, N.Y.: Cornell University, 1990.

Gonzalez, Victoria. "Somocista Women, Right-Wing Politics, and Feminism in Nicaragua, 1936–1979." Paper presented at Latin American Studies Association Conference, Chicago, 24–26 Sept. 1998.

Gordillo, Fernando. *Obra.* Managua: Editorial Nueva Nicaragua, 1989.

Gould, Jeffrey L. "For an Organized Nicaragua: Somoza and the Labour Movement, 1944–1948." *Journal of Latin American Studies* 19 (Nov. 1987): 353–87.

———. "'La raza rebelde': Las luchas de la comunidad indígena de Subtiava, Nicaragua (1900–1960)." *Revista de Historia* (San José) 21–22 (Jan.–Dec. 1990): 69–115.

———. *To Lead as Equals: Rural Protest and Political Consciousness in Chinandega, Nicaragua, 1912–1979.* Chapel Hill: University of North Carolina Press, 1990.

———. "'¡Vana Ilusión!' The Highlands Indians and the Myth of Nicaragua Mestiza, 1880–1925." *Hispanic American Historical Review* 73 (Aug. 1993): 393–429.

———. *To Die in This Way: Nicaraguan Indians and the Myth of Mestizaje, 1880–1965.* Durham: Duke University Press, 1998.

Guadamuz, Carlos José. *Y . . . las casas quedaron llenas de humo.* Managua: Editorial Nueva Nicaragua, 1982.

Guevara, Ernesto Che. *Guerrilla Warfare.* Lincoln: University of Nebraska Press, 1985.

———. *Che Guevara and the Cuban Revolution: Writings and Speeches of Ernesto Che Guevara.* New York: Pathfinder Press, 1987.

Harnecker, Marta, and Fidel Castro. *Fidel Castro's Political Strategy: From Moncada to Victory.* New York: Pathfinder Press, 1987.

Hernández, Plutarco. *El FSLN por dentro.* San José: Talleres Graficos de Trejos Hermanos, 1982.

Herrera, Miguel Ángel. "Carlos Fonseca: El anhelo de servir a la patria." MS, Managua, n.d.

Heyck, Denis Lynn Daly. *Life Stories of the Nicaraguan Revolution.* New York: Routledge, 1990.

Hodges, Donald C. *Intellectual Foundations of the Nicaraguan Revolution.* Austin: University of Texas Press, 1986.

Instituto de Estudio del Sandinismo (IES). *Carlos: El eslabón vital. Cronología básica de Carlos Fonseca jefe de la Revolución.* Managua: Editorial Nueva Nicaragua, 1985.

——. *Ahora sé que Sandino manda*. Managua: Editorial Nueva Nicaragua, 1986.

——. " 'Hacia el sol de la libertad': Selección de textos para el estudio de la historia del FSLN." Managua, 1986. Mimeographed.

Lanuza, Alberto, Juan Luis Vázquez, Amaru Barahona, and Amalia Chamorro. *Economia y sociedad en la construcción del estado en Nicaragua*. San José: ICAP, 1983.

Lozano, Lucrecia. *De Sandino al triunfo de la revolución*. México: Siglo XXI, 1985.

Mackenbach, Werner. "El problema de la nación en el pensamiento juvenil de Carlos Fonseca." MS, Managua, n.d.

Marcus, Bruce, ed. *Sandinistas Speak*. New York: Pathfinder Press, 1982.

——. *Nicaragua: The Sandinista People's Revolution (Speeches by Sandinista Leaders)*. New York: Pathfinder Press, 1985.

Meiselas, Susan. *Nicaragua: June 1978–July 1979*. New York: Pantheon, 1981.

Millett, Richard. *Guardians of the Dynasty*. Maryknoll, N.Y.: Orbis Books, [1977?].

Morales, Arqueles. *Con el corazón en el disparador (Las batallas del Frente Interno)*. Managua: Editorial Vanguardia, 1986.

Nolan, David. *The Ideology of the Sandinistas and the Nicaraguan Revolution*. Coral Gables: Institute of Interamerican Studies, 1984.

Nuñez Tellez, Carlos. *Un pueblo en armas*. Managua: Colección Juan de Dios Muñoz, 1981.

Ortega Saavedra, Humberto. *50 años de lucha sandinista*. Managua: Colección Las Segovias, MINT, 1979.

Palmer, Steven. "Carlos Fonseca and the Construction of Sandinismo in Nicaragua." *Latin American Research Review* 23 (1988): 91–109.

Pezzullo, Lawrence, and Ralph Pezzullo. *At the Fall of Somoza*. Pittsburgh: University of Pittsburgh Press, 1993.

Randall, Margaret. *Sandino's Daughters*. Vancouver: New Star Books, 1981.

——. *Sandino's Daughters Revisited: Feminism in Nicaragua*. New Brunswick, N.J.: Rutgers University Press, 1994.

Rivera Quintero, Francisco. *La Marca del Zorro: Hazañas contadas por el comandante Francisco Rivera Quintero a Sergio Ramírez*. Managua: Editorial Nueva Nicaragua, 1989.

Rothschuh Tablada, Guillermo. *Los guerrilleros vencen al los generales: Homenaje a Carlos Fonseca Amador*. Managua: Ediciones Distribuidora Cultural, 1983.

Ruiz, Henry. "La montaña era como un crisol donde se forjaban los mejores cuadros." *Nicaráuac* 1 (1980): 8–24.

Sandino, Augusto César. *El pensamiento vivo*. 2 vols. Managua: Editorial Nueva Nicaragua, 1981.

Schroeder, Michael J. " 'To Defend Our Nation's Honor': Toward a Social and Cultural History of the Sandino Rebellion in Nicaragua, 1927–1934." Ph.D. diss., University of Michigan, 1993.

——. "Horse Thieves to Rebels to Dogs: Political Gang Violence and the State in the Western Segovias, Nicaragua, in the Time of Sandino, 1926–1934." *Journal of Latin American Studies* 28 (May 1996): 383–434.

Serrano C., Dr. Alejandro, et al. *Frente a la situación nacional: Documento de la generación del 23 de Julio*. León: Editorial Antorcha, 1969.

Somoza García, Anastasio. *El verdadero Sandino, o, el calvario de las Segovias*. 2d ed. Managua: Editorial San José, 1976.

Spalding, Rose J. *Capitalists and Revolution in Nicaragua: Opposition and Accommodation, 1979–1933*. Chapel Hill: University of North Carolina Press, 1994.

Taibo, Paco Ignacio, II. *Guevara, Also Known as Che*. New York: St. Martin's Press, 1997.

Tijerino, Doris, with Margaret Randall. *Inside the Nicaraguan Revolution*. Vancouver: New Star Books, 1983.

Torres, Camilo. "Mensaje a los Estudiantes." *Revista Conservadora del Pensamiento Centroamericano* 105 (June 1969): 6.

Traña Galeano, Marcia, Xiomara Avendaño Rojas, and Róger Norori Gutiérrez. *Historia del movimiento estudiantil universitario (1944–1979)*. MS, Managua, 1985.

Vanden, Harry E., and Gary Prevost. *Democracy and Socialism in Sandinista Nicaragua*. Boulder: L. Rienner, 1993.

Vilas, Carlos M. *The Sandinista Revolution: National Liberation and Social Transformation in Central America*. New York: Monthly Review Press, 1986.

Vogl Baldizón, Alberto. *Nicaragua con amor y humor*. Managua: Ministerio de Cultura, [1985?].

Walker, Thomas W. *The Christian Democratic Movement in Nicaragua*. Tucson: University of Arizona, Institute of Government Research, 1970.

——. *Nicaragua in Revolution*. New York: Praeger, 1982.

Walter, Knut. *The Regime of Anastasio Somoza García and State Formation in Nicaragua, 1936–1956*. Chapel Hill: University of North Carolina Press, 1987.

Weissberg, Arnold. *Nicaragua: An Introduction to the Sandinista Revolution*. New York: Pathfinder Press, 1983.

Wheelock Roman, Jaime. *Las raíces indígenas de la lucha anticolonial en Nicaragua*. México, D.F.: Siglo XXI, 1975.

Wickham-Crowley, Timothy P. *Guerrillas and Revolution in Latin America: A Comparative Study of Insurgents and Regimes since 1956*. Princeton: Princeton University Press, 1992.

Wright, Bruce E. *Theory in the Practice of the Nicaraguan Revolution*. Athens: Ohio University Center for International Studies, 1995.

Wright, Thomas C. *Latin America in the Era of the Cuban Revolution*. Westport, Conn.: Praeger, 1991.

Wunderich, Volker. *Sandino: Biografía Política*. Managua: Instituto de Historia de Nicaragua, 1995.

Index

Page numbers in italics refer to quoted excerpts of Fonseca's writings.

Acosta, Luz Marina, 186–87
Agüero, Carlos, 128, 186, 188, 205; photo, 137
Agüero, Fernando, 64–65, 72, 91, 94, 95, 128
Aguilar, Cresencio, 202–3
Alemán, Arnoldo, 226
Algerian revolution, 73, 77–78, 157
Allende, Salvador, 164, 175
Alliance for Progress, 89, 90
Alonso, Julio, 51
Altamirano, Marcos, 30, 71
Alvarado, Benita, 13–14, 112
Amador Alemán, Fausto, 12–18, 25, 45, 87, 119, 124–26, 231n. 13; Fonseca's letters to, *14–15, 17–18, 158. See also* Fonseca Amador, Carlos: relationship with father
Amador Arrieta, Fausto (Faustito), 15, 124–25
Amador, Sebastián, 15, 26
APRA, 159, 179
Aráuz, Blanca, 13, 122, 154, 230n. 3
Aráuz, Pedro, 178, 186, 205
Arce, Bayardo, 174, 195, 216; photo, 140
Arellano, Jorge Eduardo, 127
Arrieta de Amador, Lola, 15, 16; Fonseca's letter to, *16–17*
Asociacíon de mujeres ante la problemática nacional (AMPRONAC), 211

Asociación de Trabajadores del Campo (ATC), 211
Atlantic Coast, 20, 124, 153, 225

Baez, Gladys, 97–98, 107, 131, 132, 198
"Bajo la sombre de Sandino," *65–66*
Baldizón, Manuel, 24, 53, 55
Baltodano, Mónica, 216
Bay of Pigs, 73, 80
Bayo, Alberto, 61
Ben Bella, Ahmed, *77–78*
Bervis, Magnus, 115
Blandón, Jesús, 30
Bocay-Raití. *See* Ríos Coco y Bocay
Bohemia, 62, 147, 148
Borge Martínez, Tomás, 29, 37, 42–45, 48, 60, 62, 72–77, 80–83, 129, 185, 203–4, 216, 225; photos, 139, 140
Browderism, 31, 160
Bryan-Chamorro Treaty, 5, 58
Buitrago Castillo, Francisco, 33–37, 72, 82, 104
Buitrago, Santos, 132
Buitrago Urroz, Julio, 76, 78, 115, 118, 119–20, 122, 125, 132, 178; Fonseca's letters to, *122–23*

Cabezas, Omar, 103–4, 115, 190, 194–95, 197, 209
Cardenal, Ernesto, 104–5, 108, 113, 156, 187

Carrión, Luis, 185, 216; photo, 140
Carter, Jimmy, 214
Carvajal, Benito, 202–3
Castañeda, Jorge, 104
Castillo, José María, 181
Castro, Fidel, 51, 61, 80, 84–85, 94, 146, 157
Catholic Church, 84, 106, 191–92, 209
Catholic Falangism, 27
Central American Common Market, 90
Central Intelligence Agency (U.S.), 128
Chamorro, Claudia, 186–87, 197–98, 202
Chamorro, Pedro Joaquín, 52–53, 85–86,
    128, 145, 156, 174, 211–12
Chamorro, Roberto, 201
Chamorro, Violeta, 219–20, 222, 226
Chinese revolution, 79, 157, 177
Comites de Defensa Civil, 215
Committee for the Liberation of Nicara-
    gua, 53, 55
Committees for Defense of the Revolution
    (Cuba), 63
Communist International, 159–60
Communist Manifesto, 38
Communist parties, 56, 94, 107, 158–61,
    163–64, 175, 179, 233n. 35; in Costa Rica,
    64, 70, 128, 160, 234n. 24; in Mexico, 73,
    159, 161, 234n. 24. See also Partido Socia-
    lista de Nicaragua (PSN)
Confederación Sindical Latinoamericana,
    158–60
Congo, 157
Consejo Universitario de la Universidad
    Nacional (CUUN), 42, 57, 62, 71–72, 93–
    94, 104
Conservative Party. See Partido Conser-
    vador Democrático (PCD)
Contra War, 223–24, 226–27
Contreras, Eduardo, 178–79, 180, 203, 205
Corinto dockworkers strike, 49
Coronel Urtecho, José, 108–9
Cranshaw, Marta, 132
"Crónica Secreta: Augusto César Sandino
    ante sus verdugos," 144, 152
Cronología de la resistencia sandinista, 144,
    146, 158, 179

Cruz, Rigoberto (Pablo Ubeda), 83, 95, 98
Cuadra, Manolo, 32, 39, 42, 45
Cuadra, Pablo Antonio, 127
Cuban Missile Crisis, 77
Cuban revolution, 6, 9, 50–51, 104, 177,
    225, 236n. 2; influence on Nicaraguan
    revolution, 56–57, 59, 61, 67–68, 77–79,
    144, 146, 157–58, 161, 227; military aid
    for Nicaraguans, 52–53, 80, 97, 164

Dalton, Roque, 63, 238n. 26
Darío, Rubén, 94, 123
Debray, Régis, 78
December 1974 raid, 181, 210
"Declarácion, 1964", 75, 80–81, 83, 84–85,
    88–89
Diaz y Sotelo, Manuel, 39
Dios Muñoz, Juan de, 196
Dirección Nacional (FSLN), 101, 119, 178,
    206, 216, 224; photo, 140
Dominican Republic, 61, 110
Duarte, Modesto, 82, 93

Earthquake of 1972, 173, 209–10
Editorial Antorcha, 87
Eisenhower, Milton, 48
Ejército Defensor de la Soberania Nacio-
    nal (EDSN), 72, 96, 97, 148–49, 153–54,
    158, 160
El Chaparral, 51, 54–57, 61, 70, 77, 79. See
    also Rigoberto López Pérez Brigade
El Estudiante, 91
El Universitario, 42, 49
Éscobar, José Benito, 70–71, 72, 114
Espártaco, 29
Espinoza, Luisa Amanda, 113, 244n. 5
Extra Semanal, 110

Federación de Estudiantes Revoluciona-
    rios (FER), 76, 91–92, 103–4, 172
Federation of Cuban Women (FMC), 63
Fiallos Gil, Mariano, 42, 48
Fonseca Amador, Carlos: on alliances, 93,
    156, 174–75, 207; arrests and imprison-
    ments of, 44–45, 48, 53, 83–84, 87, 114,

126–28, 132; on Atlantic Coast, 153; on blacks, 151, 173, 194; brothers and sisters of, 13, 15–17, 28; on Che Guevara, 69, 78, 101–2, 108, 123, 146, 147, 150, 157, 179, 184, 193; childhood of, 12, 16, 21; on Christianity, 106; on clandestinity, 88–89; on Costa Rica, 158; death of, 203–5, 254n. 37; on elections, 8, 37, 69, 88, 105, 128, 156; guerrilla campaigns of, 53–56, 81, 95–98, 201–4; health of, 16, 45, 54, 196, 201; on Indians, 21, 26, 151–52, 173, 194, 232n. 26; on internationalism, 66, 157; on land reform, 153, 190; leadership role of, 3, 34, 94, 100–101, 124, 148, 181, 185; on literacy, 34–35, 191; literary interests of, 94, 108–9, 129; and Maria Haydeé Terán, 87, 111–12, 183, 200; Marxism of, 6, 8, 29–30, 36, 38, 66–68, 103, 104, 106, 108, 109, 152, 254n. 3; personal philosophy of, 14, 40, 116–17, 153–54, 179–84, 193, 197, 199–200; photos, 135–38; and PSN, 30–32, 40, 42–43, 48, 49, 56–57, 61, 64–68, 69, 77, 86, 93, 160, 207; relationship with father, 14–18, 28–29, 38–39, 44, 45, 48, 57, 87, 125–26, 231n. 18; relationship with mother, 12–15, 18, 57, 63, 112, 231n. 21, 239 n.4; on revolutionary capacity of workers and peasants, 150–52, 161, 176, 189–90; on rural vs. urban warfare, 169–70; on Sandino, 6, 27, 37–38, 59–62, 64, 72–73, 75, 123, 143–61, 179, 181, 184, 193, 248n. 5; on security, 118–19; on Soviet Union, 45–46; student years of, 24, 25, 28–49, 54, 62, 63, 69, 70, 72, 84; on study of Nicaraguan history, 39, 83, 127, 146, 147; time in Cuba, 52, 57, 58–59, 63, 80, 112–13, 143; on vanguard party, 175–78; on violence and political change, 64–67, 69; visit to Soviet Union, 45–47; on women, 35, 36, 63, 97–98, 115–17, 198–99, 200, 224–25; on youth and students, 34–35, 40, 48–49, 101–4, 107–8

Fonseca, Estela, 15, 187, 239n. 4

Fonseca, Raúl, 13, 28

Fonseca, René, 15, 28, 125–26; photo, 136

Fonseca Terán, Carlos, 112, 183

Fonseca Terán, Tania de los Andes, 112, 183

Fonseca Ubeda, Augustina, 12–15, 18, 63, 230n. 3, 239n. 4; photo, 136

Foquismo, 78, 99–100

Frente Amplio Opositor (FAO), 213–14

Frente Democrático Cristiano (FDC), 91–92

Frente de Liberación Nacional (FLN), 73, 75

Frente Patriótico Nacional (FPN), 214

Frente Sandinista de Liberación Nacional (FSLN): alliances, 91–95, 156, 174–75, 206–7; and Atlantic Coast, 81, 124, 225; on blacks, 124; and concertación, 225; debate over name, 73; division into tendencies, 162–67, 181, 184, 185; finances of, 120–21; founding of, 73–77; and Indians, 81, 124, 225; on land reform, 123–24, 190, 223; in the montaña, 187–89, 195–96; prison culture, 129–33; reunification, 215–16; size of, 79, 101, 104, 110, 185, 205, 209, 217; urban underground, 112–21, 133, 186–87; on women, 97–98, 115–17, 124; work among peasants, 82–83, 91, 99, 187–92; work among urban workers, 92–93. See also December 1974 raid; Dirección Nacional; Federación de Estudiantes Revolucionarios (FER); Guerra Prolongada Popular (GPP); National Palace; Pancasán; Ríos Coco y Bocay; Tendencia Insurrectional ("terceristas"); Tendencia Proletaria (TP)

Frente Unitario Nicaragüense (FUN), 70

García, Rosa, 59, 63

"General Political-Military Platform of the FSLN." See Tendencia Insurrectional ("terceristas"): "Platforma General"

Gordillo, Fernando, 48, 57–58, 62, 72, 109

Gould, Jeffrey, 24, 72, 233n. 36

Guadamuz, Carlos, 116, 118, 129

Guerra Prolongada Popular (GPP), 164, 167–70, 172, 174, 177, 180–82, 185, 189, 206, 209, 214, 216

Guerrero, Marvín, 93

Guerrero Santiago, Noel, 59, 62, 73–75, 81, 240 n.30

Guevara, Ernesto (Che), 47, 61, 78, 94, 95, 99–102, 107, 108, 123, 135, 146, 150, 157, 164, 179, 182, 184, 221, 225; and military aid for Nicaraguans, 52–53, 79–80; and "new man," 179, 192–93, 195–96

Guillén, Víctor, 95–96, 100

Gutiérrez Castro, Ramón, 25, 29–33, 36, 43; photo, 140

Haslam, Chale, 51, 95

Hassán, Moises, 219

"Havana Letter," 53

Hernández, Onelio, 54–55

Hernández, Plutarco, 107, 126, 128, 178, 185

Herrera, Leticia, 107, 216

Historic Program, 122–24, 133, 153, 208, 222, 225, 226

Ho Chi Minh, 146

Huembes, Roberto, 185, 203

Ideario político del general Sandino, 144, 149, *151*, 152–*53*, *157*, 158

Independent Liberal Party. *See* Partido Liberal Independiente (PLI)

Indians, 20–23, 96–97, 232n. 26; and FSLN, 81–82, 131, 173, 225; resistance of, 25–26, 49, 131; and traditional parties, 22. *See also* Atlantic Coast; Miskito Indians; Monimbó; Subtiava; Sumo Indians

Instituto Nacional del Norte (INN), 24, 28–30, 32–33, 234n. 13

Instituto Ramírez Goyena, 38–40, 84, 121

Jérez Suárez, Julio, 72

July 26 Movement, 61

Juventud Democrática Nicaragüense (JDN), 69–70

Juventud Patriótica Nicaragüense (JPN), 70–71

Juventud Revolucionaria Nicaragüense (JRN), 70

Korea, 143, 157, 177

Lacayo, Chester, 52, 236n. 4

Lacayo, Gonzalo, 100, 121

"La lucha armada en Nicaragua," 66, *231n. 18*

La Prensa, 33, 85, 87, 125, 127, 147, 241n. 40. *See also* Chamorro, Pedro Joaquín

Lenin, V. I., 66, 146

Liberal Party (Somocista). *See* Partido Liberal Nacionalista (PLN)

Loáisiga, Isabel, 198

López, Celestina, 199

López Pérez, Rigoberto, 43, 144, 207

López, Santos, 72–73, 79, 154, 239n. 9

Los Doce, 212, 213

Mano Blanca, 215

Manos Fuera de Nicaragua (MAFUENIC), 159

Mariátegui, Jose Carlos, 60

Marín, Rufo, 126, 128, 246n. 35

Martí, Farabundo, 158–60

Martí, José, 61–62, 147, 157

Marx, Karl, 38, 66, 193

Mayorga, Silvio, 42–43, 57, 59, 62, 69, 70, 72, 76, 80, 93, 95, 97–98, 102

Mella, José Antonio, 157, 158

Mensaje a los estudiantes revolucionarios, 101–4, 107–8, 191

Mexican revolution, 39, 151

Miskito Indians, 20, 81, 96–97, 153, 194

Modesto. *See* Ruiz, Henry

Monett, Pedro, 59

Monimbó, 212

Morales Avilés, Ricardo, 116–17, 119, 129, 164, 175, 178

Movement of the Revolutionary Left (Chile), 175

Movilización Republicana (MR or PMR), 90–95

Movimiento Nueva Nicaragua (MNN), 72–73, 75
Movimiento Pueblo Unido (MPU), 212–14
Munguía, Edgard, 103–4, 201

Najlis, Michelle, 91
National Guard, 3, 5, 14, 16, 44–45, 123, 126, 150, 160, 205, 213, 215; violence of, 18, 50–51, 55, 57–58, 94–95, 97, 98, 109, 119, 130–31, 178, 180, 185, 189, 200–201. *See also* Oficina de Seguridad Nacional (OSN)
National Palace, 212
Navarro, Jorge, 40, 62, 72, 82, 114
Nicaragua Hora Cero, 92–93, 122–23, 167, 207
"Notas sobre la lucha popular contra la tiranía somocista," *82, 88, 93, 99, 100*
Notas sobre la montaña y algunos otros temas, 177, 189, 190, 192, 194, 250n. 6
"Notas y experiencias revolucionarias," *64–67, 77, 79, 82, 171–72*
Novedades, 125, 131
Núñez, Carlos, 216; photo, 140
Núñez, René, 49
Núñez, Róger, 114, 115

Obrerismo, 41
Oficina de Seguridad Nacional (OSN), 44–45, 87, 112–14, 119, 120–22, 131
Olama y Mellojones, 53, 70
Organization of American States, 214
Orientación Popular, 40
Ortega Saavedra, Camilo, 147–48, 164
Ortega Saavedra, Daniel, 129, 164, 206, 207, 216, 219, 222, 226; photos, 139, 140
Ortega Saavedra, Humberto, 126–29, 147, 164, 172, 174, 178–81, 183, 206–9, 216, 223–24, 226; photos, 137, 140

Pablo Ríos, Pedro, 75, 82
Pablo Ubeda Brigade, 187, 216–17
"Pact of the Generals," 25
Palmer, Steven, 59–60
Pancasán, 95–100, 122, 149

Partido Conservador Democrático (PCD), 26, 51–53, 64–65, 70, 72, 84, 91, 94, 95, 145, 148, 150, 155–56, 161, 163, 172, 209–10, 213. *See also* Chamorro, Pedro Joaquín
Partido Liberal Independiente (PLI), 24, 41, 43, 51–53, 70, 84, 91, 95, 155–56, 163, 172, 209–10, 213
Partido Liberal Nacionalista (PLN), 24, 26, 41, 89, 121, 155, 163–64, 214
Partido Social Cristiano de Nicaragua (PSCN or PSC), 91–94, 101, 106, 164, 210, 213
Partido Socialista de Nicaragua (PSN), 8, 36, 48, 56–57, 73, 77, 90–91, 94–95, 99, 101, 107, 155, 168, 171, 175, 210, 225–26; on Sandino, 38, 145, 234n. 24; on Somoza, 27, 48, 233n. 36; splits in, 163–64; and students, 43; on violence, 32, 53, 57, 64, 71; on women, 36. *See also* Fonseca Amador, Carlos: and PSN
Patrice Lumumba University, 107
Pomares, Germán, 51, 72, 82, 126, 191
Prado, Bertha, 34
Previo, Tomás (Colocho), 30–32
Provisional Revolutionary Government, 219–20
Punto Final (Chile), 120, 132

Ramírez, Sergio, 104–5, 219
Raudales, Ramón, 52–53
Rebel Army (Cuba), 78–79
"Retornar a las montañas," *67–68, 99, 189–90*
Revista Conservadora del Pensamiento Centroamericano, 127
Revolutionary Armed Forces (Guatemala), 99
Revolutionary Committee, 52–53
Revolutionary Directorate, 52–53
Reyna, Carlos, 93, 98, 114
Rigoberto López Pérez Brigade, 53–55. *See also* El Chaparral
Ríos Coco y Bocay, 79–83, 89, 93, 96, 98, 100, 149

Rivera, Francisco, 172, 195, 197–99
Robelo, Alfonso, 214, 219–20
Robleto, Octavio, 42, 87
Rodríguez, Fanor, 53, 59
Rodríguez Marín, Heriberto, 74–75, 118
Romero, Rodolfo, 47, 53, 56, 62–63, 76–77, 79–80
Rothschuh Tablada, Guillermo, 38–40
Rugama, Leonel, 109, 119
Ruiz, Faustino, 75, 82
Ruiz, Henry (Modesto), 100, 107, 164, 178, 181, 185–89, 201–2, 205–6, 209, 216; photo, 140
Russian Revolution, 66, 79, 151, 177

San Albino Manifesto, 149–51
Sánchez, Iván, 75, 82
Sánchez Sancho, Efraín, 178, 193–94
Sandino, Augusto César, 3, 27, 122, 133, 155–61, 220, 225; assassination of, 23, 148, 154; photo, 135. *See also* Ejército Defensor de la Soberania Nacional (EDSN); Fonseca Amador, Carlos: on Sandino
Sandino Battalion, 61, 157
Sandino: Guerrillero proletario, 144, 150, 152, *155, 157*
Schick, René, 72, 83–85, 89, 94
Segovia (Matagalpa), *14, 16, 27, 33, 34–37,* 38, 39, 191
Selser, Gregorio, 59, 148
Social Christians. *See* Partido Social Cristiano de Nicaragua (PSCN or PSC)
Somarriba, Rafael, 53–55
Somoza Debayle, Anastasio (Tachito), 3, 43–44, 83–84, 89, 94, 126, 131, 149, 173, 203, 209, 213, 220, 256n. 25; Fonseca's letter to, *44;* photo, 136
Somoza Debayle, Luis, 43–44, 71–72
Somoza García, Anastasio (Tacho), 23–24, 43, 59, 72, 148, 149
Somoza Portacarrero, Anastasio, 255n. 13
Sotelo, Casimiro, 76, 91–92, 102, 119
Southern Front, 216
Soviet Union, 45–47, 56, 91, 226

Stalin, Joseph, 46, 61, 159
Suárez, Jacinto, 89, 99–100, 129, 164
Subtiava, 49, 131
Sumo Indians, 20, 80–81, 96–97

Téfel, Reynaldo Antonio, 86
Tejada, David, 76, 94, 108, 113, 121
Tejada, René, 107, 188, 197
Tellez, Dora María, 113, 195–96, 212, 216
Tendencia Insurrectional ("terceristas"), 164, 169, 172, 177, 181, 185, 206–9, 212–14, 216, "Platforma General," 207–8, 219
Tendencia Proletaria (TP), 164, 168–69, 171–72, 175, 179–82, 185, 206, 209, 212, 214, 216
Terán, María Haydeé, 87, 94, 111–12, 121, 126–27, 183; photo, 137
Tijerino Haslam, Doris, 24, 95, 107, 113, 116–17, 119, 125, 129–31, 148, 174, 178, 183
Tirado López, Víctor, 83–84, 86, 113, 114, 188, 206–7, 216
Torres, Camilo, 106
Torres, Edelberto, 87, 94, 182; Fonseca's letter to, *55–56*
Torres, Hugo, 111, 196
Tricontinental Conference, 94, 146
Trinchera, 76
Tunnerman, Carlos, 104–5
Turcios Lima, Luis, 99, 100
Turcios, Oscar, 95, 97, 107, 119, 164, 167, 169, 178
23 July 1959 massacre, 57–58, 66, 95, 105, 114, 120

Ubeda, Pablo. *See* Cruz, Rigoberto
Unidad, 30, 49
Unión Democrática de Liberación (UDEL), 210
Unión Nacional de Acción Popular (UNAP), 29–30
Universidad Centroamericana (UCA), 71–72, 76, 91–92
Universidad Nacional Autónoma de Nicaragua (UNAN), 41–45, 48–49, 101–5

Un Nicaragüense en Moscú, 42, 45–47, 56, 236n. 47
Urcuyo, Francisco, 220
U.S. military and political intervention in Nicaragua, 13, 26, 44–45, 53, 90, 148, 200, 213–14, 220, 255n. 15

Valdivia, José, 107, 187
Vanguardia Juvenil, 24, 29
Vietnam, 78, 157, 177
Viva Sandino, 21, 144, 145, 146, 148, 149, 150–55, 157–58, 160, 161, 179

Walter, Knut, 23
Western Front, 216
Wheelock Román, Jaime, 144–45, 147–48, 164, 168, 182, 183, 185, 216, 223; photo, 140
Women: in Cuban revolution, 63, 200; in Nicaraguan revolution, 34, 62–63, 71, 97–98, 130–32, 141, 178, 181, 195, 197–98, 224–25, 253n. 27. *See also* Fonseca Amador, Carlos: on women

Yo Acuso (*Desde la cárcel yo acuso a la dictadura*), 86

MATILDE ZIMMERMANN is Assistant Professor of Latin American
History at Bridgewater State College.

LIBRARY OF CONGRESS CATALOGING-IN-PUBLICATION DATA
Zimmermann, Matilde, 1943–
Sandinista : Carlos Fonseca and the Nicaraguan revolution / Matilde
Zimmermann.
p. cm.
Includes bibliographical references and index.
ISBN 0-8223-2581-0 (cloth : alk. paper)
ISBN 0-8223-2595-0 (pbk. : alk. paper)
1. Fonseca Amador, Carlos. 2. Nicaragua—History—1936–1979.
3. Frente Sandinista de Liberación Nacional—History.
4. Revolutionaries—Nicaragua—Biography. I. Title.
F1527.F66 Z56 2001
972.8505'2—dc21   00-030849